CHOREOGRAPHIES OF SHARED SACRED SITES

RELIGION, CULTURE, AND PUBLIC LIFE

RELIGION, CULTURE, AND PUBLIC LIFE
SERIES EDITOR: KAREN BARKEY

The resurgence of religion calls for careful analysis and constructive criticism of new forms of intolerance, as well as new approaches to tolerance, respect, mutual understanding, and accommodation. In order to promote serious scholarship and informed debate, the Institute for Religion, Culture, and Public Life and Columbia University Press are sponsoring a book series devoted to the investigation of the role of religion in society and culture today. This series includes works by scholars in religious studies, political science, history, cultural anthropology, economics, social psychology, and other allied fields whose work sustains multidisciplinary and comparative as well as transnational analyses of historical and contemporary issues. The series focuses on issues related to questions of difference, identity, and practice within local, national, and international contexts. Special attention is paid to the ways in which religious traditions encourage conflict, violence, and intolerance and also support human rights, ecumenical values, and mutual understanding. By mediating alternative methodologies and different religious, social, and cultural traditions, books published in this series will open channels of communication that facilitate critical analysis.

After Pluralism: Reimagining Religious Engagement, edited by Courtney Bender and Pamela E. Klassen

Religion and International Relations Theory, edited by Jack Snyder

Religion in America: A Political History, Denis Lacorne

Democracy, Islam, and Secularism in Turkey, edited by Ahmet T. Kuru and Alfred Stepan

Refiguring the Spiritual: Beuys, Barney, Turrell, Goldsworthy, Mark C. Taylor

Tolerance, Democracy, and Sufis in Senegal, edited by Mamadou Diouf

Rewiring the Real: In Conversation with William Gaddis, Richard Powers, Mark Danielewski, and Don DeLillo, Mark C. Taylor

Democracy and Islam in Indonesia, edited by Mirjam Künkler and Alfred Stepan

Religion, the Secular, and the Politics of Sexual Difference, edited by Linell E. Cady and Tracy Fessenden

Recovering Place: Reflections on Stone Hill, Mark C. Taylor

Boundaries of Toleration, edited by Alfred Stepan and Charles Taylor

CHOREOGRAPHIES OF SHARED SACRED SITES

Religion, Politics, and Conflict Resolution

Edited by
Elazar Barkan
and Karen Barkey

Columbia University Press
New York

Columbia University Press
Publishers Since 1893
New York   Chichester, West Sussex
cup.columbia.edu
Copyright © 2015 Columbia University Press
Paperback edition, 2016
All rights reserved

Library of Congress Cataloging-in-Publication Data
  Choreographies of shared sacred sites : religion, politics, and conflict resolution / edited by Elazar Barkan and Karen Barkey.
     pages   cm. — (Religion, culture, and public life)
  Includes bibliographical references and index.
  ISBN 978-0-231-16994-3 (cloth : alk. paper)—ISBN 978-0-231-16995-0 (pbk. : alk. paper)—ISBN 978-0-231-53806-0 (electronic)
  1. Sacred space.   2. Conflict management—Religious aspects.
I. Barkan, Elazar, author, editor of compilation.   II. Barkey, Karen, 1958– author, editor of compilation.
  BL580.C46   2014
  203'.5—dc23
                                                          2014001344

Columbia University Press books are printed on permanent and durable acid-free paper.
Printed in the United States of America

Cover design: Jordan Wannemacher

CONTENTS

Introduction | 1
ELAZAR BARKAN AND KAREN BARKEY

1. RELIGIOUS PLURALISM, SHARED SACRED SITES, AND THE OTTOMAN EMPIRE | 33
KAREN BARKEY

COMPARISONS: CYPRUS/BOSNIA/ANATOLIA/ALGIERS

2. THREE WAYS OF SHARING THE SACRED: CHOREOGRAPHIES OF COEXISTENCE IN CYPRUS | 69
METE HATAY

3. RELIGIOUS ANTAGONISM AND SHARED SANCTUARIES IN ALGERIA | 97
DIONIGI ALBERA

4. CONTESTED CHOREOGRAPHIES OF SACRED SPACES IN MUSLIM BOSNIA | 130
DAVID HENIG

PALESTINE/ISRAEL

5. AT THE BOUNDARIES OF THE SACRED: THE REINVENTION OF EVERYDAY LIFE IN JERUSALEM'S AL-WAD STREET | 163
WENDY PULLAN

6. THE POLITICS OF OWNERSHIP: STATE, GOVERNANCE, AND THE STATUS QUO IN THE CHURCH OF THE ANASTASIS (HOLY SEPULCHRE) | 199
GLENN BOWMAN

7. CHOREOGRAPHING UPHEAVAL: THE POLITICS OF SACRED SITES IN THE WEST BANK | 235
ELAZAR BARKAN

8. THE IMPACT OF CONFLICTS OVER HOLY SITES ON CITY IMAGES AND LANDSCAPES: THE CASE OF NAZARETH | 270
RASSEM KHAMAISI

MUSEUMS

9. TOLERANCE VERSUS HOLINESS: THE JERUSALEM MUSEUM OF TOLERANCE AND THE MAMILLA MUSLIM CEMETERY | 299
YITZHAK REITER

10. SECULARIZING THE UNSECULARIZABLE: A COMPARATIVE STUDY OF THE HACI BEKTAŞ AND MEVLANA MUSEUMS IN TURKEY | 336
RABIA HARMANŞAH, TUĞBA TANYERI-ERDEMIR, AND ROBERT M. HAYDEN

Bibliography | *369*
Contributors | *395*
Index | *401*

CHOREOGRAPHIES
OF SHARED
SACRED SITES

INTRODUCTION

ELAZAR BARKAN AND KAREN BARKEY

SACRED SITES THAT are shared by two or more groups have long been a source of intellectual and scholarly curiosity. These sites often have a dynamic history. In India, Palestine, the Balkans, and elsewhere, we can see fluctuations between periods of peaceful sharing and of conflict over joint use. At times these sites can become the locus of communal violence. Scholarly debates on shared sacred sites often focus on the meaning of "coexistence," on the logic that reputedly underlies centuries of "sharing" and why that sharing gets interrupted by conflict. Among the studies that interrogate toleration, syncretism, and religious antagonism more broadly, scholarly explanations can often be divided to two ideal types: one that anticipates and emphasizes continuing conflict and the other that privileges peaceful coexistence. Both see periods of interruption in either coexistence or violence, but for both ideal types, the disruption is the exception that proves the rule.

In this book our aim is to explore the politics of the "choreography of sacred spaces" within the framework of state–society relations and to examine the positions, roles, and agency of various actors and institutions in an attempt to differentiate between the political and the religious features of the shared or contested space.[1] We want to understand whether sharing and contestation are politically or religiously motivated.

Do religious rules, constraints, and obligations motivate coexistence or conflict at sites, or are political imperatives more important in delineating conflict? We hasten to add that we identify the categories "religion" and "political" as a heuristic device in order to distinguish between the theological and confessional aspects of religion and the political goals of the group. In exploring from a comparative perspective the questions of when and why sites that are holy for more than one religious or ethnic group at times become politicized and turn into places of hatred and violence but in other instances remain noncontroversial, we hope to delineate the religious and the political factors that suggest the context and causality of conflict in these sites. How do we explain periods of relative tolerance and sharing that give way to distress over differences only to return to peace and calm? Which forces bring about this?

We direct our attention to the role of the state and the nature of its relationships to several religious and ethnic groups in society in order to understand when and how conflicts arise in such sacred settings. We argue that historically and in contemporary cases the importance of sacred sites lays both in the particular "choreography of daily life" around the site and in the manner in which public authorities frame the context of relations between religious and ethnic groups. Other stakeholders such as religious institutions and political activists—extremists and peace advocates—at times play critical leadership roles in instigating conflict or attempting to pacify a volatile situation. Evaluating the relationship among these constituencies provides the context for both an analysis of the phenomena of shared sacred sites as well as a policy framework.

If we want to understand what makes shared sacred sites turn contentious and violent, we need to explore the movement from relative peace to conflict as well as the postconflict situation and the reemergence of coexistence. Ethnic and religious wars, in particular around shared sacred sites, exhibit both processes of unsettling peace and creating conflict as well as postconflict processes leading to an accommodated coexistence. In this introduction we pay comparable attention to conflict and to coexistence in their various forms, underscoring a multiplicity of forms of contention and sharing. We explore issues around the definition and the practice of coexistence, the question of centrality, and indivisibility of religious sites as well as the roles of the state and other actors around the site.

Shared sacred sites, as Anna Bigelow suggests, are indices of the quality of interreligious relations; that is, they represent a proxy for understanding the larger religious/sectarian relational field in a country.[2] Shrines that remain sites of coexistence, where state actors and societal actors actively understand and promote such activities of sharing, can be seen as spaces of tolerance and cooperation while places where conflict is rampant indicate the poor nature of interreligious relations. And then there are those sites that, in the midst of conflict or in the immediate postconflict situation, maintain "sharing" in ways that are inexplicable if indeed we expect that the larger ethno-religious rivalry would dominate local conditions. In many of these places of conflict, close scrutiny will demonstrate the role of political actors, state actors, and religious and ethnic entrepreneurs acting on behalf of a particular coalition of political power attempting to destroy the modus vivendi of sharing or fostering cooperation and of pursuing local peace and economic prosperity. Indeed, rarely do religious doctrinal changes play a role in instigating conflict.

Together with the renewed rise of religion in the public sphere and the increased religious diversity of many nation-states that once attempted to build homogenous societies, states are confronted with the question of how to organize religious pluralism in a world that has gone through various iterations of modernity, secularism, and religious resurgence. Some nation-states have been or are still going through processes of homogenization: efforts to impose a singular religious or ethnic order in pluralistic societies. In this endeavor, unity is imposed through a variety of mechanisms stretching from accommodation and assimilation to violence, expulsion, and genocide. This is still the situation in many developing states of the Middle East, Africa, and Asia where oppression through homogenization is inflicted upon the "other," overshadowing a history of tolerance and coexistence. A good example is the erosion of the institutional and communal presence of Christians in the Middle East. Churches and monuments are slowly being erased from the map and from history. As churches are reconfigured into mosques, as gravestones are destroyed and tensions rise, Orthodox Christians in Turkey, Armenians, Christians in Syria and Palestine/Israel, and Copts in Egypt are emigrating, ending a rich history of sharing and belonging. Particularly brutal was the elimination of the ancient Christian community that started in the 1990s and continued during the sectarian violence after the American invasion of Iraq.[3]

The cases we consider in this volume are connected through the shared legacy of the Ottoman Empire. Whether in Palestine/Israel, the Balkans, or Anatolia, shared sacred sites were all part of the same imperial political formation for many centuries before they emerged within the realm of nationalizing states, introducing a new phase in the relations at these sites. Consequently, these sacred sites experienced different systems of rule and transitions that often produced turmoil in habitual practices and have led these spaces to reemerge as places of recharged syncretism or renewed antagonism. Across the former lands of the Ottoman Empire, many religious sites that had been abandoned or destroyed have been recently reactivated as people from various faiths insist on reviving some of the cultural and social exchanges of the past.[4]

By studying these cases both in diachronic historical manner and in their synchronic moments, it is important to reveal how changes from empire to nation-state affected the relations around sites. The transition from empire to nation-state has been studied in its many dimensions, and its effects scrutinized. Yet the impact of such a transition on shared sacred sites is hardly explored. The chapter by Karen Barkey explores the history of early shared sites in the Ottoman Empire, describing the initial proclivity for sharing that emerged in the contact between Seljuk, Byzantine, and later Ottoman frontier societies that engaged Christianity and Islam. She argues that sharing came as a result of a general proclivity for cultural accommodation on the part of imperial states as well as multiple institutional developments on the ground that brought members of different groups together into sustained relations with each other. Many of the cultural understandings and spaces that were shared in the early Ottoman centuries were carried on and have been important to a particular interpretation of Ottoman toleration.

We also want to contextualize sacred sites to demonstrate that they are not unique or different from other types of conflict such as ethnic, racial, or territorial struggles. Do sacred sites constitute a unique category that demands a distinct analysis, different but analogous to other identity conflicts such as over territory along national, racial, or ethnic divisions?[5] Interreligious atrocities are neither more nor less vicious than other forms of group violence, and since the rise of nationalism in the nineteenth century, religious violence invariably mirrors national conflicts.

One example for such analogous religious and national sacredness can be seen by comparing the sites and the histories of Kosovo and Babri Masjid in India. The region of Kosovo is sacred both for its religious history and presence and because it was the site where Ottomans defeated the Serbs in 1389. Consequently, Kosovo has been central to the Serbian church lore and politics. It is no accident that it was there that on the six hundredth commemoration of the Battle of Kosovo that President Slobodan Milosevic made his inflammatory speech that was an important cause leading to the wars and the dissolution of the Yugoslav entity. Here politics and sacred national and religious features of the space were closely interrelated. The dispute over the Babri Masjid (mosque) in Ayodhya (Uttar Pradesh) goes back to the sixteenth century and to the controversial claim that a Hindu temple of Rama was destroyed in order to build it. Disputes have erupted periodically over the last 150 years, often corresponding to heightened Hindu nationalist activism. The state and Indian courts have been closely involved in adjudicating the competing historical versions of the site's origins. In both cases, meanings are constructed and attributed to specific events and peoples, and they establish over time a communal memory that informs a religious and national "sacred identity."

It is primarily in this sense that Kosovo and Babri Masjid are similar. In these cases we see that there is no fundamental distinction between religious versus other political identity markers, such as national, ethnic, or racial. Sacred sites do have specific characteristics, but these are shaped nonetheless by political variables and are part of a larger context of the relations between two peoples and two religions.

In the next sections we discuss the three main areas of research that the essays in this book explore. We start with issues of coexistence that are fundamental to understanding the kinds of arrangements that can be found within shared sacred sites and the consequences of those arrangements. We continue by examining characteristics of shared sacred sites, including narratives, centrality, and indivisibility, to underscore how such features are theorized in the literature. And finally we discuss the various ways in which state–society relations, state structures, and the impact of state policies contribute to sharing sacred sites.

COEXISTENCE

Generally we speak of "coexistence" when two or more groups live together, respecting their differences and working out their conflicts in a nonviolent fashion. In similar ways we refer to "toleration" as a situation where differences between groups exist, but often the majority decides that it prefers to accept minorities even though there might be deep differences between them. This does not mean that coexistence and toleration are conflict free. The term "coexistence" often conveys both peace and latent conflict of interests. Thus, the expectation that coexistence means lack of conflict is misplaced. This is particularly evident by the term "peaceful coexistence," which underscores a current absence of conflict but recalls implicitly a violent past and the hope of avoiding its future renewal.

Peaceful coexistence includes respecting (or accepting) differences and resolving disagreements nonviolently. Centuries of interreligious relationship have produced extensive literature on conflict, syncretism, and tolerance as different forms of coexistence. The work of Dionigi Albera points to the long centuries of religious mixture in the Mediterranean. The evidence of mixing, of devotions shared by members of the different monotheisms living together in the Mediterranean, is remarkable in its longevity and institutional continuity.[6] Albera focuses on the shared actions and practices of the groups as well as the local institutions that provided shelter for such sharing to occur peacefully. He underscores the degree to which the sharing of sacred spaces, sacred rituals, and holy men brought about fluid relations between communities, making their relatively peaceful coexistence possible. He urges us to move away from "doctrinal and institutional discontinuity between religions." In his chapter in this volume, Albera depicts the continuity between colonial and postcolonial Algeria through the study of Our Lady of Africa. This Marian sanctuary in Algiers was constructed and operated under particular political systems, but its continuity also depended on the astute maneuvering and accommodation of the Catholic establishment in charge. The long-term survival of the sanctuary was the result of government policies, Church leadership, and continued local interest on the part of communities imbued with popular religion.

Yet we also cannot ignore that within practices of sharing there can also be long-standing intra- and interreligious dogmas and institutional arguments for exclusivity and intolerance. By claiming to be the sole source of truth, religious exclusivity cast adherents of other religions into the category of "other." This other can be someone to tolerate, to convert, or on whom to exact vengeance. These differences in regulating relations to the other are bolstered by sacred texts that are diverse enough to allow for multiple interpretations of the truth and that exclude any single "real" essential manifestation of a religion. For example, the Christian religious understanding of the role of Jews in Christian society and the teachings of the Church produced a pervasive system of beliefs that were counter to many more tolerant practices on the ground. This made it possible for anti-Judaism to be widespread in Europe before World War II and for toleration toward Jews in society occur at the same time.

The notion of coexistence then needs to be further differentiated. Historians of Western Europe have spent much time arguing over the forms of coexistence and have underscored different forms of sociability, mixed marriages, business partnerships, and shared religious sites and cemeteries as various ways of studying coexistence in the past. Historians have also argued about the meaning of coexistence, some leaning toward antagonistic and controlled forms and others toward more genuinely amicable forms of coexistence.[7] Similar studies carried out on premodern land-based empires have also stressed coexistence, meaning an ethnic and religious pluralism cohabitating under strong state management.[8]

Some of these scholarly discussions, especially those on the meaning of coexistence, also concern the field of shared sacred sites. As we will discuss in detail later, the divisions range from scholars who tend to emphasize the antagonistic nature of tolerance to those who are in favor of more contingent and fluid understandings of tolerance that are constructed on the circumstances and context of history. A more differentiated analysis is proposed by Glenn Bowman, who discusses types of coexistence indicating that these can spread from conflict to syncretism with antagonism/uneasy coexistence and peaceful amicable mutuality in between.[9] Identifying these variations along a spectrum is as important as recognizing the switches from one form to the other.

How do we then explain movement from one form of coexistence to the other? Anthropologists study various shared sites through closely observing the retelling of experiences, the changes in the sites, the administrative struggles, and the manner in which some actors foment conflict. In a series of articles on Macedonia, Bowman shows how relations between groups are altered as the daily choreographies of sharing a site change within the broader context of ethno-religious tensions and competition. He underscores the degree to which "the presence of agency necessitates close attention to what people are doing, and what they say they are doing, while they are in the process of doing it."[10] In one case he shows how the implanting of a larger cross on a site shared by Muslims and Christians started eroding the amicable mixing that had taken place for long periods of time. When larger discourses of enmity penetrate local society, when external actors interfere in the local patterns of relations, and when they manipulate the established symbols and practices, conditions of coexistence can be altered.

Similarly the meaning of various layers of conflict has to be unpacked. What does conflict over a sacred site mean?

In exploring the concept of religious conflict, we ought to ask how violent a conflict has to be in order to be included. Presenting this simplistic question aims to explicate the plurality and diversity of such conflicts. There are a great variety of conflicts around shared religious sites. It is clearly inadequate to limit a typology to a binary of conflict or coexistence. There is the self-evident distinction between varieties of violence that involve tussling among individuals, killing, sometimes massacres or even wars, and disputes over access and management of a site. Periodic outbreaks that are part of a longer and larger conflict or even perhaps single events are clearly influenced by the history and memory of violence.

If all events are considered as "conflictual," it tells us little about policies, choreography, or the ability to manage the site. It may also be useful to delineate a violent conflict that erupts as a result of failed management or control but that is not a marker for future violence and is not focused on the site. For example, the 1979 Sunni-on-Sunni conflagration in Mecca was extremely violent but was not a manifestation of a religious conflict that contested the site. Instead, it was the site as a symbolic place that served to heighten the political-religious conflict that was unleashed at the site. Major Christian sites in the Holy Land provide an example for the changing phases of conflict of a shared site. Various Christian denominations coexist in the Church of the Nativity in Bethlehem and the Holy Sepulchre in Jerusalem while engaged in an ongoing struggle for control, yet this can hardly be viewed as violent conflict. As Bowman discusses in his chapter, these are both cases of intrareligious power struggles, the history of which has not been less violent than among different religions. Yet in these sacred Christian sites the competition over the last century largely avoided serious violence. That is not to say that there have not been violent conflicts in the past. The rivalry over control of the Holy Land in the nineteenth century led, among other things, to the Crimean War. Clearly, today's struggle for control of the physical space within these Holy Land churches—which involves the Israeli government and its diplomatic relations with the Vatican, Russia, Egypt, and Ethiopia, among others as patrons of the several denominations—does not convey a "continuation" of the same conflict.

In the abstract, these concepts can obfuscate meaningful shifts. It is critical to note that the concept of coexistence as we use it displays a fluid and contingent approach to questions of history, politics, and identity. It accepts that identities are changeable and therefore can be mobilized into forms of extreme conflict as well as syncretistic embracing of the other. Many studies show in detail the particular motivating factors and actions that bring about subtle as well as dramatic change to shared shrines.[11] These are inherently empirical questions that we have to study synchronically and diachronically. While ethnographies are important to analyze particular moments and actions and their immediate articulation, the ebbs and flows of historical changes in the *longue durée*, belie the importance of fixity of identities or conflicts. Historical studies show that while these group identities may contribute to conflicts, they are also likely to further solidify in response to escalated conflicts. In Albera's piece we see the abandonment of missionary activity given the reality of postindependence Algeria, clearly changing the understanding of the role and identities of the clergymen in Algiers, whereas in Mete Hatay's essay we see the separation and solidification of identities by Greeks and Turks after the British occupation of Cyprus. In the Algerian case, the potential for conflict is evaded, but in Cyprus identities get reshaped to promote interethnic and interreligious antagonism.

Furthermore, as we will explore in this book, coexistence and conflict around sacred sites often depend on state policies. The impact of specific policies is critical in turning peaceful coexistence or dormant conflict into violence. State policies and actions by political, religious, and ethnic entrepreneurs shape the particulars of the conflict. Although political realists argue that difference and conflict are mobilized when there is structural instability, fear, and competition, empirical historical evidence points to a more complex correlation. Minorities are attacked sometimes without posing any risk to the larger society: Jews before World War II, Roma in various places, and Christians in Iraq or Egypt are pertinent examples. Animosity will still most likely be built on imagined fears, but this is distinct from real political competition among two ethnicities or religions over a concrete space.

This raises the question of whether competition among groups can be peaceful or is exclusively based on rivalry and inherent dislike, as Robert Hayden argues with his concept of "antagonistic tolerance." From

Hayden's perspective, coexistence is feasible only under a fundamental imbalance of power between the groups. In cases where there is a semblance of power parity and fear by one or both groups for their access and control of a site, the "sharing" of sites will instigate tremendous hostility, competition, and violence.[12] Hayden focuses on the inability of peoples of different religions to truly be tolerant (embracing diversity) toward each other, and he sees competition among identities (toleration of others) as fixed structural conflicts. Further, he privileges regional intergroup relations over local interactions through which people might adapt and work together in contrast to their religious and political leaders. This specific judgment of the relation between the macro and the micro, and whether it is coexistence or antagonism, is illustrated in the essay cowritten by Rabia Harmanşah, Tuğba Tanyeri-Erdemir, and Hayden in this volume. There, Hayden's category of antagonistic tolerance is explored in a situation where many might see coexistence. This speaks to the core dilemma. Harmanşah and colleagues represent politics as determining the manifestation of religious discourse, which by definition is more favorable to the powerful yet allows for accommodation by the minority to avoid conflict. Religion is once again shown to be flexible, multifaceted and not doctrinally driven but politically shaped. By concluding that it is impossible to "seculariz[e] the unsecularizable" the authors imply that religious differences are unbridgeable because the core values remains incommensurable. Would that mean the coexistence can be achieved only by erasing religion, privileging assimilation? The ethnographic details in their chapter present the negotiation of cultural religious (in this case interfaith) heterogeneity, pluralism, and the museum as one trading zone of ideas and practices that facilitates coexistence.

CHARACTERISTICS OF SHARED SACRED SITES

Other studies also focus on the characteristics of specific sites in order to understand their propensity for peaceful or conflictual coexistence. Ron

Hassner, a scholar whose work is strongly based on classifying sacred sites, reflects on the centrality and the indivisibility of sites as the main features that lead to conflict. Such a focus, as we shall see, also begs the question of who gets to define the characteristics of these sites. Before we explicate the categories of centrality and indivisibility as they emerge in some chapters in the book, we should pay brief attention to the narratives of sacred sites, which frame them as peaceful or conflictual.

NARRATIVES OF SHARED SACRED SITES

Sacred sites convey the physicality and the identity, the history and the memory, of the place. In some cases the sharing of the physical space includes the historical narrative, where both sides recognize at least some components of the others' sacred history. For example, Glenn Bowman's narration of the holy priest in Makedonski Brod comes close to a single narrative for both Muslims and Christians. The difference in the story of whether the holy man was a priest (Christian) or merely dressed as one (Muslim) is significant. But the combination of shared narrative and physical space frames the coexistence.

In other cases, the religious-historical narratives are at odds. Perhaps a most pertinent example is the current Muslim mainstream opposition to acknowledging the Jewish narrative of the Haram al-Sharif/Temple Mount or, as others refer to it, Jerusalem's Sacred Esplanade.[13] The conflict between Jews and Muslims over the site began in the 1920s, when violence erupted at the Western Wall, the western side of the Haram, and has continued intermittently ever since. The religious histories of this and other sacred sites provide the discourse for both sides to inflame nationalist sentiments and delegitimize the Other.

In cases where the narrative itself is in conflict, the choreography of sharing may be influenced by nonstate actors, either to aggravate or diminish the conflict. A one-sided narrative can be embellished to deepen the chasm and to make it politically and socially unacceptable to legitimize the other side's perspective. Thus, in the case of the al-Aqsa/Temple Mount, the spectrum seems to extend from Palestinians who reject Jewish historical affinity to the site to those who are reluctant to engage the issue, accepting that under the current power relations, validating Jewish narrative is unpatriotic. The equivalent on the Jewish side is of those who are not even politically aware that they ignore or deny an Islamic tradition concerning the Western Wall. The shared space in this case is a shared contention; each side has narrative claims on the physical site held by the other side.

CENTRALITY

In his book *War on Sacred Grounds,* Hassner presents the argument that coexistence cannot take place in central and vulnerable sites.[14] There is little doubt that the notion of centrality (in contrast to marginal sites) is critical, but what constitutes centrality? It seems centrality can arise for religious or historical reasons as well when the site is at the epicenter of a political conflict.[15] There is much overlap among these cultural, religious, historical, or political manifestations, yet different stakeholders have varying impact on the nature of the sharing/conflict in the site, depending on its character. Does the denial of access of some by others always cause violence? Not always. The nature of the conflict depends more on the political power of the denied party to resist than on "access" as an independent variable.

The delineation between central and marginal sites is critical both for analytical and policy reasons. Is there a clear division between central versus marginal sites? Hassner answers yes, making the cardinal distinction that central religious sacred spaces are more vulnerable and less divisible than other territorial disputes. In this view, central vulnerable sacred sites present particular challenges where the religious character of the site is determinative and religious leaders are uniquely situated to either exploit or resolve such conflicts.

This division raises the question of what makes a site central. One difficulty may be that every site that becomes conflict ridden is defined as central, even if it was so prior to the conflict. In many cases the religious centrality may be relatively simple to discern independent of the conflict and may be unrelated to the site's political vulnerability, as is the case in the Haram al-Sharif/Temple Mount, which derives its political centrality from its religious significance. In other cases it may be hard to delineate the political from the religious vulnerability of these sites. Indeed, it is the combination of political and religious factors that make the sites central or controversial.

What is the latitude that various stakeholders (including the state) have in shaping the meaning of a site? We believe a great deal, which is why choreography is at the heart of our inquiry. In comparing three West Bank spaces—in Hebron, Nablus, and north of Jerusalem—Elazar Barkan shows how the centrality of sites varies according to the intensity of the conflict, and how increased political conflict elevates religious devotion to a site. Thus, Joseph's Tomb, which had hardly reckoned as a Jewish sacred site, has increasingly become venerated.

It is clear that the role of politics is critical in inciting as well as in diminishing conflict and encouraging coexistence. The coexistence found in both Mecca and the Holy Sepulchre—two of the most central sacred sites in the world—demands an explanation as much as conflict does in other sites. In Mecca millions of Shia and Sunni pilgrims coexist annually. Tension is ongoing; in 1987 clashes during the Hajj led to hundreds of deaths, but at other times the tension is controlled. Should the Kaaba be viewed as a site of conflict or coexistence? One explanation might be that in these currently "nonconflictual" sites, the political authority is either too strong (Saudi Arabia) or relatively detached vis-à-vis the religion in question (Israel, and previously Jordan), and thus is not actively and consistently supporting one side (see Glenn Bowman's chapter). This suggests that conflict depends less on the religious centrality of the site and more on political choreography.

The following chapters look at sites that are central and marginal, and spaces that challenge the classical definition of a site. Is the Holy Land a site? A space? The chapter by Wendy Pullan describes the sacralization of the space outside the Haram/Temple Mount in Jerusalem and the intertwining of the religious and secular in everything from archeology to the marketplace. Rassem Khamaisi directs our attention to Nazareth, a space central to Christianity but where the competition between two minority groups (Christians and Muslims in a Jewish state) is shaped by demography and economics, and is projected on a Basilica and a mosque. In each case the political competition and conflict frame the religiosity of the space and privilege the more rigid doctrinal orthodoxy, which increases its visibility in the national discourse. Glenn Bowman explores the historical continuity in the competition for "ownership" of the space at the Holy Sepulchre between the several Christian denominations while highlighting changes in the relations between these religious communities of priests and the various successive political authorities controlling the site.

Museums are a space where culture-cum-economics creates a category that seemingly conveys the hope that the sacred can be neutralized and embedded into the public sphere in a transformed manner. The Hagia Sophia in Istanbul is the most visible example. Here again state actions can transform the museum space to either a bridge or a break between communities. But a museum established de novo on sacred land that belongs to a minority population by the state in the name of the majority can incite conflict. Yitzhak Reiter explores the ebb and flow of sacredness of the Mamilla Cemetery in Jerusalem initially as an intra-Muslim dispute before World War II, and surrounding the recent plans to build the Jewish Museum of Tolerance on part of the cemetery. The construction of a museum on a sacred old Palestinian cemetery has rallied a whole spectrum of Palestinians and some Israeli support to oppose the affront. Museums, like other institutions, do not "naturally" provide for a space of coexistence or conflict, and, as Harmanşah and colleagues show, museums also provide space for a religious public intent on peacefully and slowly reestablishing cherished rituals. This has been the fate of many museums in the post-Ottoman realm, especially in Turkey proper.

INDIVISIBILITY

A second common variable that engages the literature on religious conflicts is the question of indivisibility, which is critical in evaluating the propensity for conflict or the prevention or settlement of conflict over shared sites. Monica Duffy Toft describes indivisibility as "situations where two rational actors cannot agree that the issue over which they are bargaining is divisible."[16] Stacie E. Goddard, in contrast, views "indivisible" conflicts as malleable and dependent on the stakeholders' construction of their positions.[17] This suggests that indivisibility is a matter of degree, not typology. The distinction between the two notions of indivisibility—whether it is a matter of principle or of relative malleability—is often not analyzed explicitly but assumed to be a categorical distinction. Hassner argues that indivisibility stems from the convergence of two factors: centrality and vulnerability. The more religiously central a sacred site is—that is, the closer it is to the divine—the less divisible it becomes.[18] Therefore, these religious sites are seen as uniquely rigid and indivisible.[19] Other comparable cases of indivisibility are national territorial conflicts. Disputes in Cyprus, Ireland, and Kosovo, or between Japan and Korea are some well-known "indivisible" ethno-national examples.[20] The indivisibility of a site is often raised by politicians and others who focus on the topic with a particular goal or at a specific time, for example, to explain a political failure, to escalate a conflict, or to rally nationalist support. In each case, indivisibility stems from politics rather than the substance of the disputed issue whether it is religious, national, or ethnic conflict.

We believe that indivisibility is culturally and politically constructed. We often think of questions of partition as spatial, but indivisibility can just as much convey temporal or functional division. As Toft argues, "goods" (sites, territories) "once interpreted as indivisible in the political sphere, they are then difficult to reinterpret and present as divisible to a persuaded population."[21] The physical construction of a site does not exist in separation from its cultural construction. There ought to be a distinction between the claim that the territory or the site is indivisible and the reluctance to divide or share access, treating it all as indivisible. This ignores the extensive contrary evidence. While sites have certain continuity to believers, conflicts ebb and flow and change over time. Often by concentrating on conflict, the public and politicians overlook longer periods of coexistence that displays the malleability of the site. If, indeed, indivisibility is a construction like other concepts, then there are alternative ways in which to view what is "(in)divisible" about a site.

The highly constructed nature of indivisibility underscores the impact of politics on the interpretation of religious practices at various sites and the fact that the meaning that some central sacred sites carry for believers sometimes changes. The question is how sites are managed, choreographed, and constructed, since indivisibility is a construction that, thus, can and does change overtime. Historical evidence shows numerous examples of shifts over time. Consider the Israeli Palestinian indivisible conflict. While historically the political parties that currently lead each of the two governments (the Palestine Liberation Organization and Likud, the national liberal party) rejected compromise over any territory, today both sides agree to a principled division, though they have not agreed on the details; this is characteristic of the peace process. The indivisibility maintained as a national lore has been overtaken by politics. It is possible to speculate that the Haram al-Sharif/Temple Mount will never be shared, but it behooves us to remember that historically both religions have reinterpreted their own perspectives on "sharing" the site.[22] Jerusalem, declared as Israel's "eternal and undivided capital," has expanded continuously, especially since East Jerusalem was occupied in 1967. Its indivisibility is rhetorically religious but politically motivated, and it belies the unity of the space.

Another case in point is the recent decision by the Indian Allahabad High Court to divide the Ayodhya land into three parts between the Sunni Waqf Board, the Hindu Nirmohi Akhara, and the party representing Ram Lalla Virajman (the Ram deity), resulting in a one-part Muslim and two-parts Hindu division, a decision that the Indian state and police expected to lead to deadly violence but has had very few repercussions so far.[23] Whether the acquiescence was a matter of lopsided power relations or relative political pragmatism is a matter of opinion in part, yet while this power disparity is true throughout India's history, it has not eliminated religious violence, most instigated by the majority but at times by minorities too. The Bhagalpur riots of 1989, for example, were started

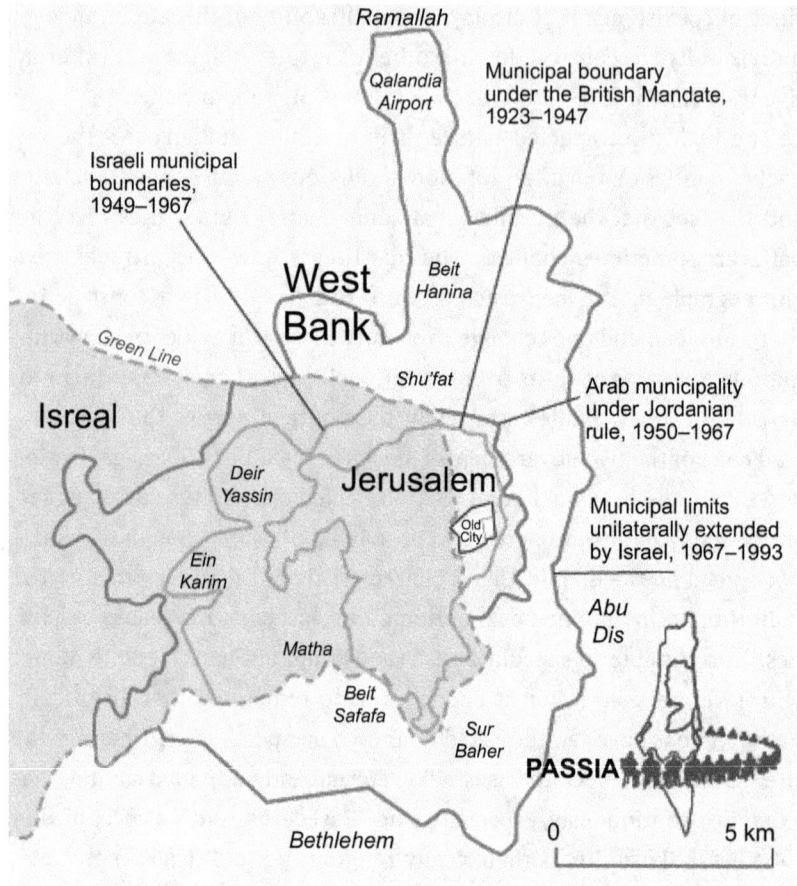

FIGURE 0.1 JERUSALEM MUNICIPAL BOUNDARIES 1947–2000.

Image reprinted by permission of the Palestinian Academic Society for the Study of International Affairs (PASSIA). http://www.passia.org/palestine_facts/MAPS/images/jer_maps/Jlem1947-2000.html.

by Muslims during Hindu processions through Bihar and were perceived as a "Muslims-stand-your-ground" type of violence. Most of the other violence by Muslims has been in the form of terrorist attacks: in 2002 on the Akshardham temple in Gujarat following large-scale anti-Muslim violence in 2006 in Varanasi, Uttar Pradesh, and in Mumbai in 2008.

The increased importance of Babri Masjid was also a result of politics, and now it looks like politics has been working once more to decrease the volatility of the site. Similarly, the shifting meaning of the al-Buraq Wall (the Western Wall) in Jerusalem for Muslims and the growing denial by Muslims of Jewish historical affinity to the Temple Mount are some of the most contentious political shifts of religious dogma. While some argue that the indivisibility stems from the essence of the site, we believe that the construction of its meaning, religious or otherwise, is temporally specific, and it changes in relation to political developments. The shift might be in the perception of vulnerability, the political feasibility of control, or the result of the predicament of sharing. Universalizing indivisibility as a characteristic of sacred sites ignores critical historical empirical evidence.

We want to understand the positions, roles, and agency of various levels of actors and institutions with a stake in the mixing or unmixing of peoples and traditions. The following chapters examine the relations of state–society relations around sites and look at why many marginal as well as some central sites remain shared and uncontested while other sites become the locus of conflict and violence.[24]

STATE–SOCIETY RELATIONS

To try to conceptualize these transformations and to envision these various instances of conflict and cooperation in a more coherent framework, we need to formulate some general propositions about the nature of state–society relations and state goals and policies. State policies are made and remade in the exchange between state actors and social actors who compose the polity and represent the field of opportunities and constraints that state actors encounter in their relations with society. Both the existing relations of social, ethnic, religious, and demographic diversity and the legacies of toleration, accommodation, or interreligious conflict influence the politics of the state. Political authorities behave within a general political culture of past and present actions and responses but also strategically within the boundaries of the bargaining power they acquire vis-à-vis existing groups within society. It is from within the structures and institutions of society that state actors both acquire their resources and their legitimacy.

On the other hand, state policies are also the products of macrohistorical transformations, changes of identity and ideology that are effected over the *longue durée* and that have implications at the more general level of the world system of ideas and political formations. That is, the historical moment and the type of political formation partly shape the cultural schema of state policies. Premodern empires, for example, were much more diverse and generally understood diversity as a given that need not turn into "sameness," but modern nation-states have been keen on homogenizing populations and have often been inimical to diversity.[25] Whether we analyze a premodern empire or a nationalizing state, we have to consider the larger political culture in which states operate since this clearly shapes the preferences and decisions of state leaders. The analysis thus necessarily evokes a diachronic understanding of the influences that shape state action. Most of the chapters in this book remark on the relatively peaceful sharing that occurred under the Ottoman Empire and only highlight the customs and meanings of daily life that were altered with the advent of nationalism. One example is Cyprus, where nationalism led to divisions that were unpredictable given the groups' prior historical accommodation with each other. Even though Cyprus is divided, nationalism did not fully succeed at tearing apart the old fabric of society as many shrines are still shared for a multiplicity of reasons. Harmanşah and colleagues show the degree of continuity between the Ottoman Empire and the Turkish Republican state in the perception of an Alevi-Bektaşi threat as introducing unauthorized pluralism into the museum as well as the discontinuity between empire and nation-state in the tremendous homogenizing and secularizing discourse of the Republic.

By introducing politics and state policies into this study, we deal with the role of the state in a variety of dimensions. We explore the ways the state in a particular space is involved in regulating, administering, and politically organizing relations around the shared shrine. A general question regarding the state would examine the degree to which it is absent or present at the site and the extent it makes demands on the local community around the shrine. The relative political involvement of the state shapes the choreography of sharing as it is organized and regulated by locals, often of religious ilk. Many scholars who have worked on shared sacred sites located in imperial and premodern settings find that the state is either voluntarily or involuntarily absent, producing a vacuum within which institutional actors have power to regulate.[26]

Historically, the coexistence between groups and the sharing of religious sacred sites has occurred under the aegis of states that were interested both in maintaining and in manipulating diversity. Historical conditions where states emerged within syncretic environments and as hybrid entities helped shape tolerant attitudes toward diversity. Thus, one general hypothesis would be that the more open a state is to ethnic or religious difference, the more likely it is for coexistence to develop and shared sites to be maintained. In such situations the agreement seems to be that violence is rare and groups tend to share in peaceful fashion. We have to acknowledge that such settings will become more contentious and violence will occur when there are wars, periods of transition, or conflict inspired by coreligionists across the border. This was the case not only during the Arab conquests and the time of the Crusades but also during the long reign of the Ottoman Empire when the rule was toleration of multiconfessional sharing, except when tensions arose, especially in relation to the neighboring empires. The "Great Serbian Migrations," for example, were organized by the Serbian Orthodox patriarch Arsenije III Carnojevic in the seventeenth century as a result of war and devastation, and they altered the balance of Ottoman/Christian Orthodox coexistence in the Balkans.

That does not mean that conflict will ensue whenever the state is present and is forcefully involved in the regulation of a site. Here we have to explore different dimensions, such as state dominance, as well as the relations that states have with dominant ethnic and religious groups within the country. We can posit that the more associated a state is with one particular group, the more likely it will be to promote the rights of that group, allowing it domination over religious sites. Yet such close association between state and dominant religious group does not indicate whether open conflict or quietude will prevail.

According to Hayden, when such a situation occurs and one group clearly dominates, conflict is not likely to occur since the minority does not pose a risk. Rather, it is perceived as a risk when one group dominates and another religious group has enough principled sources of support that it can mobilize; then the likelihood of conflict increases. Hayden describes these particular situations of competitive sharing as "manifesting the negative definition of tolerance as passive noninterference and premised on a lack of ability of either group to overcome the other."[27] Here he gives the example of Israel and Palestinians, where dominance and sharing exist but also obvious hostility and fear. This is true in many places. Yet, although in Cyprus each state is clearly associated with the dominant ethnic group and both the Greek Cypriot and the Turkish Cypriot states are rewriting the narratives of dominance and sharing, Mete Hatay shows in his chapter that there are very few local disagreements that incite violence. Focusing exclusively on conflict ignores longer periods of lack of conflict in a site.

When states are present and strong, various other forms of state–religious group cooperation might exist. We are particularly interested in exploring instances where state affinity with one dominant religion is uncontested, yet the choreography of daily life over long periods allows for coexistence. Here again we can return to the imperial example since empires did present strong affinities for one dominant religion yet allowed multiple choreographies of shared sacred sites. There are imperial examples of the opposite as well, which should lead us to think more carefully about what the content of state policy was as well as the choreography around mixing in communities.

At the height of confessionalization in the Habsburg realms, the association between the imperial state and the Catholic Church rendered the mixing of communities quite impossible, forcing separation, exile, and conversion. Among more contemporary cases are the multiplicity of shared sacred sites, Hindu temples, and Sufi *dargahs* (shrines) in India. But where relations between Hindus, Muslims and Sikhs have been fraught with tension, violence and often destruction have followed. Yet, as Bigelow demonstrates, especially for the Punjab, in many cases groups have been able to resist the divisive politics of the state. She demonstrates that the local actors were keen on sharing and self-policing their own communities in order to manage relations between groups.[28] We then need to explore more carefully the relations between different sets of actors and the state. One important set of relations that often is critical in shaping policy around these sites remains that between political and religious actors.

RELIGIOUS VERSUS POLITICAL CONTROL OF SACRED SITES

Do religious leaders possess a monopoly of defining and shaping the conflict surrounding a sacred site? There is little doubt that a consensus among religious leaders will go a long way to determine the manner in which the site is viewed. Often religious leaders are well entrenched in their communities, and their interpretation often promotes the acceptable and the politically feasible. That religious leaders ought to be part of the political negotiations over a site should be self-evident, but it would be wrong to assume they hold a monopoly over religious issues. Often religious leaders both define the discourse and are subject to political constrains by the state, in particular, over the degree to which they are allowed to play a role in the management of inter- and intrareligious relations and choreographies of sharing in mixed sites.

Religious leaders have multifaceted relations with political authorities, across the religious leadership of different communities, and with their constituencies. Most of the essays in this volume explore these relations, especially those between religious and state actors, sometimes in agreement with each other, but at other times clearly in tension. In colonial Algeria, the French state was ready to let the Catholic order establish itself and conduct missionary work as long as it did not interfere with French plans and, in fact, the Church's missionary work assisted the settlement of the region. In the Holy Sepulchre, where the different denominations of priests are not beholden to a particular settled religious community but cater more to the pilgrims, the religious leaders are adept at seeking the dominant state to negotiate their place and privileges in the Church. Glenn Bowman in his chapter shows that the demands for shared rights in the Holy Sepulchre have been negotiated at even a larger scale involving the countries representing the respective local denominations and Israel. The latter's determination to maintain control and ensure the best strategic gains from the Holy Sepulchre are clear in its international dealings. David Henig is steeped in the discourse of Bosnian religious communal actors and their interpretation of state-approved Islamic community actors' programs and guiding principles for Islamic practice. Muslims at the different shrines and pilgrimage sites bemoan their religious leaders' change of heart with regard to proper Islamic practice and the influence of Salafi intruders, which they perceive to be nefarious to the traditional Bosnian way.

In each of these cases once again we observe the changing nature of religious ideals, the reinterpretation of positions and traditions, and the "right practice"—all indications of how fluid the religious discourse can be. This is the result of the dialectical nature of political negotiations, the power relations between the various stakeholders, and public opinion, which "controls" the discourse.[29] Over time, changes occur to the political role of religion in a society and religious leaders' place in the discussion on national secular issues. This is a shift that must be considered in evaluating the role of religion versus politics in conflict management/incitement.

For example, in his book, Hassner compares Jerusalem post 1967 to the late 1980s to explain that the explosive politics in the latter period were a result of the end of earlier cooperation between political and religious leaders in Israel. While moderation among Jewish religious leaders in 1967 was critical to contain religious conflict in the 1970s, it is not clear at all that political leaders led this relative moderation. In hindsight, both nationalist and religious ideologies were less extreme in the

1960s. But the specific analysis of the various actors is beyond the available space here. It is suffice to say that it was not a one-way influence, and that the malleability of theology has to be taken into account in any diachronic analysis. The notion that it is exclusively a matter of political leaders leaves much to be explained.[30] Indeed, extreme religious leaders gain religious prominence through pushing religious extremism. This is true concerning Jews and Muslims alike. In the short run, because of the power disparity in Israel, Jewish extremism is more often successful while Muslim extremism encounters a government backlash. (See chapters by Pullan, Reiter, and Barkan.) Reiter's analysis shows that the politically extreme Muslim leadership in the conflict over the Mamilla Cemetery caused a furor and tipped the court's decision against the Muslim plaintiffs, despite their substantive case.

That cooperation between political and religious leaders is critical should be self-evident, though we ought to recognize this is not always the case, and each elite may play to its own constituency. It is questionable to assume that either the political or the religious authorities are more or less consistently peaceful. There is widespread interfaith activism and neither constituency is homogenous, so it is necessary to focus attention on the power struggle within each group—whether done politically or camouflaged as religious—to explain the conflict. In cases where religious authorities are subjugated to political authorities, whether because of authoritarianism or subscribing to a larger national–state-centric ideology, it would be hard to speak of two distinct elites that need to cooperate. In each case, the empirical evidence should be analyzed to apprehend the extent of autonomy between political and religious actors.

Contextualizing the sacred site within the conflict writ large is a matter of evaluation. But to suggest that one factor overshadows all others, while this may be true, ought to be carefully analyzed. Consider the claim that the dispute over the Temple Mount in Jerusalem was the ultimate reason for the failure of the Camp David negotiations. Was it the case or rather the convenient rationale for many to hang the failure on the uncompromising other side? Clearly, the issue was as pivotal as any, but the combustion involved other issues (refugees, specific territory), including the tempo of negotiations in the summit itself, the Second Intifada which followed in its wake, and Sharon's aggressive "visit" to the Temple Mount. Did the site provide a cause and stage for the conflict? Certainly. Whether this was the prime reason or a meaningful cipher is more a matter of judgment.

CONCLUSION

This book explores various regions of the post-Ottoman world and their diversity of forms of sharing, accommodating, and engaging in conflict between different religions and religious denominations. Most sacred sites exemplify coexistence, which include tensions embedded in sharing at moments of open conflict. The best representative cases of conflict are the holy sites in Palestine/Israel where state action directly inflamed antagonism between groups and violent conflagration resulted. The least conflictual cases are in Turkey, where the memory of competition is more implied than present, and in Our Lady of Africa in Algiers, where the state has maintained strict regulation of Muslim participation at the site but has not restricted access. The chapters on the Balkans, Cyprus, and the earlier period in the Ottoman Empire underscore that despite the divisions and tensions between groups claiming ownership and sharing the sacred space, there have not been eruptions of violence, even when political context might suggest a greater likelihood of open violent conflict. The Turkish Bektaşi and Mevlevi shrines and museums have not become the scene of hostilities, and tensions in Bosnia caused by intracommunal struggles to define a new postwar Bosnian Muslim identity and their reflection on the traditions of Orthodox-heterodox mixing is unlikely to lead to aggression.

What many of the chapters show is that, although differences exist and identities are shaped by differences, these variations do not necessarily become salient enough to incite violence as long as states, religious and political actors, and particular constituencies are not inciting conflict for political gain and remain open to negotiation and dialogue. The chapters show that political action is primus inter pares in explaining coexistence and conflict, but it is clear from the various case studies we present that the role of religious authorities, the economic benefits of interfaith mixing, and the nature and role of the museumization are critical in shaping the interests of the various interlocutors in the various sites. Political leaders at times incite violence while seeking political and nationalist gain, as do religious extremists, and both use religious rhetoric and claim religious victimization and dispossession. When conflicts are avoided or subside, states are also responsible, negotiating ancient disputes about the sharing of sacred space, such as the Holy Sepulchre.

Yet religion can also become an agent of change. Instead of arguing for separation, it can become a catalyst for sharing or nonconflictual choreography of belonging in different ways. National states have been at the forefront of homogenizing the identity of the state and as such have forced separations and amalgamations that have conflicted with cultural and religious groups and spaces. The essays in this volume show that we cannot generalize whether the interests of local actors will enable them to carve an autonomous space of coexistence (such as economic interests) or whether they will submit to the purported national interest. Our work shows that when political actors or local community members find an economic advantage to the management of a site, they are more likely to reproduce existing relations. So the shrines that provide economic opportunities in Cyprus continue to exist uncontested while the marketplace in al-Wad Street in Jerusalem has expanded despite the hardships imposed by the Israeli state and the harassment by the neighboring religious Haredi communities, which demonstrate acts and artifacts of resistance.

The volume underscores the malleability of religious sites within the political discourse and that it is the synthesis of daily life of sacred sites and high politics that constructs a choreography of these sites and determines whether it is conflictual or collaborative. The growing attention in political analysis to religion is critical, but—as the chapters that follow illustrate—this has to be done within, not in contrast to, politics.

NOTES

1. We use the term "choreography" as taken from Roger Friedland and Richard Hecht, "The Bodies of Nations: A Comparative Study of Religious Violence in Jerusalem and Ayodhya," *History of Religions* 38, no. 2 (1998) 101–49.
2. Anna Bigelow, "Everybody's Baba: Making Space for the Other, in *Sharing the Sacra: The Politics and Pragmatics of Intercommunal Relations Around Holy Places*, ed. Glenn Bowman, 25–43 (Oxford: Berghahn Books, 2012).
3. See Howard Adelman and Elazar Barkan, *No Return, No Refuge: Rites and Rights in Minority Repatriation* (New York: Columbia University Press, 2011), 238–42; William Dalrymple, *From the Holy Mountain: A Journey Among the Christians of the Middle East* (New York: Henry Holt, 1977); "Christians in the Middle East," *BBC*, December 15, 2005, http://news.bbc.co.uk/2/hi/middle_east/4499668.stm; Ethan Bronner, "Mideast's Christians Losing Numbers and Sway," *New York Times*, May 12, 2009; and Rachel Donadio "Catholic Bishops Deplore Mideast Christians' Plight," *New York Times*, June 6, 2010. For a broad view of the challenges, see Osman Mirghani, "Christians' Fears in the Arab World," *Al-Arabiya News*, March 22, 2012; and "For Arab World's Christians, An Uncertain Fate" *NPR*, August 25, 2013, http://www.npr.org/2013/08/25/215494243/for-arab-worlds-christians-an-uncertain-fate.
4. Maria Couroucli, "Saint Georges l'Anatolien, maîtres des frontiers," in *Religions traversées: Lieux saints partagés entre chrétiens, musulmans et juifs en Méditerranée*, ed. Dionigi Albera and Maria Couroucli (Arles, France: Actes Sud, 2009), 175–209.
5. Marshall J. Breger, Yitzhak Reiter, and Leonard Hammer, eds., *Holy Places in the Israeli–Palestinian Conflict: Confrontation and Co-Existence* (New York: Routledge, 2010). Note the minimal attention given to the political study of the religious and sacred sites. Can we say that the extensive violence involving religious sites is unique, or does the attention create a category that presents the appearance of difference? There is little doubt that the violence against sacred sites is specifically directed at these, but the question is whether this is analogous with sites of national significance or cultural patrimony.
6. Dionigi Albera, "'Why Are You Mixing What Cannot Be Mixed?' Shared Devotions in the Monotheisms," *History and Anthropology* 19, no. 1 (2008): 37–59.
7. Some key examples of such work are Maria Rosa Menocal, *The Ornament of the World: How Muslims, Jews, and Christians Created a Culture of Tolerance in Me-

dieval Spain (New York: Black Bay Books, 2002); Ole Peter Grell and Bob Scribner, eds., *Tolerance and Intolerance in the European Reformation* (Cambridge: Cambridge University Press, 1996); and Scott Dixon, Dagmar Freist, and Mark Greengrass, eds., *Living with Religious Diversity in Early-Modern Europe* (Surrey, UK: Ashgate, 2009).

8. Karen Barkey, *Empire of Difference: The Ottomans in Comparative Perspective* (Cambridge: Cambridge University Press, 2008). Discussions of such issues are also in Robert D. Crews, *For Prophet and Tsar: Islam and Empire in Russia and Central Asia* (Cambridge, MA: Harvard University Press, 2006); and Robert P. Geraci and Michael Khodarkovsky, eds., *Of Religion and Empire: Missions, Conversions and Tolerance in Tsarist Russia* (Ithaca, NY: Cornell University Press, 2001).

9. Glenn Bowman, "Orthodox-Muslim Interactions at 'Mixed Shrines' in Macedonia," in *Eastern Christians in Anthropological Perspective*, ed. Chris Hann and Hermann Goltz, 195–219 (Berkeley: University of California Press, 2010).

10. Ibid., 198.

11. See, for example, the essays in the collection Dionigi Albera and Maria Couroucli, eds., *Religions traversees: Lieux saints partages entre Chretiens, Musulmans et Juifs en Mediterranee* (Arles, France: Actes Sud, 2009). Published in English as *Sharing Sacred Spaces in the Mediterranean: Christians, Muslims, and Jews at Shrines and Sanctuaries* (Bloomington: Indiana University Press, 2012).

12. Robert M. Hayden, "Antagonistic Tolerance: Competitive Sharing of Religious Sites in South Asia and the Balkans," *Current Anthropology* 43, no. 2 (2002): 205–31.

13. Oleg Grabar and Benjamin Z. Kedar, eds., *Where Heaven and Earth Meet: Jerusalem's Sacred Esplanade* (Austin: University of Texas Press, 2010).

14. Ron E. Hassner, *War on Sacred Grounds* (Ithaca, NY: Cornell University Press, 2009), 31–33.

15. The sacredness of a site is increased when it is perceived to be under threat. See David Chidester and E. T. Linenthal, eds., *American Sacred Space* (Bloomington: Indiana University Press, 1995), 3; and Breger, Reiter, and Hammer, *Holy Places*, 6.

16. Monica Duffy Toft, "Issue Indivisibility and Time Horizons as Rationalist Explanations for War," *Security Studies* 15, no. 1 (2006): 36. In contrast, James D. Fearon believes there are ways of including other factors that circumvent indivisibility: "The issues over which states bargain typically are complex and multidimensional; side-payments or linkages with other issues typically are possible; and in principle states could alternate or randomize among a fixed number of possible solutions to a dispute." James D. Fearon, "Bargaining, Enforcement, and International Cooperation," *International Organization* 52, no. 2 (1998): 282.

17. Stacie E. Goddard, "Uncommon Ground: Indivisible Territory and the Politics of Legitimacy," *International Organization* 60, no. 1 (2006): 35–68.
18. Hassner is largely critical of the literature on indivisibility that views indivisibility as a result of politics, not as a cause of conflict (*War on Sacred Grounds*, 38–39).
19. Isak Svensson argues that if "the belligerents' demands are explicitly anchored in a religious tradition, they will come to perceive the conflicting issues as indivisible." See Isak Svensson, "Fighting with Faith: Religion and Conflict Resolution in Civil Wars," *Journal of Conflict Resolution*. 51, no. 6 (2007): 930.
20. Toft, in "Issue Indivisibility," centers her empirical discussion on Chechnya (37–40); see also Dan Lindley, "Historical, Tactical, and Strategic Lessons from the Partition of Cyprus," *International Studies Perspectives* 8 (2007): 224–41, http://www3.nd.edu/~dlindley/handouts/CyprusPartition.pdf. Goddard, in "Uncommon Ground," uses Ireland as an empirical case study. Japan has ongoing conflicts with Russia over the Northern Islands, over the Senkaku/Diaoyutai Islands with China, and over the Takeshima/Dokdo islands with South Korea.
21. Toft, "Issue Indivisibility," 39.
22. Yitzhak Reiter, Nazmi Ju'beh, *Contested and Shared Holy Sites in Palestine/Israel: Towards an Inclusive Narration.* (unpublished ms.)
23. Nivedita Menon, "The Ayodhya Judgment: What Next?" *Economic & Political Weekly*, July 30, 2011; and Shahira Naim and R. Sedhuraman, "Ayodhya Heads to Supreme Court," *Tribune* (India), September 30, 2010, http://www.tribuneindia.com/2010/20101001/main1.htm
24. "Mixing" is term preferred by Glenn Bowman in his discussion of shared sites, and "unmixing" was used by Rogers Brubaker as a way to talk about the separation of peoples after the collapse of multiethnic empires.
25. Aron Rodrigue, "Difference and Tolerance in the Ottoman Empire," interview by Nancy Reynolds. *Stanford Humanities Review* 5, no. 1 (1996): 81–92.
26. Many of the articles in *Religions traversees* discuss situations of an absent state where coexistence and sharing was mostly a local phenomenon. See Albera and Couroucli, *Religions traversees*.
27. Hayden, "Antagonistic Tolerance," 206.
28. Anna Bigelow, *Sharing the Sacred: Practicing Pluralism in Muslim North India* (Oxford: Oxford University Press, 2010).
29. A central claim by Hassner is that politicians have to include religious leaders in the conflict management of sacred sites, and that they should not ignore the religious component by treating it merely as ideology. While it is clear that leaders of every group of stakeholders in a conflict should be included, it is not at all clear that religious beliefs are more critical to the process than nationalist

or racial beliefs when these incite conflict. The suggestion that political leaders who co-opt religious leaders are somehow better able to manage the religious conflict assumes that the goal of political leaders is to control the conflict, and religious leaders have somehow to be enticed to participate (Hassner, *War on Sacred Grounds*, 3). There is no empirical or analytical reason to support this. Often the two constituencies share goals—either pursuing conflict or coexistence—and cooperate on a set of issues, of which a particular site, as central as it might be, is only one of a set of issues involving the sides, including mundane political considerations of power, coalition building, recognition, and relative standing in the community. There are many religious leaders who participate in interfaith cooperation.

30. "If they can mobilize influential religious leaders who are able to redefine the meaning, value, or parameters of a sacred site in a manner conducive to conflict resolution." (Hassner, *War on Sacred Grounds*, 4) While the sentiment of cooperation between religion and politics is right, this vision needs to be expanded. In evaluating the role of religious leaders in this conflict, Hassner's analysis ignores the consequences of two decades of occupation, the intervening wars, the intifada, the mounting religious extremism globally—certainly among Muslims and among Jews—the growing entitlements many Israelis felt of intertwined religious and nationalists ideologies, and the growing Palestinian national movement that had lacked almost any independent voice before 1967 but by the mid 1980s had become formidable. These are only some of the factors that provide the context for the growing volatility around the site and the city, which make the explicit separation of religious from political causes unwarranted.

1

RELIGIOUS PLURALISM, SHARED SACRED SITES, AND THE OTTOMAN EMPIRE

KAREN BARKEY

PERHAPS ONE OF the most salient problems shared by our contemporary world and the field of social science relates to ethnic and religious conflict and coexistence. The question of what makes certain societies relatively tolerant of ethnic and religious diversity while others appear prone to conflict, violence, and even genocide remains unanswered. Many scholars want to understand how people of different religious and ethnic backgrounds manage to live together, cooperating across social boundaries, but also sometimes engage in life-threatening conflict. In this book, the sharing of sacred space—which has occurred freely in many mixed societies—is taken to reside at the heart of understanding both peaceful coexistence and violence.

Shared sacred sites are holy for multiple religious groups (groups that may also be ethnically or nationally distinct) and serve not only as places where persons are brought together to variously respect the site but also as sites where they are forced by their coexistence to mediate and negotiate their otherness. These sites are often "indices of the quality of interreligious relations" in larger national contexts.[1]

Possessing tremendous religious, ethnic, and linguistic diversity, the Ottoman Empire gave rise to many forms of coexistence (peaceful or otherwise) that offer us a genuine laboratory of research possibilities that have yet to be exhausted. There is ample proof that the Ottoman case is still relevant to discussions of diversity and that the *millet* organization of religious communities is understood as a relatively successful historical example of ruling diversity.[2] While there is apparent agreement that the *millet* system of organizing diverse communities under a common religious umbrella and incorporating them into the state through their own religious hierarchy worked relatively well, such an institutional focus faces the danger of oversimplifying the day-to-day complexity of interreligious relations.[3] For this reason, we need to look beyond the *millet* system and self-consciously rethink diversity as a dynamic and capacious concept. Diversity flags difference, indicating boundaries and relations within sites as varied as markets, religious institutions, and political, legal, and administrative organizations, among others. There are so many locations and institutions where difference was negotiated and managed in the Ottoman Empire that a true study of its diversity would be deservedly path breaking.

It is by now an accepted fact that the first three hundred years of the empire were tolerant of diversity. Toleration in the Ottoman Empire was an organizational by-product of state society relations in which both the state and religious community leaders were interested in intercommunal peace and order and in the maintenance of boundaries within a flexible system of negotiation. Islam provided an initial cultural blueprint for how to rule non-Muslim "peoples of the Book"—that is, Christians and Jews—in a Muslim polity: the empire would offer protection in return for the subordination and special taxation of its religious minorities. The Ottomans adapted and adjusted Islamic teachings to address the needs of the state. Examples of conflict and persecution can nonetheless be found at the local level: both individual and communal cases of local violence occurred and are inscribed in the archives. Yet these were not allowed to spiral out of control, and state officials acted quickly to punish culprits and establish local peace. As both state and social actors benefited from accommodation and coexistence, toleration became the norm. Political leaders, scholars, and public intellectuals of the time wrote about

Ottoman diversity and its positive characteristics.[4] Local pashas sometimes declared their own small-scale edicts of toleration, interfering in Christian confessional struggles.[5] As they watched the religious divisions caused by the Reformation and religious wars, the Ottomans were eager to exhibit their state policies of accommodation, especially at the borders with Europe. Most sensitive to these confessional struggles were the local high-ranking officials who were wary of these religious tensions spilling over into the Ottoman lands they governed.

While this form of toleration provided a general and pragmatic understanding of diversity, the proof of a wide-ranging construction of mutual coexistence and forbearance can be found at many sites and sets of relations. Groups related to each other in their everyday activities, frequently engaging with one another on economic, social, and cultural levels. When they encountered disagreement, they had multiple legal forums to resolve their issues. They also interacted with one another in religious contexts, navigating issues that pertained to cohabitation in mixed neighborhoods, such as the intrusion of religious symbols and sounds upon the other, participation in each other's ceremonies, and cohabiting spaces of worship.

One approach to uncovering the workings of diversity is through the history of the numerous shared sacred sites that existed in the vast dominions of the Ottoman Empire. These sites were sacred places—churches, shrines, and mausoleums—shared by more than one religious and ethnic group. Looking at the manner in which shared sacred sites became places of coexistence, conflict, and cooperation is one way to evaluate the quality of interreligious relations in the empire. Given that many of these sites remain shared in the post-Ottoman world raises the significance of this phenomenon as well. These spaces of sharing have survived numerous religious and ethnic wars, several nationalizing regimes, and efforts aimed at creating a forced homogeneity, which only reinforces the fact that coexistence and toleration are possible in the *longue durée* and that the forbearance necessary for coexistence between groups can pass down through generations, even though conflict might temporarily and abruptly interrupt peace.

This chapter explores toleration and coexistence by proceeding in three interrelated sections: First, I rethink the conceptual language of coexistence, toleration, and violence in order to apply them to the long history of Ottoman pluralism, where toleration set the stage for centuries of coexistence in various religious, legal, and social contexts. Second, I explore key debates on the sharing of sacred sites and discuss how we can bring some of the analytic dimensions used in the toleration discussions to bear on sacred sites. I argue that to understand the manner in which sacred sites were shared in the Ottoman Empire, we need to focus on state policies, boundary relations across groups, and the construction of identities. Doing so will enable us to develop a methodology for historical ethnography, which will in turn allow us to understand the manner in which relations across boundaries change over time as well as how they manifest themselves in the practical negotiations of the day to day. Third, I analyze the historical circumstances that provided the context for the sharing of sacred spaces in the Ottoman Empire.

This chapter then demonstrates that during the reign of the Seljuk and Ottoman empires the larger context of toleration and accommodation to diversity, especially of Christians across the frontiers, promoted the sharing of sacred sites between Muslims and Christians. While churches and monasteries were often converted to Islamic buildings, mixed worship became the rule in many places as openness to the other was encouraged by state authorities. I also show that Ottomans made a concerted effort to build institutions that were inclusive of the diversity of the empire, often positioning their foundations within reach of Christians and Jews. I also raise several issues not fully resolved and require further research and analysis.

DEFINING COEXISTENCE, TOLERATION, AND VIOLENCE

Debates around toleration and coexistence have broad significance, especially as the former is often contested and the latter takes various and contradictory forms. These remain relevant concepts to the study of shared sacred sites since sharing occurs under an umbrella of coexistence, whether tolerant or violent. Generally, we speak of coexistence when two or more groups live together while respecting differences and working out conflicts in a nonviolent fashion. We categorize a situation as tolerant when variance between groups is marked, but the majority decides they will live together even if their differences are irreconcilable. Toleration comes from the Latin word *"tolerare,"* which means to endure. In this sense, scholars have understood toleration "to signify no more than forbearance and the permission given by the adherents of a dominant religion for other religions to exist, even though the latter are looked upon with disapproval as inferior, mistaken, or harmful."[6] Toleration, then, usually refers to the actions of public authorities, whereas the term "tolerance" refers to the understanding and consideration that local populations may develop toward each other. Toleration represents that state policies aim at ensuring coexistence and that different groups can earn their livelihood and live in peace together. Tolerance represents the more organic, social, and civic notions of living together among people who recognize differences in their everyday lives. These two do not always coincide. One can be present without the other. Historians and political philosophers have primarily carried out historical and analytic work on toleration within the geographical confines of Western Europe. More recently, toleration has been explored in various geographical contexts, and the analytic boundaries of its study have stretched to the social sciences more generally. In this chapter I do not intend to review the field, although I will highlight those studies that have provided useful concepts and mechanisms for understanding coexistence.

There was a time when historical studies of toleration in Western Europe were written to stress more long-term trends of persecution and violence. Particularly in the classic work of Robert Moore, *The Formation of a Persecuting Society*, there is a tendency to see connected histories of intolerance, with every episode of violence becoming more important and widespread.[7] This reminds us of many conflicts where it is said that ancient hatreds and long-term historical animosities endure, flaring up from time to time and causing the collapse of multicommunal societies.[8] Here the assumption is that hatred and violence are deep-rooted between groups and will erupt into violent action at every possible juncture. There is also the assumption that difference is marked by inflexible and fixed markers with conflict across boundaries dependent on these essentialist notions of identity. As we will see, this view is similarly embedded in parts of recent anthropology scholarship.

These rigid assumptions might mostly be a part of the past. In his work on the Reformation in Europe, historian Bob Scribner argues that "there were moments or circumstances in which intensified persecution could be mobilised for various reasons, yet it was not possible for this to be continuous over time or across an entire society."[9] He adds that "persecution which is both extensive and intensive is socially dysfunctional in the long or even medium term, and persecution may be more a matter of short term political conjunctures or expedients."[10] In *Communities of Violence*, David Nirenberg reconsiders the function of violence. Rather than just viewing violence as part of an explanation of a "persecutory *longue durée*," he emphasizes its role in the immediate setting, its multiple meanings, and the various tasks it performs in regulating community relations.[11] His intervention makes violence part of relations on the ground while also making it visible within a contained time and space. Violence and persecution are conceptualized as episodes within the broad temporality of coexistence. This makes sense theoretically if we take a Simmelian view of conflict, understanding it as an integral component of sociability; conflict then is essential and omnipresent but also serves a positive function in social relations.[12]

Recently historians of Western European religious coexistence have produced studies where the complicated, contingent, and often historically unique configuration of toleration and persecution is clearly demonstrated.[13] These scholars show that there were multiple ways in which coexistence and conflict could become complementary in the unfolding of the Western European history as rulers, subjects, and members of different communities found ways of organizing social relations.[14] They stress the role of both public authorities (usually the state) and boundaries between groups in their work. By analyzing different modes of coexistence across confessional boundaries, Keith Luria demonstrates the dramatic ways in which French Catholics and Huguenots began peacefully coexisting after the Edict of Nantes (1598), when a powerful monarch pushed them toward accommodating one another. Drawing on Luria's study of France, we can identify three forms of coexistence that help us to conceptualize relations across religious boundaries: (1) cooperation at the local level; (2) tense coexistence around issues of governance and participation in civic life; (3) and violent conflict.[15]

In the first case, cooperation in social, cultural, and economic affairs as well as intermarriage and participation in each other's baptisms and funerals was common. In the second, boundary relations were negotiated and separation was instituted and monitored leading to the separation of sacred spaces, churches, cemeteries, and so on. This second form, according to Luria, emerged from a negotiated boundary when each side respected the rights of the other and when public authorities were present to maintain the boundaries between groups. It was also the form of negotiation that enabled a Huguenot minority to remain and coexist within a Catholic majority. The third form, violent conflict, historically reemerged after the Revocation of the Edict of Nantes in 1685 and renewed the persecution of Protestants.[16] Luria argues that during this period the state and the Church succeeded in constructing stricter barriers making confessional identity hold a place of primary importance, and therefore fostered this kind of violent conflict between groups.

Luria's work shows the dialectical manner in which religious identities can become set and lead to violent conflict in some places and during some periods, while in other places and times they change to allow for relations across boundaries and the flexibility of sharing. On the one hand, his work demonstrates how, after the Edict of Nantes, Protestants and Catholics in many places were able to bypass these fears and establish forms of coexistence that established fluid and permeable boundaries. On the other hand, he also reveals the manner in which each religion constructed a sense of its own absoluteness and a fear of contamination by the other. For example, in Poitou, the Capuchin mission was able to provoke significant rupture and violence through the use of public rituals, separation of sacred spaces, and conversions, resulting in the division of people of different religious denominations. It is here that we see public and religious authorities at work reinforcing religious absoluteness and difference. Such evidence is repeated in the work of others. For example, Benjamin Kaplan shows that in the later period of confessionalization in Europe, public and religious authorities promoted a perception of absolute difference; intolerance and piety became closely associated as religious prejudice demonstrated that one was really pious.[17]

What emerges most forcefully from these studies is the degree to which religious and public authorities play an integral role in engendering toleration, coexistence, and conflict. Religious authorities can force separation, intolerance, and conflict in the name of piety; conversely, in the name of state-making, public authorities may practically choose to promote toleration and coexistence to consolidate political power. Scribner argues that public authorities typically make pragmatic choices: "In changed circumstances, toleration was a privilege that could be withdrawn; or it was no more than a working political compromise that could be altered if and when circumstances allowed."[18] Yet we cannot attribute toleration or persecution completely to state makers and religious authorities. At the local level, publics were able to bypass the authorities. Left to their own devices, communities separated by confessional difference often found ways to cooperate, share, and coexist in peace. Wayne Te Brake focuses on the mechanisms of action that people in such situations espouse to maintain relations across boundaries and avoid conflict. Given a certain necessity to live in relative peace, he argues that even in places where oppression was relatively high, coexistence at the level of communities happened because those who were oppressed found ways to dissimulate and remain concealed and because those outside the community of dissenters showed indifference, toleration, and even complicity.[19]

In summary, the role of religious and public authorities, historical circumstances and the passage of time, the nature of identities, and the actual mechanisms of coexistence at the community level are all essential to the definition and practice of toleration. Since I will argue that the same explanatory variables are useful when seeking to understand the practices of coexistence at shared sacred sites, a brief discussion on the importance of public authorities (specifically the state), the role of social relations across boundaries, and the historical circumstances that help formulate identities is useful before we initiate our more focused discussion.

PUBLIC AUTHORITIES

States can choose to initiate violence and maintain conflict, or they can work to make inter- and intrareligious accommodation and sharing possible, depending on their political needs. First, states as political formations operate within certain cultural and ideological understandings that are the products of their history and their relations to the social structures on the ground. The difference between national states and empires discussed in this introduction is a case in point. Empires, as polities open to diversity, developed a variety of policies and solutions to accommodate diversity by keeping it manageable, productive, and subject to top-down control. Nation-states have been much more ruthless with regard to diversity, forcing the assimilation and homogenization of ethnic, cultural, and linguistic differences. Consequently, empires have been more open to the presence of diversity and, as we shall see, of shared sacred sites, whereas nationalizing states have tried to impose their supremacy over these spaces.

Second, given their larger cultural and institutional context, states make political and strategic decisions about the potential for conflict and harmony given existing diversity on the ground. As state makers get involved in creating legibility and organizing relations on the ground to maintain their rule, they often make decisions about accommodation, conflict, and coexistence in their land.[20] Decisions such as the Edict of Nantes in France (1596) or the Edict of Tolerance in the Habsburg Empire (1782) were decisions made by state makers either to contain civil violence and restore peace or to improve the economic conditions of the empire. Similarly, much is made of the narrative that Sultan Beyazid II in 1492 dispatched vessels to bring Jews and Muslims who were expelled during the Spanish Inquisition to the Ottoman lands and offer them opportunities to prosper. Such state decisions are seen as positive examples of coexistence and open up the way for more community interaction and accommodation.

BOUNDARIES AND THE POLITICS OF IDENTITY

The next area of emphasis concerns boundaries and the politics of identity. Following Fredrik Barth and Charles Tilly, I see identity as unfixed, allowing for the possibility of change and mixing while also recognizing the manner in which social actors politicize identity to instill categorical distinctions of *us* versus *them*. Boundaries are objective markers that define access to resources and rewards as well as subjective distinctions that actors have in their minds about access. Adopting a Barthian perspective might help us to clarify the relations between groups; Barth proposed that boundaries define groups, as opposed to the cultural and religious contents of each side. Boundaries matter because they help define difference.[21] Often when we look at the differences between peoples separated by boundaries, we see that they bear many similarities and that the separation itself is what intensifies difference. Therefore, boundaries are crucial to the management of difference. In a similar vein, Rogers Brubaker developed the notion of groupism in ethnic and racial analysis to denote that groups as entities become reified in public discourse and acquire a categorical existence of their own.[22] As Charles Tilly argues,

> Identity is in fact not private and individual but public and relational. . . . Any actor deploys multiple identities, at least one per tie, role, network and group to which the social actor is attached. So to assert an identity as a Chechnian or a Croat is not to summon up primeval consciousness but to draw a boundary separating oneself from specific others (in the instance, most often Russian, Serb or Muslim,) to claim solidarity with others on the

same side of the boundary, and to invoke a certain sort of relationship to those on the opposite side.[23]

Asserting that identities are public and relational allows for the possibility of change; individuals possess many different identities that they can pick from and between, depending on their social context. Boundaries that are fluid and easily crossed enhance flexible identities and allow for coexistence between groups. On the other hand, if boundaries are rigid and codified with "go" and "no-go" zones, identities become fixed, and conflict can easily erupt over issues of differential access. Of course, public authorities are involved in shaping boundaries and religious authorities as well, even if differently.

HISTORICAL METHODS

State policies, boundaries, and identities change over time, and the best way to capture these changes is to adopt a methodological perspective that promotes both historical and ethnographic sensibilities. While change can be demonstrated using diachronic analysis, which stresses transformation over time, synchronic analysis is better to unpack and disentangle relations among actors in a particular setting at a particular time. The best work combines the two, as William Sewell Jr. has argued in his defense of Clifford Geertz.[24] As we have already seen, the policies of state authorities and religious institutions change over time, providing the constraints and the opportunities available for accommodation and sharing at the communal level. Yet at any given moment, local forces, particular needs, and mentalities also operate within the case that shape the way people act, enter into peaceful agreements, or conflict. To understand such local contexts deeply, Geertzian close readings, "thick descriptions," and historical and present-day ethnographic studies of sites are needed. This is obviously very difficult to accomplish in the historical context since the type of local knowledge on social interaction crossing boundaries, the daily intelligence on how people live and accommodate to each other, is rarely the stuff of archives. It is indirectly gleaned from travelers' reports, biographies, and personal materials that can also be less reliable. As we rethink sacred sites, the importance of combining diachronic and synchronic temporalities together will become even more salient.

DEBATING COEXISTENCE, TOLERATION, AND VIOLENCE: APPROACHES TO THE STUDY OF IDENTITY WITHIN SHARED SACRED SITES

Analyses of the role of public authorities, of boundaries between groups, and of the manner in which identity becomes significant at moments of inclusion or exclusion from groups, spaces, and events are equally powerful ways to understand the politics of sacred sites. Yet the field of sacred sites is divided in its understanding of what is occurring in these shared spaces. Two perspectives remain at odds with one another: the first focuses on sharing in sacred sites as a nonthreatening form of coexistence and cooperation, while the second interprets sharing as a tension-filled and contested coexistence in which groups are just waiting for the first opportunity to assert their dominance. Different approaches to sharing are summarized in the book's introduction; however, it is beneficial to discuss them here in terms of identity politics. Most critical for the topic at hand are the following two different visions of identity in the study of sacred sites since they seem to have locked the field out of more innovative work.

Robert Hayden, who published in 2002 a seminal article in which he developed the concept of "antagonistic tolerance" (AT), emphasized a negative definition of tolerance, seeing it as the result of two or more groups achieving a kind of parity wherein each antagonistic group is unable to overcome the other. The groups therefore share the expectation that one day they will be able to either suppress or expel the other.[25] The AT model, as it is now known, "predicts that 'tolerance,' in the passive sense of permitting a subordinated group to manifest its religion and associated practices, occurs when dominance is clear."[26] For Hayden, this type of tolerance is only strategic acquiescence rather than genuine sharing. Writing in this volume, David Henig describes the AT perspective best:

> The idea of antagonistic tolerance simultaneously accommodates conflict and sharing as inevitable modalities in the pragmatics of social life in a multiethnic fabric. Put in this way, latent conflict supplies an inherent condition in the processes of making and sharing sacred sites, and sharing is understood only as a temporal moment expressing actual processual relations rather than a fixed quality of intergroup stasis based on long-lasting difference, antagonism, and pragmatic acceptance.[27]

In this view, identities are fixed, differences remain, and groups are inevitably driven toward separation even if they are temporarily amicable toward each other. The recent work of Ron Hassner, *War on Sacred Grounds*, remains within this identitarian framework, asserting that the characteristics of religious sites—their centrality, vulnerability, and indivisibility—make them contested and, as a result, always within the realm of potential violence.

Such perspectives have been criticized as essentialist and unresponsive to the multiple dimensions and multivocality of identities, the diversity within particular identities, and the transformation of identities over time. As Tilly rightly argues, identities are public, changeable, and expressed in the relations among people. Therefore, it is important to examine relations on the ground and acknowledge that situational identities possess a certain degree of autonomy and flexibility. Many social anthropologists stress the role of agency, the complexity of social relations, the strategies on the ground, and the meanings that actors give to their actions. They are committed to investigating continuity in historical and contemporary contexts through the methodological joining of diachronic and synchronic analyses.

Such a perspective sees shared sacred sites as potentially multivalent, enabling a number of groups (both within a single religion and spanning two or more communities) to gather. Sites reveal more than just a dichotomous outcome; local and sensitive investigation discovers open conflict, antagonism between groups, uneasy coexistence, amiable mutuality, and forms of syncretism.[28] Coexistence or antagonism depends very much on how people perceive the formation of inclusive or exclusive communities within sacred sites. Whether the site is perceived as building community and open to other influences determines how people engage with one another. How people practice their religions, how they understand and communicate their practices, and how their practices impact upon others at the sites are vital to our understanding of how space can be negotiated and shared between two or more potentially antagonistic groups. As described in our discussion of toleration and persecution, outcomes, especially conflict or violence, are usually not sustained over long periods of time. Relations at mixed sacred sites change over time according to political forces and interests surrounding the sites. The long tradition of sharing at sites strewn over the territories of the Ottoman Empire—stretching from the southern borders of the Holy Roman Empire through Hungary and the Balkans, to Yemen and Eritrea in the south, controlling much of North Africa and western Asia—demonstrates the diversity, complexity, and multivocality of the many groups that inhabited these lands.

COEXISTENCE AND SHARING SACRED SITES IN THE OTTOMAN EMPIRE

The context for coexistence and the sharing of sacred spaces in the Ottoman Empire was established early on, during the period of conquest and colonization, especially 1299–1453. The coexistence that emerged in the early centuries of Ottoman rule was the joint product of pre-Ottoman relations between the Byzantine and Seljuk empires, Ottoman state strategies of colonization and incorporation, and local predilections for cultural fusion. Important too was the role of various religious leaders and institutions in spreading a new Islamic vision, but tempering it within an

Islamo-Christian frame of reference. The Ottomans took their time, starting from a small principality and expanding through military conquest and alliances, both military and matrimonial.

The conquests that set the small principality on its path to empire were started with Osman, the first ruler, in 1299 and reached their apogee in 1453 with the conquest of Constantinople, the Byzantine capital. During this period the Ottomans conquered the Balkan Peninsula and expanded their reach in the Anatolian heartland. The combination of demographic, sociopolitical factors and expansive cultural fusion made for the military and sociocultural success of the early rulers. As used here, "cultural fusion" does not imply Islamic religious zeal and Holy War against the infidels or a strong sense of ethnic unity that helped organize fighters around their leaders. Rather, military conquest was facilitated by a fluid and dynamic frontier region where the boundaries between Islam and Christianity were famously porous; Islam and Christianity were both relatively undemanding, and Islam was mostly forbearing.

Ottomans were treading on fertile ground when they assembled what was by far the most inclusive and syncretic force of the region. Beginning as a small state appearing out of the breakdown of the Seljuk Empire (1077–1307), they had vast knowledge and experience managing diversity and accommodation and had developed the political culture of a frontier society on the move. Because their emerging state was small and had serious demographic disadvantages, their policy of expansion necessitated political and social accommodation (*istimalet*) as a pragmatic solution. When the Ottomans became a more established empire, their early virtues, such as the acceptance of diversity and multivocality of projects, remained key ingredients of their political form. Many premodern, land-based empires were multireligious and multiethnic political formations that included much diversity; they understood different populations as separate and did not force them to assimilate. It is in this vein that the Ottoman Empire's political culture was also open to diversity, by force of circumstance, historical antecedent, and a cultural understanding of the politics of empire and expansion. This overall description of Ottoman relations with diversity is fully applicable to the fourteenth and fifteenth centuries and extends with some exceptions to the eighteenth century. In this part of the chapter, I consider the initial institutionalization of relations that opened the way for accommodation to diverse religions and shared sites.

Moving beyond these imperial considerations, it is important to consider boundaries between groups located at different sites and their impact on identity construction in order to understand the propensity for the common usage of sacred sites and lands. Seljuk and early Ottoman relations at the frontier demonstrate that boundaries were recognized and accepted but were also "used" in ways that were fluid and porous. Physical, mental, and cultural boundaries were crossed, and identities were affected by the crossings. It is not that Muslims were not Muslims or Christians were not Christians, or that they became a truly syncretic whole (some syncretism was certainly apparent), but more that the porousness of boundaries demonstrated how similar peoples were to each other even if they belonged on the other side of the boundary. Clearly, Barth's identification of boundaries as more significant for identity construction than the content of cultural information and traditions is a useful anthropological insight that guides us in this work.

The Anatolian territory had been fertile ground for frequent population movements, frontier raids, and skirmishes as well as cooperation and coexistence between Christians and Islamic peoples since the Battle of Manzikert in 1071.[29] Such friction and fusion at the frontiers had created cultural mixes that paved the way for alliances across groups. Historians such as Keith Hopwood write about the political and cultural exchanges between the Seljuk and Byzantine empires, providing examples of emperors who crossed frontiers, visited each other's traditional cultural places, and were renowned for their multifaith landscapes from the eleventh century on. Nevra Necipoglu argues that Byzantine-Seljuk relations were not just relations of warfare but that these two groups hired each other's soldiers and mercenaries, maintained commercial relations, and married each other freely in sites of coexistence. She quotes twelfth-century Byzantine historian Niketas Choniates: "These islands were inhabited by colonies of Christians who, intermingling with the Turks of Ikonion [Konya] by means of barks and light boats, not only strengthened their mutual bonds of friendship but also maintained strong commercial ties. Allied with their neighbors, they looked upon the Romans [i.e., the Byzantines] as their enemies. Thus custom, reinforced by time, is stronger than race and religion."[30]

Friendship and enmity created alliances that sometimes defied imagination. Choniates was eager to show that Christians were getting along better with the Turks than with their fellow Christians by explaining the relations of Christians and Turks on the islands of Beysehir Lake as representative of peaceful coexistence.

Accommodation to the other was made in both physical structures and in spiritual and emotional configurations. In the Seljuk Empire, churches were maintained close to the Seljuk palaces to provide places for the Christian entourage of the sultans to pray and to ensure that their religious needs were met.[31] Moreover, myths, legends, and holy figures were appropriated by both cultures. Their myths and legends emphasized interfaith alliances and passions, crossing geographical and cultural frontiers. Christians and Muslims told analogous narratives and cohabitated, adopting each other's characteristics. For example, what became an important monument to the mythical Muslim warrior Seyyit Battal Ghazi (located at Nakoleia/Seyyit Gazi) was turned into a pilgrimage site for all who considered themselves of frontier heritage. There are various narratives of the life and prowess of Seyyit Battal Ghazi, especially romanced epics that emphasize the relation between this Muslim warrior and a Christian woman. Seyyit Battal is supposed to have laid siege to Amorion, where the daughter of the local castellan (castle-governor in the Byzantine Empire) fell in love with him but accidentally caused his death. It is said that the two lovers were buried together in the mausoleum, a Christian woman and a Turkish man.[32] The Byzantine tale of Digenis Akrites was based on the Arab-Byzantine wars, but Digenis himself was "the offspring of a cross-frontier love-match" between a converted Arab emir and a Byzantine noblewoman.[33] The assimilation of such narratives into the folklore of populations who interacted in their daily lives must have made these stories and their carriers more alike.

Additionally, pre-Ottoman Anatolia was the site of many conversions of religious sanctuaries associated with Christian holy figures and saints into Muslim sites with Muslim figures, but with Christian worship continuing in these places and considered sacred by both religions.[34] Many of these sites were associated with Khidr, "who is identified in Muslim tradition as the unnamed companion of Moses who holds the secret to immortal life (Qur'an 18:60) and who occupies a unique place in Muslim belief for his role as an elusive figure both of immortality and esoteric knowledge."[35] There have been various interpretations of how Khidr linked Christianity and Islam. Ethel Sara Wolper writes that "in his visitation to the sites of the figures of Saint George and Saint Theodore, Khidr served to mark the continuity and significance of these figures within a newly formed sacred landscape."[36] F. W. Hasluck, studying the materials of sixteenth-century visitors to Elwan Celebi Tekke near Corum, argued that Khidr was the ambiguous cultic transitional figure that transformed the Christian site into a Muslim one.[37] Along the tracks of this saintly figure's travels, Anatolia was strewn with ambiguous sanctuaries shared by Muslims and Christians. Oya Pancaroglu, studying the image and identity of dragon slayers (Saint George and Khidr are both identified as dragon slayers) in medieval Anatolia, maintains that "the web-like complexity of these identifications is evident particularly in the case of the dragon-slaying saint-hero whose legend and iconography readily traversed the fluid cultural boundaries between Christian and Muslim societies of medieval Anatolia."[38] Today in modern Turkey the tradition of Khidr continues under the name of Hidrellez, marking the beginning of spring, but also bringing the stories of Khidr, the Prophet Elijah, and the story of Saint George together. The mix of these figures and the particular days of the festivals are remarkable remnants of the days where the mixed sanctuaries helped bring Muslims and Christians together.

It is no surprise, then, that Michel Balivet identifies a "Turco-Byzantine crucible" that comes about after the Seljuk invasion of Anatolia and continues until the takeover of Constantinople in 1453. During this time many social and cultural exchanges were carried out, based on profound similarities in religion and mysticism, but also in scientific, popular and literary understandings.[39] What the Byzantine Empire began with Seljuk Turks extended to Ottomans and the lands they conquered in Anatolia and the Balkans. By the time the Ottomans rose to become the new regional power, Muslims and Christians had found multiple ways to accommodate each other across frontiers and in shared territories and sanctuaries. Fikret Adanir attests to this trend, stressing the resemblance between Turkic *yuruks* and Vlach and Albanian nomadic elements in the Balkans as conquests unfolded and Turks encountered their counterparts in the Balkans. Such similarity could facilitate exchange and cooperation as well as conquest.[40] Travelers of the fourteenth century assert that Asia Minor was a densely inhabited and prosperous space. They stress considerable agricultural and artisanal production, and the development of towns and commercial activity, partly as a result of conscious Ottoman policy and partly as a result of local interactions. Elizabeth Zachariadou argues that this level of development and growth can be explained by the number of mixed marriages between Muslims and Christians and the relative ease with which Christians left their lands to seek protection in Muslim lands.[41]

The opportunity for such openness and syncretism also signals the lack of a strong hegemonic Islamic project. The early symbiosis, the cultural syncretism and tolerance of the Ottoman rulers, indicates that while they were certainly mindful of their Muslim origins, they were not fully decided upon the form and the structure that their religiosity would take. The dervish orders of Sufi mystical saints that traveled into the West alongside Ottoman warriors represented one way of thinking, different from another more orthodox view of Sunni Islam. As a result of the absence of a standard framework for thinking about religion, the new conquerors of Anatolia and the Balkans were independent from rigorous and inflexible models of religion and less interested in the separation of religions. The cooperation between the conquering Ottoman leaders and the dervishes was neither fully planned nor thought out in religious terms. On-the-ground strategic thinking; immediate responses to local, regional, and economic stimuli; and the maintenance of open channels of communication across mixed networks of people produced cooperation and critical cross-religious interactions.[42] Such pragmatism emerged from shared historical and local understandings. Neither syncretism nor the decisive conversions of the Byzantine peasantries were planned.[43] There is no doubt that this indifference to religion would change; the religious arteries of the empire would come to harden and orthodoxy would prevail. By then, however, some mixed traditions, such as shared practices at shrines and ceremonies, were set and had taken on a life of their own.

Notwithstanding such versions of pragmatism, the Islamic blueprint of how to behave with conquered populations and how to manage peoples of different religions was indisputable yet adaptable to context. The indifference of the Ottomans to religion during the incipient stages of empire building needs to be discussed and adjusted in the context of Islamization and conversion. The conquest of Byzantine Anatolia and the Balkans by Turkish forces was neither easy nor pleasant. Speros Vryonis Jr., in his important work on the decline of medieval Hellenism in Asia Minor, describes the dominion of the Turks to be harsh and intransigent.[44] While Vryonis's perspective was long accepted, new research has altered part of the narrative of the initial encounters and the political and cultural changes of the period. The colonization and Islamization of the Balkan Peninsula started early with the first footholds of the Ottomans in the Balkans in 1354. However it was achieved, whether by conversion or by immigration, the Islamization of different Balkan populations was progressive, took time, and was not enforced simply by the sword.

Islamization came in many forms. Among them were the early work of colonizing dervish orders that were received relatively openly in the Balkans; the *devsirme*, the levy on young boys from Christian Balkan families; and the conversion of Christians both voluntary and forceful. No doubt numerous voluntary and forced marriages between Christian women and Muslim men promoted the spread of Islam in the countryside. Islamization was also encouraged in part by a heterodox understanding of Islam, which included an active dervish-based proselytism that was achieved via pious foundations and also within Islamo-Christian sanctuaries.[45] Hasluck's work points to the impact of advancing Ottoman forces and the conversions of religious spaces as additional elements of the Islamization trend. But his work also indicates that the manner in which these places were inhabited by dervishes served to open peripheral sites to local Christian populations, especially as they became in some way useful, imbued with healing power.[46] As Yuri Stoyanov writes: "During this advance the dervish orders took a number of Christian churches, saints' tombs and sanctuaries, thus greatly contributing to the evolving process of Christian-Islamic interaction and syncretism which had already began in Anatolia earlier in the Seldjuk period and was to reach a new scope of development and intensity in the Ottoman Balkans."[47] Under the influence of the dervish leaders, interactions between Christianity and Islam led to the sharing of sanctuaries and traditions, especially by rural and illiterate populations that were tucked away from elite influences.[48] Crypto-Christianity remains another less explored but fruitful area of sharing where religious rites such as baptism or pilgrimages to saints' tombs and shrines prepared the ground for further Christian and Islamic interfacing.

The discourse on Islamization in the early Ottoman Empire includes the conversion of peoples as well as of churches and monuments important to the conquered populations. Examining the historical record on conversions, for example, there is ample evidence that numerous religious properties survived the conquests unharmed.[49] Historians refer to the monastery of Saint John Prodromos near Serres or the monastery of Saint Athos as good examples of survival. Further research, however, shows a more complex situation in which rural monasteries survived but many urban monasteries were converted into Islamic property. According to Anthony Bryer, urban monasteries were six times more likely to become converted than rural ones. For urban cases, the numbers are harsh: out of 417 urban monasteries known within the borders of the Byzantine Empire in the twelfth century, 80 still existed at the eve of the Ottoman conquest, 20 remained after 1453, and 6 continued to modern times. In the rural case, of the 283 rural monasteries, 158 existed on the eve of the Ottoman conquest, 91 survived after, and 62 continued into the modern period.[50]

To understand the situation with the conversion of churches and monasteries in the Balkans and in Constantinople, we have to turn both to the political and pragmatic reasons for conversion as well as to the law. On the one hand, the politics of conquest necessitated a measured and deliberate approach to the conversion and confiscation of religious properties since rule was initially established on lands with a majority Christian population. On the other hand, Islamic law demanded that if conquest was made by force and without surrender, all lands and religious buildings could be confiscated and converted. As Rossitsa Gradeva notes, the reality was always somewhere in between. An Islamic blueprint guided the conquerors, but politics always framed the decisions rulers made. The demands of Hanafi law, one of the four schools of Sunni jurisprudence, were less stringent than those of other schools of Islamic interpretation. Ottomans who abided by Hanafi law therefore, were allowed some leeway when dealing with members of other religious groups, and with issues such as the restoration of churches and monasteries that had been demolished.[51] Ottomans also let the local politics of the region guide many decisions regarding the restoration and building of churches. For example, we can see how politics played a role when Ottomans allowed the construction of churches in Bosnia in the mid-sixteenth century, as the empire sought to counter Catholic influence by fostering more Orthodox expansion.[52] In some important cases, individual grandees could promote and pay for the restoration or rebuilding of a church.[53]

Aleksandar Fotic, a scholar who has studied the application of Ottoman law in the Balkans, argues that while we should pay attention to the state's political needs, we must also attend to the efforts of Ottoman lawmakers to standardize, define, and coordinate the land practices of conquered regions with the sharia. This was particularly evident in the rapid and concerted effort to confiscate and sell monasteries during the reign of Selim II (1566–1574). The need to create a legible and ordered land structure was made more appealing by the financial benefits of confiscating monasteries, ordering their sale, and then allowing the monasteries themselves to buy back the property, clearly a financial ruse to increase the cash to the treasury.[54] As a result, the confiscation and then repossession of monastic properties could become part of a process of negotiation between the state and the religious leadership of the Balkans.[55] In many areas demographic changes also helped the process of conversion. In big cities such as Constantinople, where Muslims established new neighborhoods (*mahalles*), or where Christians either converted or moved, unused churches were converted to mosques.[56] In rural areas the same principles of depopulation, conversion, and Islamization led to people changing the function of churches to mosques.

Given that political and pragmatic goals worked in tandem with demographic changes to affect the landscape of the cities and countryside, as church bells were replaced with minarets and the conquest of Christianity by Islam was reaffirmed, we need to ask how the relations between different religious and ethnic populations proceeded. It is certainly impossible to generalize, but Gradeva presents a variety of cases that give the reader a flavor of how complex the situation was on the ground. As much as state officials were the final arbiters of when and how buildings and peoples should coexist, Gradeva also shows that members of the Muslim community often took it upon themselves to complain about the Christian presence in a Muslim ward or the continuing use of a building for religious rites. In this way their local intransigence made relations difficult. Nevertheless, even though the law mandated that a church that had been converted to a mosque could never again be used as a Christian sanctuary, there are examples of local Christians continuing to use the space and locals looking the other way.[57] What the appropriation of buildings also brought was some nearly syncretic behavior, especially at the level of popular religion. When Muslims took over buildings, they often also took on the characteristics and distinctiveness of the building and of the Christians who had used it as their sanctuary.[58]

Over time, the spread of the Islamic legal system also promoted the process of colonization and incorporation by spreading a kind of Pax

Ottomanica that ensured the security of the people throughout the region. As one of the main institutions of the state, the Islamic court and the *kadi* (magistrate) spread across the empire, providing an Islamic legal framework for the dissemination of justice. Used by Muslims and Christians alike, the court brought different religious groups together. Svetlana Ivanova and Rossitsa Gradeva show the importance of many Muslim orthodox and heterodox religious institutions in the spread of Islam: the *vakif* (pious foundation) institutions in the colonization of the Balkans, the *kadi* court, and local Muslim schools and soup kitchens (*imarets*) all contributed to this swelling of Muslim Ottomans. The by-product of such transformation was in the creation of a syncretistic Islamic culture with strong Christian elements in it. The strategic locations of the *vakif* institutions in the Balkans, their proximity to Orthodox Christian settlements, monasteries, churches, and community organizations, promoted relations with the Christian populations and provided institutional bases for interaction. Given the degree to which the *vakif* was embedded in the religious and social fabric of society and the ways in which traditions and acts of welfare were disbursed regardless of religion, the *vakif* linked groups and created an environment for coexistence.[59] Many of the *imarets* of Rumeli that were established in the fifteenth and sixteenth centuries continued to act as charitable organizations throughout the empire's tenure and provided food for everyone, Christians and Muslims alike, until the end of World War II.[60]

Parallel to such institutional coexistence, the two faiths increasingly came to use the same sacred space through locales that had been consecrated to the memory of ambiguous religious figures.[61] Dervish lodges (*zaviyes* and *tekkes*) established by the dervish orders became sites of religious mixing. Lodges were usually built at the tomb of the founder of the order who came to be seen to have saintly powers, by Christians and Muslims alike, although often under different names. Such locations of heterodox Islamic practice, more fluid and open to religious mixing, became magnets for both Christians and Muslims.[62]

It is also important to show the long history of continuity that these mixed locales experienced throughout the period of the Ottomans, some displaying shared ceremonies and rituals at key sites into the contemporary era. Dionigi Albera's work shows this long continuity, especially in the tradition of sharing of meanings and symbols across the monotheisms of the Mediterranean.[63] Exploring the religious mixture and interfaith expressions in Mediterranean history, he argues that "syncretism is not necessarily an ephemeral stage preceding the repression or the assimilation of other groups, nor is it confined to some historical situation" but instead "people of different religions have long lived intermingled.... The history of this region has been characterized by a long-term proliferation of traffic, contacts, and borrowings."[64]

In the contemporary world many locations in the territories of the Ottoman Empire still share sacred spaces. For example, shrines dedicated to the Catholic Saint Anthony of Padua, present in both in northern Albania and Istanbul, attract not only Christians but also Muslims. Enforced by the state, Communist atheism in Albania during the 1960s resulted in the destruction of the shared sanctuary. However, the Catholic saint's cult survived; the shrine was rebuilt in the 1990s and today is again frequented by both Christian and Muslim pilgrims. In Istanbul, as in Albania, the shared devotion at the shrine of Saint Anthony of Padua is historically linked to the presence of the Franciscan settlers during the Middle Ages and today attracts both Muslims and Christians of various denominations. The Catholic Church of Saint Anthony of Padua is open to interfaith prayers, and on Tuesdays the Mass is conducted in Turkish, to appeal to Muslims.[65] Maria Couroucli shows the continued importance of Saint George as a popular saintly figure to whom Christian and Muslim devotions continue until today. She follows the yearly ceremonies at the Monastery of Saint George in Büyükada, Istanbul, to assess the religiously mixed devotions.[66] Many more sites of mixed devotions still exist in Istanbul, especially Greek Orthodox churches, which are known to have *ayiasmas* (Holy Water), and have experienced a resurgence of interest and participation.

The post-Ottoman world in the Balkans is similarly strewn with examples of inter- and intrafaith sharing in areas that have even experienced wars and ethnic cleansing. Ger Duijzings, who has done work on pilgrimages in Kosovo and other areas of the Yugoslav territories, concentrates on those pilgrimage sites, churches, and monasteries that have had a continued, if sometimes interrupted, history of sharing. Focusing on relations between groups, he compares different ways in which pilgrimages and sharing of religious spaces occur in three locations: (1) in Gracanica, a Serbian Orthodox monastery on Assumption Day, between Christians and Muslim gypsies; (2) in Zociste Monastery, where the Serbians are trying to assert their presence among the Albanian Muslims; and (3) in the Ostrog Monastery (near Niksic), where on important religious days Muslim pilgrims from Serbia, Montenegro, Kosovo, and Bosnia have visited from time immemorial. In each of these cases, sharing occurs with or without tensions but with struggles often associated more with the material gains to be made from a space rather than with direct religious contention.[67] Similarly, Glenn Bowman looks at three sites in Macedonia where a tradition of sharing has occurred. In particular, the study of Sveti Nikola shows the ways in which throughout the long history of this Orthodox Church, both Muslims and Christians have claimed it to be theirs, providing different yet analogous histories of the space. Yet at the time of Bowman's ethnographic work, the church functioned as a church for the Orthodox community and a *türbe* (mausoleum) for the Sufi Muslim pilgrims who visited the site. Not only did the space accommodate both religions, but the caretakers of the church made sure that both Christians and Muslims felt welcome, adjusting the religious décor according to the identity of the visitors. Looking at the history of this shrine diachronically, and by synchronically analyzing the contemporary relations within and around the shrine, we can gather a lot of intelligence about what sharing constitutes and how it happens over time and in the present.[68] Examples of shared sacred sites abound in the new studies carried out by anthropologists and historians. We also have examples of conflict around sites from the territories of the Ottoman Empire, such as the Dome of the Rock, the tombs of the patriarchs, and other sites located in Palestine-Israel where the conflict between these two peoples for the land has added to the politics of the shrines.

CONCLUSION

The narrative of first Seljuk then Ottoman domination in Anatolia and the Balkans demonstrates the role of public authorities, boundaries, and identities in preparing the ground for the sharing of many sacred sites throughout centuries. Both the Seljuk and the Ottoman states were open to diversity as they encountered it at the frontiers and in their lands. They made efforts to accommodate this diversity within the limits of their interests as empires—that is, the creation of ordered and legible polities open to multiple groups that could coexist in relative peace. They perceived no harm at having different ethnic and religious groups participate in practices and ceremonies that were similar, in some sense offering people the freedom to enter each other's sanctuaries. In many ways they let sharing happen on the ground, especially as heterodox religious figures transcended boundaries and attracted locals of diverse religion and ethnicity to follow them. Yet the Ottoman state was also strategic about what it allowed, establishing, for example, a blueprint for rules of coexistence at the Holy Sepulchre.

The historical establishment of these shared sanctuaries happened during times at which public authorities were tolerant of mixing but also at times and locations where boundaries and identities were less rigid, less inscribed in separation. The fluidity of boundaries came from the frequent movement of populations that shared similar traditions and geographical circumstances, and the diversity of identities that were just self-evident but not of great schismatic importance. What Bowman explains about the present-day proclivity of people toward coexistence seems to have also been the case in historical perspective,

> insofar as both intercommunal amity and inter-communal antagonism are discursively constructed it seems vital, in the midst of the war of words evident in debates over the "clash of civilizations" and "antagonistic tolerance" to show that there is nothing natural or necessary in hating your neighbour, and that people, when they perceive interaction and

amicability as working for rather than against them, are fully capable of mixing with, and embracing, the other.[69]

It is then possible to say that even though Ottoman centuries exhibit both conversions of peoples and of churches, from the very early establishment of the empire, the politics of empire allowed for enough cultural tolerance and flexibility that people of different religions and ethnicity could engage in various choreographies of sharing sacred sites.

NOTES

1. Anna Bigelow, "Everybody's Baba: Making Space for the Other," in *Sharing the Sacra: The Politics and Pragmatics of Intercommunal Relations around Holy Places*, ed. Glenn Bowman, 25–43 (New York: Berghahn Books, 2012).
2. The *millet* organization was a form of indirect rule of religious communities in which communities were ruled by their own religious leaders and provided with internal autonomy. There are arguments that question the formal existence of such institutional arrangements, though it is clear that the Ottoman state and religious authorities established contracts that defined relations between them.
3. For a discussion of the issues related to the *millet* system, see chapter 4 in Karen Barkey, *Empire of Difference: The Ottoman in Comparative Perspective* (New York: Cambridge University Press, 2008).
4. This is a short summary of a much larger argument from *Empire of Difference*.
5. Susan Ritchie, "The Pasha of Buda and the Edit of Torda: Transylvanian Unitarian/Islamic Ottoman Cultural Enmeshment and the Development of Religious Tolerance," *Journal of Unitarian Universalist History* 30 (2005): 48–49.
6. Perez Zagorin, *How the Idea of Religious Toleration Came to the West* (Princeton, NJ: Princeton University Press, 2003), 5.
7. Robert Moore, *The Formation of a Persecuting Society* (Oxford: Blackwell Publishers, 1998).
8. Lloyd Rudolph and Susanne Rudolph, "Modern Hate: How Ancient Animosities Get Invented," *New Republic*, March 22, 1993, 24–29.
9. Bob Scribner, "Preconditions of Tolerance and Intolerance in Sixteenth-Century Germany," in *Tolerance and Intolerance in the European Reformation*, ed. Ole Peter Grell and Bob Scribner, 32–47 (Cambridge: Cambridge University Press, 1996), 43.
10. Ibid.

11. David Nirenberg, *Communities of Violence: Persecution of Minorities in the Middle Ages* (Princeton, NJ: Princeton University Press, 1996), 11. His study is also an argument against the more romanticized versions of Iberian history where the notion of "convivencia" has become of the understanding of Jewish, Muslim, and Christian relations until 1492. The work of Maria Rosa Menocal, *The Ornament of the World: How Muslims, Jews, and Christians Created a Culture of Tolerance in Medieval Spain* (New York: Black Bay Books, 2002), represents best this view.
12. See Kurt H. Wolff, ed. and trans., *The Sociology of Georg Simmel* (New York: Free Press, 1950), 58–64.
13. For example, in Ole Peter Grell and Bob Scribner, eds., *Tolerance and Intolerance in the European Reformation* (Cambridge: Cambridge University Press, 1996), see especially Heiko Oberman, "The Travail of Tolerance: Containing Chaos in Early Modern Europe," 13–31; and Scribner, "Preconditions of Tolerance and Intolerance in Sixteenth-Century Germany," 32–47. See also Ira Katznelson and Gareth Stedman Jones, eds. *Religion and the Political Imagination* (Cambridge: Cambridge University Press, 2010); and Alfred Stepan and Charles Taylor, *Boundaries of Toleration* (New York: Columbia University Press, 2014).
14. See Didier Boisson and Yves Krumenacker, eds., "La coexistence confessionelle à l'épreuve: Études sur les relations entre protestants et catholiques dans la France modern," in *Chrétiens et sociétés, documents et Mémoires*, no. 9 (Rhône-Alpes: Religions, Sociétés et Acculturation du Laboratoire de Recherche Historique, 2009); Olivier Christin, *Confesser sa Foi: Conflits confessionnels et identités religieuses dans l'Europe moderne* (Seyssel: Champ Vallon, 2009); Olivier Christin, *La paix de religion: L'autonomisation de la raison politique au XVIe siècle* (Paris: Seuil, 1997); Gregory Hanlon, *Confession and Community in Seventeenth-Century France: Catholic and Protestant Coexistence in Aquitaine* (Philadelphia: University of Pennsylvania Press, 1993); and Keith Cameron, Mark Greengrass and Penny Roberts, eds., *The Adventure of Religious Pluralism in Early Modern France* (Oxford: Peter Lang, 2000).
15. Keith P. Luria, *Sacred Boundaries: Religious Coexistence and Conflict in Early Modern France* (Washington, DC: Catholic University of America Press, 2005).
16. Ibid.
17. Benjamin J. Kaplan, *Divided by Faith: Religious Conflict and the Practice of Toleration in Early Modern Europe* (Cambridge, MA: Harvard University Press, 2007). See also Wayne Te Brake, "Emblems of Coexistence in a Confessional World," in *Living with Religious Diversity in Early-Modern Europe*, ed., Scott Dixon, Dagmar Freist, and Mark Greengrass (Surrey, UK: Ashgate, 2009), 53–80.
18. Scribner, "Preconditions of Tolerance and Intolerance," 39.

19. Wayne Te Brake, "Emblems of Coexistence in a Confessional World," in *Living with Religious Diversity in Early-Modern Europe*, eds. Scott C. Dixon and Mark Greengrass, 53–80 (Surrey, UK: Ashgate, 2009).
20. On legibility, see James C. Scott, *Seeing Like a State: How Certain Schemes to Improve the Human Condition Have Failed* (New Haven, CT: Yale University Press, 1998), 11–53. "Legibility" refers to the intention of the state to get a handle on the diversity within its realm and to increase order and control, enabling the administration to run smoothly and taxes to flow unhindered.
21. Fredrik Barth, "Introduction," in *Ethnic Groups and Boundaries: The Social Organization of Cultural Difference*, ed. Fredrik Barth, 9–38 (London: Allen & Unwin, 1969).
22. Rogers Brubaker, "Ethnicity Without Groups," *Archives Européennes de Sociologie* 43, no. 2 (2002): 163–89.
23. Charles Tilly, "Micro, Macro or Megrim," in *Stories, Identities and Political Change* (Lanham, MD: Rowman & Littlefield, 2002), 76.
24. William H. Sewell Jr., "Geertz, Cultural Systems, and History: From Synchrony to Transformation," *Representations*, no. 59 (1997): 42.
25. Robert M. Hayden, "Antagonistic Tolerance: Competitive Sharing of Religious Sites in South Asia and the Balkans," *Current Anthropology* 43 (2002): 205–31.
26. Robert M. Hayden, Hande Sozer, Tugba Tanyeri-Erdemir, and Aydin Erdemir, "The Byzantine Mosque at Trilye: A Processual Analysis of Dominance, Sharing, Transformation and Tolerance," *History and Anthropology* 22, no. 1 (2011): 1–17, at 3.
27. See chapter 4 in this volume.
28. See Glenn Bowman, "Orthodox–Muslim Interactions at 'Mixed Shrines' in Macedonia," in *Eastern Christians in Anthropological Perspective*, ed. Chris Hann and Hermann Goltz, 195–219 (Berkeley: University of California Press, 2010).
29. Keith Hopwood, "Christian–Muslim Symbiosis in Anatolia," in *Archeology, Anthropology and Heritage in the Balkans and Anatolia: The Life and Times of F. W. Hasluck (1878–1920)*, ed. David Shankland, 13–30 (Istanbul: Isis, 2004).
30. Quoted in Nevra Necipoglu, "The Coexistence of Turks and Greeks in Medieval Anatolia (Eleventh–Twelfth Centuries) *Harvard Middle Eastern and Islamic Review* 5 (1999–2000): 58–76, at 58.
31. V. Macit Tekinalp, "Palace-Churches of the Anatolian Seljuks: Tolerance or Necessity?," in *Byzantine and Modern Greek Studies* 33, no. 2 (2009): 148–67. Even though Tekinalp is shy to add the label of tolerance on the rulers of the empire, I think that letting others worship is also a tolerant a practice.
32. Hopwood, "Christian–Muslim Symbiosis in Anatolia," 26.
33. Ibid., 25; and Keith Hopwood, "The Turkish-Byzantine Frontier," in *Acta Viennensia Ottomanica, Akten des 13*, ed. Markus Kohbach, Gisela Prochazka-Eisl,

and Claudia Romer, 153–61 (Vienna: Institut für Orientalistik, University of Vienna, 1999), 155–56.
34. F. W. Hasluck, *Christianity and Islam Under the Sultans*, vol. 1 (Oxford: Clarendon Press, 1929).
35. Ethel Sara Wolper, "Khidr, Elwan Celebi and the Conversion of Sacred Sanctuaries in Anatolia," *Muslim World*, 90 (2000): 309–22, at 309.
36. Ibid., 316.
37. Hasluck, *Christianity and Islam Under the Sultans*, 1:47–49.
38. Oya Pancaroglu, "The Itinerant Dragon-Slayer: Forging Paths of Image and Identity in Medieval Anatolia," *Gesta* 43, no. 2 (2004): 151–64, at 151. See also A. Yasar Ocak, "XIII-XV Yuzyillarda Anadolu'da Turk-Hiristyan Dini Etkilesimler ve Aya Yorgi (Saint Georges) Kultu," *Belleten* 55 (1991): 661–75.
39. Michel Balivet, "A la maniere de F. W. Hasluck: A Few Reflections on the Byzantine-Turkish Symbiosis in the Middle Ages," in *Archeology, Anthropology and Heritage in the Balkans and Anatolia: The Life and Times of F. W. Hasluck (1878–1920)*, ed. David Shankland, 13–30 (Istanbul: Isis, 2004), 124–25.
40. Fikret Adanir, "The Ottoman Peasantries, c.1360–c.1860," in *The Peasantries of Europe from the Fourteenth to the Eighteenth Centuries*, ed. Tom Scott (London: Longman, 1998), 277.
41. Elizabeth Zachariadou, "Notes sur la population de L'Asie Mineure Turque." *Byzantinische Forschungen* 12 (1987): 223–31, at 228.
42. Chapter 2 in my book *Empire of Difference* details these mixed networks and traces their origins.
43. As Cemal Kafadar discusses the origins of this syncretism, he says: "No one ever theorized it, either. It appears to have been shared insight deriving from the cumulative experiences gained through the fusion of Islamic elements with pre-Islamic beliefs of the Turks on the one hand and Anatolian Christianity on the other." Cemal Kafadar, *Between Two Worlds: The Construction of the Ottoman State* (Berkeley: University of California Press, 1995), 72. See also Omer Lutfi Barkan, "Osmanli Imparatorlugunda bir iskan ve kolonizasyon metodu olarak vakiflar ve temlikler I: Istila devrinin kolonizator Turk dervisleri ve vakflyeler," *Vakiflar Dergisi* 2 (1942): 283–304; and Speros Vryonis, *The Decline of Medieval Hellenism in Asia Minor and the Process of Islamization from the Eleventh through the Fifteenth Century* (Berkeley: University of California Press, 1986), 359.
44. Vryonis, *Decline of Medieval Hellenism*.
45. Barkan, "Osmanli Imparatorlugunda"; and Vryonis, *Decline of Medieval Hellenism*.
46. Hasluck, *Christianity and Islam Under the Sultans*.
47. Yuri Stoyanov, "On Some Parallels Between Anatolian and Balkan Heterodox Islamic and Christian Traditions and the Problem of their Coexistence and

Interaction in the Ottoman Period," in *Syncretismes et heresies dans l'Orient seljoukide et ottoman (XIVe–XVIIIe siècle)*, ed. Gilles Veinstein, 75–178, Collection Turcica 9 (Paris: Peeters, 2005), 97.

48. Ibid., 98.
49. N. Oikonomides, "Monasteres et moines lors de la conquete ottoman," *Sudost-Forschungen* 35 (1976): 1–10; and Nevra Necipoglu, "Byzantine Monasteries and Monastic Property in Thessalonike and Constantinople During the Period of Ottoman Conquests (late Fourteenth and Early Fifteenth Centuries), *Journal of Ottoman Studies* 15 (1995): 122–35.
50. Anthony Bryer, "The Late Byzantine Monastery in Town and Countryside," in *The Church in Town and Countryside*, ed. D. Baker (Oxford: Oxford University Press, 1979), 233–34. See also Necipoglu, "Byzantine Monasteries," 125. Similar results can be found in other areas, for example, in Trebizond, which is outside the Byzantine realm at the time but is conquered by the Ottomans. See Heath Lowry, "Privilege and Property in Ottoman Macuka in the Opening Decades of Tourkokratia: 1461–1553," in *Continuity and Change in Late Byzantine and Early Ottoman Society*, ed. Anthony Bryer and Heath W. Lowry (Birmingham, UK: Dumbarton Oaks, 1986).
51. Rossitsa Gradeva, "Ottoman Policy Toward Christian Church Buildings," *Etudes Balkaniques* 4 (1994): 14–36.
52. Ibid., 28.
53. Bernard Lory, "The Vizier's Dream: 'Seeing St. Dimitar' in Ottoman Bitola," *History and Anthropology* 20, no. 3 (September 2009): 309–16.
54. Aleksandar Fotic, "The Official Explanations for the Confiscation and Sale of Monasteries (Churches) and Their Estates at the Time of Selim II," *Turcica* XXVI (1994): 33–54. See also Eugenia Kermeli, "Central Administration Versus Provincial Arbitrary Governance: Patmos and Mount Athos Monasteries in the 16th Century," *Byzantine and Modern Greek Studies* 32, no. 2 (2008): 189–202.
55. Kermeli, "Central Administration Versus Provincial Arbitrary Governance."
56. Suleyman Kirimtayif, *Converted Byzantine Churches in Istanbul* (Istanbul: Ege Yayinlari, 2001).
57. Gradeva, "Ottoman Policy," 32.
58. Ibid., 34.
59. Svetlana Ivanova, "Muslim Charity Foundations (Vakf) and the Models of Religious Behavior of Ottoman Social Estates in Rumeli (late 15th to 19th Centuries)," *Weiner Zeitschrift zur Geschichte der Neuzeit*, 5, no. 2 (2005): 44–68; and Rossitsa Gradeva and Svetlana Ivanova, "Researching the Past and Present of Muslim Culture in Bulgaria: The "Popular and "High" Layers," *Islam and Christian-Muslim Relations* 12, no. 3 (July 2001): 317–37.

60. Ivanova, "Muslim Charity Foundations," 52.
61. Michel Balivet, "Aux origines de l'Islamisation des Balkans Ottomans," *Les Balkans a L'Epoque Ottomane La Revue du Monde Musulman et de La Mediterranee* 66 (1992): 11-20.
62. Gradeva and Ivanova, "Researching the Past and Present," 321.
63. Dionigi Albera, "'Why Are You Mixing What Cannot Be Mixed?' Shared Devotions in the Monotheisms," *History and Anthropology* 19, no. 1 (2008): 37-59.
64. Ibid., 37-40.
65. Dionigi Albera and Benoit Fliche, "Les pratiques dévotionelles des musulmans dans les sanctuaires chrétiens: Le cas d'Istanbul," in *Religions traversées: Lieux saints partages entre Chrétiens, Musulmans et Juifs en Mediterranée*, ed. Dionigi Albera and Maria Couroucli, 141-74 (Arles: Actes Sud, 2009).
66. Maria Couroucli, "Saint Georges l'Anatolien: Maîtres des frontiers," In *Religions traversées: Lieux saints partages entre Chrétiens, Musulmans et Juifs en Mediterranée*, ed. Dionigi Albera and Maria Couroucli, 175-208 (Arles: Actes Sud, 2009).
67. Ger Duijzings, *Religion and Politics of Identity in Kosovo* (New York: Columbia University Press, 2000); and Ger Duijzings, "Pilgrimage, Politics and Ethnicity: Joint Pilgrimages of Muslims and Christians and Conflicts over Ambiguous Sanctuaries in Yugoslavia and Albania," in *Power and Prayer: Religious and Political Processes in Past and Present*, ed. M. Bax and A. Koster, 80-91 (Amsterdam: VU University Press, 1993), 86.
68. Bowman, "Orthodox-Muslim Interactions."
69. Glenn Bowman, "Identification and Identity Formations Around Shared Shrines in West Bank Palestine and Western Macedonia" (Processus Identitaires Autour de Quelques Sanctuairs Partages en Palestine et en Macedoine), in *Lieux saints en partage: Explorations anthropologiques dans l'espace méditerranéen*, ed. D. Albera and M. Couroucli, 27-52 (Arles: Actes Sud; Canterbury, UK: University of Kent, 2009), http://kar.kent.ac.uk/28168/1/couroucli.pdf.

COMPARISONS

CYPRUS/BOSNIA/ANATOLIA/ALGIERS

2

THREE WAYS OF SHARING THE SACRED

CHOREOGRAPHIES OF COEXISTENCE IN CYPRUS

METE HATAY

During the latest Muslim Kurban Bayramı holiday, many Turkish Cypriots milled in the narrow streets of north Nicosia, near the Lokmacı checkpoint, which had opened in 2008 after several decades of closure.[1] On the other side of this checkpoint is Ledra Street, a busy shopping area, and Turkish Cypriots on holiday were taking this new opportunity to shop in the wealthier and more attractive shopping areas of Cyprus's south, or to visit its trendy cafes, restaurants, and bars. During the four-day holiday period, many Turkish Cypriot families patiently queued at the checkpoints, presenting their passports or identity cards to be allowed to cross the divide. Turkish Cypriot customs officers checked that those persons returning from the south had not exceeded their shopping quota while their counterparts on the other side of the checkpoint similarly rummaged through the handbags of Greek Cypriot visitors returning from the north to ensure that they were not bringing with them illegal goods purchased in the occupied areas. In the meantime, other Greek Cypriot policemen and customs officers were handing out what they called the *bayram* gift of the Greek Cypriot government to the Turkish Cypriots.

This unexpected present was a handsomely designed, expensively printed book published by the Public Information Office of the Republic of Cyprus (RoC). It included many colorful photographs showing Muslim heritage sites on the island, mainly in the south. The book's introduction proudly proclaimed that it intends to illustrate the affluent cultural heritage of Cyprus, "which bears the marks of various cultures, including Islam."[2]

However, if one examines it more carefully, the main purpose of this expensive gift turns out to be more complex than it looks. The book repeatedly describes a purported period of peaceful coexistence between Turkish Cypriots and Greek Cypriots before the 1974 division of the island. To add to the assertion's legitimacy, the book also includes a preface by Dr. Tarek Radwan, a professor at the Al-Azhar University in Cairo, who states, "The present volume highlights the reality of peaceful coexistence that prevailed for centuries between the Christian Greek and Muslim Turkish ethnic communities." More importantly, Dr. Radwan claims that the book "also draws attention to the understanding, on the part of the government of Cyprus, of the importance of the cultural wealth enjoyed by the island; an understanding that has led to the policy of renovating and preserving mosques and other shrines and places of worship."[3] As becomes clear from Radwan's preface, the gift's main aim is more than just to provide information on Muslim places of worship in the areas controlled by the RoC; in fact, the book shows the efforts of the Greek Cypriot government in repairing and maintaining them. This appears to be why the book was published in both a Turkish version for a local, Turkish Cypriot audience and an English version aimed at an international audience. These political aims became clear in the book's claims that the "other" side fails to make the same efforts for Greek Cypriot religious heritage in the north.

The choices of Muslim heritage sites used in the book are themselves interesting. For instance, most of the restored mosques presented in the book were once churches that had been converted into mosques following the Ottoman conquest in 1571. Clearly, according to this book, more priority was given to these kinds of mosques for restoration than to later structures originally built as mosques. Although one may perhaps argue that these mosques converted from churches were from earlier periods and had more historical value, the book's significant section on the origins of the Muslims in Cyprus provides opportunity for an alternative interpretation. The section that discusses the origins of Cypriot Muslims is reminiscent of the previous focus on mosques converted from churches. According to the narrative offered in this chapter, the majority of the island's Muslims are descended, in reality, from Christian converts—a historical fact that also conveniently explains why they peacefully coexisted with Greek Cypriots.

Within the context of Cyprus's ongoing conflict—as the material above demonstrates—"peaceful coexistence" is a term often bandied about but little understood. It is a term with definite political connotations and, for some, has become a type of religious doctrine. At the same time, close examination shows that even supporters of this thesis clearly understand it in different ways. For Greek Cypriots, the thesis that Cypriots had always lived together peacefully became official doctrine after 1974, when the Greek Cypriot state wished to show that the "Cyprus problem" had been created not by Cypriots but by Turkey's invasion and occupation.[4] This thesis has primarily taken the form of attempting to "show" that Turkish Cypriots are "really" crypto-Christians and, as a result, all Cypriots are "brothers." To prove this case, they generally tend to concentrate on certain shared sacred sites frequented by both communities.[5] A good example of this official rhetoric of coexistence may be found in Greek Cypriot president Dimitris Christofias's 2010 Easter address. The president wanted to send a message to Turkish Cypriots, saying he looked forward to the day when all Cypriots celebrated Bayram and Easter together again. The message of Easter was a message of love, he noted, adding, "often Turkish Cypriots undertake pilgrimages as do Greek Cypriots," and referring to an incident when he went to Apostolos Andreas Monastery to pray and met a family of Turkish Cypriots who had come to light a candle. This was how people bonded for decades, he said.[6]

For Turkish Cypriots, in contrast, the "peaceful coexistence" thesis primarily refers to a period of Ottoman "tolerance," before Greeks began to develop strange notions about nationalism and Hellenic identity. According to this narrative, Turkish Cypriots saved the Greeks from Latin slavery, returned their freedom to them, and restored their church's position. This thesis also claims that the same Greeks have been unfaithful since the departure of the Ottomans and have tried to systematically destroy Turkish Cypriots. In a similar vein as the Public Information Office's Bayram gift, discussed earlier, the Turkish Cypriot administration also continuously uses the tools of a "politics of heritage" to produce books and pamphlets demonstrating that they care about the "other's" heritage, and that, contrary to Greek Cypriot claims, it is mainly Turkish Cypriot heritage that has been systematically attacked and destroyed by Greek Cypriots since the early 1960s. In order to do this, they also prepare pamphlets (although not as flashy as the Bayram gift) with photographs of destroyed mosques, cemeteries, and villages.

Of course, the terms "tolerance" and "peaceful coexistence" themselves emerge within the context of present-day politics and are a projection into the past of current understandings of what it might mean to live with difference. As such, the terms are also empty signifiers when applied to Cyprus's past, ambiguously incorporating friendship and pragmatic neighborliness and having minimal knowledge of and immersion into the other's beliefs, traditions, and practices. In the context of Cyprus, they also—as noted earlier—tend to imply that present differences must be superficial since people managed to get along so well in the past. If Turkish Cypriots are "really" converted Greek Cypriots, difference disappears. Or, in a similar thesis, Cypriots really all belonged to one basic common village culture until nationalists came along and told them that the minimal differences of language, dress, and practice that they observed between the religious communities were actually important.

This essay attempts to complicate this picture by looking at sites where the everyday practices of "peaceful coexistence" always threatened to break down. These were religious sites believed by one or both communities to have efficacious powers, especially the ability to heal the sick. Because of the alleged power of such sites, they were one of the main draws enticing people to cross or to adopt the practices of the other. As such, these were dangerous sites where people were called to define and maintain their identities and to submit to certain kinds of authority.

This essay traces this historically complex relationship between efficacious power and legitimate authority, or between acts and the right to interpret those acts.

I outline three basic types of sites: (1) what I call spaces of (temporary) submission, where members of both communities knew of and believed in the efficacious power associated with the site, but where the site clearly "belonged" to one community and its clergy; (2) contested shared spaces, where members of both communities believed in the power of the site but where there was an unresolved dispute, usually based on competing accounts of the site's origins, over which community could legitimately claim authority; and (3) economic spaces, or those sites believed by only one community to have efficacy but which may have been tolerated by the other community for pragmatic reasons, usually the economic benefit that their presence brought. While these categories reflect real differences in the way the sites were used by members of the two communities at a given moment, the distinctions drawn here may also be seen as heuristic ones, since the categories themselves are not static. For instance, a shared site that was founded with economic motivations can change with time and, within a new economic and political situation, may become a contested space or place of temporary submission. The remainder of the essay describes these sites and the practices that surrounded them. In the conclusion, I use these sites to reflect on how the variety of practices and attitudes toward them can help us think about debates over tolerance and its varieties.

THE ESTABLISHMENT OF ISLAM IN CYPRUS

While the presence of Muslims in Cyprus predates the Ottoman conquest of 1571, it was only postconquest that the foundation for the emergence of a significant and more stable Muslim society was established.[7] However, there is no concurrence among scholars regarding the number and demographic composition of the Muslim community in that period. Many affirm that the first Ottoman Muslims on the island were soldiers from the campaign who remained behind, augmented by settlers (mainly farmers and heterodox tribes) who were brought from Anatolia as part of a traditional Ottoman policy for populating newly acquired territories.[8] Others have insisted that an important portion of the island's Muslims were Christian converts.[9] In light of recent evidence extracted from the Ottoman records, we know now that both of these claims are partly correct. According to Ottoman historian Ronald C. Jennings, who carried out a detailed study of Ottoman court documents from Cyprus, there were indeed some cases of conversion to Islam on the island during Ottoman rule, but "the level of conversion cannot be measured precisely." He highlights instead the large number of records concerning settlers arriving in Cyprus from other provinces of the Ottoman Empire, and he notes that he never encountered evidence that might confirm instances of conversion en masse.[10]

Moreover, during this era, there was no monolithic identity among the Muslims of Cyprus. Towns were usually dominated by mainstream orthodox Sunni Islam, which had been rationalized and codified into law and systematic theology, regularly supervised by the ulema, while a form of Islam often labeled as "folk" or "popular" predominated in the rural areas.[11] This folk Islam consisted of both orthodox and heterodox elements, including traces of superstitious magic and mysticism as well as some practices and beliefs shared with Christian neighbors.[12] It is important to note that many studies have shown that, prior to the development of powerful nationalist movements in the twentieth century, Cypriot communities participated in a practice, widespread throughout the Levant, of worshipping at Muslim and Christian shrines virtually without making any distinction between them.[13] Apart from present-day Greek Cypriot scholars, some European travelers and observers who witnessed these practices also interpreted them as definite proof of the crypto-Christianity thesis regarding the origin of the island's Muslim population. Nonetheless, we should keep in mind what Hasluck observed for early twentieth-century Anatolia:

> European travelers in Asia Minor, mainly classical archaeologists and very seldom orientalists, are generally better acquainted with Christianity than

with Islam. Consequently, the divisions of the Christians are more obvious to them than those of the Mahommedan populations. By most the latter are regarded as a single whole, and any divergence they may notice from orthodox Sunni practice suggests to them that the population in question has been affected by Christianity that is, it represents an originally Christian population half-converted to Islam.[14]

Some Turkish Cypriot historians believe that the heterodox elements apparent in folk Islam allowed a creeping process of religious syncretism.[15] On the other hand, historian Charles Beckingham, whose work focused on Islam in Cyprus, defends the view that for the people of Cyprus and for others in the eastern Mediterranean and many parts of the Ottoman Empire, Islam and Christianity "did not present themselves as two mutually exclusive systems of belief, but rather as two ways of conciliating supernatural forces." Rather, he claims that

> the Orthodox Cypriot did not become a Muslim when he prayed at the shrine of the forty (Kirklar, Ayii Saranda) at Tymbou . . . nor did the Cypriot Muslim become a Christian when he sought the aid of the Holy Cross at Stravrovouni, or of St. Andrew at his monastery on the extreme eastern promontory of the island. They were simply testing the efficacy of another means of getting a good harvest or curing an illness.[16]

To avoid confusion, I should reiterate that "peaceful coexistence" and cooperation was usually the norm between Orthodox Christians and Muslims in Ottoman Cyprus (especially in the rural areas). Turkish Cypriot historian Altay Nevzat has noted that "even in the tumultuous year of 1821 there is evidence that cooperation could still occur even under the most precarious of circumstances." He asserts that this situation still held even at the beginning of British rule.[17]

Although some "hybrid" or "crypto-Christians" still lived on the island into the British period, the phenomenon of shared sacred sites and peaceful coexistence should not be ascribed only to crypto-Christians' interaction with their former brethren. The dynamics of and motivations for crossing religious boundaries were more complex, and while those who crossed were sometimes assimilated, the majority remained and thought of themselves as remaining within the boundaries of their faiths. Instead of fully crossing, they borrowed from the other side's habits, mimicked the other, or submitted temporarily when needed. In some cases, they permanently adopted practices associated with the other denomination or faith and hybridized their own ways of behaving to create a kind of a third way.

SPACES OF (TEMPORARY) SUBMISSION

According to the definition I introduced earlier, spaces of (temporary) submission belonged to one religious community but allowed others to participate in worship at particular times and for particular purposes. Although some members of the other community may still visit these sites today, the rise of secular nationalism in the second quarter of the twentieth century tended to erode the bicommunal nature of these sites so that they have become more homogeneous to the degree that they have been abandoned by the other community. A site belongs to the other community if one's own religious group makes no claim on the site and possesses no legend about the site's foundation that could serve as the basis for contesting the site's legitimate ownership. Persons visited these sites in the full knowledge that the sites belonged to the other community. The legitimate authority of one community over this kind of site was always recognized by those who temporarily submitted to it, and the site's power or efficacy was not challenged. Although there were many sites in Cyprus with alleged miraculous powers, only certain locations became shared shrines thanks to the other community's recognition of the sites' efficacy. It is beyond the scope of this essay to investigate the reasons why only certain sites were chosen to be shared by both communities. Instead, we will concentrate on what kind of sites fell into this category, what practices were associated with them, and how these sites were choreographed by those who administered them. Finally, we will look at how new power structures that emerged with the rise of nationalisms in the island disturbed the way these sites were used.

Persons who visited these sites usually did so out of need or hope. Anthropologist Maria Couroucli, who studied a contemporary shared pilgrimage site, claims that "people who gather there do so as individuals hoping to receive help in their everyday problems, not primarily as members of a religious community celebrating its identity."[18] For example, in Cyprus the same kind of need drives instances in which objects are shared among different faiths: "Christian peasants often reposed great faith in Moslem amulets containing verses from the Qur'an as effective against sickness, death and the evil eye."[19] People who had malaria did not scruple about visiting *türbes* (shrines) belonging to the other community because of simple desperation.[20] Muslims frequently visited miracle-working icons in order to receive cures for their illnesses. For example, according to some villagers from the Limassol District, the Panagia (Mother Mary) church of Doros village in the southern foothills of Cyprus used to be regularly frequented by anyone who had a serious eye illness. The people believed that if they spent a night in the church, their eyes would be cured.

Historian Sir Harry Luke, who was the private secretary for the British high commissioner of Cyprus in the first quarter of the twentieth century, claimed that, "paradoxically as it may seem, Christians and Moslems in the Near East, while hating the doctrines of each other's faiths, take not unkindly to each other's superstitions."[21] Turkish Cypriot archaeologist and folklorist Tuncer Bağışkan reiterates Luke's analysis and claims that local people treated certain votive sites "as hospitals, and people buried in them as doctors. They believed that sick people would recover their health if they visited such sites and made vows; if they tied fragments of their clothing to the grave, to the grille of a *türbe*'s window, or to the tree near the votive site."[22] Similar expectations and motivations were at play when Muslims visited certain monasteries and worshipped certain icons. Luke describes what he witnessed during his stay at Makharias Monastery: "I saw two unattended Turkish women among the worshippers, conspicuous by their *charshaf* [head covering] and veiled faces. When the ceremonies were over and the crowd had dispersed, the pair were given leave to spend the night in the church, hoping by the intercession of the saint to be cured of their epilepsy."[23]

Alleged miracles or wonders attributed to certain saints attracted people from both faiths to tombs or other sites associated with the saints. One such miracle was relatively recently attributed to the shrine of the Apostle Andrew (Apostolos Andreas). The shrine only became a popular destination for pilgrimage after the miracle of Maria Georgiou in 1912. It is claimed that Maria saw Saint Andrew in a dream seventeen years after her son had disappeared. The saint told her that if she wanted to find her missing son, she should go to the neglected chapel of Apostolos Andreas at the tip of the Karpasia Peninsula in Cyprus. On the boat journey to Cyprus, she explained the reason for her journey to a fellow passenger who happened to be a traveling Sufi dervish. He asked Maria how she would identify her lost son if she saw him, so she told him about a peculiar birthmark he bore on his shoulder. The dervish threw off his shirt to expose the same marks and fell on his knees before his mother. This reunion immediately guaranteed the saint's popularity for years to come. Luke described what could be seen at the formerly abandoned chapel a few years later:

> An impressive stream from all corners of the island now converges upon the chapel at the season of the *panegyris* [religious festivals]. Generous gifts fill the monastic coffers; the modern church above the medieval chapel chocked with *ex voto* offerings; the accommodation for pilgrims was enlarged (if scarcely bettered); the managing committee of the monastery built a carriage-road and installed a telephone. Such are the results of a modern miracle.[24]

Muslims probably also attended Christian sacred sites because of certain holy personages who could be equally respected and endorsed by the Islamic faith. Anthropologist Dionigi Albera suggests that "among the saints who act as bridges between religions, Mary has perhaps the dominant role."[25] For instance, some elderly people have informed us that before the Cyprus conflict reached their villages in Larnaca District, pregnant women who had previously miscarried used to visit Panagia (Mother Mary) church in Civisil village. To ensure a healthy birth, they used to borrow the belt that was tied onto the icon of Mary and replace it with their own.

Certain sites were not only visited by individuals from different faiths who wished to meet their own needs; they could also serve as meeting places for different faith groups whose members were faced by a common danger or concern, such as natural disasters that would affect them collectively. For instance, in some villages of Cyprus, farmers belonging to one religious group, accompanied by their own clergy, did not hesitate to collaborate with the other community during times of drought in order to bring an end to natural disasters by visiting certain sacred sites and holding either shared or parallel ceremonies. Until the late 1940s, at Rizokarpasos (Dipkarpaz in Turkish) village on the Karpasia Peninsula during times of drought the Christian inhabitants used to make procession with their icons, singing hymns and praying, from their village to the Turkish Cypriot village of Kaleburnu, which was situated near a chapel called Saint Anna. The village priest usually led the procession while holding the Gospel. The Muslim inhabitants of Kaleburnu, headed by their *hodja* (Muslim preacher) holding the Qur'an, used to wait for the Christians at the entrance to their village, where they joined the procession to the chapel of Saint Anna and all prayed together to God to send rain and multiply their crops.[26] Such multireligious group gatherings took place not only during the Ottoman period; Chris Schabel describes a similar gathering to meet the threat of plague during the fourteenth century under the Crusader Kingdom of Cyprus.

> All the sects of Christians again joined in their own groups, singing in their own languages: "Greeks, Armenians, Nestorians, Jacobites, Georgians, Nubians, Indians, Ethiopians, and many other Christians," we are told, "each of whom had a different rite and a different tongue, as well as the Latins." Barefoot, fasting on bread and water, they all gathered in the cathedral and walked in procession and the legate "provoked the people of such devotion that, at God's command, many infidel Saracens, Turks, and Jews living there burst into tears and walked barefoot with the Christians' procession." After another inspiring sermon, the plague ceased.[27]

We should remember, however, that this kind of multicommunal group gathering took place during exceptional times of collective suffering; accordingly, they were generally considered to be unusual events. In that sense, these events differed from peasants' regular visits to certain sacred sites that belonged to the other community, which had become part of the texture of everyday life.

It is important to add that the caretakers of these sanctuaries also played an important role in attracting people from different faiths. Until recently, many monks or Sufi dervishes have been believed to possess special powers for curing people from certain illnesses. For instance, Sheikh Ali Faik Efendi, who was the sheikh of a *tekke* (dervish lodge) in Larnaca until 1940, was believed to have special healing powers, which he transmitted by breathing over those who were seeking help. According to Bağışkan, an endless number of Turkish and Greek Cypriots came to the *tekke* to be cured. The sheikh was especially famed for curing mental illnesses: "In the building adjacent to the *türbe* he would read charms to the sick and blow on them, and then work charms by means of his amulets."[28]

The existing historical evidence supports my claim that management or authority at these places of what I have called temporary submission was usually monopolistic, and that persons from the other community who frequented them observed the rituals of the local clergy. Although sometimes people belonging to other faiths were allowed to perform their own rituals, the control and administration of the site belonged to only one faith. Albera claims that "common attendance requires an interaction with specialists from another religion who manage the shrine and may administer ritual acts. The attitude of the clergy is not monolithic. On a more or less voluntary basis, the local clergy often respond positively to the request of worship by 'foreigners,' sometimes with a more or less secret aim of conversion."[29] During the Ottoman period, fear of the central Muslim authority meant that, although Christian clergy may have had the secret aim of converting those "others" who were using the spaces under their control, they made no overt attempts to effect conversion and instead "tolerated" the attendance of Muslims, resigned to influencing them without imposing a conversion strategy. Whatever the real aim of the clergy at these sites, those who came from the other faith were always open to the unintended consequences of intermingling and always carried the risk of adopting the doctrines of the other faiths on a more permanent basis. I agree with Albera that "the adoption of some items of another religion generally does not imply an intention of conversion," and this was usually the case in Cyprus. However, I also agree with his analysis that in some cases "the conversion can be the result of crossing over," but "this depends mainly on the political context and on the strategy of the religious specialists," which adequately describes the case in Cyprus.[30]

Due to these interfaith crossings and the general negligence on the part of the central religious authorities, a small hybrid community gradually formed in Cyprus alongside the distinctly Christian and Muslim communities. Persons adhering to a blend of Islamic and Christian beliefs, customs, and practices were usually called "in-between," "half-and-half," or "linen-cotton" (a literal translation of *linobambaki*).[31] Until the British period, the majority of this hybrid populace maintained its official Muslim status in order to avoid the penalty for Muslim apostates—death. They continued, however, to practice Christianity together with Islam. During the Ottoman period, members of this group were usually marginalized and ridiculed by the main religious communities. R. L. N. Michel, who wrote about them at turn of the twentieth century, claims that most Cypriots treated their practices as "a religion of hypocrisy, with no little contempt and distrust."[32] According to Costas M. Constantinou, "they have been viewed at best as exotic anomalies or crypto-believers; at worst traitors and crude opportunists whose ethno-religious normalization was necessary and inevitable."[33] His hypothesis is that the advent of modern governmentality and biopolitics that coincided with British rule in Cyprus "has made it more difficult for individuals to use ethno-religious identities flexibly and pragmatically, including their use as a tactic to resist the policies of the ruling elite." The British administrators initially preserved the Ottoman religious divisions (*millet* system) but progressively finessed them into ethnic divisions "on the basis of which modern governmentality could be exercised."[34]

These newly introduced British categories forced members of the hybrid community to choose sides, and although the majority chose or were convinced to identify themselves officially as Greek Cypriots, some found themselves behind the rising walls of Turkish identity, generally because of the timely intervention of the local Muslim elite to convince them to choose the "right" religion. It should be noted that during this struggle between the elites of the communities to add members to their community or at least to prevent the loss of members, numerous means were used, including ostracization and economic inducements. For example, Greek Cypriot theologian Benedict Englezakis claims that after the church ordered moneylenders to cease lending to hybrid villages, those villagers converted to orthodox Christianity.[35] Those who were convinced to identify with one side or the other were usually celebrated in heroicomic ways.[36] "It became standard practice upon a 'conversion' for church bells to be rung and guns fired in the middle of the night, for baptism to take place, and for a man (for it was typically a man) to be paraded through the village eating a large chunk of pork."[37]

Whether it was due to the British administration's biopolitics or not, the new 1940s ethnonationalists in Cyprus had become so obsessed with homogeneous identity that even the most innocent attempt to cross religious boundaries, now rigidly policed by the new ethnonationalist forces within each community, ended up provoking their ire. Rising nationalism had also affected the longstanding process of religious syncretism, and it became more and more unacceptable for Turkish Cypriots to seek comfort at the island's Christian shrines. An article from a Turkish Cypriot newspaper in 1954, illustrates the atmosphere at the time:

> Some of our birdbrains, forgetting that they're Muslims, make offerings to idols at the monasteries, thinking that they'll help them! It seems these Orthodox saints have found the cure for everything! They give children to infertile women! They bring together couples in love! They find hus-

bands for old maids and widows! They heal rheumatism, insanity, blindness, cross-eyedness, lameness, even people on their deathbeds! Because of this, one should leave offerings at the idols of these saints!

We're Muslims, but we also tend to imitate the religious traditions of the Christians. This is not good! We don't let anything touch our religion, and certainly not our nation! In that case what business do we have with the monasteries? If it's really necessary to make offerings in fulfillment of promises to God, we have Hala Sultan Tekkesi, Kirklar Tekkesi, Hazreti Omer Tekkesi! We take pride in our Muslimness, we brag about our Turkishness. Then we go and give our goats and kids to the monasteries and make the monks fatter. If this practice isn't hypocrisy and an insult to our religion, then for the love of God, what is it? . . . Hoping for help from idols! It's time to erase these superstitious beliefs from our minds! Because worshipping idols and waiting for miracles from them is what the Christians do.[38]

Following the intercommunal strife that began in December 1963, each community departed toward a separate future. In response to the clashes, Turkish Cypriots retreated into armed enclaves while Greek Cypriots took over the bicommunal republic that had been founded three years earlier. The durable physical division of the communities, however, took place only in 1974, when the Turkish army intervened to restore the constitutional order that had been destroyed by the Greek Cypriot coup that ousted the first president of Cyprus, Archbishop Makarios III, from his post. Instead of restoring the arrangements established in 1960, Turkey divided the island and created two new ethnically homogenous spaces. After the flight of Greek Cypriots from the northern side of the barbed wire, all the Christian religious sites, apart from a handful of functioning churches and a monastery, were either desecrated or turned into mosques, cultural centers, or museums. It is telling that the Apostolos Andreas Monastery, which had become so popular with both communities after the miracle of 1912, ended up being the only Greek Cypriot monastery that continues to function under Turkish Cypriot rule. Although today most of its visitors are Greek Cypriots from the southern part of the island and foreign tourists, one can still see some old Turkish Cypriots paying visits to the site and bringing their offerings or lighting candles. Additionally, and somehow paradoxically, a few Turkish settlers from Anatolia who were resettled in the area after 1974 have also begun to enlist the efficacy of the saint by joining in some of the ceremonies of Apostolos Andreas. Recently, on a visit to Cyprus, one of the Turkish ministers also made a stop at the monastery as part of Turkey's new charm offensive politics, to light a candle in the church and make a wish for a peaceful settlement to the island's conflicts.

CONTESTED SHARED SPACES

Contested spaces were spaces claimed and used by both communities, places where parallel but not always syncretistic forms of worship existed. These were also sites whose efficacy was recognized by both communities, but unlike in the first case, the sources of this efficacy are contested. While in the first case Muslim Cypriots may also have acknowledged the efficacious power of a particular Christian saint, contested sites were ones where different saints of different faiths were said to have imbued the site with its power. However, these were sites that tended to have been administered by only one community at any given time, so that persons from the other religious community who wished to worship there had to do so with the toleration of those controlling the site. The difference with the first case is that those persons of the religious group not in control of the site normally claimed to be its real owners and so engaged in their own rather than the other group's practices at the site.

The competition over the shrines emerges clearly not only in the different foundation myths for the sites advanced by each religious community but also in the stories and legends that each community tells to describe certain events that involve the other religious group that uses them. These stories act both as warning signs for those others and as constant reminders of where limits are set and who actually wields authority at the site.³⁹ For instance, according to one story told by the Muslims about the Kırklar Tekkesi (Tekke of the Forty Saints), a sacred sword hung in the *tekke*.⁴⁰ "Tradition has it," Bağışkan remarks, "that a priest made fun of the *shaykhs* attached to the *tekke*, and an invisible force grasped the sword and cut off the priest's head."⁴¹ This story was supposed to serve as a warning to Orthodox visitors who doubted the essentially Muslim nature of the site.

The sites in Cyprus that come under this heading belonged exclusively to various Sufi dervish orders, and they were all *türbes* or *tekkes*. It is also important to point out that all of these shrines' foundation myths refer to a time that predates the Ottoman conquest of the island. The shrines usually consist of a *tekke* built near a *türbe* where at least one saint's or martyr's tomb (*şehida*) is situated. The Muslim foundation myths usually assign these tombs to Muslim martyrs who were killed fighting infidels during the Arab raids of the seventh century. For Christians, these tombs belong to Christian holy persons usually believed to have been killed in the same Arab raids. Hasluck claims that "the motive for the 'discovery' of such tombs is consciously or subconsciously political. At the back of the mind of the conquering race lies the idea of substantiating a prior claim to the conquered soil."⁴²

Only fourteen Sufi *tekkes* survived from the Ottoman period and continued to function into the twentieth century. Of these, three were known to be used by Christians as well. Turabi *tekke* was for Muslims the grave of the African companion of Hala Sultan, the Prophet Muhammad's aunt who also died in Cyprus. In Greek, this site was known as Ayios Therapon, a legendary dark-skinned Christian saint. Hazreti Ömer *tekke* is for Muslims the grave of the Muslim commander Ömer, who died during the early Arab raids; this site is known to Christians as Ayios Phanontes, an unknown foreign saint. The Tekke of the Forty Saints is known in Turkish as Kırklar *tekke* and in Greek as Agioi Saranda, both names having the same meaning. For Muslims, these forty saints were martyrs who died during the Arab raids in the island, while for Christians these are saints who died defending the island against these same Arab invaders. All of these *tekkes* were built on former Christian sacred sites.

Unlike the places I have called "spaces of (temporary) submission," both faiths made claims to these places, but only one faith was in control at any given moment. It remains difficult to discern from the evidence available to us at what point the parallel use of these sites began, or the circumstances that made this possible. Although some common practices existed, these sites also were spaces where each community performed its own rites, at different times or on different occasions. The tolerance of other practices that we associate with these sites contrasts sharply with the strict prohibition against use by the other community, which was in force for a significant number of churches converted into mosques during the Ottoman period. In other words, given prohibitions present in other sites that might be claimed by both communities, what characteristics are common to these shared sites that may have allowed the toleration of other ritual practices?

According to Hasluck, greater tolerance for other practices could be explained by the hidden intentions of the heterodox Sufi orders who administered these kinds of sanctuaries. He also claims that these "ambiguous sanctuaries," following the Muslim conquest, were appropriated by heterodox Sufi orders, such as the Bektaşis. He writes that in appropriating the sites, the Sufi orders did not cleanse the spaces of Christians who had previously been using them but rather attempted to absorb these groups into Bektaşism with the intention of converting them.[43] In other words, the Sufi orders who allowed Christians to use the sites may have had missionary aims. Although Şefki Koca, a well-known specialist on Bektaşism, claims that two of the Cypriot shared shrines I mentioned earlier were Bektaşi *tekkes* until the nineteenth century, we know, on the basis of Evkaf (a Muslim religious foundation) records, that the administrators of these sites in the early twentieth century were mainly Nakşibendi.[44] It is possible that the Bektaşis developed the habit of allowing Christians to use the sites while they were in control, and that their approach was simply adopted without interruption by the new order that most likely took over during the second quarter of the nineteenth century, when the Bektaşi order was suppressed. During that period, Sultan Mahmut II attempted to centralize religious institutions through the institutions of Sunnism and the suppression of certain heterodox Sufi orders. Nakşibendis, who were closer to Sunnism, were allowed to take over certain religious sites. In Cyprus it appears that one of the main motivations for the Nakşibendis to allow Christians to continue worship in these sites after this period was the economic benefit the order received (as in my category of economic spaces, discussed later).

One important example is the shrine of Kırklar Tekke/Agioi Saranta, located between the Greek village of Tymbou (Kırklar in Turkish) and the Turkish village of Ayia Kebir (Dilekkaya in Turkish) in Nicosia district. Certain historians claim that it played a significant role in the effort to Islamize the nearby villages.[45] Until the 1940s, Kırklar *tekke* was famous for its festival and fair, which was set up at the entrance of the building each year on March 9. On this day the neighboring villagers, both Christian and Muslim, would travel on foot or by donkey to the festivities, where they set up stalls to sell nuts, morsels in syrup, fruit juices, and other kinds of food.[46] While Muslim villagers prayed in the *mesjid* (mosque), Christians preferred to visit the tombs in the *türbe* and light candles. Since they bought these candles at the site, the dervishes controlling such sites generated significant income for their *tekkes* from such activities.[47]

Another case that supports the claim that economic reasons encouraged tolerance is the Turabi *tekke*, where Christian pilgrims had to pay an entrance fee. Greek Cypriot historian Costas P. Kyriss claims, however, that in 1884 a citizen complained that the sheikh in charge of the Turabi *tekke* demanded one piastre from each Christian pilgrim. The complainant asked the government either to forbid this charge or to separate the part of the monument containing the saint's tomb from the administration of the rest of the complex and grant it to the Christians for their exclusive use as a cultic center.[48] This petition demonstrates how demands, rights, and expectations can change with sociopolitical situations. This kind of appeal was most likely not possible on the island before 1878, when Cyprus, although still an Ottoman province, came under British administration. This case also demonstrates Albera's claim that "the freedom to enter into a sanctuary belonging to another religion depends on the socio-political context and on power relations between religious groups."[49]

The category of "contested sites" fits well into Robert M. Hayden's antagonistic tolerance (AT) thesis.[50] These spaces were claimed by both communities, but one community had the power to control the spaces and tolerate the others. Those others who believed in the efficacy of the site visited the place, but always in compliance with the rules set by those who controlled the shrines. They tactically, rather than voluntarily, accepted the limitations on their activities. While believing in the power of the site, they did not totally submit themselves to the authority controlling it. This at least tacit resistance marks the crucial distinction between "contested sites" and the first category, "spaces of (temporary) submission," in which visitors to the sites recognize both the legitimate authority of the controlling clergy and the efficacy of the place.

Religious activities at *tekkes* and *türbes* controlled by the Sufi orders had already nearly died out by the 1950s. Banned in Turkey by government decision in 1925, they similarly ceased to function in Cyprus, although mainly because of a lack of interest and financial means.[51] For many Turkish Cypriots, the once venerated visitors to these holy sacred sites rapidly became objects of derision, even a source of "embarrassment," and by the 1950s, "the Muslim shrines [were] tending to become sites for picnics more than anything else."[52] The only remaining active *tekke* was that of the Mevlevis in Nicosia (now a museum), which had a couple of residents who kept the building open mainly for tourists to visit. Although these sites were mostly abandoned by Turkish Cypriots as they became more secularist and nationalist, that same nationalistic pride also urged them to prevent Greeks from attending these sites. Although we can only speculate, it is probable that this "nationalization" of these spaces was one of the reasons that almost all of the sites were targeted and burned down or otherwise destroyed by Greek Cypriot extremists during intercommunal clashes in 1963.

ECONOMIC SPACES

Certain religious spaces, such as churches located in entirely Muslim villages, were tolerated because of their economic benefits. According to Glenn Bowman, economic benefit also encouraged the tolerance of Christian sites in Jerusalem during the Mamluk and Ottoman periods: "Substantial payments were demanded from religious authorities resident in Jerusalem and the holy places to maintain their residence and their hold on those sites. Pilgrimage was clearly good business for the local authorities, and allowing and fostering the presence of a diversity of churches ensured the most expansive, and hence lucrative, catchment area for the pilgrimage."[53]

Immediately after the second Tanzimat decree in 1856, Christians felt freer to build churches in places where they had not previously been allowed to build. There was a massive campaign of church construction throughout the island during this period. Most of these churches brought abundant economic benefits to the impoverished villagers through festivals and fairs that were arranged around the churches. George Jeffrey, Cyprus's Curator of Antiquities in 1903, mentions how one Turkish Cypriot village sponsored a new church to be built in their village: "Pigeana, a Moslem village, possesses a Christian church which has been completely rebuilt lately, it is said at the expense of the Moslem villagers (!) for the purpose of encouraging a 'panegiri' or fair in connection with it."[54] My own grandmother comes from a village that similarly had a functioning church without having any Christian inhabitants. Apparently, the church was reconstructed from an earlier structure in the 1880s, and the older villagers claim that their grandparents had helped in the construction of the church in exchange for assistance in building the mosque in the same village.[55]

The church in my grandmother's village was built on top of a cave. Apparently the bones attributed to the Iliofotoi saints, rumored to have healing powers, had been discovered there. Pilgrims used to bring their sick relatives to be touched by the bones.[56] Once a year, clergy arranged a festival and fair in front of the church, which provided a wonderful income opportunity for the Muslim inhabitants of the village, who hosted the pilgrims and sold them their agricultural produce and other products. When the Muslims of Alifodes talk about their village, the annual Christian festival holds an important place in their memories of a happier period before their lives were touched by the "Cyprus problem."

Some of the villagers who had earlier migrated to Nicosia say that they made certain to time their yearly holidays in order to be in the village during the Ayioi Iliofotoi festival. Women nostalgically recall preparing different kinds of food, such as sweetmeats and *böreks* (savories), for the event. Men recall the ovens full of *kleftiko* (thieves' meat) that they prepared for the Greek Cypriots, and the butchers who slaughtered as many animals for the festival as they normally would for the entire year.[57]

However, since these particular villagers were themselves known for their Muslim piety, their cooperation with the church should be taken not as an instance of syncretism but as a pragmatic form of religious coexistence. Their contributions to church events and to caring for the church buildings and grounds were not given on religious grounds but for social and economic reasons. They acted as custodians of sites associated with another religious heritage, but they did not spiritually identify with it in any formal sense.[58]

This case, then, is typical of sites in my third category. Those who do not recognize the efficacy of a site (and this lack of belief immediately sets this category off from the first two) may still allow it to function and even actively encourage and support it if they believe that the site will generate economic benefits. I mentioned earlier that most of these sites continued to function until the "Cyprus problem" reached them. In the previous case, the Turkish Cypriots abandoned the village and sought refuge elsewhere, but the church continues to function today without the village that once surrounded it. Following the flight of the Turkish Cypriot villagers in 1963, the whole village surrounding the church was looted and razed. In other cases that fit into the category of economic spaces, however, the opposite occurred: the church was destroyed by the same Turkish Cypriot villagers who had originally encouraged its construction and regularly supported its upkeep.

CONCLUSION

What, then, can we learn from these examples? Can they model any practices that are useful today? What might the management of difference during the prenationalist period in a place like Cyprus tell us about how difference is understood after the emergence of competing nationalisms? It should be noted that in the examples given here, the term "submission" is every bit as important as "tolerance." Submission—or the recognition both of the potential efficacy of a site and of another authority's right to control that site—became particularly threatening with the rise of rival nationalism. As this coincided with the end of Ottoman rule, submission at these sites began to be interpreted not as temporary but as crypto, in other words not as a strategy but as an identity. The presence of Muslims at Christian sites began conveniently to be interpreted as an expression of crypto-Christianity by nationalist Orthodox Christians; in turn, this appeared threatening to Turkish Cypriot nationalist leaders and intellectuals, as we saw in the quote regarding Apostolos Andreas. In addition, religious authorities at these sites often used the presence of the other— as well as the interpretation of the other's submission as crypto-Christianity—to attempt to convert them or bring them into the right path. In the 1950s the argument that Muslims in Cyprus are actually converted Christians (and in many cases crypto-Christians) would be used to argue that the political claims of the Turkish Cypriot minority did not need to be taken into account. In the latter nationalist period, then, it was not tolerance of the other but submission to the other's practices and authority that appeared threatening to nationalist leaders and intellectuals. It was the act or potentiality of crossing—in other words, the attraction of the other—that in certain periods laid the grounds for understanding and in other periods needed to be erased.

This willingness not only to tolerate but to submit was made possible, however, under a particular regime in which Islam was the religion of the state, and crossing or even temporary submission did not imply the threat of conversion (for the Muslims). There were layers of submission, and within this regime Muslims were clearly more comfortable than their Christian neighbors with the possibilities of crossing, which appeared relatively nonthreatening to Muslim elite because of the absolute ban on conversion. Temporary submission became threatening when religious identity was linked to ethnonational identity, and when these two religio-ethnic groups were incorporated asymmetrically into new modes of politics. In these cases the practices of crossing were discouraged, but the sites themselves have survived, for the most part, the conflict that divided the island.

If spaces of temporary submission were sites that were accepted as belonging to the other community, what we have called economic spaces were ones in which the site belonged to one's own community but tolerated the beliefs and practices of the other community for pragmatic reasons. While spaces of submission were spaces in which one mimicked the other community or temporarily applied its practices because of belief in the site's possible efficacy, economic spaces may be seen as sites of toleration of difference without this toleration affecting one's own belief.

Between these two are what we have called contested spaces, where both submission and toleration are partial. These were sites with mixed heritages, sites where the rights of one community to control the site were contested, if not always challenged. Interestingly, these sites of heterogeneous origin were both the ones at which significant conversion is known to have occurred as well as the sites that have been most negatively affected by the rise of nationalisms and the eventual intercommunal conflict that divided the island. We see in the Balkans, Israel, and South Asia that such sites have been the sources of heated dispute, even violence, depending on the regime in power and the relation of the claimants to these sources of power.

What we can see from these examples is that both submission and toleration were primarily strategic acts, and contest emerged only in cases where historical rights of a particular community over a site were challenged. Submission and toleration were made possible through the acknowledgment of difference and its potential efficacy, which in turn was clearly made possible under particular hierarchies of power. This is an aspect of prenationalist everyday life that is erased or denied in current discourses of peaceful coexistence or Ottoman tolerance in Cyprus. In the first discourse, submission is no longer strategic but is attributed to a crypto-Christianity that implies an ultimate sameness. And in the second discourse, any form of submission is attributed to the benevolence of the state. Both of these discourses ultimately deny that believers of another faith may not only recognize difference but may also see its power or benefits to them. They deny the strategies of everyday life that give us a more complex picture of how people may have lived together or beside each other, sharing or contesting spaces, in the past.

NOTES

This essay is part of a European project, Identity and Conflict: Cultural Heritage and the Reconstruction of Identities After Conflict (2008–2012), funded under the 7th Framework Programme. For their comments, thanks to Rebecca Bryant and the participants at the Choreography of Sacred Spaces conference in Istanbul in May 2010. The latter event was organized by Karen Barkey and Elazar Barkan of Columbia University's Center for the Study of Democracy, Toleration and Religion.

1. Known in English as the Feast of the Sacrifice, Kurban Bayramı is one of the two most important holidays and an opportunity for visiting family and friends and for travel.
2. Press and Information Office of Cyprus (PIO), *Muslim Places of Worship* (Nicosia: PIO, 2008), 1.
3. Ibid., 1–2.
4. Yiannis Papadakis, "Nationalist Imaginings of War in Cyprus," in *War, A Cruel Necessity? The Bases of Institutionalised Violence*, ed. R. Hinde and H. Watson (London: I. B. Tauris Academic Studies, 1995), 54–67.
5. Costas P. Kyriss, "Symbiotic Elements in the History of the two Communities of Cyprus," in *Proceedings: International Symposium on Political Geography* (Nicosia: Cyprus Geographical Association, 1976); and Costas P. Kyriss, *Peaceful Co-Existence in Cyprus Under British Rule (1878–1959) and After Independence*. (Nicosia: Public Information Office, 1977).
6. Stephanos Evripidou, "Christofias: Solution Will Heal Wounds and Cleanse Souls," *Cyprus Mail*, April 1, 2010.
7. The Islamic connection with the island can be traced back to the early years after the death of the Prophet Mohammed when, in the seventh century, a series of Arab raids, some leading to intermittent periods of settlement, began. See İ. H. Danişmend, "İslam ve Türk tarihinde Kıbrıs." *Türk düşüncesi* 8, no. 9 (1958): 15–16.
8. See, e.g., Cengiz Orhonlu, "The Ottoman Turks Settle in Cyprus," in *The First International Congress of Cypriot Studies: Presentations of the Turkish Delegation*, ed. H. İnalcık (Ankara: Institute for the Study of Turkish Culture, 1971), 76–77;

and A. E. Özkul, *Kıbrıs'ın sosyo-ekonomik tarihi 1726-1750* (İstanbul: İletişim, 2005), 40–43.
9. Kyriss, "Symbiotic Elements."
10. Ronald C. Jennings, *Christians and Muslims in Ottoman Cyprus and the Mediterranean World 1571-1640* (New York: New York University Press, 1993), 137–38.
11. Altay Nevzat and Mete Hatay, "Politics, Society and the Decline of Islam in Cyprus: From the Ottoman Era to the 21st Century," in Middle Eastern Studies 45, no. 6 (2009): 911–33.
12. Ibid.
13. Charles Fraser Beckingham, "The Turks of Cyprus," *Journal of the Royal Anthropological Institute of Great Britain and Ireland* 87, no. 2 (1957): 165–74. The general distinction between the Bektaşi and Nakşibendi sects is that while Nakşibendis are closer to Sunnism, Bektaşis tend to be more heterodox, and they place an emphasis on Ali and the doctrine of the Twelve Imams, which is also of defining importance in certain branches in Shiism.
14. Frederick William Hasluck, "Heterodox Tribes of Asia Minor," *Journal of the Royal Anthropological Institute of Great Britain and Ireland* 51 (1921): 310–42.
15. Historian Ahmet Erdengiz suggests that most of those who originally settled in Cyprus, such as the Janissaries and members of Turcoman tribes of rural Anatolia, were Alevi-Bektaşi. While today's Turkish Cypriots hardly identify themselves as Alevi-Bektaşis, they nevertheless, Erdengiz suggests, inherited their cultural heritage. Ahmet Erdengiz, "Kıbrıslı Türklerin Alevi kimliği," in *Halk bilimi sempozyumları III*, ed. Fatma Kükrer (Ankara: KKTC Milli Eğitim ve Kültür Yayınları, 2001), 240–44.
16. Beckingham, "Turks of Cyprus," 173.
17. Altay Nevzat, *Nationalism Amongst the Turks of Cyprus: The First Wave* (Oulu, Fin.: Oulu University Press, 2005), 78.
18. Maria Couroucli, "Sharing Nostalgia in Istanbul; Christian and Muslim Pilgrims to St. George's Sanctuary" (paper presented at the international conference Sharing Sacred Space: Religion and Conflict Resolution, February 14–15, 2008, Columbia University, New York).
19. Harry Luke, *Cyprus: A Portrait and Appreciation* (London: George G. Harrap, 1957), 147.
20. Tuncer Bağışkan, *Ottoman, Islamic and Islamised Monuments in Cyprus* (Nicosia: Cyprus Turkish Education Foundation, 2009).
21. Luke, *Cyprus*, 145.
22. Bağışkan, *Monuments in Cyprus*, 404.
23. Luke, *Cyprus*, 145.
24. Ibid., 138–41.

25. Dionigi Albera, "'Why Are You Mixing What Cannot Be Mixed?' Shared Devotions in the Monotheisms," *History and Anthropology* 19, no. 1 (2008): 46.
26. Kyriss, *Peaceful Co-Existence*, 20.
27. Chris Schabel, "Religion," in *Cyprus: Society and Culture 1191–1374*, ed. Konnari Nicolaou and C. Schabel (Lieden: Brill, 2005), 158.
28. Bağışkan, *Monuments in Cyprus*, 74.
29. Albera, "Why Are You Mixing," 52.
30. Ibid.
31. Such people numbered around 1,200 at the outset of British rule. Samuel White Baker, *Cyprus, as I Saw It in 1879* (London: Macmillan, 1879), available at http://www.gutenberg.net/etext/3656.
32. R. L. N. Michel, "A Muslim–Christian Sect in Cyprus," *Nineteenth Century Journal*, no. 63 (1908): 751–62.
33. Costas M. Constantinou, "Aporias of Identity: Bicommunalism, Hybridity, and the 'Cyprus Problem,'" *Cooperation and Conflict* 42 (2007): 249.
34. Ibid., 256.
35. Benedict Englezakis, *Studies on the History of the Church of Cyprus, 4th to 20th Centuries* (Aldershot, UK: Variorum, 1995), 437–38. Similarly, Turkish Cypriot historian Ahmet An noted that one wealthy Muslim merchant, after hearing of the conversion of two villages to Christianity in the remote Tylliria region, assembled a group of notables to visit nominally Muslim villages in the region to speak to them of the importance of their religion and to circumcise the males, some of whom were forty years old and had not yet been circumcised. They also distributed supplies of wheat and grain and financed the construction of a mosque and school. Ahmet An, *Kıbrıs'ın yetiştirdiği değerler (1782–1899)* [Valuable persons raised in Cyprus, 1782–1899] (Ankara: Akçay Yayınları, 2002), 81–82.
36. Constantinou, "Aporias of Identity," 256.
37. Rebecca Bryant, *Imagining the Modern: Cultures of Nationalism in Cyprus* (London: I. B. Tauris, 2004), 66.
38. "Ah, bu adakçılar!" (Oh, these votive worshippers!), *Halkın sesi*, August 5, 1954. Author's translation from the Turkish.
39. This rule, by the way, also applies when stories are told about sites that fall into the other two categories of economic spaces and spaces of temporary submission.
40. According to archaeologist and folklorist Tuncer Bağışkan, Muslims in the past enjoyed relating a popular myth about the site to its Greek Orthodox visitors. Bağışkan, *Monuments in Cyprus*, 303.
41. Ibid.

42. Frederick William Hasluck, "Graves of the Arabs in Asia Minor," *Annual of the British School at Athens* 19 (1912–1913): 182–90; at 189.
43. Frederick William Hasluck, "Ambiguous Sanctuaries and Bektashi Propaganda," *Annual of the British School at Athens*, 20 (1913–1914): 94–119.
44. Şefki Koca, *Kıbrıs'ta Bektaşi dergahları* (İstanbul: Cem Dergisi, 2001).
45. See Church of Cyprus on this matter: "Religions Symbiosis in an Importan[t] Archaeological Side: Agioi Saranta/Kirklar Tekke at Tymbou," (English summary), www.churchofcyprus.org.cy/documents/English_Summary.doc.
46. Bağışkan, *Monuments in Cyprus*, 302–7.
47. Ibid.
48. Kyriss, *Peaceful Co-Existence*, 15.
49. Albera, "Why Are You Mixing."
50. Robert M. Hayden, "Antagonistic Tolerance: Competitive Sharing of Religious Sites in South Asia and the Balkans," *Current Anthropology* 43, no. 2 (2002): 205–31.
51. Hizber Hikmetağalar, *Eski Lefkoşada semtler ve anılar*, 2nd ed. (Istanbul: Fakülteler Matabaası, 2005), 30–32.
52. Charles Fraser Beckingham, "Islam and Turkish Nationalism in Cyprus," *Die Welt des Islams* 5, no. 1–2 (1957): 81, doi:10.1163/157006057X00027.
53. Glenn Bowman, "'In Dubious Battle on the Plains of Heav'n': The Politics of Possession in Jerusalem's Holy Sepulchre," *History and Anthropology* 22, no. 3 (2011): 371–99.
54. George Jeffrey, *A Description of the Historic Monuments of Cyprus* (Nicosia: Government Printing Office), 417.
55. Costas M. Constantinou and Mete Hatay, "Cyprus, Ethnic Conflict and Conflicted Heritage," *Ethnic and Racial Studies* 33, no. 9 (2010): 1600–1619.
56. Magda H. Ohnefalsch-Richter, *Greek Customs and Mores in Cyprus* (Nicosia: Laiki Cultural Centre), 80–81.
57. Constantinou and Hatay, "Cyprus, Ethnic Conflict," 1600–1619.
58. Ibid.

3

RELIGIOUS ANTAGONISM AND SHARED SANCTUARIES IN ALGERIA

DIONIGI ALBERA

THIS ESSAY DEALS with Muslim attendance at an important Marian sanctuary in Algeria, Our Lady of Africa in Algiers, from the mid-nineteenth century to the present, and examines the sanctuary's relationship to a changing political environment. I analyze how the political background frames the context for the choreography of daily life at this Catholic site, paying attention to the complexity of the interplay between different forces and interests in the colonial and, later, postcolonial state. Moreover, I take the issue of proselytism into account as a key factor in order to understand the political context and the symbolic repercussions of Muslim attendance at a Christian sanctuary.

Located in the upper part of the town, in a panoramic position, the huge sanctuary of Our Lady of Africa is a central element of the urban landscape of Algeria's capital. When one looks from the seaside to "Algiers the white," it is impossible to avoid noticing this imposing building with neo-Byzantine cupolas. This prominent Catholic site of pilgrimage also attracts the Muslim faithful. Such interreligious choreography of daily life has persisted for more than a century. These manifestations initially developed in the context of the French colonial state, where a Christian minority dominated a vast Muslim majority. But things changed abruptly after Algeria's independence in 1962. The postcolonial state was built with a strong orientation toward the homogenization of the population from a linguistic and religious point of view: the Algerian nation was conceived as Arab and Muslim. Almost all of Algeria's Christians and Jews abandoned the country, and the Catholic presence became very marginal. Thus, the supremacy of Islam became overwhelming from a demographic and symbolic point of view. Moreover, during the civil war of the last decade of the twentieth century, distress over differences extended even to the physical elimination of several Christians by jihadist groups. Yet daily life at Our Lady of Africa has traversed all of these turbulent periods without losing its character as a place where different (and conflicting) religious groups can experience a pacific coexistence.

To grasp the meaning of this astonishing continuity of religious pluralism, it is necessary to consider the intersection of the choreography of daily life at the sanctuary with more official religious choreographies established by religious leaders and institutions. This is done by adopting a historical perspective that takes into account the evolution of the political and religious environment of the mixed attendance at this shrine.

THE CHURCH AND THE COLONIAL STATE

The birth and growing influence of the sanctuary of Our Lady of Africa was situated for almost a century in a political context characterized by an unstable balance of power and a somewhat conflicting alliance between the Church and the colonial state. Since the beginning of the conquest of Algeria, the Church allied with the French army. As a matter of fact, among the aims of the original French expeditions was the restoration of Christianity in Africa. This intention was clearly mentioned in the plan of conquest proposed by the minister of war to the French king, Charles X.[1] However, in the new political climate inaugurated by the July Monarchy, the missionary dimension of the conquest was somewhat put aside.

The Vatican immediately showed a great interest in the horizons opened by the French expedition and made every effort to impose its presence on the spot.[2] In the following years a number of Catholic congregations made their appearance in Algeria. Yet the Church's plans to start a proselytizing campaign were slowed by the French state, which feared that the missionary zeal could endanger the establishment of peace in a country that had already experienced the turmoil of lengthy indigenous movements of resistance and rebellion. In the next decades, moreover, French plans to create an "Arab Kingdom" under the Second Empire (1852–1870) and the secular orientations of the Third Republic (1870–1940) contributed to limiting the freedom of action of the Church.

The conflict between priests and generals became a recurrent feature of the political maneuvering in colonial Algeria. This conflict, however, never succeeded in suppressing the substantive alliance between the Church and the state. While ambiguous, and with wide grounds of dissension, this alliance remained strong for more than a century. On the one hand, French domination of the country was essential to ensure the presence of the Church. Thus, the Vatican was forced to accept the conditions imposed by the French state on apostolic work. On the other hand, an increasingly massive migration of European settlers made the presence of the Church valuable for the colonial government since it became clear that priestly action was a crucial instrument to ensure the integration of the newcomers into the colonial state.

Beginning in the 1830s the French authorities decided that Algeria should be a territory of settlement. The state tried to promote the installation of European settlers on land confiscated from local people. Besides colonizers from the metropolis, this political initiative aimed primarily at the recruitment of incomers from Switzerland and Germany. The results of this sponsored settlement were relatively weak. However, starting from the first years after the occupation, there was a massive unorganized arrival of people from Italy, Spain, and Malta. The common Catholic affiliation of these disparate groups was an important lever to ensure their integration into the colonial state. On its side, the Church was well aware of the political repercussions of the establishment of a religious mapping of the colonial territory. In its negotiations with the authorities, the ecclesiastical hierarchy did not fail to recall the Church's essential contribution to the assimilation of these heterogeneous groups of European newcomers.³

The Algerian country was gradually organized in an ecclesiastical grid inspired by the logic of the religious structure of Catholic Europe: dioceses, parishes, churches, seminaries, charitable institutions, religious congregations, and so on. Along with the transformation of some synagogues and mosques into churches (for instance, in Tlemcen, Algiers, and Constantine), several new religious buildings were erected.⁴ By 1838 the creation of the diocese of Algiers was already decided upon. At the beginning it covered the entire northern belt of the country, and it was later subdivided into three sections through the erection of the bishoprics of Oran and Constantine in 1866 (both the new ecclesiastical provinces were meanwhile subordinated to Algiers, which was then transformed into an archbishopric).

The first bishop of Algiers, Antoine-Adolphe Dupuch (1838–1845), set up the clerical mapping of the territory. His work was completed by his successors, Louis-Antoine-Agustin Pavy (1846–1866) and Charles Martial Lavigerie (1867–1892). A symbolic elaboration was necessary to establish the legitimacy of the new Church of Algeria. A first strategy was based on the assertion of the existence of strong ties with the ancient Christian presence in North Africa. From this point of view, twelve centuries of Muslim life did not seem to represent more than a parenthesis, an almost insignificant digression, if compared to a Christian continuity over the millennia. To situate the Christian presence in a fictitious descent from this distant past, the Church employed a rhetoric based on the celebration of African martyrs of the early centuries and on lexical choices that referred to the new Catholic districts by ancient religious designations. From this perspective the current population of Algeria (mainly the Berber component) was seen as being composed of descendants of the ancient Christians who were converted by force to Islam, thereby justifying the Catholic missionary zeal (which was nevertheless obliged to remain quite discreet, due to the restraints imposed by the French authorities).⁵

Alongside this reinvention of the African past of the Algerian Church, some modern themes were also mobilized to consolidate the Catholic presence on Algerian soil. Among these, the cult of the Virgin Mary, with the accents that it was manifesting during the nineteenth century, had a very important role. Several new places of worship, sometimes linked to supernatural manifestations, were devoted to the Virgin. Some urban sanctuaries (such as Our Lady of Santa Cruz in Oran [6]) and rural chapels (e.g., in Misserghin) acquired a great reputation. Their influence soon went beyond the Christian sphere since they also attracted the Muslim faithful. Yet the paramount efforts to establish a Marian choreography were concentrated in the capital of the colony. The most conspicuous result of this endeavor was the creation of the sanctuary of Our Lady of Africa in Algiers.

THE BIRTH OF THE SANCTUARY

The first bishop of Algiers, Mgr. Dupuch, had a strong devotion to the Virgin and encouraged the special dedication of the new Church of Algeria to the Mother of God. A native of the diocese of Bordeaux, he was a regular pilgrim at Our Lady of Verdelais, a renowned sanctuary located about forty kilometers from the town. In his early years in Algiers, he planned to create a pilgrimage to Mary and ordered the building of a small shrine next to a seminary he had founded on a hill near Algiers. At the time of the French conquest, a statue of Mary was discovered in a locked cabinet in the port of Algiers. The bishop interpreted this as a divine sign. This statue was placed in the mihrab of a mosque in Algiers that had been transformed into a church.[7]

Bishop Dupuch also had an important role in relation to the statue that later became the central symbol of the devotion to Our Lady of Africa. During a tour in France in 1840, he visited an institute of the Ladies of Sacred Heart, near Lyon, where he received the gift of a bronze statue of the Virgin to be placed on the top of the Algiers cathedral. This cathedral was originally a mosque (the Ketchaoua Mosque). It was transformed into a church in 1832 and in the 1840s underwent restoration. In the meantime, Bishop Dupuch intended to locate the statue on the minaret of a mosque in the upper town that had also been transformed into a church (known as Sainte-Croix). But apparently this project was met with opposition from the military authorities. The French military leaders feared the reactions of Algerian people to this ostentatious demonstration of the new assignment of this religious building. The statue thus ended up being transported to a Trappist monastery in the outskirts of the city. As we will see, this bronze statue would later be moved to the new religious edifice consecrated to the cult of the Virgin Mary in Algiers, and would become a crucial iconographic symbol of the devotion to the "Black Madonna" in this context.

In 1845 Bishop Dupuch left his office (in the face of financial difficulties and open conflict with the French authorities[8]) and was succeeded by Mgr. Pavy. The new bishop was also very attached to the Marian cult and was a regular visitor to French shrines dedicated to the Virgin, starting with his attendance at Our Lady of Fourvière, on a hill overlooking the town of Lyon, where he was born. Pavy was the true founder of the shrine of Our Lady of Africa and the successful entrepreneur of the pilgrimage linked to it. In several texts, he presents himself as the only person who conceived of the project, adding that he was subsequently assisted by a committee composed by several members of the colonial elite of Algiers. He announced the creation a new great Marian pilgrimage center during a homily in Algiers cathedral on the occasion of the feast celebrating the proclamation of the dogma of Mary's Immaculate Conception in 1854.[9]

But later priestly chronicles also highlight the role of two women who were the receptacles of a divine inspiration that fueled the foundation of the holy place (according to a common model in the ecclesiastical narratives of the birth of centers of Marian piety in the nineteenth century Europe). Agarithe Berger and Anna Cinquin, two humble workers from Lyon who followed the bishop when he was appointed to Algiers, are presented as two secular saints whose lives were under the sign of prayer, asceticism, and charity. Their efforts to instigate the pilgrimage are seen as the result of an "illumination from above."[10] In particular, there were some attempts to develop a hagiographic portrait of Agarithe Berger following the pattern of Bernadette of Lourdes and Mélanie of La

Salette.¹¹ The story of the foundation of Our Lady of Africa has it that the two pious women started by placing a small statue of the Virgin in a narrow uninhabited valley near the town. This place began to be attended by other Christian women who came to say their prayers before the statue. The bishop decided on the edification of a small shrine at the spot, which was then known as Notre-Dame du Ravin. As the number of pilgrims increased, Agarithe Berger and Anna Cinquin would eventually convince the bishop that Algeria needed a Marian pilgrimage comparable to that of Our Lady of Fourvière, to which they were attached. The bishop promptly agreed and decided on the construction of a chapel at the top of a hill overlooking the city that was near the valley. This chapel was inaugurated in 1857 and received the bronze statue given in 1840 to Bishop Dupuch.

The chapel was but a temporary stage in the strategy devised by the bishop. He bought a huge area of land around it in order to build a much larger sanctuary. His biographer observed that "no location could be more appropriate: close to town, easy to get, with a beautiful vegetation, a stunning view, a majestic crown of mountains, nothing was lacking to make here one of the finest pilgrimages in the world."¹² The work on the foundation of the sanctuary, which was already identified as Our Lady of Africa by Pavy and the committee that assisted him, started in 1858.¹³ To cover the costs, the bishop launched a fundraising campaign that lasted several years.

The project was sustained by an explicit intellectual elaboration. In 1858 the bishop published a book in which he retraced the history of the Marian cult in North Africa since antiquity and appealed to the Catholic world to help the project of the sanctuary.¹⁴ In these texts the prelate exposed the multivocality of the symbol of the Virgin as he handled it, and he made clear the ambitious pastoral projects that he linked to the creation of this new holy site. Several other works published in the following years diffused the ideas of Pavy in various forms, including poems.¹⁵

In the bishop's works, Mary appears first as a liberator from the threat of the Moors. She is presented as the patron of religious orders such as the Trinitarians and the Mercedarians, which were especially effective since the Middle Ages in the redemption of Christian captives in North Africa. After the French triumph the Virgin Mary could now been addressed as Our Lady of Victories (this was precisely the title given to a mosque converted into a church in Algiers) because, according to the bishop, the Virgin had clearly patronized the victory over the Muslims of North Africa, putting an end to intimidation by Barbary pirates. The bishop develops a lengthy rhetoric of self-victimization that transformed a violent military conquest into an act of justice and reparation justified by centuries of unilateral terrorization, extortion, and slavery suffered by the pacific Europeans on the Mediterranean Sea.

Mary also served as a bridge with the traditions of the ancient African past when several religious sites were devoted to her. The neo-Byzantine style of the new sanctuary explicitly sought to renew the link with this ancient past, materializing some features of Justinian's epoch. Moreover, the project proposed by the architect Jean Eugène Fromageau also highlighted the points of contact between Byzantine and Moorish architecture. Some elements of the latter were therefore "Christianized."

At the same time, the establishment of a Marian pilgrimage in Algiers was aimed at building a different, synchronic bridge across the Mediterranean, connecting North Africa with the Marian pilgrimages that were then flourishing in Southern Europe, often in remote places, on hills and mountaintops. In particular, the bishop proposed to join both shores of the Mediterranean through the devotion to the Mother of God, providing a pilgrimage to Our Lady of Africa that would mirror the important pilgrimage to Notre-Dame de la Garde in Marseilles.

There are striking parallels with Marseilles's paramount Marian sanctuary, which was without doubt a model for its Algerian counterpart. Notre-Dame de la Garde is also situated on a hilltop overlooking the town. It is highly probable that this location influenced the choice of Pavy when he acquired the area where first the chapel and then the basilica were built in Algiers. In Marseilles a monumental edifice was also under construction in a similar eclectic neo-Byzantine style. The new imposing sanctuary was replacing a small chapel built in the Middle Age, which acquired popular devotion over several centuries and had experienced a growing success in the first part of the nineteenth century. A fundraising campaign had also been launched in Marseilles to collect the resources for the new sanctuary that was consecrated in 1864.

Pavy believed that the recent proclamation of the dogma of Mary's Immaculate Conception was generating a renewed movement of devotion to the Virgin in Catholicism, and that Algeria might be associated to this development. This link was made clear by the fact that it was precisely on the day of the proclamation of this dogma that he announced the founding of the new Marian pilgrimage in Algeria. Here, in a country composed of foreigners from different countries, there was a need to establish a "center of brotherhood" capable of giving the sense of a common development, in the name of Mary, to a conglomerate of people without roots. The birth of a great Marian pilgrimage would also encourage morality by sanctifying Christian family life.

Pavy attributed to the Virgin an apostolic role among Muslims. They venerated her as the mother of a great prophet. In his historical work on Mary's cult in North Africa, Pavy attentively analyzes all the passages of the Qur'an that refer to Mary. The bishop mentions with satisfaction that the Qur'an seems to even confirm the dogma of the Immaculate Conception of Mary. On this point, he cites some Qur'anic verses that were inscribed in a mosque in Algiers (which had been subsequently converted into a church), where it is said that Mary is "exempt from all sin." On the whole, he suggests that, thanks to the Islamic attention to her, the Virgin will one day open the Muslims' eyes to the divinity of her son, making their conversion possible.[16]

The bishop hoped that the future sanctuary would become, thanks to all these multifarious vocations, "the ark of the covenant of piety in Algeria." Pavy wanted this to be a place where young and old, soldier and sailor, French, Spanish, Maltese, German, and Italian, would kneel, "accompanied from time to time by the Native."[17] The exact meaning of this statement is not clear: it may express a vision of the future religious life at the sanctuary or, more probably, it may refer to a plural (and multifaith) frequentation of the provisory chapel.

Pavy successfully obtained funding for the erection of the sanctuary, but he died in 1866, when the new building was not yet completed. His successor, Mgr. Lavigerie, resumed the supervision of the works. The imposing edifice was finally inaugurated with an impressive ceremony in 1872. To make clear the links between the sanctuary and the establishment of the French colonial order, among the ex-votos offered to the Virgin on this occasion were some swords and other objects belonging to the French generals who had been the protagonists of the conquest of Algeria.

The following year, in May 1873, at the moment of the first council of the new African Church, the bronze statue of the Virgin was transferred from the temporary chapel to the church in a magnificent ceremony that, under the seal of Mary, illustrated the power of the new Church of Africa and its renewed relationship with a distant past. Ecclesiastical sources affirm that a huge number of people covered the hill of Our Lady of Africa; in addition to the Christians, there were also many Muslims and Jews, "attracted by such a spectacle."[18] Various orders of clergy and members of fraternities attended a solemn procession, organized in an articulated choreography, where several symbols of continuity with the African Church of antiquity—such as the canons of the ancient African councils, the work of Church doctors from Africa, the relics of St. Augustine and St. Monica—were ceremoniously exhibited.[19]

In 1876 Pope Pius IX attributed to the new church the title of minor basilica along with the right to put a crown on the statue of the Virgin. This dual recognition from the Vatican ratified the rapid success of the creation of this new form of worship and gave further impetus to popular devotion through indulgences attached to this new status. As evidenced by contemporary sources, Our Lady of Africa already attracted a large number of pilgrims, whose ex-votos already covered the walls of the sanctuary.

The articulated web of meanings and values that the ecclesiastical entrepreneurs put at the heart of this pilgrimage was transposed through the materiality of the sanctuary, which became richer and richer in the following decades. The eclectic architecture of the basilica combined a dominant Byzantine form with some Moorish influences (for example, the tower bell fashioned after a minaret and the external Hispano-Moorish ceramics). The sanctuary was inhabited by a host of saint figures (Saint Augustine, Saint Monique, and several saints devoted to the redemption of the captives), who were materialized through altars, statues, and paintings. Moreover, the symbolical topography of the sanctuary was enriched by certain relics (those of Saint Augustine and Saint Monique) and by the tombs of the "fathers" of this devotional center: Dupuch, Pavy, Agarithe, and Anne. The bronze statue of the Virgin, which was brought from Lyon to Algiers in 1840, rapidly became the most important symbol of the new shrine. The statue originated as a copy of a statue made by Edmé Bouchardon (1698–1762), a leading sculptor in eighteenth-century France. Mary was represented with a smiling face and hands outstretched in a posture that is typical of what has been called the Faithful Virgin. An engraving that reproduces the statue in the chapel shows that the Virgin stands on a globe while stepping on the head of a serpent. Her clothing reproduces the ordinary style of the representation of Mary in European art. In the basilica, the statue of the Virgo Fidelis was transformed into "Our Lady of Africa" by dressing her in a gigantic robe embroidered in the sumptuous style of Tlemcen. Both the serpent and the globe disappeared.[20] The name attributed to the statue, her dark bronze visage that made her a Black Madonna, and the local style of the robe can be seen as elements of a successful strategy of enculturation of the cult.

THE ISSUE OF PROSELYTISM

As we have seen, the symbolic apparatus deployed in the sanctuary included a missionary action directed at Muslims. In 1858 Pavy founded a prayer association whose general aim was the conversion of Muslims spread throughout the world, especially those inhabiting Algeria.[21] The center of the association was established in the temporary chapel of Our Lady of Africa and was then transferred to the future church of the same name. Each member of the association had to recite a daily number of prayers to this end. Moreover, a weekly Mass was celebrated at Our Lady of Africa with this intention. The ranks of the association were opened to the Catholic faithful residing in France and in other European countries. Two years later the association based at Our Lady of Africa had already acquired twenty-seven thousand adherents. By 1863 there were sixty thousand, and in successive years the number grew to eighty thousand.[22] The recitation of a special prayer for the conversion of the Muslims, specially composed for the members of the association, which was used to open an indulgence of one hundred days, ended with these words: "Our Lady of Africa, pray for us and for the Muslims."[23]

To emphasize the link between the sanctuary and the prayer association, these words were inscribed inside the basilica, at the bottom of the apse above the altar. They are still present today, although, as we shall see, the meaning given to them has radically changed. The activities of the prayer association for the conversion of Muslims continued for several decades and, after experiencing a decline in the early twentieth century, received a new impetus in 1923 by Archbishop Augustin-Fernand Leynaud.

Besides the prayers, the Algerian Church developed more concrete initiatives to convert Muslims to Catholicism. Charles Martial Lavigerie, the influential prelate who headed the Church of North Africa with a firm hand from 1867 to 1892, accentuated the association between Our Lady of Africa and missionary activity. In the previous decades the military authority had constantly hampered Christian proselytizing. Apostolic action had to be very discreet, and it did not produce significant results. Upon his arrival in Algeria, Lavigerie mobilized new energies in this direction.[24] In 1868 he founded the Society of Missionaries of Africa (initially called Society of Missionaries of Our Lady of Africa). Two years later the Congregation of the Missionary Sisters of Our Lady of Africa (White Sisters) was created. The first order (whose members were commonly called White Fathers) experienced a rapid expansion and was instrumental in converting people in Algeria and in sub-Saharan Africa. Despite the subsequent change of name, the order was clearly placed under the patronage of Our Lady of Africa. By 1869 the first White Fathers missionaries pronounced their oath in this church. A few years later caravans of the missionaries directed to Central Africa received their blessing in this basilica. From 1873 on the management of the sanctuary was assigned to the Missionaries of Africa and, in 1876, Lavigerie required members of the order to recite daily the prayer to Our Lady of Africa.[25]

Another instrument of proselytism was the creation of orphanages for Arab children. While his predecessors already had moved in this direction, Lavigerie put a strong emphasis on the foundation of orphanages, the responsibility of which was soon assigned to the White Fathers in a clearly apostolic move. From 1872 on, the White Fathers were also involved in the management of Arab Christian villages. The archbishop had bought a large agricultural field 180 kilometers west of Algiers in order to establish a place for converted orphans and to create exemplary Christian families under the supervision of the Fathers and Sisters. In the following years, however, this project resulted in complete failure.

The missionary activity that Lavigerie entrusted to the White Fathers in Kabylia was more successful. This region had been the last stronghold against French colonization. It was gradually taken over by the French army in 1857, despite vigorous local resistance that continued with an uprising in 1871. Missionary work started here in the 1870s and lasted several decades, producing thousands of conversions.[26] A narrative that attributed ancestral Christian origin to this population (which would have been only barely changed on the surface by the Arab-Muslim invasion) seemed to legitimize missionary work even in the eyes of the colonial authorities. Lavigerie regarded Kabylia as "another Lebanon," and the Kabyle people as a sort of Maronites still unaware of their true identity.

A MIXED ATTENDANCE

As we have seen, the sanctuary of Our Lady of Africa was at the heart of the conversion directed at the entire African continent generally and toward Algeria in particular. Since the 1850s the shrine was the basis of an association devoted to a "crusade of prayers" for the conversions of the Muslims.[27] This was made visible through the inscription of the last sentence of the prayer in the apse of the basilica. We have also seen the strong association of the basilica with the missionary orders created by Lavigerie. Some ecclesiastical writings of the 1870s mention with satisfaction the attendance of young converted Arab orphans and their veneration for the Virgin Mary. The first converted orphans were baptized in the Basilica of Our Lady of Africa, and the first marriage between two converted orphans was celebrated here.[28]

Another type of "indigenous" attendance at the sanctuary was nevertheless becoming more important. Even here some "infidels" did not confine themselves to being spectators of the grand Catholic ceremonies but crossed the threshold of the churches looking for supernatural assistance. This phenomenon seems quite precocious at Our Lady of Africa, which was particularly known for its spiritual power. Many episodes of miraculous healings occurred in the sanctuary, and thousands of votive offerings were accumulated in the space of just a few years. Pavy seems to allude to a Muslim presence as early as 1858 in relation to the provisory chapel.[29] This phenomenon is clearly attested to in the 1880s by a book on the pilgrimage to Our Lady of Africa in Algiers, which I have already quoted from several times. It was published for the first time in 1885 and written by a White Father, Father Michel, under the control of Cardinal Lavigerie.[30] In a chapter that lists several miraculous events that occurred in the sanctuary, a paragraph titled "The Negro Who Has Found a Job" describes the visit, on May 4, 1881, of

> a negro who appears in the sacristy of Our Lady of Africa, taking with one hand a beautiful candle, and, the other, a sheet of paper on which is sought, for the negro, the permission to enter the shrine of Mary. The chaplain asked the negro the reason for his visit and his offering, and this poor heathen, who had heard of the merciful goodness of Mary, answered immediately in its incorrect, but very touching language: "I promised, in my head, the Mother of Africa that if I found a job, I'd give her a candle. She gave me what I asked for, and I gave her what I promised her."[31]

The visit of this pilgrim who seems to come from far away, gives the writer the opportunity to mention that the attendance of this shrine by other *infidels* who recognize the power of the Virgin was fairly common. Both Muslim and Jewish women used to visit the sanctuary, where they accomplished devotional actions: "Many times Muslim women came to light candles before the statue of the Immaculate Virgin, and Jewish women were to ask for their children, and this repeatedly, the strings of the Virgin Mary, blessed by the chaplains of Our Lady of Africa."[32]

As Pavy rightly foresaw some years before, the Virgin Mary could be a powerful channel of communication with Islam. She is a familiar figure for any Muslim, and several traits ascribed to her are held in common with Christianity. Mary has a very significant place in the Qur'an, which mentions her nativity, her presentation to the Temple, the Annunciation, the virginal conception, and the birth of Jesus. Mary is presented as a model of confidence in God, of modesty and piety.[33] The appeal of the Virgin Mary for Jewish women seems, on the contrary, decidedly devoid of any theological basis.

The hope of being able to convert the Algerian people probably explains the rather warm welcome that the priests made to these "infidels." Yet the latter did not seem animated by a desire to explore another religious universe, with its meanings, rituals, and dogmas; their search did not generally include the possibility of a conversion at the end of the road. On the contrary, they were oriented toward an instrumental and quite magical recourse to the supernatural power of the shrine and of the leading saint figure that inhabited it.

A pastoral letter from Bishop Leynaud dated January 6, 1923, describes similar phenomena of mixed attendance that seems more consolidated. By the time of this letter, the archbishop restores the association of prayers "for the conversion of Muslims and other infidels in Africa," which was founded and maintained by his predecessors, and had then ceased to be active. He adds:

And yet the Divine Mother of Jesus clearly attracts more each day, at the foot of her Divine Son, the hearts of Muslims around us. Every day, in fact, especially when the weather is beautiful, a large number of indigenous men, women, children, visit the Basilica and pray in their own way:

— Are you Christian? the chaplain requests to a young woman, kneeling near the Holy Table.

— No, I'm Muslim.

— What are you doing here?

— I pray Meriem to find a sober, serious and hardworking husband.

Another day, a woman gesticulates and shouts, looking at the image of Mary: "I am ill, I suffer, Meriem must heal me!"

Beside her, a man in his thirties stands with respect: "I ask Meriem baraka, blessing."

Two other natives of the Sahara have come to see Meriem to put an end to the drought: "Everything is burned in the corn, they say, no fruit, no barley, what will become of us, if Meriem does not protect us?"

Finally here is a young native of Algiers, 12 years old: "I have received the graduation certificate," he says to the chaplain who asks, "and I came to say thank you to Mary."

Every day, I repeat it, the same examples recur; particularly on Sundays, we see together, among Christians, face veiled Muslims women, who approach the altar of Our Lady of Africa, to deposit a candle, make their devotions and listen to evangelical speech.[34]

A missionary spirit clearly influenced this outline of a "clerical ethnography." The archbishop added that attendance on the part of Muslims was a sure sign of mercy by which the Virgin "calls the dear souls of Muslims to the Christian Truth." According to him, the day in which a general movement of Muslim conversion will occur may not be too far away. To hasten its coming, the prelate decided to restore with a new fervor the association of prayers for the conversion of Muslims founded in 1858 by Pavy.

These narratives demonstrate how two bishops, sixty-five years apart, were hoping that Marian piety among Muslims could generate a process of conversion to Christianity. As a matter of fact, all these missionary expectations regularly failed. However, as Pavy predicted, the devotion to Our Lady of Africa was an important factor of unity among the European Christians of disparate origins who, in their pilgrimages, were "accompanied from time to time by the Native." Indeed, Muslims frequented the basilica throughout all of the twentieth century. Our Lady of Africa became a very popular figure in Algiers, where she was often defined as "Lalla Africa" or "Madame l'Afrique." In the early 1950s Emile Dermenghem described Muslims' devotional practices at the shrine, including the circumambulation carried out by women around the statue of the Madonna.[35] This author also depicts the pious weekly circuit accomplished by devout Muslim women in Algiers. Each day they visited a particular shrine. After having been at many Muslim holy shrines during the week, on Sunday they preferred to go to Our Lady of Africa.[36]

If the sanctuary of Our Lady of Africa became a kind of "ark of the covenant" for different religious groups present in Algiers, this took place at the level of an ordinary practice at the margins of religious structures. Muslims were attracted by the spiritual magnetism of certain Christian holy places and neither worried very much about theological distinctions and dogmatic boundaries nor considered the possibility of a formal conversion. The mixed attendance at Our Lady of Africa is part of a multifaceted, everyday religious practice. In twentieth century Algeria, incursions of the faithful to religious spaces pertaining to other religions have been many-sided. Indeed, in a parallel perspective, Emile Dermenghem observed in the 1950s that "it is common for afflicted Jewish and Christian women to go to Muslims marabous."[37] The same author also mentions the frequentation by Muslim women of a synagogue that was previously a Muslim shrine:

> There is in Algiers, rue Sainte, a small synagogue on an old marabou: when the last Muslim *oukil* [custodian], Sheikh Khider died in the last century, without a successor, he left, by title deed, the local to a rabbi friend, with the clause that Muslims would be allowed to come. The curious is that Muslim women continue to come, when a *thâleb* [Muslim religious expert] told them that this could help to cure sterility or avoid repudiation. They revolve seven times around the *teba*, the podium of the readers of the Torah, which is roughly in the middle of the room and that even during the office, without caring the assistants and without the latter care of them.[38]

THE SANCTUARY IN THE POSTCOLONIAL FRAMEWORK

A series of transformations in the last fifty years have profoundly changed the context of the devotion to Our Lady of Africa. After a long war with France, the independence of Algeria in 1962 led to the forced departure of almost the entire population of European origin—that is to say, more than one million people. With them, thousands of Jews and Algerians (mostly from Kabylia) who had converted to Christianity also abandoned the country. The spread of a more austere and legalistic Islam had already been felt in the 1930s by the movement of the Oulémas, led by Cheikh Abdelhamid Ben Badis. It was pursued by the Algerian nationalist movement and further stressed by the influence of Wahhabis and the rise of fundamentalism until the civil war of the 1990s. Meanwhile, the Catholic Church developed a new attitude toward Islam.

Starting in the 1950s the focus shifted from proselytizing to a simple testimony of a Christian presence, along with engagement in endeavors of social progress. During the war of liberation, the Church took a cautious attitude and condemned the violent excesses of the French army. The archbishop of Algiers, Léon-Etienne Duval, took a position in favor of the independence of the country. This led the authorities of the postcolonial state to accept the presence of the Church. Several Christian buildings were damaged or transformed (into mosques, libraries, etc.), thus reversing the transfers that had taken place more than a century before, when some mosques became churches, but some churches kept their Catholic character. Moreover, some of these Christian places, like Our Lady of Africa in Algiers, continued to attract Muslim faithful.

In the decades after independence, the Christian presence in the country has been reduced to a few thousand people, many of whom are there on behalf of European government and social agencies. The greater part of this residual Christian presence was severely reduced when, in the turmoil of violence that infected the country in the 1990s, many Europeans decided to leave. Several priests were killed in a series of terrorist attacks. In the single diocese of Algiers, nineteen of the two hundred religious who were living there were murdered during this period.[39]

Yet Muslim devotion to the Virgin survived the shocks of the 1990s civil war. Even in the most risky moments of the black decade, which left nearly two hundred thousand victims dead, several Muslims continued their devotions to Our Lady of Africa. In 1997 and 1998, when the guerrilla war reached its climax, the attendance dropped to an average of twenty people per day (around seven thousand yearly). In 1999 it was around sixty-five people per day. The Father Henri Maurier, in an article published in the journal of the Missionaries of Africa in 1999, presents these data and also gives an interesting account of his experience at Our Lady of Africa:

> Three missionaries of Africa, Paul Marioge, Etienne Desmarescaux, Henri Maurier, keep the sanctuary, with a community of four Franciscan Missionary Sisters of Mary, one of them ensuring the maintenance and decoration. Our ministry is not properly a parish one [here the Christians are rare], but is aimed at the reception of people who are almost all Muslim. Women, girls and grandmothers, sometimes alone, sometimes with their children or husbands, come to pray Our Lady, mainly for women's problems. "How do I do?" is someone asking. — "Mary is a mom, talk to her as a mother, women understand each others."
>
> But men and boys are no exception. Some just want to see a beautiful building and are interested in its history and its architecture. Others are happy to find here a place of silence and peace. Couples come to meet. Students of both sexes are asking for the documentation: "We have to make a presentation on Christian Education"; it is a professor of psychology and comparative education who requests it. And then there are grieving persons, of all ranks, who want to talk: "It is only with you that one can talk about that!" Finally there are all sorts of questions about religion, about the religions, or on the Christian faith. "I do not want my religion imposed upon me," said a young Kabyle man.
>
> Many questions arise: "Who is Mary? Is she buried here?" [because there are in Algeria pilgrimages to the "marabous," Muslim holy men

buried there]. "What is the Bible? Why four Gospels . . . ?"—"How do I become a Christian"? Visitors look at length at the Stations of the Cross, so we project to decorate the nave of frescoes depicting the parables of Jesus [someone even said "do not forget the episode of the adulterous woman!"]. Meanwhile, since last year, one can meditate before the eight frescoes depicting the life of St. Augustine, born in Thagaste and bishop at Hippo (Annaba). Augustine is the most famous ancient Algerian in Christendom; Algeria, in search of its roots, is interested in him. A short biography is available for visitors, who can get an idea of the work of a bishop. These frescoes are crowned with a phrase of Augustine: "Brotherly love comes from God and is God himself," in French, Arabic and Kabyle. These words are very strong in the difficult context of the country, where people are killed in the name of Allah.[40]

Attendance increased during the subsequent years. During a visit I made in 2003, officials stated that the basilica attracted an average of one hundred people each day, of which less than 5 percent were Christian. So it can be estimated that forty thousand people visited it annually. My observations and the conversations I had with the Fathers in charge of the basilica confirmed the same. The priests explained that Muslims come to pray to Madame Africa (as her name is often spelled), asking for her assistance in matters of different natures (suffering, disease, fertility). In several cases, young couples make the visit. Generally the pilgrims light candles and made offerings. They bring various gifts (money, flowers, small cakes, carpets) to the sanctuary when wishes are fulfilled. It was possible to see, inside the church, ex-votos and prayer slips left by the Muslims. Often Muslims talk about their problems with Christian priests. It is a sort of confession, as a member of the clergy of the basilica suggested during a dialogue I had with him.

In an article published in 2007 by the journal of the Missionaries of Africa, the White Father Paul Marioge, rector of the Basilica of Our Lady of Africa in Algiers for twelve years, adds further detail to his activity during the black decade, when Muslims accounted for almost all visitors:

The presence of Muslims, modest when the French were in number, became more evident after the mass exodus of 1962. The terrorist violence of the 1990s completed the disappearance of European visitors. Algerians continued to come, and more and more numerous in recent years. This presence may surprise those who have no idea of popular Islam, or those who pay little attention, or even commiseration, to it! Myself, I was surprised to find myself the rector of a church frequented by so many believers of Islam, indeed highly disturbed by the evils of terrorism, and experiencing a spontaneous urge to address to the sky, and implore the protection of Mary. I took the event as it was; my mission is to help people who are all creatures of the same Creator and merciful saviour.

People come to Notre Dame of Africa as we go to Lourdes, with all that is in the heart, great pain, suffering physical or moral: they are sick, they would heal, or is the child who is sick, or they did not have children and they would have, or they only have boys and they would still have a little girl [or vice versa], a woman may even be beaten by her husband, or the pilgrim finds himself without work and without resources, or he wants to pass a test, and then there are also young people who love each other, who come to share the pangs in their heart, and also their wishes for a successful marriage. It is the humanity of always and everywhere.[41]

Father Marioge proposes a poignant testimony of the choreography of daily life at the sanctuary, giving some details about his interaction with the Muslims who come to Our Lady of Africa, and on the practices they accomplish at the shrine:

Their questions? Questions of trust: how does one pray here, because people are aware that this is not the place of the traditional prayers of Islam. They are open to prayer from the deep of their heart, to dialogue with God, with Mary, with Sidna Aissa. Many are burning a candle; some of them wet their face with holy water! Others bring flowers, or incense, or perfume.... The lovers put a prayer slip beneath the statue, women desiring to have children bring a doll that represents their wishes, and others come with a sick child. Our visitors are slipping their hands on the stones of the wall, they would like to touch the statue, as in Lourdes people touch the rock of the cave.

If the wish has been fulfilled, they come to thank with a gift, an offering, a bouquet of flowers, embroidery, or a rug. The newlyweds offer a statue representing the couple in holiday clothes. Some offer an ex-voto.[42]

According to the priest, an encounter is possible between the Church and what he defines as popular Islam. The latter is far removed from the rigidity of the official Islam. Popular Islam is not so preoccupied with prohibitions concerning alcohol, and it manifests mainly in the cult of the Muslim saints. The cult of the Virgin Mary appears as a privileged ground for interaction with Muslims, but on this issue the vision of the Church is now very different from that proposed by the nineteenth-century ecclesiastics:

> Thus, parallel to the official Islam without being confused with it, there is a popular Islam, more human, making the dialogue easier. The relationship with God is less rigid, and practices set apart from puritanical severity without difficulty. The man has no qualms about enjoying a good glass of wine, or to request a cold beer. The woman does not hesitate to prepare a hot toddy in order to heal faster a bad cold or a flu threat. The little cross would be almost carried and the sound of bells (now forbidden) is remembered with regret, church music is appreciated, and the other too! The priests are respected, and the sisters even more. In short, we feel respect and sympathy for Christianity, as they like pilgrimages to marabous, they have the worship of medals, images, processions with banners and oriflamme, all things that make people very close to Islam brotherhoods, that with which the official Islam struggles vigorously.

The story of Our Lady of Africa is just beginning. The popular Islam likes to stop at the mystery of the strange fecundity of the saint Virgin. The Archbishop of Algiers Henri Teissier, sixth successor of Cardinal Lavigerie, the founder of the White Fathers, is aware of the privileged role of this place in the encounter between Algerian Muslims and the Church that is present in Algeria.[43]

As these statements clearly show, the appreciation of Muslim attendance at Our Lady of Africa is now situated in a repositioning of the Church in Algerian society, as expressed by Mgr. Henri Teissier, archbishop of Algiers between 1988 and 2008. It is a Church that has lived in turmoil, survived in suffering, and redefined its relationship with the Muslim population. The weakness is now perceived as a condition for the dialogue with the other, with the Muslim people of Algeria, in a civic, respectful, and fraternal engagement. The encounter takes place mainly in the field on everyday collaborations and the sharing is rooted in the soil of a common humanity.[44]

This new approach involves a revisitation of history. The Church of Algeria is detaching itself from missionary trends of the past and is attempting to recover moments and features that suggest a more respectful attitude. For example, out of the initiatives by Cardinal Lavigerie to create the White Fathers, it retains the emphasis on the knowledge of local languages and immersion in local society. The words engraved in the Basilica of Our Lady of Africa ("Our Lady of Africa pray for us and for Muslims") now acquire a different meaning. The missionary intentions that marked this sentence in the past are completely evicted. Now this phrase is perceived as the utterance of a communion of prayer before the Virgin, which foreshadowed the Catholic opening to other religions operated by Vatican II and, more generally, the disposition of contemporary interreligious dialogue. This sentence is regularly quoted when people of different backgrounds refer to Our Lady of Africa, and everybody interprets it as a poignant testimony of centuries of dialogue between the religions.

THE RESTORATION OF THE BASILICA

In recent years the peace process, which has included the surrender of several armed groups and the politics of reconciliation initiated by the Algerian president Abdelaziz Bouteflika, has reduced tensions within the political climate. The lives of the priests are no longer directly threatened and in general their movements are less constrained. The borders of

Algeria are also relatively more open and the number of foreign visitors to the country has increased. In addition to European travelers, there is also the new arrival of migrants from sub-Saharan Africa. Many of them are Catholic, and this has increased the small flock at the local Church. All this resulted in, among other things, a subsequent increase in attendance at Our Lady of Africa, which witnessed about sixty thousand visitors per year in 2005 and 2006.

The global context of the relations between Islam and Christianity, however, has been recently upset by tensions around the issue of proselytism in which the Catholic Church has found itself unexpectedly involved. The origins of the phenomenon are linked to the actions of neo-evangelical Protestant missionaries who have been very effective, particularly in Kabylia. The conversions, initiated mainly in the 1990s, remained mostly underground and emerged in public debate with a press campaign in 2004. The media controversy has been particularly fierce, with journalistic and political statements often exaggerating the extent of the phenomenon and attributing it to the imperial designs of the United States, charging the superpower with creating a pretext for interference in the internal affairs of Algeria. Conversions were also seen as a factor that could encourage the threat of secession of Berber Kabylia. The discussion has continued in subsequent years. The Catholic Church has sought to avoid the confusion, noting that its attitude in these matters is very different from that of Protestant "colleagues." As a matter of fact, in recent decades the attitude of the Church of Algeria has been very prudent on the issue of conversion. Applications for baptism by Muslims are subject to a meticulous examination to verify the sincerity and the depth of the intention to change religion. But this vindication was not met with much success. In particular, the Algerian Arab press has tended to stress a generic "Christian threat." Some articles denouncing the conversions have also showed photographs of Archbishop Teissier. The embarrassing example of the action of evangelization carried out by the Catholic Church in the past is also explicitly recalled. In particular, many commentators point out the continuity between the missionary work undertaken by the White Fathers between 1873 and 1954 in Kabylia and the contemporary activity of Protestant missionaries in the same context.

The state has taken a position on this issue by enacting a law in 2006 that sets the conditions for the exercise of non-Muslim worship. This law drastically regulates these cults, requiring that any activity carried on outside worship places approved by the state and requiring statements to be made to the state authorities before any religious event can take place. Proselytizing to Muslims is punishable by imprisonment of two to five years. The consequences of this law have been severe, and not only for the Protestant community. Father Peter Wallez, a priest of the Diocese of Oran, was sentenced in 2008 to one year of jail (later suspended) and fined 200,000 dinars for having prayed the day after Christmas with a small group of Christian African migrants outside of a place recognized by the government. A policy to restrict or delay the renewal of visas has also impacted Catholics priests and nuns, thereby hampering their activities.[45]

Rather unexpectedly, if one considers its past status as a symbolic center of the Catholic proselytism on the African continent and its daily attendance by Muslims for more than a century, the Basilica of Our Lady of Africa did not significantly appear in the debate over Christian proselytizing, past or present. On the contrary, this shrine has been at the heart of a multilateral endeavor devoted to its repair. Along with other contributors, there has been direct involvement by Algerian authorities in the restoration of this sanctuary, damaged by age and by the earthquake of 2003.

Restoration work began in 2007. The intervention was the result of international cooperation, and several bodies were involved in the process. On the Algerian side, the city of Algiers contributed up to 600,000 euros. The European Union gave 1 million euros. The French state, the municipality of Marseilles, the General Council of Bouches-du-Rhône, and the region Provence-Alpes-Côte d'Azur contributed additional funding. Several Algerian and French enterprises also subsidized the works. The initiative came within the framework of a Mediterranean cooperation initiative driven by France.

The company that performed the work is based in Provence and also recently restored the Basilica of Notre-Dame de la Garde in Marseilles. The mirroring between the two shrines that is the result of a strategy initiated in the mid-nineteenth century by the Archbishop Pavy, who conceived of these centers of pilgrimage vis-à-vis one another, is continuing in renewed forms. Jean-Claude Gaudin, mayor of Marseilles, who led in 2006 a cooperation mission of three hundred French people in Algiers, spoke about the similarities between the two churches. He emphasized the correspondence between the two cities and their basilicas, which were constructed at the same time, in the same Romano-Byzantine style, and in similar positions overhanging the towns. "In Marseilles, people who are not of Christian religion care for Notre-Dame de la Garde. We felt the same state of mind here," he stated.[46] As a matter of fact, during the twentieth century the Marseilles sanctuary became an ecumenical symbol of the town, attended by non-Christian faithful, including several Muslims. It is a new parallelism between the two shrines that Pavy might not have predicted.

The basilica was solemnly reopened in December 2010 in the presence of Algerian and French dignitaries after extensive restoration work that amounted to more than 5 million euros.[47] The local and national press in France and Algeria have relayed echoes of the restoration of the basilica. For many observers, Our Lady of Africa appears to function as a timeless symbol of encounter between religions. It is a haven of peace, a cease-fire in the relations between Christianity and Islam symbolized by the friendly patronage of the Virgin; its openness to Muslim presence and the sentence written in the apse suggests an old fraternal conversation.

CONCLUSION

Over almost 150 years, there has been an astonishing level of stability in the mixed attendance at Our Lady of Africa, in spite of changing contexts. Here the sharing of the same religious space by distinct religious groups has been and remains quite uncontroversial, even in times of hatred, violence, and distress over religious differences. Such a peaceful choreography of daily life is embedded in a complex history of power relations and in a web of (often contradictory) symbols and meanings.

It is a partial, subaltern, and yet resistant choreography that has gained an interstitial space among more powerful and coherent choreographies. This weak choreography is made of tactical movements on a ground that is dominated by superior strategies and that is defined by the dialectical relationships between the state, religious hierarchies, and civil society.

The context in which a multireligious choreography was installed in the sanctuary is that of the French colonial experience. A central feature of this context was the existence of a somewhat disputed alliance between the Church and the state. The former took advantage of the French conquest in order to affirm its presence into the country, but also suffered under the control of political and military authorities, which generally restricted the ecclesiastical proselytizing fervor.

Within this general framework, the creation of Our Lady of Africa shrine stemmed from an elaborated project devised by the Church aimed at establishing a major pilgrimage center. The result was a stratified choreography with a diversified layer of symbols and meanings, which summarized the multifarious connotations linked to the founding of the Catholic Church of North Africa. This miscellaneous assortment included the activation of (more or less invented) historical links with a very far Christian past, a (rather Durkheimian) pastoral attention to the cohesion of the European settlers of different national backgrounds, a clerical geopolitical construction of a Catholic Western Mediterranean under the seal of Marian devotion (and under the umbrella of the French colonial empire), and a missionary project of conversion of African Muslims. All these aspects took on a semiotic form at the shrine through the materiality of religious objects and activities. The architecture of the basilica, the statues, the altars, the relics, the ornamentation, the rites, the prayers, and the processions were all part of a complex, formal choreography. A component of the sanctuary's semiotics was related to a strategy of enculturation that was aimed at facilitating the acclimation of the Church on African soil and the diffusion of its credo. Among the acculturative elements there were, for instance, the Moorish architectural elements of the building and the statue of the Virgin Mary (with her brown visage, her robe that echoed a local style, and her denomination referring to Africa).

On the whole, this formal choreography was the result of a strategy, in the meaning that Michel de Certeau attributes to this notion, which is to say, a conscious plan fulfilled by a conquering institution that affirms its control on a place as a part of an expansive action.[48] Yet in the interstices of this rich and powerful choreography is also the development of an informal choreography characterized by spontaneous interfaith attendance at the sanctuary that had no direct links with the Church's proselytizing campaigns.

This phenomenon is a manifestation of a cult of the Virgin Mary widespread among Muslims, who in several areas often frequent Christian sanctuaries. This devotion is well documented in the Middle East and the Balkans since the Middle Ages and has some theological ground in the founding texts of the Islam.[49] Embracing some items of the Christian religion generally does not imply a path toward conversion (even if in very sporadic cases the conversion could be the result of this crossing over). Muslim Marian devotion is but a chapter in a complex web of interfaith conversation among Christians, Jews, and Muslims across the Mediterranean.[50] In the monotheistic religions, interfaith devotions draw on a vernacular range of practices and beliefs that present significant convergences in a context in which the mediation of more concrete intercessors remedies to the distance of God.

In Algiers, Muslim people (and also some Jews) rapidly adopted the supernatural resources offered by the semiotics of the new sanctuary as a part of the repertoire of an eclectic devotional practice that seemed more attentive to the efficacy of the shrine than to its religious affiliation. It was, in de Certeau's terms, a tactical infiltration on a terrain controlled by institutional strategy. This joint attendance required the mediation of religious personnel who were in command of the shrine and who decided to what extent those accretions could be tolerable variations of the common ritual stock. The Catholic clergy responded positively, interpreting Muslims' attention to Mary as a possible vehicle for their conversion. Yet even in this case, priestly action was hampered by the constraints put in place by the colonial state.

The political context changed dramatically with the war of liberation and the creation of the new Algerian state. The changing attitudes of the Church, which renounced its close association with the European colonials and its proselytizing attitudes toward the Muslims; the massive departure of the Christian population; and the establishing of a postcolonial state with a strong orientation toward an Islamic nationalism were all factors that powerfully transformed the environment of the religious life at the sanctuary. Yet the informal choreography of daily life was not severely altered at Our Lady of Africa. The basilica continued to be attended every year by thousands of Muslims, who represented almost all of the people frequenting the shrine. Several manifestations of an eclectic, vernacular religiosity that crosses religious borders carry on now, in spite of the strong pressures to create a monolithic religious nationalism, and even in the framework of the bloody conflicts that occurred especially in the 1990s. During the last decades the attitude of the Catholic personnel at the shrine was devoid of any explicit missionary ambition, and their warm welcoming of Muslim faithful was mainly in a spirit of interreligious dialogue and fraternal engagement.

Some central semiotic forms of the past official choreography (such as the close association of the Virgin Mary to the military conquest of the country or the centrality of this shrine for fueling missionary activity devoted to the conversion of the Muslims in the African continent) are now completely hidden. Some other items have been recuperated and translated into the new cultural and political context. For example, the Mediterranean dimensions of the sanctuary, with its strong links mainly with Southern France and Marseilles, can now be rearticulated within the Mediterranean agenda of European and French politics.

The shrine of Our Lady of Africa is now a symbol of interreligious coexistence and dialogue, which can be appropriated by different actors (politicians, journalists, associations) both in Europe and in Algeria. From this point of view, the reinterpretation of the missionary inscription in the apse, which has unanimously become a sort of nineteenth-century forerunner of the tolerant spirit of Vatican II, is the most significant example of the overall shift of the religious meaning of the basilica. One could speak of a triumph, in the long run, of the sanctuary's informal interfaith choreography that developed in the interstices of the ecclesiastical routine and has now become a central feature of sanctuary life.

NOTES

1. *Notice sur le pèlerinage de Notre-Dame d'Afrique à Alger*, 2e édition revue, corrigée et augmentée avec une préface de Monseigneur Leynaud, Archevêque d'Alger (Alger: Papeterie, Imprimerie E. Gaudet 1924), 46–47.
2. Karima Dirèche-Slimani, *Chrétiens de Kabylie 1873–1954: Une action missionnaire dans l'Algérie coloniale* (Paris: Ed. Bouchène, 2004), 23.
3. Michèle Baussant, *Pieds-noirs: Mémoires d'exils* (Paris: Stock, 2002), 214–15.
4. Ibid., 209.
5. Jean de Prats, *L'Église africaine ancienne et moderne* (Tours: Alfred Mame et fils, 1892).
6. On this sanctuary, see Mathieu Chanoine, *La Vierge de l'Oranie au XIXe siècle: Histoire du pèlerinage de N.-D. du Salut à Santa-Cruz* (Oran: D. Hentz, 1900), and the wide-ranging synthesis of Baussant, *Pieds-noirs: Mémoires d'exils*.
7. See *Notice sur le pèlerinage de Notre-Dame d'Afrique*, 50–53.
8. An ecclesiastical point of view on this controversy was presented in *Documents relatifs à la position de Mgr Dupuch, ancien et premier Evêque d'Alger* (Bordeaux: Henry Faye imprimeur de l'archevêché, 1851).
9. Louis-Antoine-Augustin Pavy, *Histoire critique du culte de la sainte Vierge en Afrique, depuis le commencement du christianisme jusqu'à nos jours* (Alger: Bastide Libraire, 1858); and Louis-Antoine-Augustin Pavy *Histoire de Notre-Dame d'Afrique: Appel de Mgr L.-A.-A. Pavy, évêque d'Alger, en faveur de cette chapelle*, 4 vols. (Paris: E. Repos Libraire, 1864).
10. See *Notice sur le pèlerinage de Notre-Dame d'Afrique*, 64.
11. Several articles signed L. J. Christus, published in the *Revue de Saint Augustin et de Sainte Monique* during the 1870s, established a hagiographic portrait of Agarithe Berger. Drawing on them, Lady Herbert of Lea (a Roman Catholic convert who was well connected with the Victorian political and religious milieus) wrote a biography of this woman for the Anglophone readers. See Mary Elizabeth Herbert, *A Saint in Algeria* (London: Burns and Gates, 1878).
12. See *Notice sur le pèlerinage de Notre-Dame d'Afrique*, 102.
13. The name "Our Lady of Africa" explicitly recalled that of a church that the Portuguese built in Ceuta in the fifteenth century. Still today, Nuestra Señora de Africa is the patron saint of Ceuta.

14. Pavy, *Histoire critique du culte*; and Pavy, *Histoire de Notre-Dame d'Afrique*.
15. See, for example, Jacques Jasmin, *La Bièrges, poème dédié à Monseigneur Pavy, évêque d'Alger* (Agen: Imprimerie Prosper Noubel, 1860); Casimir Melcion-D'Arc, *Notre-Dame d'Afrique, Vierge libératrice* (Alger: Typographie Duclaux, 1862); Antoine Ricard, "La piraterie barbaresque et Notre-Dame-d'Afrique," in *Revue du monde catholique*, vol. 4 (Paris: Victor Palmé éditeur, 1862), 161–71; and Antoine Ricard, *Quelques années en Afrique, souvenirs, par l'abbé H. B.* (Toulouse: Cluzon, 1861).
16. On Mgr. Pavy's views on Islam, see also his homely "Sur le Mahométisme," in *Collection intégrale et universelle des orateurs sacrés*, ed. Jacques Paul Migne (Paris: Imprimerie catholique du Petit-Montrouge, 1856).
17. Pavy, *Histoire de Notre-Dame d'Afrique*, 53.
18. *Notice sur le pèlerinage de Notre-Dame d'Afrique à Alger*, 153.
19. Ibid., 154–55.
20. The engraving and a photograph of the statue in the basilica are reproduced in *Notice sur le pèlerinage de Notre-Dame d'Afrique*, 83–84.
21. *Notre-Dame d'Afrique et l'association de prières pour la conversion des musulmans* (extrait du *Messager du Sacré-Cœur de Jésus*) (Le Puy: Imprimerie M.-P. Marchessou, 1862).
22. *Notice sur le pèlerinage de Notre-Dame d'Afrique*, 196–97.
23. The full text is as follows: "O Holy and Immaculate Heart of Mary, so full of mercy, be touched by the blindness and the profound misery of the poor Muslims. You, the Mother of God, made man, get them the knowledge of our Holy Religion, and the grace to embrace it loyally, so that through your powerful intercession, we are all united in the same faith, the same hope and the same love of your divine Son, our Lord Jesus Christ, who was crucified and died for the salvation of all men, and who resuscitated full of glory, and reigns in the unity of the Father and the Holy spirit, for ever and ever. So be it. O Our Lady of Africa, pray for us and for the Muslims. So be it" (See *Notice sur le pèlerinage de Notre-Dame d'Afrique*, 198).
24. Charles Lavigerie, *Recueil de lettres publiées par Mgr l'archevêque d'Alger, délégué apostolique du Sahara et du Soudan sur les œuvres et missions africaines* (Paris: Plon, 1869).
25. Jean-Claude Ceillier, *Histoire des missionnaires d'Afrique, Pères blancs: De la fondation par Mgr. Lavigerie à la mort du fondateur, 1868–1892* (Paris: Karthala, 2008), 67–68.
26. Dirèche-Slimani, *Chrétiens de Kabylie*.
27. *Notre-Dame d'Afrique et l'association de prières*, 14.
28. Ibid., 198.

29. He also says that some "indigenes" were then contributing to the fundraising campaign for the pilgrimage centre. See Pavy, *Histoire de Notre-Dame d'Afrique*, 45n2.
30. The second edition was augmented including other documents.
31. *Notice sur le pèlerinage de Notre-Dame d'Afrique*, 295.
32. Ibid., 296.
33. Michel Dousse, *Marie la musulmane* (Paris: Albin Michel, 2005).
34. *Notice sur le pèlerinage de Notre-Dame d'Afrique*, 211–12.
35. "We know that the Moorish women have a great veneration for the Black Madonna, Our Lady of Africa, Lalla Africa. They remain a long time before the Virgin, offering candles, votive offerings, and celluloid babies, and are distressed if they are prevented from turning around her." Émile Dermenghem, *Le culte des saints dans l'islam maghrébin* (Paris: Gallimard, 1954), 126.
36. Ibid., 125–26. According to Dermenghem, on Monday some Muslim women also used to attend (along with Christian faithful) the small shrine of Notre-Dame du Ravin, near to Our Lady of Africa. On that day a nun kept this shrine open for some hours (see 126n2).
37. Ibid., 126.
38. Ibid., 125.
39. Henri Teissier, *Chrétiens en Algérie: Un partage d'espérance* (Paris: Desclée de Brouwer, 2002), 63.
40. Henri Maurier, "Notre-Dame d'Afrique," *Voix d'Afrique*, no. 45 (1999), http://peres-blancs.cef.fr/hmaurie.htm.
41. Paul Marioge, "Une dévotion mariale populaire en terre d'Islam," *Voix d'Afrique*, no. 74 (2007) http://peres-blancs.cef.fr/devotion_mariale.htm.
42. Ibid.
43. Ibid.
44. Teissier, *Chrétiens en Algérie*, 138.
45. See Karima Direche-Slimani, "Évangélisation en Algérie: Débats sur la liberté de culte," *L'année du Maghreb* 5 (2009): 275–84; Karima Direche-Slimani, "Dolorisme religieux et reconstructions identitaires: Les conversions néo-évangéliques dans l'Algérie contemporaine," *Annales. Economies, Société Civilisations* 5 (2009): 1137–62; Amine Kadi, "Les chrétiens d'Algérie sous pression," *La Croix*, April 6, 2008, http://www.la-croix.com/Religion/Actualite/Les-chretiens-d-Algerie-sous-pression-_NG_-2008-04-06-670031; and Julia Ficatier, "La Pentecôte de fraternité des catholiques d'Algérie," *La Croix*, May 13, 2008.
46. See "Notre Dame d'Afrique fait peau neuve," *Bab el Oued Story*, http://babelouedstory.com/thema_les/souvenir/12456/12456.html. Accessed September 16, 2013.

47. The day before the inauguration, an Algerian tribunal condemned four Kabyle Protestants for praying in an unauthorized place.
48. Michel de Certeau, *The Practice of Everyday Life* (Berkeley: University of California Press, 1984).
49. See Alexandra Cuffel, "'Henceforward All Generations Will Call Me Blessed': Medieval Christian Tales of Non-Christian Marian Veneration," *Mediterranean Studies* 12 (2003): 37–60; Dionigi Albera, "La Vierge et l'islam: Mélange de civilisations en Méditerranée," *Le Débat*, no. 137 (2005): 134–44; and "Combining Practices and Beliefs: Muslim Pilgrims at Marian Shrines," in *Sharing the Sacra: The Politics and Pragmatics of Inter-Communal Relations Around Holy Places*, ed. Glenn Bowman (Oxford: Berghahn Books, 2012), 10–24.
50. See Dionigi Albera, '"Why Are You Mixing What Cannot Be Mixed?' Shared Devotions in the Monotheisms," *History and Anthropology* 19, no. 1 (2008): 37–59; and Dionigi Albera and Maria Couroucli, eds., *Sharing Sacred Spaces in the Mediterranean: Christians, Muslims, and Jews at Shrines and Sanctuaries* (Bloomington: Indiana University Press, 2012).

4

CONTESTED CHOREOGRAPHIES OF SACRED SPACES IN MUSLIM BOSNIA

DAVID HENIG

Everyone knows that his or her perspective is contested, and that each view has always been contested. No perspective has really ever had the privilege of being considered to be the authoritative, let alone self-evident, truth about the Balkans. What is self-evident, and is therefore where the hegemonic discourse is located in my view, is that everything about the Balkans is contested, including explanations for that state of affairs.

—SARAH GREEN, NOTES FROM THE BALKANS

THE SHARING OF sacred spaces by divergent social actors is by no means a new phenomenon. Yet shared holy places have recently attracted the attention of many scholars. Indeed, during the second half of the twentieth century many holy sites became the repositories and articulations of core collective identities' rhetoric and claims. A "sharing turn" in the study of holy sites ensued from a considerable increase in the nationalization and politicization of sacred spaces in the past decades, such as the Church of the Anastasis in Jerusalem, or Ayodhya in Uttar Pradesh, India, to name just a couple of examples.[1] However, religious nationalism is a collective identitarian frame with teeth.

Many authors have convincingly argued that the political cosmologies and metanarratives of nation-states are often harnessed to religion and the sacred as a fertile symbolic source of their teleologies and identitarian frames of reference.[2] Sacred spaces, their orchestration and sharing, come to epitomize for both popular and academic discourses the manner in which the religious and nationalistic cosmologies intermingle and forge a terrain in which collective identities are contested, enacted, and negotiated. This is no less true for the politics of shared sacred sites in the Balkans, a region so deeply influenced by the legacy of the Ottoman Empire that contributed so much to the subject of this book.

The dominant perspective in the current scholarship on shared sacred sites focuses on interreligious or intercommunal forms and practices of sharing.[3] Less attention, however, has been paid to intracommunal and intrareligious disputes and contestations between divergent actors involved in the social field around a sacred site. In this chapter, I illustrate how processes such as the politicization of sites or their regulation and administration through the state religious apparatus also emerge in intracommunal and intrareligious social fields. The material discussed here is based on extensive ethnographic research in Muslim Bosnia.

As I have argued elsewhere, sacred landscapes in Bosnia-Herzegovina have undergone tremendous transformations in the past two decades.[4] The postsocialist liberation of religious expression and conduct after several decades of suppression and control, further encouraged by the war and postwar public ethnonational identity rhetoric and the proliferation of various foreign Islamic humanitarian organizations in Bosnia-Herzegovina, opened public debates questioning the authenticity and practice of Bosnian Islam and what it means to live a Muslim life. Special attention in the debates has been paid to the discourses on renewed Bosniak traditions and to the choreography of Muslim holy sites in particular.[5]

In this chapter, I discuss how these transformations of the Muslim sacred landscape intertwine with the social field around the sacred sites by documenting the contingency of their regulation, administration, and "sharing," with special attention paid to choreographic shifts.

Specifically, I seek to document the complex nature and choreography of Bosnian Muslims' relations with holy sites in the context of debates on sacred landscapes in the Balkans and the Mediterranean that have recently been hotly contested.[6]

SACRED SITES IN THE BALKANS

Sacred landscapes in the Balkans have recently attracted the attention of many authors.[7] The main theme has become the politics of the sharing of holy sites among various religious constituencies. In particular, scholars emphasize how various holy sites acquire a multivocal character and a capacity to accommodate religious differences. Hence, the prevailing and dominant scholarly views on Balkan holy sites are anchored to a politics of sharing and difference between (ethno-)religious communities, such as Serbs (Orthodox Christians); Croats (Roman Catholics); and Bosniaks, Kosovo Albanians, and Macedonian Torbeshis (all Muslims). The thought-provoking concept of "antagonistic tolerance," proposed by Robert Hayden and based on a comparative analysis of competitive sharing of sacred sites by multiple ethnoreligious groups, continues to gain importance in the field.[8]

Hayden relies on the negative definition of tolerance proposed by such moral philosophers as John Locke when he defines "antagonistic tolerance" as "passive noninterference ... premised on a lack of ability of either group to overcome the other" combined with "attitudes of strategic calculation of the value of tolerating others."[9] The idea of "antagonistic tolerance" entails both effectively sharing holy sites and "a pragmatic adaptation to a situation in which repression of the other group's practices may not be possible rather than an active embrace of the Other."[10] This analytical perspective takes as the unit of analysis chiefly an ethnoreligious group and thus emphasizes a sociology of intergroup relations and boundaries, where sharing and difference, the processes of inclusion and exclusion, and other contrasting dichotomies emerge on an ad hoc basis from the needs of actually sharing holy sites without ever erasing boundaries between groups.[11] The idea of antagonistic tolerance simultaneously accommodates conflict and sharing as inevitable modalities in the pragmatics of social life in a multiethnic fabric. Put in this way, latent conflict supplies an inherent condition for the processes of making and sharing sacred sites, and sharing is understood only as a temporal moment expressing actual processual relations rather than a fixed quality of intergroup stasis based on long-lasting difference, antagonism, and pragmatic acceptance.[12] This view highlights the fact that the differences between those who share a holy site are continuous and profound. Hayden argues directly that the conviction that "identities are fluid or changeable does not mean that distinctions between groups are easily removed."[13]

However insightful and challenging, such a perspective is somewhat biased toward the epistemological trap of groupism; that is, it has a tendency to ascribe agency to entities such as ethnic or religious groups, which are then taken for granted and considered as basic constituents of social life.[14] The very same trap of "groupism" (by which I mean specifically sectarianism) can be found in Hassner's prominent work on shared sacred spaces. Hassner asserts, for example, that "sacred places invite conflict with rival groups who strive to compete for access or legitimacy or who simply wish to inflict harm on their opponents."[15] As I have argued elsewhere, such analytical essentialism often reduces complex social fabrics to their collective identitarian dimensions while overlooking at the same moment other related processes taking place on the ground.[16]

Recently many anthropologists have spent a great amount of time arguing about the danger of essentializing collective identities.[17] These debates suggest that one possible escape from the trap of essentialism might be found in an engaged and detailed ethnography that makes any taken-for-granted-essence uncertain, fractured, and ambivalent by embedding it in historical contingencies and power relations. Therefore, I shift my perspective on the Bosnian sacred sites from groupism, with its emphasis on top-down control over defining and regulating consistent, approved practices, toward the grassroots activities of divergent social actors who intersubjectively construct and negotiate the more fluid meanings and practices involved in actually sharing sites from day to day. Such a perspective enables researchers to move through various scales—bottom-up/top-down, micro/macro, indivisible/shared, identity/difference—without essentializing the processes that constitute social life. In other words, degrees of conflict and sharing need to be analyzed as a result of specific and contingent processes in which interactions among social actors are not merely proxies for interactions between social groups.

Indeed, Albera has likewise argued for shifting the analysis of holy sites in the Balkans and in the Mediterranean at large toward an examination of greater social complexity and the broader scale of historical continuity that these sites often entail.[18] Albera calls for a more focused perspective on sacred sites per se, and for tracing the agency of various actors in the processes of making a sacred site without necessarily focusing on their ethnicization or ascribing any group-like characteristics to them. In a similar vein, Bowman has developed and ethnographically instantiated the issues of agency involved in the study of holy sites thus:

> The presence of agency necessitates close attention to what people are doing, and what they say they are doing, while they are in the process of doing it. It is vital to attend to who is saying what to whom and who is listening; long-term historical processes are characterized by silencings as well as debates. It is important to examine both if we want to really know what goes on in "sharing."[19]

Based on his comparative research of shared holy sites in Palestine and in Macedonia, Bowman points out that preexisting antagonism cannot provide the foundational logic for intercommunal interactions. He nevertheless observed another dynamic that respected the contingency of specific situations and the constantly shifting power relations among multiple social actors involved in the process of sharing the sites. Thus, sharing a holy site might lead to antagonism, tension, and mixing, or it might not. As Bowman concludes, "we must attempt to see what happens on the ground while syncretistic practices are occurring."[20] I concur with Bowman's cautionary note since it does not impose any proxy for interactions that take place around the holy sites.[21] More importantly, though, tracing the agency of social actors in the process of sharing a holy site enables researchers to move through various scales of analysis, switching from intercommunal to intracommunal relations and contestations, and shifting from a perspective that focuses on essentialized groups to one that pays attention to actors and to the contingent aspects of sharing.

Scholars of the (post) Ottoman sacred landscapes have paid very little attention to intracommunal perspectives and voices. By an intracommunal perspective I specifically mean an intraconfessional one. As Barkan and Barkey point out in their introduction to this volume, the history of intrareligious disputes has been as violent as interreligious conflicts, and we can find comparative parallels and processes with the intercommunal case studies. Even more importantly, Barkan and Barkey pose a crucial question: how are sacred spaces choreographed, regulated, or administrated? Choreography-oriented analysis enables us to shed light on modes of intrareligious sharing, competition, or rivalry over sacred sites. As I argue, choreographic shifts, in particular, generate power shifts, discontents, or resistance in sacred sites. Transformations or revisions of choreography entail changes, imbalances, or conflicts that can be exploited and enacted, as Barkan and Barkey argue in the introduction, by divergent "political actors, state actors, and religious and ethnic entrepreneurs acting on behalf of a particular coalition of political power attempting to destroy the modus vivendi." Social actors who seek to change power relations around a site frequently push explicitly for future changes in choreography while simultaneously taking advantage of the present contradictions inherent in every particular arrangement of a site's choreography.

In this chapter, I analyze choreographic shifts in Bosnian Muslim sacred sites at the grassroots level as a means to achieve a more nuanced analytical framework. Based on ethnographic fieldwork in Muslim areas of the Central Bosnian highlands conducted between 2008 and 2012, I examine processes of contestation among Bosnian Muslims over the choreography, appropriation, and meanings of sacred sites in order to shed light on intracommunal interactions and relations. By attending ethnographically to the theoretical argument discussed here, I believe my analysis can be used comparatively for further and much-needed ethnographic study of intracommunal or intraconfessional choreography of sacred spaces in the Balkans at large.

The veneration of holy sites in Muslim Bosnia has a long history.[22] In the Central Bosnian highlands, where I carried out my fieldwork, the veneration of multiple holy sites, including tombs, caves, water springs, hills, and trees, is closely associated with Muslims' personal notions of well-being.[23] Bosnian Muslims believe that their actions on the sites, such as visitation, praying, or maintaining the sites, bring them individual blessing (*bereket*), fortune, luck (*sreća*), and the good life, as such. In this chapter, I introduce and subsequently contrast the annual pilgrimage to the Karići holy site with the Ajvatovica pilgrimage and the annual venerations of outdoor sacred sites (*dovište*), known as prayers for rain (*dove za kišu*). These two examples follow Barkey and Barkan's call for examination of "everyday lives around holy sites," and neatly illustrate the manners in which the sites assemble diverse actors, the specific administrative practices and forms of orchestration of the sacred landscape, and the merging of local Bosnian Muslim politics and practice with globalized forms of Islam. In turn, I illustrate how these sites have become critical scenes of contestation in the transformative processes affecting the choreography of intracommunal sharing of Muslim sacred spaces in postwar Bosnia-Herzegovina. In doing so, however, let me move along the scale of analysis and begin by introducing the key actor in the process of orchestrating, administering, and transforming the sacred spaces in Muslim Bosnia: the Islamic Community of Bosnia and Herzegovina (Islamska Zajednica Bosne i Hercegovine).

BOSNIAN MUSLIM BODY POLITICS: ISLAMIC COMMUNITY OF BOSNIA AND HERZEGOVINA

In 1878, after the Congress of Berlin, the Austro-Hungarian Empire took over the territory of Bosnia-Herzegovina from the Ottoman Empire. Bosnian Islam was soon institutionalized in the Austro-Hungarian political structure with the establishment in 1882 of the Islamic Community (Islamska Zajednica), headed by its own representative grand mufti or *reis-ul-ulema* (religious leader). The Islamic Community (IC) thus gained autonomous legal status, and the link to Istanbul, the heart of Ottoman institutionalized Islam and the center of religious authority, was eventually severed.[24] Within this newly created bureaucratic hierarchy, the IC began to control and authorize both specific Islamic practices and Muslim religious life overall. After the Second World War, the newly formed Socialist Federal Republic of Yugoslavia acknowledged the status of the IC and adopted it into its own state bureaucratic structure. Under the new state socialist mode of governing, the IC was charged with regulating and controlling all manifestations of Islamic religious knowledge and expression in the public sphere, including the organization of collective piety (i.e., venerating the sacred sites), religious training, the appointment of new imams, and the construction of new mosques throughout the federation. Through the work of the IC, the Yugoslav state gained easy access to the very religious infrastructure of Muslim lives. As anthropologist Ger Duijzings reminds us, "Islamic community . . . was co-opted by the Communist system more than the Catholic and Serbian Orthodox churches: its close symbiosis with the regime was facilitated by Tito's benevolent attitude towards the Muslim world as one of the leaders of the Conference of Non-aligned States."[25]

In Bosnia-Herzegovina, as Tone Bringa has pointed out, a pragmatic coexistence between Islam and the communist ideology of the state came into force. Islamic scholars "encouraged Muslims to put their obligations to the state before their obligations as practicing Muslims," yet "the leaders could also use the socialist state discourse to reinforce their own power base."[26] One such an example is the ban of dervish orders in 1952, which was imposed by the IC itself with silent support and approval from the Yugoslav government, and which resulted in the closure of dervish lodges (*tekija*) and confiscation of their property. Although many dervish orders have been restored or founded following the 1989 post-Yugoslav religious liberation, the relationship between the IC and dervish orders continues to be far from ideal, and many tensions persist. The dervish sheikhs with whom I worked in 2009 and 2012 in the highlands described the relationship to me in terms of the IC's "hostility" toward the orders, and as a history of "exploitation" and "looting." Another example of the pragmatic coexistence between the Islamic Community and the socialist state that affected "everyday lives around sacred spaces" was the IC's politics of abandoning the practice of outdoor religious gatherings (*dove*) in some regions. In other cases the dates of such gatherings were rescheduled from traditional Tuesdays to Saturdays or Sundays as a concession to the new working calendar of the socialist state. The Islamic Community of Bosnia and Herzegovina thus gained power and generous support from the state in exchange for conformism, and its uniquely powerful position in the state's body politic continues to the present day. During and especially after the war in Bosnia-Herzegovina, the IC became a guarantor of "collective Bosniak identity" and "tradition" in the public rhetoric associated with ethnonational politics in Bosnia-Herzegovina. Furthermore, the IC continues to administer the Muslim sacred landscape and plays a key role in the "reinvention" and revitalization of many of those holy sites that were abandoned by the IC in the past decades.

CONTESTED SACRED SITES IN THE CENTRAL BOSNIAN HIGHLANDS

KARIĆI

Dova na Karićima is the annual three-day pilgrimage during which Bosnian Muslims worship Allah and commemorate Hajdar-dedo Karić at the place of the wooden mosque called Karići, at the top of a plateau. Although there are no written historical records about Hajdar-dedo Karić, his cult remains alive through a tremendously vivid oral tradition, the annual communal pilgrimage, and Muslims' individual visits (*zijáret*) in search of blessing (*bereket*).[27] It is believed that Hajdar-dedo Karić was one of the messengers of Islam who were brought to the Balkan peninsula during the early period of Islamization in the fifteenth century. In the narratives Hajdar-dedo Karić is portrayed as a wise, knowledgeable Islamic scholar, effendi, or imam, and a dervish sheikh (a leader of a sufi brotherhood). There are several repeating motifs used to describe him in the local narratives: a scholarly person (*učenjak*), the founder of the mosque/holy site in Karići thanks to a dream revelation, a friend of God (*evlija*, from Arabic *walī*), and a person who performed miracles (*keramet*) during his life.[28] The very first tomb (*mezar*) next to the mosque, situated to face in the direction of Mecca and constructed with a small pit in the middle, is almost certainly Hajdar-dedo's since this kind of gravestone (*nišan*) was usually made for individuals who performed miracles during their lifetimes. The rainwater that collects in the pit is considered to be healing and is used not only to treat illnesses but for good luck, blessing, and good fortune in general.

Good luck and divine power are associated with the place as a whole. There are stories told that during the Second World War, the Četnik troops tried to burn down the wooden mosque but were unable to set it alight by any means. Another story claims that no Muslim community (*džemat*) has dwelt on the plateau for the last 150 years, and that the mosque and pilgrimage site are used only during the pilgrimages. The nearest residents were a few Serbian (Orthodox) households. In the past, these Orthodox families cared for the mosque and even held the key, although they did not participate in the pilgrimage or worship at the site. I heard one story repeated even in the more distant villages: During the time when the Karići mosque was abandoned through most of the year, the Orthodox families desperately struggled with poor harvests and sick livestock. When they searched for help, an Orthodox cleric told them that most likely a sacred object near their homes needed their care; undoubtedly, the object was the Karići mosque. When the families began to take care of the mosque, all their bad luck vanished.

It is worth mentioning that during the state socialist period, when religious gatherings were generally subjected to close control or suppressed altogether, the Karići pilgrimage was neither sanctioned by the state power nor banned by the Islamic Community, despite high levels of Muslims attendance.[29] In 1993, during the Bosnian war (1992–95), a Yugoslav

National Army tank drove through the ancient wooden mosque. At the time the region was barely accessible because of the many landmines scattered around the pilgrimage site during the war. Therefore, local Muslims temporarily organized the annual gathering in a nearby provincial town mosque. After the war the landscape was slowly demined, the wooden mosque was eventually rebuilt in 2002, and the pilgrimage fully restored again.

Although the restoration of the mosque was initiated by a group of local Muslim patriots, the land and the mosque are officially owned and maintained by the IC. The IC is also responsible for organizing and setting the dates in July for the Karići pilgrimage. The date is counted according to the old Julian calendar as the week of the eleventh Tuesday after Jurjevdan (May 6). The pilgrimage usually begins with Saturday's noon prayer and lasts until the Sunday midday prayer. Only male Muslims are allowed to attend the Karići pilgrimage. The pilgrimage gathering involves reciting the Qur'an, singing *ilahija* (songs in praise of Allah), and other performances, such as reciting verses from *mevlud* both in Turkish and Bosnian, *tevhid* for the Ottoman as well as Bosnian martyrs (*šehide*), and a collective devotional prayer, *kijam zikr* (*qiyam dhikr* in Arabic).[30] *Kijam zikr* is performed by dervishes and led by a dervish sheikh. Other pilgrims usually observe rather than take part in this form of prayer because dervishes in the territory of the former Yugoslavia have been historically perceived ambivalently as the Islamic "other-within."[31] The devotional *zikr* prayer was also performed as part of the pilgrimage under socialist Yugoslavia. I return to this significant fact later since, as I have already pointed out, all dervish orders in Bosnia-Herzegovina were officially banned in the 1950s by the IC itself, with the Yugoslav state's assistance, for being "devoid of cultural value," and this ban lasted until 1989.[32]

While the dervish lodges in the western parts of Central Bosnia, the traditional cradle of Bosnian Sufism, managed to maintain a certain degree of continuity, this longevity was interrupted for dervish lodges in the northern parts of the country.[33] Karići has been, consequently, publicly presented and understood for a long time solely as a place of Muslim annual pilgrimage rather than a place associated with dervish worship. In the late 1980s, however, a dervish group of the Rifa'i order, which I have also studied, was formed in the region.[34] The group actively aligned itself with the legendary figure of Hajdar-dedo Karić in its bid to gain authenticity by restoring the severed link between living Sufism and its historical traces in the region. Although the dervish group has recently begun to forge links with a Kosovo dervish lodge through its sheikh's "spiritual lineage" (*silsila*), the dervishes still consider the Karići site as their spiritual cradle and Hajdar-dedo Karić their spiritual forefather because he brought Sufism to the region.

AJVATOVICA

Although this chapter primarily explores how Muslim sacred landscapes in the Central Bosnian highlands have been transformed along with the choreography for managing the major pilgrimage site of Karići and the local pilgrimages known as prayers for rain, it is important to introduce another pilgrimage site, the Ajvatovica. The Ajvatovica is a significant holy site in Muslim Bosnia that in many respects shapes the ways village Muslims in Central Bosnia reflect on post-Yugoslav changes of intracommunal sacred geographies. Indeed, my village friends often juxtaposed Karići and the Ajvatovica pilgrimages both in casual, everyday conversations as well as in the pilgrimage narratives I collected during my research. The great majority of villagers, however, have never made the pilgrimage to Ajvatovica for reasons I discuss later.

The Ajvatovica pilgrimage site, near the village Prusac, boasts legends similar to those attached to the Karići site, legends that go back to the seventeenth century and invoke the legendary messenger of Islam in the region, effendi Ajvaz-dedo, who likely was also a dervish sheikh. However, unlike the Karići pilgrimage site, Ajvatovica was officially banned during the socialist period beginning in 1947.[35] The pilgrimage was renewed in 1990, mainly through the engagement of the IC, a media campaign conducted by such outlets as the IC's weekly Preporod and the efforts of the SDA political party (Party for Democratic Action), led at the time by the first Bosniak president, Alija Izetbegović. Moreover, because the region where the Ajvatovica pilgrimage site is located had been controlled and defended during the war by the Bosnian army, it came to be portrayed in public rhetoric as a holy land emblematic of a threatened Muslim community's historical continuity and cultural heritage.[36]

While conducting my research on the Muslim sacred landscapes in Central Bosnia, I soon discovered that the present manner in which the Ajvatovica pilgrimage is orchestrated plays a significant role in Muslim public politics, which are dominated by the IC, and in many conversations I had with local Muslims. I was characteristically told that, whereas the Karići pilgrimage actually continued uninterrupted, the IC now promotes Ajvatovica as the biggest annual Muslim gathering in Europe, with a long and continuous tradition, despite the official ban imposed in 1947. The orchestration and choreography of the Ajvatovica pilgrimage, including the related parade, "The Days of Ajvatovica" (Dani Ajvatovice), recall aspects of religious pilgrimage, political gatherings, and folkloric parades. The festival is composed of various events, concerts, and lectures that are widely advertised by the IC, using billboards and other public media to reach the wider Bosnian public. These sources describe the Ajvatovica pilgrimage as a "manifestation of tradition and long lasting continuity of Bosniak [Muslim] identity and culture" or as the "largest Muslim gathering in Europe."[37] Many people I spoke with during my fieldwork often emphasized that the Ajvatovica pilgrimage used to be an all-male gathering. When it was renewed in 1990, however, it was promoted, in accord with the nationalized rhetoric prevalent in the public sphere at the time, as a gathering for all Muslims. In my village friends' views, the inclusion of female participants in the pilgrimage, and of tourists and foreign folkloric groups more recently, betrays what for them constitutes the Bosniak tradition of religious gathering (*dove*). Thus, the manner in which the Ajvatovica pilgrimage was reorchestrated during the last decade caused it to very quickly become a powerful instrument in post-Yugoslav public political discourse to channel, symbolize, and articulate the collective identity of Bosniaks (Muslims).

CHANGING CHOREOGRAPHY, CONTESTED MEANINGS

During my stays in mountain villages and my visits to the Karići site during the pilgrimages, male Muslims often drew me into their friendly conversations (*mehábet*) about their memories of making pilgrimages and their strong emotional attachment to Karići. In conversation, each person tended to give his individual experiences a common narrative form, usually starting from the exact date when he visited Karići for the first time and continuing by recounting all of the important dates in the history of the site that intersected with his own biography. For example, Fadil, a pious Muslim in his late sixties, explained to me that as soon as he could walk long distances as a child, his father brought him to Karići. When I asked Fadil how many times he had visited the holy site so far, he answered that he has never neglected to go, and neither did his father. He singled out particular Karići pilgrimages, such as the one the year his father died, the year when the war in Bosnia-Herzegovina broke out, or the year when the site was destroyed and later rebuilt. Younger pilgrims, however, revealed different memories. Male Muslims in their forties often told me that they had attended the pilgrimage for the first time only after the end of Yugoslav communism, and many of them had not attended until after the 1990s war, when they realigned themselves with the renewed and liberated Islamic tradition and the political discourses on Bosnian Muslim identity. A dervish sheikh in his mid-fifties from Herzegovina offered a slightly different perspective:

> I visited Karići for the first time in 1981. I remember very vividly how I met old men in very old traditional clothes, fezzes wrapped in a golden cloth which they brought from hajj, and with beautifully decorated horses. It

was astonishing. They were so nice. Today it is different, these gatherings [*dove*] are one of the last expressions of living Bosnian Islam. It is not like Ajvatovica.

It soon struck me how frequently village Muslims employ this juxtaposition of Karići and Ajvatovica in their narratives. The juxtaposition succinctly sheds a contrastive light on the profound transformations of intracommunal choreography that have affected sacred sites in Muslim Bosnia. In their often very passionate conversations, the narrators pass quickly from pride to anger to melancholy when they consider how the Muslim sacred landscape has changed in response to the new manners of organizing pilgrimages. Both the Karići and Ajvatovica pilgrimages operate as rhetorical and materialized tropes through which village Muslims try to comprehend these changes.

I also compared recent media coverage for the Ajvatovica and Karići pilgrimages; the latter hardly received any attention in the public sphere in general, and in the mass media in particular. Muslims of diverse backgrounds from the region blamed the IC, its imams, and Bosniak politicians for overlooking the Karići pilgrimage in favor of Ajvatovica; at the same time, however, they were proud of the fact that the Karići pilgrimage had not yet been "polluted" by any significant innovations. In conversations during the pilgrimage in 2008, I was characteristically told:

> Today, the Ajvatovica is like many other gatherings [*dove*] you can attend, all are just one big parade [*teferić*]. Whereas Karići is the place where people come to pray and contemplate together, to have a conversation [*mehabet*] but not a party [*teferić*], and it has always been like this. Karići has had continuity! I tell you what, these Bosnian gatherings [*dove*] aren't what they used to be. Today, people say that they are going to a pilgrimage but they mean a parade [*teferić*]. And Ajvatovica? Ehh, that's for tourists. Only Karići still continues in the way of a traditional Muslims' gathering [sing., *dova*] as it used be everywhere here. Even a few decades ago you could meet so many hajis in the Karići, the golden fezzes were just everywhere. Indeed, in the past people said, "Karići, this is our little hajj."

This narrative, presented by a male Muslim in his late thirties, embraces rather eloquently some of the intracommunal tensions and the contradictory ways in which the sacred sites are perceived because of the manner in which they are presently administered and orchestrated. Indeed, in the great majority of narrative reflections and conversations I encountered in the region, Bosnian Muslims critically reflected on how the pilgrimages are organized and choreographed. Turning now to the actors' critical perspectives on the orchestration and management of pilgrimages to holy sites will allow us to gain insight into the changing dynamics of power relations, shifting hierarchies, and the agency of various actors in the process of making and maintaining those sacred sites.

DEBATING CHOREOGRAPHIC SHIFTS

AJVATOVICA

It appears to village Muslims that the Ajvatovica pilgrimage is advertised and promoted by the IC everywhere with a very expensive and conspicuous program of events. The significant and oft-repeated motif of discontent with the current ways the Ajvatovica pilgrimage is orchestrated emphasizes the pilgrimage's increasing politicization. But the process of politicization (the expression usually used is "*sve je politika*"—everything is politics) meant for my friends specifically the political contest between different local Muslim alliances (i.e., intracommunal) rather than ethnonational (i.e., intercommunal) politics associated with sacred spaces. In particular, many of my Bosnian friends bitterly objected to the ways some Bosniak politicians and Islamic clerics exploit the pilgrimage to promote themselves in the public sphere or for their own factional political gains.

The main target of discontent, however, is the IC itself. The IC is in charge of orchestrating all pilgrimages and religious gatherings, and thus figures as the official state-sanctioned authority and guarantor of the Bosnian Islamic tradition. One brand of criticism of the IC's involvement in the orchestration of pilgrimages such as the Ajvatovica comes from various networks of new Bosnian Muslims—Salafists—who adhere to a very scripturalist understanding of Islam. These are usually called in the vernacular *"vehabije"* (Wahabis). The Salafi Muslims regard all local pilgrimages as a heretical practice of idolatry (*širk*) and accuse both the Bosnian IC and village Muslims of breaking with Islamic orthodoxy.[38] Salafists' discontent is distinct from that usually expressed by male Muslims in the villages where I carried out my fieldwork. My village friends pointed out on various occasions that, according to tradition, Bosnian pilgrimages should be all-male Muslim gatherings, like the Karići pilgrimage, so the IC had no business changing the Ajvatovica pilgrimage to invite both men and women, or tourist and folkloric ensembles. For this reason, some of my friends have decided never to make the pilgrimage to Ajvatovica.

Many local dervish communities—yet another actor involved in sharing the sites—feel rather uneasy, for different reasons, about the ways the Ajvatovica pilgrimage is choreographed. Over the past few years, folk groups from Turkey have been invited to the Ajvatovica pilgrimage to perform "classical Turkish sufi music" alongside "whirling Turkish dervishes," presented as a contribution to the performance of "traditional Bosnian Islam." Only a few Bosnian dervish orders, such as the Nakşibendi, which is aligned with the IC, have been invited. All Bosnian dervishes affiliated with other orders have been pointedly excluded from the orchestration of the pilgrimage. Several dervish sheikhs explained to me the IC's agenda. By inviting Turkish folk groups, the IC denied Bosnian Sufism's viable living tradition in order to relegate a fossilized version of the tradition to the distant historical realm of Ottoman folklore. The interviewed sheikhs also often recalled the fact that the same Bosnian IC had been historically hostile to Bosnian dervishes, especially in early socialist times, resulting in the official ban and closure of their sanctuaries (*tekija*). In the late 1970s a few dervish groups were restored in Bosnia, but this was limited to conformist orders (the Nakşibendi order in particular) willing to submit to de facto surveillance by the IC and the state secret police. The allegiance of the Nakşibendi order to the IC became an important factor in the process of renewing Bosnian Islamic traditions, including Sufism, after the breakup of Yugoslavia and the liberation of religious practice. As a result of this history, the IC, as the state-approved dominant actor in the religious sphere, along with the officially tolerated Nakşibendi order claim joint authority to decide what is Islamic, traditional, or genuine sufi teaching, on the one hand, and how to appropriately choreograph veneration of sacred spaces, on the other.

KARIĆI

The Karići pilgrimage has escaped the heavy hand of the IC and is orchestrated in a modest way. Still, every year it attracts up to a thousand pilgrims, and in the first postwar years it was even up to several thousand pilgrims. As I have argued earlier, village Muslims from the region and beyond view the choreography of the Karići pilgrimage with melancholy and nostalgia. They find at Karići the continuation of traditional and genuine Bosnian Muslim pilgrimage practices while fearing that change is imminent. It is not surprising, then, that in recent years multiple tensions and competing meanings over how the Karići pilgrimage is orchestrated have emerged as a result of the wider choreographic transformation affecting sacred landscapes in post-Yugoslav Bosnia.

Indeed, in the summer of 2009 the local branch of the IC invited a group of Turkish Sunni Muslims from a Turkish Islamic aid organization to attend the Karići pilgrimage. As part of their "social aid" in Bosnia-Herzegovina, this group organized in local mosques throughout the region summer schools for children to study the Qur'an.[39] Some of the Turks also took part in the Karići's program by reciting the Qur'an and *mevlud*. At the time of the night sermon, one of the Turkish guests gave a short speech about the importance of Hajdar-dedo Karić; the even greater importance of the sultan Mehmet al-Fateh, who conquered the Bosnian lands more than five centuries ago; and the ways the sultan spread Islam in the region. The Turkish effendi also emphasized how the sultan established intimate and enduring family ties between Turkey and Bosnia-Herzegovina. This speech sharply contrasted with the very brief speech about the facts of Hajdar-dedo Karić's life given by the local imam, who represented the IC. He did not speak of Hajdar-dedo Karić as someone who brought Islam to the region, nor of the relations between Sufism and the sacred site; he simply treated the Karići pilgrimage as a traditional gathering of Bosnian Muslims who have survived various past aggressions on the part of the peoples around them.

Many pilgrims, however, reacted to the imam's speech with discontent, although their reactions were also contradictory and ambiguous. In his speech, the pilgrims argued, the imam had detached himself from the long-standing local narratives about Hajdar-dedo Karić and so, by implication, also from the ways Muslims in the region conceive of themselves as specifically Bosnian Muslims. In their views, the speech confirmed yet again the IC's ongoing campaign to marginalize the Karići site in favor of politicized sites such as the Ajvatovica. The majority of the pilgrims also rejected the Turkish guest's speech. Although he included Hajdar-dedo Karić, he did so by embedding the regional historical narratives into a grand narrative of postimperial Ottoman nostalgia that places Turkey at the center and constitutes Bosnia and Karići as a mere periphery that needed to be civilized by the Ottomans. Many pilgrims angrily disapproved of the way the pilgrimage had been organized: "Did they come to Turkify (*turćit*) us again?"[40] They were deeply disappointed that the IC had brought these Turkish guests and enabled them to intervene in the choreography of the pilgrimage.

The local group of dervishes introduced another voice into this chorus of discontent and added yet another dimension to the intracommunal contest over orchestrating the Karići pilgrimage. Despite their engagement with restoring the damaged Karići mosque in the early postwar years and their strong attachment to Hajdar-dedo Karić's role in bringing Sufism to the region, they have participated neither in the organization of the pilgrimage nor in the gathering at all in recent years. They refused to attend after the local imam, representing the IC, did not allow them to lead the devotional prayer (*zikr*). Instead, the *zikr* prayer was led by a sheikh of the Nakşibendi order who is closely allied to the IC; moreover, he was not from the region. The local group of dervishes interpreted the denial to participate in the pilgrimage—to share the site—as a consequence of its involvement in translocal dervish networks affiliated to the Rifa'i order (with its center in Kosovo, it is considered by the Bosnian Ulema to be Shi'a oriented). Thus, the dervishes explained, their inclusion in the pilgrimage would pose a threat to the local IC's authority. Indeed, Ger Duijzings has argued, based on his fieldwork in Kosovo under socialist Yugoslavia, that there is a long history of asymmetric relations within the IC between what he calls the Bosnian-dominated official Islam (Sunni of the Hanafi interpretation) and various heterodox (Shi'a) dervish orders, especially in Kosovo, such as the Rifa'i order.[41] In the post-Yugoslav period, when the links between many Bosnian and Kosovo dervish orders have been reestablished and even intensified, these old tensions gain new meanings in Bosnian Muslim political struggles over control of sacred authority, conduct of Muslim practice, and choreography of sacred spaces. Put differently, in the years of postsocialist religious liberation, the Bosnian IC has tried to maintain a complete monopoly over appropriating and administrating the Bosnian sacred landscape and sacred authority in the face of proliferating and multiplying interpretations of Islam and Muslim practice. The IC has been willing to employ any means to accomplish this end, including the exclusion of dervishes from the orchestration of the pilgrimage and, thus effectively, from sharing the sacred site.

CHOREOGRAPHIES OF "LITTLE TRADITION" CONTESTED: PRAYERS FOR RAIN IN CENTRAL BOSNIA

Outdoor prayers for rain (*dove za kišu*) provide another venue where contestation over the choreography of Muslim sacred sites in the Central Bosnian highlands can be analyzed. Prayers for rain in Central Bosnia occur annually when Muslims make pilgrimages to the holy sites (*dovište*) in the local sacred landscape, such as tombs, hilltops, springs, caves, and lime trees. These gatherings have been recognized as a distinctively

Central Bosnian ritual practice.[42] The prayers have historically been correlated to the cycle of agricultural production, with its corresponding fertility rituals and regenerative symbolism, and they are orchestrated according to the local ritual calendar.[43] The days recognized as Jurjevdan and Alidjun have acquired particular importance in the ritual calendar. The dates are derived from the Orthodox Christian celebration of St. George's day and St. Elijah's day according to the Julian calendar (May 6 for Jurjevdan and August 2 for Alidjun). Both dates are pivotal for the pastoral and agricultural work schedules in many Central Bosnian villages.[44]

Even the choreography of this somewhat distinctively regional ritual practice and the sacred spaces associated with it wound up in a fatal embrace with the IC's authority to enforce first the restrictive socialist policies that marked the Yugoslav period, and then with the imperatives of the turbulent Muslim politics that has dominated in postwar times. There were approximately sixty sites in use in the Central Bosnian highlands before 1945. After 1945 the restrictions imposed on various religious practices, such as prayers for rain, by the socialist state with the assistance of the IC, had caused nearly half of the sites to no longer exist. Nonetheless, many of these sacred sites continued to be venerated semiclandestinely in defiance of the restrictions. In the wake of the post-Yugoslav religious liberation and the war in the 1990s, rain prayers have more or less recovered their earlier significance and many sites have been revived, often explicitly to demonstrate the Bosniak sense of tradition and collective identity.

However, veneration of the outdoor sacred sites has also generated intracommunal tensions between local Muslims and the dominant state-approved religious body politic. Following the historian Muhamad Hadžijahić, we can trace these tensions all the way back to the fifteenth century.[45] Hadžijahić provides us with an example of fatwa issued by an Ottoman jurist in which the jurist disapproves of St. George's day and the associated ritual activities, referring to them as infidel practices and beliefs. The example brought to light by Hadžijahić illustrates not only a vivid continuity of certain practices. It also points to a continuity of intracommunal tensions over practices such as prayers for rain among village Muslims and their legitimation, control, and choreography by the Islamic authority and the body politic.

In the late 1980s Tone Bringa studied an annual prayer for rain in the village of Dolina in Central Bosnia. In her succinct ethnography, Bringa describes a continuous tradition of organizing these gatherings (*dova*) exclusively for women.[46] Furthermore, Bringa argues that "the prayers for rain, which are clearly a fertility ritual, should be the concern of women."[47] It was somewhat surprising, then, that all of the two dozen outdoor prayers I attended in the highlands during 2008 and 2009 were entirely all-male gatherings. When I later asked Muslim women in the villages about this seeming choreographic disparity, I learned from them that it is the local custom (*adet*) for men to attend the ritual since women are busy in their homes preparing the feast that usually follows the gatherings.

Today the choreography of prayers for rain falls under the competence, control, and approval of the local branch of the Bosnian IC. The gathering usually consists of a recital of the Qur'an, the midday prayer, and a prayer for rain. In recent years a sermon and a collective prayer commemoration of the souls of Bosnian Muslims who died during the recent wars (*šehide*, or martyrs) have become obligatory components of the ceremony.

Many village Muslims, including local dervishes, continue to conceive of the prayers for rain as significant agricultural and fertility rituals that govern the tempos of their agricultural activities and shape the local sense of belonging and identity. Local dervishes have actively participated in the rain prayers along with village Muslims and have even assisted, in some cases, with their postsocialist revitalization. The dervishes support the practice of prayers for rain at the outdoor sites at least in part because they associate the sites, like the Karići site, with the spiritual continuity of their own orders and practice. During my fieldwork I learned from several dervish sheikhs that some of the outdoor sacred sites around which the prayers are orchestrated are associated in local narratives and legends with dervish messengers of Islam in the early history of Islamization in the region. Indeed, some of the sites are known in the vernacular as Sheikh's tekke (Šejhova tekija), Sheikh's spring (Šejhova voda), or Sheikh Feruh's tomb (Šejh Feruhovo turbe).

On the other hand, the IC treats the rain prayers differently. Many of its imams see these gatherings solely as a way to debate, channel, and authorize the discourses on religious orthodoxy and the political identity of Bosnian Muslims. There are also imams who concur with the aforementioned fatwa that the veneration of outdoor sites is an impermissible infidel form of religious conduct.

After one of the prayers in the highlands in 2009, I interviewed the imam who led the gathering. He belonged to the younger generation of Bosnian clerics who have in recent decades acquired their religious training in Saudi Arabia. When we met he was surprised that I was interested in these pilgrimages, and he ironically remarked, "It would be better to abandon such heretical [*bogomil*] traditions." Then he added, with strong disapproval in his voice, "What a folk Islam, I don't understand why people still care." Village Muslims, as well as dervishes, for their part, take an ambivalent stance toward these orthodox imams who have adopted a scripturalist interpretation of Islam during their studies in the Gulf and now promote a normative Islam that seems alien to local people. During my fieldwork I was often told that anyone who has not been born in the region and has not grown up there can hardly understand the importance of rain prayers within the vernacular cosmologies of village Muslims. One villager's reaction against the imam neatly and straightforwardly captures this ambivalence. "He is not traditionalist but revolutionist. He is not interested in any tradition. If so, then it is the dead tradition contained in the books. He is from the outside, he does not understand what people care about and strive for here."

On another occasion the very same villager who had disapproved so strongly of the orthodox imam offered a contrary evaluation of the local imam who had led another prayer for rain: "He is a good effendi, one of us, he does not pretend anything. The effendi is from here, not like those young imams today who don't respect our tradition, the tradition of Bosnian Muslims. Contrarily, they try to impose various foreign novelties from Turkey or Arabia where they studied. This is not good."

Nevertheless, the intracommunal tensions outlined here must not be interpreted simply as a conflict between the modernist IC and parochial regional traditionalists. The ways that village Muslims apprehend and enact what constitutes correct Muslim practice or, in this specific instance, the choreography of the sacred site are inevitably multivocal and often contradictory. The choreography of prayers for rain was also contested especially in those mountain villages where new mosques had been built only recently, often thanks to foreign Islamic "humanitarian aid organizations" from the Gulf, and were administered by the IC.[48] Here the prayers have very often been administratively relocated from the outdoor holy sites to the mosques, a move that has generated multiple tensions in both local village politics and in Muslim politics more broadly, often driving a wedge even between village neighbors. When I visited one such village where a dispute over the relocation of the rain prayer from the outdoor holy site to the newly built village mosque still raged, one villager described the conflict this way: "We have a new mosque even with a balcony so why should we climb to the hills forevermore. We should follow progress, we ought to be modern!"

Here the trope of "being modern" gains a specific meaning. It was later explained to me that being modern means "adjusting the traditional custom [adet], not abandoning it." Nonetheless, on that very day I observed approximately two hundred men of various ages gathering at the local holy site about an hour's walk into the hills to pray for rain. However, the potential danger of these tensions lies elsewhere. As I have argued, the choreography of prayers for rain is to a great extent under the control and competence of the IC, and any decision needs the approval of its respective local branch (medžilis). In this particular village, the dispute had intensified because the newly appointed village imam, the representative of the IC, was not from the region. Moreover, he had also studied in Saudi Arabia, and his attitude to prayers for rain was rather dismissive, to the point that he decided not to attend the prayer. As a result, some of the villagers did not hesitate to call him a Wahabi (Vehabija), and eventually both village factions, despite their differing opinions about the orchestration of the rain prayer, were united in their discontent with the imam and joined together to invite another imam who would not question the choreography of the prayers, let alone their validity as a practice, to the outdoor holy site. However, as the last example illustrates, even a small choreographic shift—in this case, a spatial one (relocation from outdoor to indoor)—can profoundly transform the ritual practice and escalate into unprecedented open intracommunal conflicts.[49]

CONCLUSION

In this chapter I have documented the complex nexus between the choreography of Muslim sacred spaces and the transformations of sacred landscape in the Central Bosnian highlands. The material discussed here illustrates that an intracommunal analytical perspective on the processes involved in sharing sacred sites is as important and fertile as the intercommunal one. By attending to "who is saying what to whom and who is listening" rather than taking collective identitarian frameworks as a proxy for interactions and relations "around the sites," I have shown that these sacred sites are not necessarily venerated, worshiped, or shared by Muslims strictly as members of an ethnoreligious group.[50] On the contrary, these sites in Muslim Bosnia entail a complex nexus of (power) relations cutting across multiple scales. The sacred sites in the Central Bosnian highlands assemble female and male, village and urban Muslims, or Sunni Muslims and dervishes of divergent cults. Yet the sites are intricately entangled in the state-level bureaucratic field as their administration, and thus their appropriation, involves the IC, international Islamic organizations, and the state. On the other hand, these sites operate as a point of significance in local cosmologies in which the notions of blessing (*bereket*) and well-being are attached to the sites. Moving on the cosmological scale, the sites have been invested in the cosmologies of post-Yugoslav nationalism with identitarian and political values of a new significance. Therefore, in order to fully examine the "choreography of daily life around the site," and the dynamics and the contingency of the mechanisms that are elaborated to regulate (both formally and informally) that sharing, we need to pay close attention to what is happening on the ground while social actors assemble, and to the regulatory and administrative forms of power intervening in the choreography.[51]

I started this chapter with an epigraph from Sarah Green's splendid ethnography of the Greek-Albanian borderland, yet another fecund example of a space of significance that also requires careful management, administration, and contested orchestration of the relationship between people and space across many scales.[52] Borders, like sacred sites, are zones of ambiguity and contest, especially when put into the service of nation-states that use them to essentialize and divide, and to manage inside-outside relations between people and place. In political cosmologies of nation-states, borders, like holy sites, often become "sacralized," and as such they need to be appropriated, controlled, and—if necessary—contested. The reason I am drawing a parallel with Green's work here becomes evident when reading from the epigraph again: "everything about the Balkans is contested, including explanations for that state of affairs."[53] The story Green tells us about the nation-state borders illustrates how this contest between people and space in the historically highly contested post-Ottoman region, in the Balkans, replicates on multiple scales. It inevitably includes the scholarly debates about the nation-states, intercommunal relations, and sacred sites. What I have tried to do in this chapter, however, is to show a cross-cutting perspective that would allow us and urge us to move the analysis through relational scales. Or, as Green puts it, "to switch to and fro between scales, to switch the sound off and switch it back on again repeatedly, to try to understand the relations between them, rather than the fragmentations."[54]

Such a perspective reinvigorates the need of ethnographically rich, grassroots contributions to the choreography of sacred spaces and is suitably inclusive since it accommodates a wide range of "sharing forms," at both inter- and intracommunal levels. Moreover, it enables researchers to move beyond the collective identitarian categories that have tended to hold sway whenever the problem of sharing has been examined toward closer examination of how sites are affected by the contingent confluence around them of divergent actors with sometimes contradictory commitments involved in multiple intertwined processes frequently working at cross-purposes. Indeed, sacred sites need to be conceived of as relational fields in which the construction of difference does not always follow the collective identitarian frames of reference. Choreography as a heuristic device for analysis enables us to begin comparing such interrelations and connections on multiple scales. I have presented here material to show how, during the Ajvatovica and Karići pilgrimages and during the local prayers for rain, multiple actors and discourses assemble and interact.

One possible danger in the choreography-centered analytical framework, in my view, is the temptation to present transformations of choreography as something irreversible, and, indeed, inevitable (as a shift "from–to"), especially conceived as a tendency of actors within shared sites to work against the modus vivendi. My illustration helps to clarify the central argument of this book by showing how sacred spaces are choreographed, regulated, and administered in a way that can only be properly understood if we provide nuance to the choreography framework and pay particular attention to what I call choreographic shifts in order to accommodate into our analysis the contingency of sharing by divergent actors in its restorative, conservative, and innovative modes.[55]

Choreographic shifts shed nuanced light on the dynamics of transformations in choreography of sacred spaces that unfold in multiple directions, oscillating between amity and enmity as well as across continuums of individual–collective and divided–shared. However, these shifts always need to be contextualized ethnographically and situated in historical, political, and temporal contexts. I have shown that even seemingly tiny choreographic shifts—such as changing the venue *from* outdoor *to* indoor, deciding to include all Muslims or limit attendance to a particular segment (male only, for instance), including or excluding dervishes, aligning a ritual with or detaching it from specific historical narratives, or inviting another imam—might generate power shifts, momentary discontents, or resistance in sacred sites, but also might not. To conclude, I argue that in our analysis of choreography of sacred sites, we need to take the notions of contingency and choreographic shifts seriously in order to trace the actions around the sacred sites.[56] Sharing of sacred sites thus needs to be analytically apprehended as a result of particular actions and processes rather than proxy for interactions and relations that impose categorical boundaries to the eventful dynamics of social life.

NOTES

1. Peter van der Veer, *Religious Nationalism: Hindus and Muslims in India* (Berkeley: University of California Press, 1994). See also Glenn Bowman, "'In Dubious Battle on the Plains of Heav'n': The Politics of Possession Jerusalem's Holy Sepulchre," *History and Anthropology* 22, no. 3 (2011): 371–99.
2. Bruce Kapferer, *Legends of People, Myths of State: Violence, Intolerance, and Political Culture in Sri Lanka and Australia* (Washington, DC: Smithsonian Institute Press, 1988), 1–26.
3. Examples include Ron E. Hassner, *War on the Sacred Grounds* (Ithaca, NY: Cornell University Press, 2009); Dionigi Albera and Maria Couroucli, eds., *Sharing Sacred Spaces in the Mediterranean: Christians, Muslims, and Jews at Shrines and Sanctuaries* (Bloomington: Indiana University Press, 2012); and Glenn Bowman, ed. *Sharing the Sacra: The Politics and Pragmatics of Inter-Communal Relations Around Holy Places* (Oxford: Berghahn, 2012).
4. David Henig, "'This Is Our Little Hajj': Muslim Holy Sites and Reappropriation of the Sacred Landscape in Contemporary Bosnia," *American Ethnologist* 39, no. 4 (2012): 752–66.
5. See Dženita Sarač Rujanac, "Ajvatovica: A Bridge Between Tradition, National and Religious Identity," *History and Anthropology* 24, no. 1 (2013): 117–36.
6. I wrote the bulk of this chapter, and its ethnographic part in particular, with the debates on Bosnian Muslim politics and the competing discourses on Muslim practice articulated around local sacred sites in mind. See Henig, "'This Is Our Little Hajj.'" In my original text, therefore, I paid more attention to Muslim politics and the competing rhetoric of divergent actors. In this version, I use the same ethnographic material, but I focus primarily on highlighting choreographic aspects of intracommunal sharing that are employed to maintain, negotiate, transform, or appropriate the sacred sites in Muslim Bosnia, leaving aside more explicitly ideological stances taken by competing actors.
7. For examples, see Tone Bringa, *Being Muslim the Bosnian Way: Identity and Community in a Central Bosnian Village* (Princeton, NJ: Princeton University Press, 1995); Jill Dubisch, *In a Different Place: Pilgrimage, Gender, and Politics at a Greek Island Shrine* (Princeton, NJ: Princeton University Press, 1995); Ger Duijzings, *Religion and the Politics of Identity in Kosovo* (New York: Columbia University

Press, 2000); Robert M. Hayden, "Antagonistic Tolerance: Competitive Sharing of Religious Sites in South Asia and the Balkans," *Current Anthropology* 43 (2002): 205–31; Dionigi Albera, "'Why Are You Mixing What Cannot Be Mixed?': Shared Devotions in the Monotheism," *History and Anthropology* 19, no. 1 (2008): 37–59; Karolina Bielenin-Lenczowska, "Visiting of Christian Holy Places by Muslims as a Strategy of Coping with Difference," *Anthropological Notebooks* 15, no 3 (2009): 27–41; and Glenn Bowman, "Orthodox–Muslim Interactions at 'Mixed Shrines' in Macedonia," in *Eastern Christians in Anthropological Perspective*, ed. Chris Hann and Hermann Goltz (Berkeley: University of California Press, 2010): 163–83.

8. Hayden, "Antagonistic Tolerance"; and Robert M. Hayden, Hande Sozer, Tugba Tanyeri-Erdemir, and Aydin Erdemir, "The Byzantine Mosque at Trilye: A Processual Analysis of Dominance, Sharing, Transformation and Tolerance," *History and Anthropology* 22, no. 1 (March 2011): 1–17.
9. Hayden, "Antagonistic Tolerance," 206.
10. Ibid., 219.
11. Ibid., 207.
12. For example, see Hayden et al., "The Byzantine Mosque at Trilye."
13. Hayden, "Antagonistic Tolerance," 207.
14. Rogers Brubaker, "Ethnicity Without Groups," *Archives Européenes de Sociologie* 43, no. 2 (2002):164.
15. Hassner, *War on Sacred Grounds*, 149.
16. David Henig, "'Knocking on My Neighbour's Door': On Metamorphoses of Sociality in Rural Bosnia," *Critique of Anthropology* 32, no. 1 (2012): 3–19; and Cornelia Sorabji, "Bosnian Neighbourhoods Revisited: Tolerance, Commitment and Komšiluk in Sarajevo," in *On the Margins of Religion*, ed. F. Pine and J. Pina-Cabral (Oxford: Berghahn, 2008): 97–112.
17. For example, see Pnina Werbner, "Essentialising Essentialism, Essentialising Silence: Ambivalence and Multiplicity in the Construction of Racism and Ethnicity," in *Debating Cultural Hybridity: Multi-Cultural Identities and the Politics of Anti-Racism*, ed. P. Werbner and T. Modood (London: Zed, 1997), 226–54; and Anthony P. Cohen, ed. *Signifying Identities: Anthropological Perspectives on Boundaries and Contested Values* (London: Routledge, 2000).
18. Albera, "'Why Are You Mixing?'" 53–56.
19. Bowman, "Orthodox–Muslim Interactions," 196.
20. Ibid., 199.
21. Ibid.
22. Muhamed Hadžijahić, "Sinkretistički elementi u Islamu u Bosni i Hercegovini," *Prilozi za orijentalnu filologiju* 28–29 (1978): 301–28.

23. See Bringa, *Being Muslim the Bosnian Way*, 169–77.
24. Francine Friedman, *The Bosnian Muslims: Denial of a Nation* (Boulder, CO: Westview Press, 1998).
25. Duijzings, *Religion and the Politics of Identity*, 112.
26. Bringa, *Being Muslim the Bosnian Way*, 199–200.
27. Enver Mulahalilović, *Vjerski običaji Muslimana u Bosni i Hercegovini* (Sarajevo: Starješinstvo Islamske Zajednice, 1989), 192–96.
28. As founding narratives, these motifs are characteristic for such charismatic living saints and sheikhs in other parts of the Muslim world and in the Central and South Asian context in particular; see Pnina Werbner and Helene Basu, eds., *Embodying Charisma: Modernity, Locality and the Performance of Emotion in Sufi Cults* (London: Routledge, 1998); and Stephen M. Lyon, *An Anthropological Analysis of Local Politics and Patronage in a Pakistani Village* (Lampeter, UK: Edwin Mellen Press, 2004).
29. Mulahalilović, *Vjerski običaji Muslimana u Bosni i Hercegovini*, 192–96.
30. *Mevlud*—honoring the birth of the Prophet Mohammad; *tevhid*—collective prayer for the souls of the dead; and *zikr*—remembrance of God's names and dervish recitation and praise of God.
31. Bringa, *Being Muslim the Bosnian Way*, 22; and Duijzings, *Religion and the Politics of Identity*. 107.
32. Duijzings even argues that "the official Islamic Community, in particular, was co-opted by the Communist system, more than the Catholic and Serbian Orthodox churches. . . . It was sometimes compared with a melon: green [the color of Islam] outside but thoroughly red inside." Ibid., 112. See also Bringa, *Being Muslim the Bosnian Way*, 221; and Hamid Algar, "Some Notes on the Naqshbandī Tarīqat in Bosnia," *Die Welt des Islams* 13, no. 3-4 (1971): 196.
33. See Algar, "Some Notes"; D. Čehajić, *Derviški redovi u Jugoslovenskim zemljama sa posebnim osvrtom na Bosnu i Hercegovinu* (Sarajevo: Orijentalni institut, 1986); and Bringa, *Being Muslim the Bosnian Way*.
34. Several authors, such as Popović and Duijzings, have pointed out that in the 1980s many dervish orders flourished in Yugoslavia and were often involved in the larger process of a so-called Islamic revival in Bosnia. However, this term seems to be rather misleading since it refers to Islam and Muslims generally, yet what happened in Bosnia in the 1980s was rather the emergence of political Islam in the terms of debates over collective identity. See Alexandre Popović, "The Contemporary Situation of the Muslim Mystic Orders in Yugoslavia," in *Islamic Dilemmas: Reformers, Nationalities and Industrialisation: The Southern Shore of the Mediterranean*, ed. Ernest Gellner, 240–54 (Berlin: Mouton, 1985); Cornelia Sorabji, "Islamic Revival and Marriage in Bosnia," *Journal of the Institute of*

Muslim Minority Affairs 9, no. 2 (1988): 331–37; and Duijzings, *Religion and the Politics of Identity*.

35. See Mulahalilović, *Vjerski običaji Muslimana u Bosni i Hercegovini*, 192–96.
36. See Rujanac, "Ajvatovica."
37. These quotes were taken from a website which no longer exists.
38. See Onder Cetin, "Mujahidin in Bosnia: From Ally to Challenger," *ISIM Newsletter* 21 (2008):14–15.
39. By "social aid" I mean an intersection of Islamism and humanitarianism; that is, a *da'wa* activity (call to Islam) modified to address local needs and problems. See Jonathan Benthall and Jérôme Bellion-Jourdan, *The Charitable Crescent: Politics of Aid in the Muslim World* (London: I. B. Taurius, 2003).
40. The verbs "*turćit*" or "*poturćit*" come from the period of Islamization and the spread of Ottoman cultural patterns, and mean "to Turkify oneself." The verbs' usage today is rather ambivalent or even negative. Noel Malcolm, *Bosnia: A Short History* (London: Macmillan, 1994), 59. For a similar argument in contemporary Bulgaria, see Kristen Ghodsee, *Muslim Lives in Eastern Europe: Gender, Ethnicity, and the Transformation of Islam in Postsocialist Bulgaria* (Princeton, NJ: Princeton University Press, 2010).
41. Duijzings, *Religion and the Politics of Identity*, 106–31.
42. Hadžijahić, "Sinkretistički elementi u Islamu u Bosni i Hercegovini"; and Bringa, *Being Muslim the Bosnian Way*, 247.
43. For example, Benthall and Bellion-Jourdan, *The Charitable Crescent*; and Bringa, *Being Muslim the Bosnian Way*, 226.
44. See Henig, "'Knocking on My Neighbour's Door'."
45. Hadžijahić, "Sinkretistički elementi u Islamu u Bosni i Hercegovini."
46. Bringa, *Being Muslim the Bosnian Way*, 172.
47. Ibid.
48. Harun Karčić, "Islamic Revival in Post-Socialist Bosnia and Herzegovina: International Actors and Activities," *Journal of Muslim Minority Affairs* 30, no. 4 (2010): 519–34.
49. See Bowman, "Orthodox–Muslim Interactions."
50. Ibid., 198.
51. Ibid.
52. Sarah Green, *Notes from the Balkans: Locating Marginality and Ambiguity on the Greek-Albanian Border* (Princeton, NJ: Princeton University Press, 2005).
53. Ibid., 140.
54. Ibid., 141.
55. See Bowman, "Orthodox–Muslim Interactions."
56. Ibid.

PALESTINE/ISRAEL

5

AT THE BOUNDARIES OF THE SACRED

THE REINVENTION OF EVERYDAY LIFE IN JERUSALEM'S AL-WAD STREET

WENDY PULLAN

WITH THE PROTRACTED conflict between Israelis and Palestinians embedded in Jerusalem, the possibility of shared space has become fraught with resentments and misunderstandings. Christian, Jewish, and Muslim faiths share some common traditions or overlap in their use of a number of sacred sites that have become major centers of contestation.[1] Disputes have raged and over the centuries different types of accommodation have been attempted with varying degrees of success. The term "status quo" emerged to describe designated long-standing holy places and the rights of their adherent faiths, but many sites endure an uneasy truce and periodically are the scene of violence.[2] While the status quo was effectively legalized by Israel at the beginning of its occupation in 1967, the situation has become increasingly radicalized in response to the First Intifada in 1987.[3] It has escalated again since 2000, after the failure of the Oslo Accords, through the years of the Second Intifada, and with the growing influence of the Jewish settler movements.[4] With its large number of holy places, Jerusalem is particularly affected. Historically, there have been examples of holy places that were venerated by more than one faith where certain common traditions were recognized.[5] Today, however, boundaries have been firmly drawn, and any threat to those boundaries only fuels the wider Israeli/Palestinian conflict. Christian sites do figure in this contest, but the heaviest disputes concern the relationship between Jews and Muslims and their holy places.

In Jerusalem's walled Old City, the Muslim and Jewish site of the Haram al-Sharif/Temple Mount is central to both religions, and to the conflict.[6] Policing is pervasive and worshippers of the different faiths are kept apart by an elaborate combination of regulations, custom, surveillance, and security. Muslims worship on top of the plateau, where the Dome of the Rock and al-Aqsa Mosque, as well as many other shrines, draw the faithful.[7] Below, along the southwest retaining wall of the enclosure, is the Kotel Ha-Maaravi or Western Wall, where Jews pray at the last remains of the Second Temple.[8] The two sites stand together, one poised above the other and well in view of each other, but each has different constituencies, faiths, practices, architecture, and access routes (see figures 5.1, 5.2).

The Haram, sometimes referred to today as the fifth quarter of the Old City, is a compound defined by an enclosing wall and accessed by well-guarded gates; it is adjoined on two sides by the Muslim Quarter and on the south by the Jewish Quarter. The Kotel area is a large plaza on the edge of the Jewish Quarter, abutting the Muslim Quarter to the north.[9] All access streets to the Kotel plaza end in checkpoints heavily monitored by Israeli security personnel and, for all intents and purposes, it has become a compound. Both of these sites—Haram and Kotel—are restricted to their own religious adherents; as such, they are excellent examples of religious segregation. Together they present the kind of close proximity combined, at least superficially, with detached interest that is common throughout much of Jerusalem. When this fragile separation is breached, long and violent repercussions may result, as when Israel's Ariel Sharon entered into the Haram area in 2000, provoking the Second, or al-Aqsa, Intifada. These areas, with or without violence, have become associated with how we picture Islamic and Jewish Jerusalem; they are what the world sees on television, computer screens, and in vivid pictures in the printed press. They are both iconic and highly controlled.

In the thoroughfares of the Muslim Quarter that surround the Haram and lead to the Kotel, a different choreography takes place. These are narrow city streets and alleyways, and many of them are at the center of urban neighborhoods (figure 5.1). Although Israeli security cameras

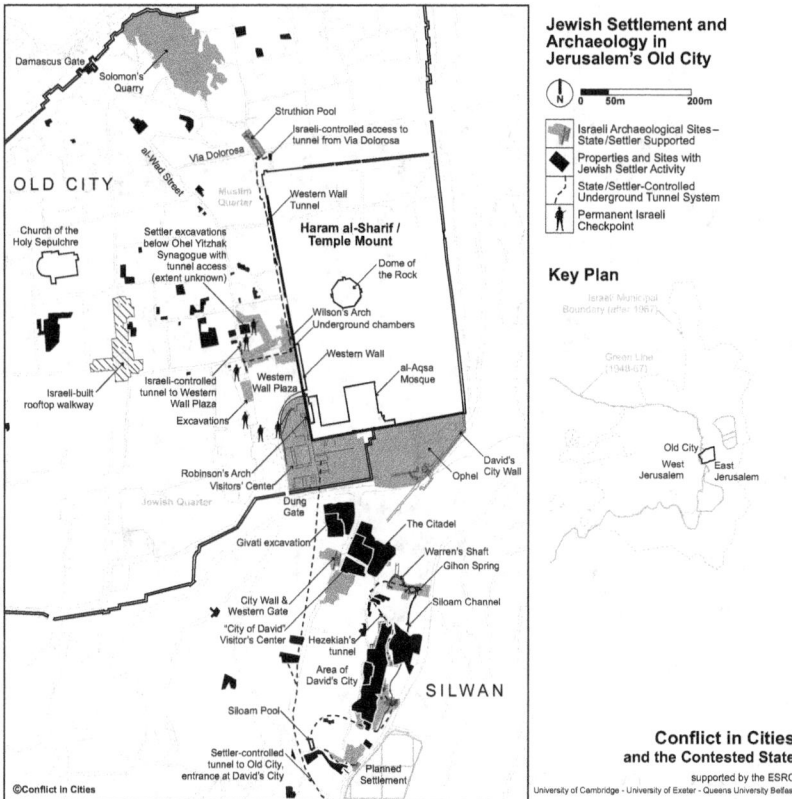

FIGURE 5.1 MAP OF JERUSALEM'S OLD CITY AND SILWAN, SHOWING JEWISH SETTLEMENTS AND ARCHAEOLOGICAL SITES NEAR THE HARAM AL-SHARIF.

(Conflict in Cities)

abound and there are periods of military presence and restricted access, much of the time people come and go with relatively minimal levels of control. A number of the streets provide access to the holy places, and auxiliary religious institutions such as small mosques and synagogues, madrasas and yeshivas, have grown up along these routes, heralding the proximity of the main sites. Some of these religious sites are recently "rediscovered" or invented, and the authenticity of even the more established ones may be contested. In this essay, I concentrate upon what adherents believe about the sites and their religious values rather than trying to determine facts about them with historical accuracy. In

FIGURE 5.2 THE WESTERN WALL (KOTEL HA-MAARAVI) WITH THE HARAM AL-SHARIF ABOVE. THE DOME OF THE ROCK IS VISIBLE ON THE LEFT.

(Conflict in Cities)

addition to religious institutions, the area is filled with residential and commercial structures, places of everyday life in Jerusalem's Old City. Tariq al-Wad, or al-Wad Street, is an active example (figure 5.3).

It runs the length of the Muslim Quarter from Damascus Gate in the north to the Kotel and Jewish Quarter in the south. As the key thoroughfare along the western edge of the Haram al-Sharif, it functions as both a border and a connector between Muslim and Jewish sacred terrains. At one point it is crossed by the Christian Via Dolorosa, which attracts Western tourists. It accumulates a mixture of religious sites, people, and practices, and if the Haram and Kotel are particularly segregated, al-Wad Street is heterogeneous.

These are highly charged urban spaces; along with religious affiliations, national and ethnic identities are formed in a topography where much of Jerusalem's present conflicts play out. Because Tariq al-Wad is a market area, its ostensibly more secular nature can accommodate a looser and sometimes more personal competition of sacred topographies.

AT THE BOUNDARIES OF THE SACRED | 167

Many aspects of the street culture display a combination of political allegiance and religious identity in, for example, the decoration and signage of the buildings, the goods for sale, the graffiti on the walls, and the sounds of taped sermons. The topography has been marked with various endorsements of national aspirations that are underlain with and supported by recent socioeconomic development. Above all, it is an environment where spatial experience is articulated by a potent mix of imagery, materiality, and aurality. A color, a bit of song, a specially draped piece of fabric, or even a scent immediately cues the cultural richness of a particular community. Many of these are expressions of religious allegiance, but, notably, they also promote—often subversively—national ambitions. Benedict Anderson and others have focused on the role of political narratives in forming such imagined communities.[10] My study of the Tariq al-Wad area does indeed reveal the envisioning of communities, but here it is material culture and the spaces that contain its many variations that are particularly significant for determining religio-political affiliations.

FIGURE 5.3 VIEW OF AL-WAD STREET.

(Conflict in Cities)

Although al-Wad Street is essentially a market—a secular area by modern standards—it is important to ask how its situation at the edge or boundary of a crucial shared sacred site affects the way both inhabitants and visitors act, and how this peripheral area in turn contributes to the playing out of religious conflicts centered on the threefold pieties of Jerusalem's major faiths. This border area acts as a transitional zone on the way to and from more holy domains and, in this sense, not only separates but also communicates between or mediates secular and sacred territories. It also functions as a rich topography of religio-political life grounded in everyday practices. Most of all, it is home to various groups who wish to assert their religio-political identities connected to the sacred sites proper and yet, for a variety of reasons, see fit to do this outside the holy sites.

This essay explores how al-Wad Street has become a new arena of conflict in Jerusalem. I concentrate less upon political policy than upon the cultural construction of the various sites and artifacts in the market street that both emerge from and enable intense levels of popular partisan political participation. It reflects not a polarization of sacred and profane but more nuanced conditions at the boundaries of the sacred, where religious practices and beliefs permeate mundane situations and everyday acts. In contrast to this environment, I also consider a recent attempt to interpret an archaeological site, known as the Western Wall Tunnel, as a holy place. This relatively new creation has been isolated from these quotidian settings and delineated from the world of the street. There we find a contrasting mode of intervention for asserting religious and national claims beneath the major holy places.

THE PERMEABILITY OF "SACRED SPACE"

While modern discourse tends to regard sacred and secular space as opposing modes of being, the patterns found in al-Wad Street do not fit easily into one category or another, and it is important to consider why experience on the ground may contradict the dominant theories of sacred space. The modern distinction between sacred and profane was initially made by Emile Durkheim in the nineteenth century and further developed in the mid-twentieth century by Mircea Eliade.[11] In his major studies, Eliade explains the sacred and profane as "two modes of being in the world, two existential situations assumed by man in the course of history.... In the last analysis, the sacred and profane modes of being depend upon the different positions that man has conquered in the cosmos."[12] And he further contends that "the idea of the sacred place involves the notion of repeating the primary hierophany which consecrated the place by marking it out, by cutting it off from the profane space around it."[13]

Although Eliade's theories have been questioned over the latter part of the twentieth century, the polarizing notions of sacred and profane have remained prominent.[14] As opposed and absolute terms, they may be referred to in modern times as "sacred" and "secular," with the latter deriving from *saeculum*—an other, separate, and different space. "Profane," on the other hand, simply comes from *profanum*, outside the temple, and is thus relational. The post-Enlightenment opposition of sacred and secular tends to reflect its own neutral disposition of space itself, which favors clear divisions without bleeding borders, where rich or ambiguous differentiation has little place.[15] This concept fundamentally opposes certain philosophical stances for which space is a continuity, where the world is "a single horizon that embraces everything contained in historical consciousness."[16] It is likewise not reflected in recent theories that stress the interrelatedness and multiplicity of meanings in space.[17]

The boundaries of sacred space may be permeable points of transformation. This is not to belittle the special qualities of religious sites, nor is it meant to devalue the significance of the sacred center of a holy place for those who venerate it; rather, the center is made visible and understood by its wider orientation rather than by a hard break with the profane. There prevails a deep reciprocity between the typicality of praxis and the uniqueness and intensity of the ritual or symbolic mediation with the divine. So everyday life and space become major players in configuring religious experience. If we see the sacred and the profane not as opposed phenomena but as part of a continuous but differentiated structure, they reflect certain broader, contemporary spatial conceptions, offering a more credible platform for talking about sacred space today. This is the direction I will follow for the present discussion in order to interpret the activities observed in al-Wad Street in Jerusalem's Old City. This approach will help to explain these events as being, at one and the same time, part of both the holy places and the mundane world. Furthermore, such thinking may encourage alternatives to the common practice of designating spaces in cities as only sacred or only secular, consequently severing them completely from surrounding areas.

This thinking is especially important in conflict situations where contested holy places are regularly assigned to separate combatant groups; enforcing such measures requires establishing highly controlled formal authorities and administrations that often are not effective. Intense conflict management intervenes when holy places are disputed and violent, often leading to imposed divisions that fragment space or regiment its use in a way that is not in keeping with the practice and rituals associated with the site.[18] Some major shrines are administered so as to accommodate competing religious discourses rather than allow one to monopolize the site, although it would be fair to say that it becomes overwhelmingly difficult to maintain such diversity when religious differences emerge as surrogates for political disputes.[19] But it is also worth noting that the city itself may provide a more integral structure for accommodating diversity, even when there is a spillover of religious activities into areas where they might be unexpected. In Jerusalem's Old City, where many holy sites are highly regulated with military checkpoints at every entrance, the immediate areas beyond them in Tariq al-Wad remain remarkably mixed. Since there is no question that these boundary areas are highly contested, the mixing of populations does not necessarily indicate that urban space can be benignly shared, but it does demonstrate that space is elastic even when it is saturated with intense religious content.

PALESTINIAN AL-WAD STREET

Al-Wad Street extends almost the length of Jerusalem's walled city, running north–south from Damascus Gate until the entrance of the Western Wall Plaza. Because it runs along what in ancient times was known as the Tyropean Valley (both the Arabic *al-wad* and the Hebrew *ha-gai* mean valley), it has a topographical integrity that was recognized by the Romans when they constructed it as the eastern branch of the Cardo Maximus.[20] Today it is the main street of the Muslim Quarter, cutting through its densely populated fabric. Most importantly, it runs parallel to the western boundary wall of the Haram al-Sharif, linking into feeder streets that lead to the gates of the sacred Muslim compound (figure 5.1). Today the street presents a choice at its south end, either to continue through the Israeli checkpoint into the Kotel or to climb some steps and take a roundabout route, first to the east and then veering to the west, to continue into the Street of the Chain between the Muslim and Jewish Quarters (figure 5.4).

Tariq al-Wad and the streets leading from it into the Haram are major routes for Muslims on their way to Friday prayers, and most weeks they are thronged with people before and after the midday service. They act as a vestibule to the sacred compound, and many of the smaller cross streets have Mamluk religious or semi-religious structures that were built on either side during the Middle Ages to contain madrassas, pilgrims' hospices, dervish centers, and a large covered market with two bath houses.[21] Most of these structures themselves contain tombs and small mosques, and the combination of activities housed in these enclosures demonstrates that the Mamluks mixed different functions, oriented toward both the living and the dead, some more sacred and some more profane, in the immediate environment of the Haram. The building complexes engage well with the urban setting, forming a thick architectural rim on the edges of the sacred precinct and providing a transition along the side streets from the markets and residential areas of the city into the holy compound.

Today the al-Wad Street area responds to the politics of the Israeli/Palestinian conflict in ways that are rapid, acute, and visible. With the building of the separation barrier by the Israelis and the related imposition of closure policies that both predate and reinforce it, the area has been transformed. In the Jerusalem region, the barrier (or wall, as it is

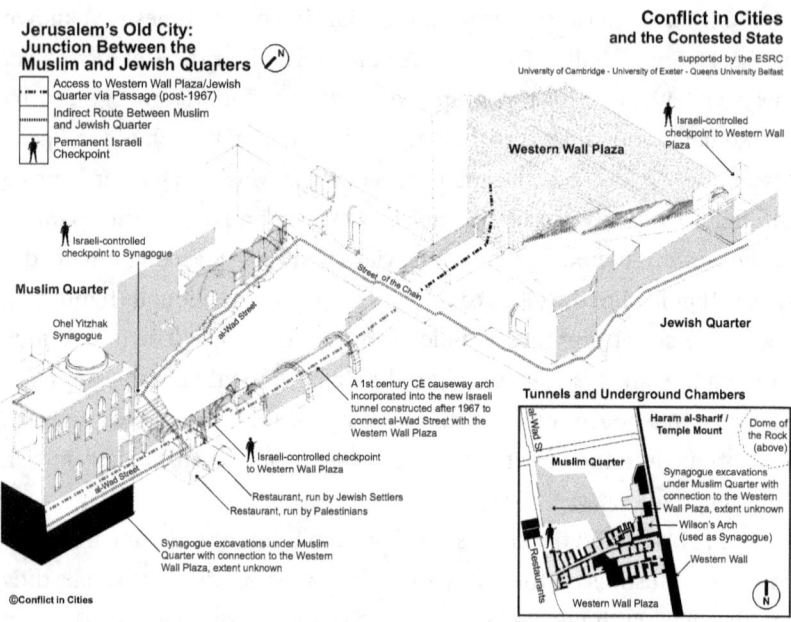

FIGURE 5.4 ANALYTICAL VIEW OF THE JUNCTION BETWEEN THE MUSLIM AND JEWISH QUARTERS, AND PLAN OF SUBTERRANEAN CHAMBERS BENEATH THE JUNCTION.

(Conflict in Cities)

more commonly known) separates the Palestinian city from its hinterland in the West Bank.[22] The process of closure has been accretive, with checkpoints used in one way or another since the early years of the occupation and policies for separation accelerated by the Oslo agreements of 1991 and 1993.[23] However, Israeli-imposed closure policies that culminated in late 2005 have resulted in great changes: many Palestinians with Israeli-determined Jerusalem residency and identity cards had been living in West Bank towns and villages but rushed back to the city in order not to lose their status and rights with the closing of the city.[24] In many cases they did this without promise of employment or homes. The influx has affected the Old City and especially the Muslim Quarter, where low housing costs have attracted migrants from across the border, increasing the population by an estimated five thousand people in its already overcrowded thirty-one hectares. This has particularly affected al-Wad

AT THE BOUNDARIES OF THE SACRED | 173

Street, which for many years had been a quiet thoroughfare with a few local food shops and the odd stall selling tourist goods. Now shops are open along its whole length, many casual vendors sell herbs and vegetables on the street, and, especially on Fridays and Saturdays, it is crowded with shoppers. Superficially, this market street looks vibrant and prosperous, yet the reasons for its apparent urban success feed off the chaos and bias introduced by the occupation.[25]

In many ways, the goods for sale in the market reveal the situation for Palestinians in the Muslim Quarter. A closer look shows that among the piles of vegetables and baked goods, and the cheap clothes and household items made mostly in China, are many things that can be described as having Islamic content. In fact, the shops with Islamic goods have become so prevalent that nearly half of all market units sell them (figure 5.5).

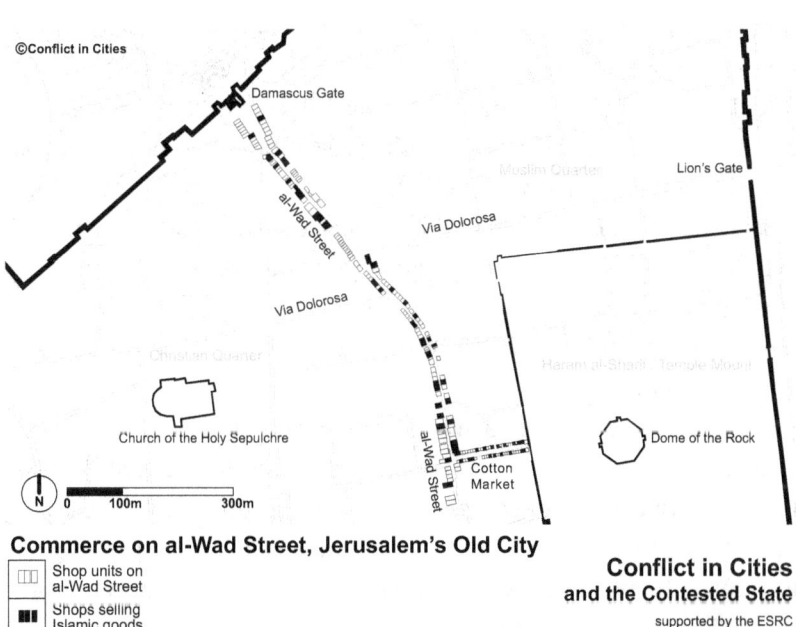

FIGURE 5.5   MAP OF AL-WAD STREET SHOWING SHOPS THAT SELL ISLAMIC GOODS.

(Conflict in Cities)

Many merchants sell the *hijab*—not just head scarves but various forms of long, loose-fitting garments that are traditional women's clothing have become common. Prayer beads, Qur'ans and their decorated cases and stands, plaques with proverbs from the Qur'an and Hadith, veiled dolls, and call-to-prayer clocks are also widely available. Islamic perfumeries that specialize in scent without alcohol have sprung up. A selection of these items may be obtained in even the most unexpected places: the hardware shop sells head scarves; the local grocer carries prayer beads. Many of them use signs that display a photo of the Dome of the Rock or al-Aqsa Mosque beside the name of their shop. Put simply by one market vendor: "We know who we are."[26] A number of merchants indicated in interviews that their businesses profit from the new emphasis on Islamic content on the street and among its shoppers.

Linking Tariq al-Wad with the Haram, the vaulted Cotton Market (or Suq al-Qattanin) contains a great concentration of Islamic goods. Built in 1336–1337 and lauded for its monumental architecture in the fifteenth century, it was known as a *qaysariya*, a market for precious goods like silk and cotton; nonetheless, by the nineteenth century it was abandoned and filled with rubbish.[27] Although the British restored it in the twentieth century, it never flourished as a market; suggestions for making it a folk museum or a city farm were never adopted. Now, in the early twenty-first century, it has been revived as an active market and an important entrance to the Haram al-Sharif, and it provides a location for Palestinian institutions including al-Quds University's Old City premises and the center for Israeli Muslims who wish to make the Hajj in the adjacent Hamam al-Ayn.

Today the Cotton Market no longer contains luxury items, but desirable objects of the contemporary Islamic trade, like digital Qur'ans, DVDs of sermons, jihadi computer games, and light boxes depicting Islamic holy places may be found. Concentrations of small sparkling objects catch the eye and recall *qaysariya* in the gleam of glass prayer beads, the gold print on Qur'an covers, and the silky fringes of veils (figure 5.6).

Few items are made in the workshops of Palestine. They come instead from other Arab countries or are mass produced in the factories of the Far East.[28] But in these markets along the Friday processional route to

FIGURE 5.6 PRAYER BEADS AND OTHER GLITTERY OBJECTS FOR SALE IN THE COTTON MARKET.

(Conflict in Cities)

the Haram, they are transformed into souvenirs with layered identities. On al-Wad Street, and particularly in the Cotton Market, the shops and stalls are encrusted with colorful and glittery goods. Some items visible among the goods, like jewelry and key rings with the map and colors of Palestine, display overt nationalism, but most are Islamic.[29] These items represent a global surge in Islamic culture and its accoutrements; at the same time, their prominent display likely reflects the Israeli authorities' greater tolerance for expressing religious rather than political identity.

In accord with these observations we may further identify two important aspects of the souvenirs: first, they acquire a level of value incongruent with their inherent worth as merchandise. They bring to mind what Michael Billig claims in *Banal Nationalism*, that "small words . . . offer constant, but barely conscious, reminders" and become, in turn, extremely important to those who repeat or reread them.[30] In the al-Wad Street markets, small objects may be banal, but national aspirations clearly underlie each one. Each mundane item is like a forbidden fruit, a national symbol or metaphor fought for and won, whose meaning emerges through its religious content. One merchant, for example, thrusting a handful of small glass prayer beads in my face, declared, "Here is Palestine."[31] Although many shopkeepers complain that they make very little money and are under regular assault by the Israeli authorities, more than one stated that it is important to keep the shops open in order to retain a Palestinian presence on the street.[32]

Second, most objects tend to be of a personal nature, appealing more to women than men as ornaments for the home and the body. By simply purchasing cheap but appealing accessories that combine national and religious iconography at micro scale, a Palestinian woman can assert her domestic role as part of a national struggle. One is reminded of Susan Stewart's interpretation of the miniature as a metaphor for the interior, and the gigantic for the state and collective.[33] Yet, with sovereignty denied, the larger state body in this case is incomplete and abstract. Instead the small-scale souvenirs and the glittery market itself offer some links between individuals and the community in a manner that is immediate, concrete, and easily shared. Empowered by purchasing these small and intimate goods, individuals are able to participate in a wider political community and to affirm Palestinian identity expressed as Islamic content.

On Friday mornings, Tariq al-Wad becomes a major pedestrian thoroughfare for Muslims making their way in this processional route to Friday prayers in the Haram al-Sharif. At times of unrest, Palestinians are vetted by Israeli soldiers and border police at Damascus Gate. Age and gender restrictions are often applied to prevent younger males from entering, but at almost all times, under the closure protocols, West Bank Muslims are barred from Jerusalem and thus excluded from the Haram.[34] Palestinians from inside Jerusalem have responded to this situation in large numbers, taking on the responsibility of populating the religious sites in order to make up for those who are prohibited from being there. The influx of worshippers has helped to increase business in the shops and stalls near the Haram, making them more lucrative for their owners. As well, impromptu markets have sprung up on Fridays along the footpaths into the gates to the Old City that lead to the Haram; one route into Lions' Gate even traverses an Islamic cemetery. Men smoke and drink coffee in a small café in the Cotton Market until almost the last minute before the service begins, then rush into the compound. Many come without prayer carpets, and a glimpse through the gate shows them waiting around with no intention of praying, there only to add their bodies to the crowd and represent those who are forbidden, against their own wishes, to be present.

One distinct group of visitors is Muslims from the north of Israel who are Israeli citizens, and therefore free to pray at the holy places of Jerusalem (figure 5.7). The prominence of these religious tourists is recent, stemming largely from the vacuum of political and economic power created in Palestinian Jerusalem as a result of the separation barrier and closure policies. Islamic religious and political groups from northern Israel have stepped into this void.[35] They have developed package tours to bring in groups by coach for the day to pray at al-Aqsa; sermons, often with political content, are included in the tour and sometimes delivered by Sheikh Raed Salah, leader of the Islamic Movement in the north of Israel.[36] The internal tourists are also taken to Islamic sites in the Old City, and then to eat and shop in the Muslim Quarter, very often in al-Wad Street and the Cotton Market. The merchants in the market report that much of their business comes from the north. Some merchants even suggest that the religious tourists purchase their products specifically in order to support the Palestinians of Jerusalem.[37]

FIGURE 5.7 RELIGIOUS TOURISTS FROM THE NORTH OF ISRAEL VIEWING THE DOME OF THE ROCK; AL-WAD STREET IS BELOW.

(Conflict in Cities)

This new form of tourism in Jerusalem lies in the gray area between religion and politics. Certainly, many of the Israeli Muslims travel there for religious purposes; at the same time, they regard their involvement with al-Aqsa as a demonstration of renewed interest in religion within a system that offers them scant possibilities to assert their identity in other ways.[38] And the more frequently that the slogan "protect al-Aqsa" appears in graffiti and is heard in the Palestinian street, the more these visits can be perceived as actions to support Islamic Jerusalem against encroachment by Jewish settlers and unwanted interference by the Israeli authorities. Palestinians regard the pressures on Muslim Jerusalem as an existential threat, and many believe it is their religious duty to counter it.[39] One member of a tour group from Taiba, in Israel's north, when asked where she was from, claimed that her real home was "here" while pointing toward the Dome of the Rock (figure 5.7).[40] These tours enable Israeli Muslims to participate in the struggle for Jerusalem's Islamic holy places, offering them a political identity that has been denied in Israel. Souvenirs from the Old City market authenticate that connection and commemorate Islamic tourists' experiences and actions in Jerusalem from a distance after they return home. Stewart acknowledges that the souvenir is incomplete when she writes that it is rooted "in a context of origin through a language of longing."[41] Buyers of Old City trinkets may ultimately see their longing as the desire for a nation. For the time being, however, as much as that desire remains unfulfilled, small purchases made near the Haram help to preserve and enhance that yearning.

Activity in al-Wad Street and its markets follows in a general sense the received Palestinian religio-political narrative; at the same time, the area allows more personalized interpretations that suit smaller groups and individuals and still conform to the protocols that are appropriate for the area. As an edge between the sacred terrain of the Haram and the rest of the city, al-Wad Street is both a testing ground and a repository for slightly unexpected and ad hoc practices. To what extent this feeds the radicalization of the Palestinian street is not clear. Nonetheless, the area certainly provides fertile ground for the expression of otherwise restricted identities.

JEWISH SETTLEMENTS AND ARCHAEOLOGY IN THE MUSLIM QUARTER

The al-Wad Street area has become the destination for certain Jewish groups who are also motivated by its proximity to the holy places, in this case, the Temple Mount (now the Haram) and the Kotel. Unlike the Palestinians, these people engage very little in commercial activities; rather, they focus on residential, institutional, and archaeological sites. At its southern extremity, al-Wad Street ends at a checkpoint inside a tunnel leading into the Kotel and Jewish Quarter; normally only Jewish Israelis or foreigners pass beyond this point (figure 5.4). The checkpoint is not heavily used since many more Jewish Israelis and Jewish tourists enter the Kotel area from the west via Jaffa Gate, or coaches and taxis take them to Dung Gate in the south. But Jewish presence in al-Wad Street and the Muslim Quarter has been established in the form of settlement by radical right-wing groups who buy property there. Their aims are ideologically extreme, based on the belief that they are divinely entitled to settle in all parts of Eretz Israel (the biblical Land of Israel) without regard for other inhabitants or other rights and claims on land and buildings.[42] While they have bought property in many locations throughout the Christian and Muslim Quarters, and the map shows a fragmented pattern of holdings, they tend to cluster around al-Wad Street mainly because it is so close to the Temple Mount (figure 5.1). It is common to find groups of yeshiva students, settler families, and the ubiquitous security guards; a number of the men carry weapons. Settlement in the Muslim Quarter continues with the support, both explicit and tacit, of the Israeli government. The home of former Israeli prime minister Ariel Sharon, part of which forms a prominent bridge over the al-Wad Street market, is a constant reminder of that official encouragement (figure 5.8).[43]

Other more modest structures function as family homes, synagogues, and yeshivas. The settlers buy and occupy whatever they can procure: a flat, a whole floor, sometimes only a room, occasionally an entire building.[44] This means that they often share entrances, courtyards, or stairwells with Palestinians, and friction is inevitable. Sometimes interactions are malicious; portions of the market are roofed in wire net to protect shoppers from objects hurled down from above.[45]

Not all of the Jews who pass through the Muslim Quarter are settlers. Al-Wad Street has long formed a direct pedestrian route to the Kotel for the residents of orthodox neighborhoods in West Jerusalem and, especially before prayers on Fridays at sunset, many use it to traverse the Old City (figure 5.3). Some of these people are antinationalists and are there for purely religious reasons.[46] But others, including settlers and tourists, may follow al-Wad Street from Damascus Gate in the north, pass through the checkpoint at its southern end, cross the Western Wall Plaza, and arrive at new nationalist holdings south of the Old City in Palestinian Silwan or, as Israelis often refer to it, David's City.[47] On the map, the spatial contiguity of settler properties and archaeological sites shows the extent

FIGURE 5.8 MUSLIMS RETURNING FROM FRIDAY PRAYERS; ARIEL SHARON'S HOME SPANS THE STREET ABOVE.

(Conflict in Cities)

to which Jewish territory has been consolidated in the Old City and its environs (figure 5.1).

Jewish collective memory of the destruction of the Second Temple, which has characterized much Jewish theology and ritual ever since, is regularly invoked in the Wad Street area and often exploited to legitimate nationalist undertakings. Before the Islamic conquests in the seventh century, the Haram al-Sharif was the precinct of the ruins of Herod's or the Second Jewish Temple, believed to have been built on the site of Solomon's or the First Temple. After the destruction in 70 CE, the ruins were venerated by Jews who returned regularly to weep over them. Little more than biblical description is known of the First Temple, but Roman period archaeological remains have been found, and the outer retaining wall of the Haram is understood to have been the enclosure of the whole Temple Mount platform. Just as al-Wad Street runs parallel to the western edge of the Haram and feeds access roads to the Islamic compound today, a similar thoroughfare ran parallel to the Jewish sacred enclosure in Roman times. Today al-Wad Street leads through the checkpoint and out into the large plaza of the Western Wall. Here the Kotel, an exposed piece of retaining wall, is considered the major and most sacred of the remains of Herod's Temple (figure 5.2). Many orthodox Jews even today do not enter the grounds of the Haram since they believe that the Holy of Holies was lost there in the destruction of 70 CE and that a Jew must not risk treading on it unwittingly. Needless to say, Muslims would not welcome Jewish worshippers in the Haram. Because of this situation, religious Jews find certain places outside and along the edge of what is today the Haram very attractive. In some cases, these sites have only recently been "rediscovered" and deemed sacred; for example, farther north along the retaining wall, another smaller section is exposed, sometimes called the Little Kotel. The site is not consecrated, as the large Kotel is, and prayers are held mostly on an ad hoc basis, often by yeshiva students. This wall stands in the middle of a Palestinian residential neighborhood, and Jewish worship there tends to be provocative and disruptive for local inhabitants. Most immediately, the conflict involves confrontations between residents and students, but behind these local manifestations is Israeli government support for Jewish worship at the site. This is seen by

Palestinians as a contravention of the delicate status quo that determines the use of the holy places.[48] The situation is indicative of the problem of extending sacred territories in Jerusalem, for whatever reason.

Unlike the impressive Muslim buildings of the Haram al-Sharif, the primary Jewish holy places in Jerusalem are essentially ruins and fragments, reminders of the past. Their condition as ruins usually requires that some reinforcement or even reinvention is necessary if they are to be recognized and used as holy places, and new religious narratives and practices may need to be furnished to make the sites convincing. At the same time, the outwardly secular pursuit of archaeology has become the favored channel for concretizing shifting memories, and it seemingly legitimizes what may be regarded as dubious holy sites. Much has been written about the Israeli affinity for archaeology and, indeed, the religious and political agendas of Holy Land archaeology since the nineteenth century.[49] In more recent years, the settler organizations have become particularly proficient at using their excavations and tourist sites to demonstrate the historical longevity and religious auspiciousness of the Jewish people, and thereby to Judaize present day Jerusalem; the al-Wad Street area is central to their strategy.[50] If we return to the map of settler sites (figure 5.1), it is clear that the combination of settler property and archaeological excavations constitutes a continuous and intense swath of control running through the city in the al-Wad Street area and south to Silwan. The vertical implications are also profound; in the Muslim Quarter, settlers tend to own property above street level and on the rooftops, and to occupy archaeological sites underground, thus sandwiching the Palestinians, whose commercial, social, and religious life exists mostly at street level (figure 5.8). A number of underground sites connect and extend existing ancient and medieval cisterns and chambers. Tunneling in the al-Wad Street area alarms Palestinian residents who worry about subsidence of their properties. There has been widespread concern for digging underneath the Haram.[51] The combination of settlement and archaeology both oversees and undermines the Palestinians at street level, who fear they will be squeezed out completely.

Perhaps the most notorious of the subterranean sites is the Western Wall Tunnel, an excavation of linked passages and chambers that form a major route running along the outside of the base of the Haram al-Sharif's western retaining wall (figures 5.1 and 5.4).[52] Now located below ground level, this was an ancient commercial street with shops on both sides. Under the Romans, it ran along the Temple Mount wall underneath two large vaulted causeways (known as Wilson's Arch and Robinson's Arch) that formed the entrances, above, to the temple compound.[53] After 1967 the tunnel was extended to the full length of the retaining wall, and in 1996 it opened as a major tourist site that allowed visitors to enter from the Western Wall Plaza and exit in the Via Dolorosa, in the middle of the Muslim Quarter. The opening immediately provoked major rioting, during which seventy-five Palestinian civilians and fifteen Israeli soldiers were killed.

The tunnel now connects via underground passages to excavations located directly on al-Wad Street, beneath the Ohel Yitzhak Synagogue (completed in 1904; figure 5.4), which had been abandoned by its congregation during the Arab uprising of 1929.[54] Since 2004 it has been enlarged and restored by the settler group Ateret Cohanim.[55] Its main entrance is from al-Wad Street, and the building presents an imposing and active Jewish religious site in this Palestinian neighborhood. Across the street and just a few meters from the checkpoint to the Jewish Quarter, a kosher restaurant has been established, presumably to attract the tourists who visit the synagogue as an important example of the restored Jewish presence in the Muslim Quarter.[56] Opened between the Jewish and Muslim Quarters in the post-1967 period, the checkpoint is effectively closed to Palestinians; however, Israelis and foreigners can make forays into the Muslim Quarter to see the synagogue. An alternative underground entrance to Ohel Yitzhak connects to the main Western Wall Tunnel that is accessed from the Western Wall Plaza. Together the two routes complete a controlled circle that allows tourists to be shepherded into a Muslim Quarter made to look, for all intents and purposes, Jewish. Like many colonial incursions, the development contributes little indigenous life of its own to the city street and, unsurprisingly, drives local Palestinian commerce from this part of the Muslim Quarter.

The Jewish religious content of the Western Wall Tunnel has been made uncompromising and unambiguous. Whereas most ancient sites in

Israel are managed by the Israel Antiquities Authority, the tunnel is under the auspices of the Ministry of Religion and managed by the Western Wall Heritage Foundation, a charity established in 1988 by the government of Israel.[57] Since the tourist site is intended to attract foreign and Israeli Jews, it targets the desired audience with a strong religio-nationalist message by permitting entry only from the Western Wall Plaza, requiring preregistration by credit card, and allowing visits only by organized tours. At the entrance, male visitors are asked to cover their heads according to Jewish custom, and in chambers identified for worship, men and women pray separately in the orthodox fashion. Prayers are directed east toward what had been the temple; one chamber is particularly significant because worshippers believe it to face directly through the earth to the location of what had been the Holy of Holies, lost when the temple was destroyed nearly two thousand years ago (figure 5.9).

FIGURE 5.9 WORSHIPPERS PRAY IN THE DIRECTION OF THE HOLY OF HOLIES IN THE WESTERN WALL TUNNEL.

(Conflict in Cities)

FIGURE 5.10 INSIDE THE WESTERN WALL TUNNEL.

(Conflict in Cities)

During one of my visits, the tour guide asked whether the group would like time to stop and say a prayer there, assuming a level of piety and unified religious affiliation in a group of unconnected, mostly foreign, English-speaking visitors. The tunnel is rendered simply and monumentally in bare rock, without decoration, helping to equate the present religious experience with the fundamental properties of the earth itself (figure 5.10), conforming to anthropologist Nadia Abu El-Haj's observation that "the historical is produced as transparent by eliminating as much as possible any signs of the production and restoration process."[58]

The tour guides emphasize the archaeologists' professional need to reach the bare rock as a basis of truth. For some, such a fundamental response recalls not just ancient times but, ultimately, an ahistorical act, a discovery of what is God-given in the primordial nature of the earth itself. Yet it is worth remembering that the place that today commands this veneration was simply a Roman street outside the temple compound, inauspicious and commercial. Unlike the Muslims who encrust al-Wad Street with religious souvenirs to search for inspiration in the quotidian aspects of their cause, the Jews have spurned the memory of the market street in order to attain and expose the wondrous appeal of bedrock itself. Yet in both instances a newly radicalized topography is being choreographed by bestowing religious significance on what is seemingly secular.

RELIGIO-POLITICS, SACRED SPACE AND THE URBAN EVERYDAY

Both Palestinian and Israeli activities in the boundary areas of al-Wad Street are choreographed to articulate and bolster their claims to the holy places of the Haram al-Sharif/Temple Mount. In practice, their religious and national aims are opposed but firmly intertwined, and they are sometimes difficult to distinguish. The Palestinian focus on Islam is symptomatic of increased worldwide interest and activism and has often been connected to the "recent forcing of nationalized communities upon . . . sacred spaces."[59] More specifically, in Jerusalem the new religiosity masks nationalistic goals that are unrealized and to some extent unexpressed. As for Israel, its official attitude to Jerusalem initially concentrated on the city's political status, a stance typical of secular Zionism, but even that interest, Tamar Mayer argues, was absent or minimal until East Jerusalem was captured in the 1967 war.[60] At that point, the holy places became integral to the national equation, and "every soldier's duty was to defend the [Western] Wall."[61] More than ever, this sort of refrain is heard in right-wing Israeli circles today in an uncanny echo of Sheikh Salah's call for Muslims to protect al-Aqsa.

For all the similarities of increasingly emotional and militant religious and political concerns, there are some key variations in the nature of the urban spaces that have developed around the holy sites. Clearly, the Palestinian markets, with their adjacent residential and institutional courtyards, form a living city that is multifunctional and incorporates both religio-political activism and the mundane repetitiveness of everyday life. The market retains a high capacity to contain many conflicting scenarios, often at micro scale, and it readily accommodates practices of survival, dissent, resilience, resistance, and oppression. Historically markets have always been more than places to buy and sell goods; since the ancient agora in Greece, their role has been economic, religious, political, and social, with a complex architecture and ritual topography that developed over time to embody aspects of civic order. In a broad sense, al-Wad Street and the Cotton Market are residues of this history, so it is not surprising to encounter a mixture of religious doctrines and political proclamations amid the Palestinian shops and stalls, signage, and consumer goods.

It would be fair to say that even the extreme and controversial presence of the Jewish residential settlements in the Muslim Quarter also depends upon the capability of the markets to be sufficiently flexible to absorb, at least to some degree, such contentious everyday activities. Both Jewish and Muslim groups present an odd combination of radical ideologies couched in mundane practices, and, as Hannah Arendt has well demonstrated, associating banality with the benign is often misleading and can be dangerous.⁶² Nor, as Billig points out, should we simply assign either positive or negative judgments upon nationalism, favoring the anticolonial over the fascist. Banal nationalism is neither innocent nor harmless, no matter what its ideological guise.⁶³ Since the national expressions of both Jews and Muslims in al-Wad Street are so often everyday practices rooted in a mundane setting, it is worth attaching the same warning to what manifests as vibrant urban life but clearly has underlying intents. Ordinary urban structures—streets, courtyards, and markets—have formed a frontier around the primary holy places of Haram and Kotel, and they absorb and accommodate religious praxis in the secular setting so well as to make it a primary zone of political conflict.

The Western Wall Tunnel presents a different setting with a choreography that contrasts markedly from that observed in the market streets. The quasi-religious, cave-like spaces have been developed and administered for Jewish visitors, Jewish worship, and Jewish national sensibilities. The isolation of these underground passages and chambers supports such a homogeneous purpose, and the monumental, even monolithic, physical qualities of the spaces take on their own minimalistic aesthetic, offering little possibility for incorporating other contrary religious or political imagery. In the tunnel there is an attempt to enhance what is believed to be a fragment of the temple and to symbolically restore its integrity and make it whole again in a way that is relevant today. Yet a fragment cannot so easily represent the whole from which it was torn or be reunited with its lost context, and the effort to make it do so often results in abstract and unsituated interventions that depend upon "simulated integrity."⁶⁴ All the same, such fragments can also acquire their own strange potency. In his discussion of fragmentation as a modern phenomenon, Dalibor Vesely states: "An object taken out of its context, and an artificial ruin often initiate symbolic meaning and reference more powerfully than does the piece intact in its original setting."⁶⁵ He goes on to quote Diderot: "One must ruin a palace in order to make it interesting."⁶⁶ The great popularity of the tunnel, with its Jewish visitors, confirms this. Not simply a place of prayer, as is the Ohel Yitzhak Synagogue that stands above, but wedged underground between the Haram al-Sharif and the

Muslim Quarter, the tunnel has been created today as a reconnection with the long-buried Holy of Holies, to expose it as something forbidden yet significant.[67] Even secular people are encouraged to feel the mysterious power of connection with the hallowed earth.[68]

Continuing through the passage, the guide's explanation of how the rock was cut in order to let people pass eventually brings visitors back to a more ordinary sense of history. At the exit visitors find themselves among security guards and then enter into the middle of the Muslim Quarter, perhaps feeling more empowered after the experience of the tunnel. Zygmunt Bauman reminds us that the taboos associated with a sacred place may be accompanied by the suppression of the human "other" to establish a "we/they" duality that remains obstinate even outside specifically religious circumstances.[69] Here at ground zero of a city that suffers extremely high levels of political conflict, such a persistent frontier is easily transferred from the exclusivity of religious space back into the political space of the nation.

The tunnel has been reconstituted as a sacred place by the imagination of a certain ideological community, and, since it was a market street in ancient times, its authenticity may be questioned. It has been manipulated for tourist use even though it is presented as a found holy site.[70] But fashioning it in an exclusivist manner helps it to conform to some of the basic assumptions about sacred space that I outlined in my introduction and have tried to bring into question in this essay. In Eliadian terms, the tunnel is cut off from the profane space around it. Applying this idea to the contested arena of cities like Jerusalem, Ron Hassner has argued that the perceived dangers of desecrating a sacred place make it impossible to share it with members of a different religion without affecting the site's integrity. In consequence, he concludes that holy sites of any significance are indivisible.[71] Many aspects of the tunnel and its related underground chambers have been configured and presented to support such an assertion: the physical separation from its aboveground surroundings, the systems of controlled entry and participation that privilege one ethno-religious group, the archaeological transformation of its ancient existence as a commercial street into an ahistorical holy place, the dramatic and monolithic stone passages, and the exclusively Jewish narrative to interpret definitively a place that has multicultural meanings. The tunnel is manipulated and controlled in order to make it appear sacred, and in doing so, it becomes indivisible.

Al-Wad Street market, on the other hand, is, in Hassner's terms, divisible. Every square centimeter is contested, and violence is a regular threat, but the varied topography and everyday practices mean that it incorporates a range of religious discourses. Al-Wad Street market is permeable and flexible; while it refers to the holy sites it flanks, it is also, at least potentially, open to the tempering aspects of the city. Neither the tunnel nor the market has traditionally been understood as a holy place. In fact, being borderlands of Haram and Kotel, they are similarly liminal spaces; each space reveals a concentrated effort to claim it for the popular pieties and ideologies of its constituent people. But from an urban and topographic point of view, the market is open to the tempering capacities of the city while the tunnel has been closed against anything that disrupts its rigid order.

CONCLUSION

Sacred space clearly gives orientation to a city. While there may be attempts to posit its bounds in an incontrovertible way, associated activities and meanings bleed out beyond the holy places so that adjacent portions of the city become implicated in their rituals and practices. In a city such as Jerusalem, where holy places are major focal points for conflict, a complex topography emerges in which areas adjacent to the sacred both make connections and act as contested theatres for religious and national identity; effectively, they constitute frontier areas where urban everyday life is incorporated into key aspects of the conflict.[72] Both communities are empowered by the contingencies of their location: one takes advantage of market goods, the other of archaeology. But the transactions in these spaces are not simply defined by interactions between embattled peoples. The physical settings and the artifacts found in them are themselves contentious in their configurations, connections, consumption, use, and meanings. The places do not only have a major role in how the conflict proceeds, they also act and are acted upon reciprocally with the players. Ideologies and meanings fluctuate back and forth between religious and political, partly in keeping with common forms of practice in the area but also governed by the sorts of action available to those involved. Hence, the tunnel is an elaborate site established and condoned by the state while the markets provide strongly subversive possibilities.

There are no obvious solutions to the conflicts here. None of the problems can be divorced from the wider political situation. There is no question that the illegal and often violent Jewish colonial settlement in the Muslim Quarter feeds the conflict, and state support for Jewish projects allows the settler sites to achieve a level of scale and control that is unattainable for any Palestinian initiative. Any comparison between the two always needs to recognize the asymmetry of the situation. Nonetheless, it is also apparent that there is power in the street, especially in the harnessing of everyday life. Moreover, it is also evident that heavy regulation may function in a space like the tunnel, which is designed for control, but would have only limited effectiveness in the markets. The many days of unrest, rioting, and military crackdowns show that the tipping point in the markets is always close at hand. Yet, true to the nature of everyday life, al-Wad Street is relatively open and changing and may hold further surprises.

NOTES

This article forms part of a larger research project, "Conflict in Cities and the Contested State," supported by the Large Grants Programme of the Economic and Social Research Council (ESRC) of the United Kingdom (RES-060-25-0015). Further information may be found on the project's website: www.conflictincities.org. I should like to thank Nadera Karkaby for her fieldwork in Jerusalem and the north of Israel. She and Lefkos Kyriacou are responsible for the maps and drawings; between them they have made a significant contribution to the visual depictions in this essay. I have presented this research in various versions, including the Columbia University conference Choreography of Sacred Space, in Istanbul; the Jerusalem: City Portraits conference at the

University of Venice; and at seminars at the Max Planck Institute for the Study of Religious and Ethnic Diversity and the Cambridge University Department of Sociology. I am grateful for comments and advice that emerged from discussions in these sessions.

1. For an extended investigation of contested Muslim and Jewish holy sites in Jerusalem today, see Wendy Pullan, Maximilian Sternberg, Lefkos Kyriacou, Craig Larkin, and Mick Dumper, *The Struggle for Jerusalem's Holy Places* (London: Routledge, 2013).
2. Established in modern times by the Ottomans and then again the British; see L. G. A. Cust, *The Status Quo in the Holy Places* (1929; facsimile ed., Jerusalem: Ariel, 1980); see also David E. Guinn, *Protecting Jerusalem's Holy Sites: A Strategy for Negotiating a Sacred Peace* (Cambridge: Cambridge University Press, 2006), 21–37; Michael Dumper, *The Politics of Sacred Space: The Old City of Jerusalem in the Middle East Conflict* (Boulder, CO: Lynne Rienner, 2002), 106–10.
3. *Protection of Holy Places Law*, vol. 1–2, "Jerusalem and the Holy Places," June 27, 1967; *Israel Ministry of Foreign Affairs* website, www.mfa.gov.il/MFA/Foreign+Relations/Israels+Foreign+Relations+since+1947/1947-1974/14+Protection+of+Holy+Places+Law.htm.
4. Guinn, *Protecting Jerusalem's Holy Sites*, 39–70.
5. Suleiman Ali Mourad, "The Symbolism of Jerusalem in Early Islam," in *Jerusalem: Idea and Reality*, ed. Tamar Mayer and Suleiman A. Mourad, 86–102 (London: Routledge, 2008).
6. For Jews, the walled compound of what the Bible calls Mount Moriah is known as the Temple Mount; although this is primarily a historical term referring to the site of the destroyed Jewish temples, it is used frequently today and still carries great meaning for Jews. Palestinians often call the area "al-Aqsa," referring to the Prophet Muhammad's Night Journey at the further mosque, or *al-aqsa* in Arabic, as described in the Qur'an. For Muslims, the compound is officially known as the Haram al-Sharif (Noble Sanctuary). Because this essay is primarily concerned with the Haram as a Muslim holy site today, this is the term that will be used, except when specifically referring to Jewish references to it.
7. This is Islam's third holiest site; for a selection of primary sources see F. E. Peters, *Jerusalem: The Holy City in the Eyes of Chroniclers, Visitors, Pilgrims and Prophets from the Days of Abraham to the Beginnings of Modern Times* (Princeton, NJ: Princeton University Press, 1985), chap. 5.
8. Today this is Judaism's most holy site of prayer; for a selection of primary sources see ibid., chap. 1–3.
9. The small space in front of the Kotel was enlarged into an open plaza in the days after the 1967 war; to do so, the Palestinian Mughrabi Quarter was demolished.

10. Benedict Anderson, *Imagined Communities: Reflections on the Origin and Spread of Nationalism*, rev. ed. (London: Verso, 2006); and Michael Billig, *Banal Nationalism* (London: Sage, 1995).
11. Emile Durkheim, *The Elementary Forms of the Religious Life* (New York: Free Press, 1965).
12. Mircea Eliade, *The Sacred and the Profane: The Nature of Religion* (New York: Harcourt, 1959), 14–15. Eliade's ideas on sacred space are presented most comprehensively in *The Sacred and the Profane*; the themes are reiterated often in Eliade's large oeuvre on the subject; see also *The Myth of the Eternal Return* (London: Arkana, 1989); *Image and Symbol* (Princeton, NJ: Princeton University Press, 1991), chap. 1; and *Patterns in Comparative Religion* (London: Sheed and Ward, 1958), chap. 1 and 10.
13. Eliade, *Patterns in Comparative Religion*, 368. See also ibid., 20.
14. The significance of the Eliadean understanding to modern scholarship should not be underestimated; a former student and colleague, Jonathan Z. Smith, calls him the giant who "taught all of us how and what to see"; Smith, "The Wobbling Pivot," in *Map Is Not Territory* (Leiden: Brill, 1978), 90. At the same time, Smith points out a number of problems in Eliade's ideas (88–103); see also Smith, *To Take Place: Toward Theory and Ritual* (Chicago: University of Chicago Press, 1987), 3; and Wendy Pullan, "'Sacred Space' as Mediation," in *The Church in the Industrial Landscape*, ed. Kees Doevendans and Gertjan van der Harst (Zoetermeer: Uitgeverij Boekencentrum, 2004), 247–63.
15. Pullan, "'Sacred Space' as Mediation," 248.
16. Hans-Georg Gadamer, *Truth and Method* (London: Sheed and Ward, 1975), 271.
17. Doreen Massey, *For Space* (Los Angeles: Sage, 2005).
18. Guinn, *Protecting Jerusalem's Holy Sites*; and Ron E. Hassner, *War on Sacred Grounds* (Ithaca, NY: Cornell University Press, 2009), 69–88.
19. John Eade and Michael J Sallnow, eds., *Contesting the Sacred: The Anthropology of Christian Pilgrimage* (London: Routledge, 1991); and Yitzak Reiter, "Contest of Cohabitation in Shared Holy Places?," in *Holy Places in the Israeli–Palestinian Conflict: Confrontation and Co-Existence*, ed. Marshall J. Breger, Yitzak Reiter, and Leonard Hammer, 158–77 (London: Routledge, 2010). Since Reiter wrote about coexistence at the Tomb of Samuel, the site has become a center for Jewish settlers, and the Muslim worship curtailed.
20. The Cardo Maximus is visible in the sixth century mosaic map found on the floor of the Church of St. George in Madaba, Jordan.
21. This is well documented in Michael Hamilton Burgoyne, *Mamluk Jerusalem: An Architectural Study* (London: British School of Archaeology in Jerusalem and World of Islam Festival Trust, 1987).

22. Omar Yousef, Rassem Khamaisi, Abdallah Owais, and Rami Nasrallah, *Jerusalem and Its Hinterland* (Jerusalem: International Peace and Cooperation Center, 2008). On the developing power vacuum in Palestinian Jerusalem, see Hillel Cohen, *The Rise and Fall of Arab Jerusalem: Palestinian Politics and the City Since 1967* (London: Routledge, 2011). Israel claims that the barrier is intended for security; the Palestinians regard it as part of a land grab. In the cities, it is a wall up to eight meters high, constructed of concrete, ostensibly to prevent sniping. In nonpopulated areas, it is a combination of security roads and wire fence to aid surveillance. It is built on Palestinian land. The closure policies involve a combination of physical barriers and separation with a disciplinary regime.
23. For a timeline of the wall 1995–2011, see "The Separation Wall and the Permit Regime in the 'Seam Zone,'" *Hamoked*, http://www.hamoked.org/timeline.aspx?pageID=timelineTheWall. For different points of view on the wall and its effects on Jerusalem, see Robert D. Brooks, ed., *The Wall: Fragmenting the Palestinian Fabric in Jerusalem* (Jerusalem: International Peace and Cooperation Center, 2007); and Israel Kimhi, ed., *The Security Fence around Jerusalem: Implications for the City and Its Residents* (Jerusalem: Jerusalem Institute for Israel Studies, 2006).
24. The identity cards are issued by the Israeli authorities and based on a census carried out in 1967. The blue Jerusalem card is coveted not only for the right to live in the city but also for Israeli social welfare benefits and the freedom of movement between the West Bank and Jerusalem.
25. Some of this is manifested economically; many of the shop owners complained about the high municipal tax (*arnona*) levied by the Israeli authorities and the little benefit they received from it. This and the following observations about al-Wad Street have benefited from interviews with the merchants and shoppers carried out by Conflict in Cities (CinC) in 2005 and again in 2009–2010.
26. CinC interview, October 20, 2009.
27. The Cotton Market structure is well documented in Burgoyne, *Mamluk Jerusalem*, 273–98. On *qaysariya*, see Al-Umari, in ibid., 277, 298n20. The history of the building is discussed in Burgoyne, *Mamluk Jerusalem*, 277.
28. One shopkeeper states: "We sell products from different places: from Egypt we get the *helal* [Islamic decorations] and *fawanies* [Islamic lights], from Jordan we get music, from Makkah we get Islamic perfume. We also make perfume with holy land infusions" (CinC interview, November 4, 2009). But on examination of many of these goods, one finds "China" stamped on the bottom.
29. Several shopkeepers spoke of the religious atmosphere of the route to the Haram. A few shops still sell Jewish and Christian souvenirs for tourists, reminiscent of an earlier, more relaxed time.

30. Billig, *Banal Nationalism*, 93. Much of Billig's interest is in the American experience.
31. CinC interview, October 20, 2009.
32. Nir Hasson, "Israeli reining in Old City merchants," *Haaretz*, August 21, 2009, www.haaretz.com/hasen/spages/1108762.html; CinC interviews 2009–2010; and CinC interview, October 23, 2009.
33. Susan Stewart, *On Longing: Narratives of the Miniature, the Gigantic, the Souvenir, the Collection* (Durham, NC: Duke University Press, 1993), xii.
34. During Muslim feast days, West Bank children and older men and women are sometimes admitted.
35. CinC interviews with Islamic tour organizers, November 2009. Package tours are organized by a number of groups, including the Northern Islamic Movement, the Southern Islamic Movement, El Bayarek, and al-Aqsa Association as well as certain mosques. Most tours are on Fridays or especially on Saturdays, the Jewish Sabbath, when Palestinians in Israel often do not work. On Muslim religious holidays extra tours are organized with reports of up to five hundred buses converging on Jerusalem.
36. On the Islamic Movement in Israel, see Michael Dumper and Craig Larkin, "Political Islam in Contested Jerusalem: The Emerging Role of Islamists from within Israel," *Conflict in Cities*, Working Paper 12, 2009, http://www.conflictincities.org/PDFs/WorkingPaper12_10.11.09.pdf.
37. CinC interview, October 23, 2009.
38. CinC interview, November 21, 2009.
39. Shaykh Salah became prominent by leading controversial excavations under al-Aqsa Mosque to rehabilitate what is known as the Marwani Prayer Hall; the effort culminated in Ariel Sharon's visit in 2000, with upward of one thousand aides, to inspect the hall; see Dumper and Larkin, "Political Islam in Contested Jerusalem."
40. CinC interview, September 4, 2010.
41. Stewart, *On Longing*, 135.
42. The main settler groups in the Old City have strong links to groups in the West Bank and are well represented in the Israeli parliament, ministries, and departments. On the settler organizations, see Dumper, *The Politics of Sacred Space*, chap. 3; Idith Zertal and Akiva Eldar, *Lords of the Land: The War Over Israel's Settlements in the Occupied Territories 1967–2007*, trans., V. Eden (New York: Nation Books, 2007); Gershom Gorenberg, *The End of Days: Fundamentalism and the Struggle for the Temple Mount* (Oxford: Oxford University Press, 2000); and Meir Margalit, *Seizing Control of Space in East Jerusalem* (Jerusalem: Sifrei Aliat Gag, 2010).

43. Many of the settler reclamations in the Old City have been extensively reported and documented; see the Israeli newspaper *Haaretz*, especially different views in articles by Nadav Shragai and Meron Rappaport, www.haaretz.com. See also Palestinian Academic Society for the Study of International Affairs, "Jerusalem Settlement Activities and Related Policies," June 2009, www.passia.org; and Margalit, *Seizing Control*.
44. In some cases the settlers have reoccupied houses that belonged to Jews before 1948; this contrasts with the policies for Palestinian property lost in 1948, which remains in Jewish hands. The settlers buy Palestinian property as well, in a complex series of carefully timed transactions using middlemen. Sometimes their techniques are coercive; the Palestinian vendors are no longer able to remain in the Old City, and most leave the country.
45. Wendy Pullan, "Frontier Urbanism: The Periphery at the Centre of Contested Cities," *Journal of Architecture* 16, no. 1 (2011): 15–35.
46. Some Jews believe that a Jewish state cannot be established without the coming of the Messiah.
47. On David's City and its grooming as a tourist site with religious content by the settler group El-Ad, see Wendy Pullan and Max Gwiazda, "The Biblical Present in Jerusalem's 'City of David,'" in *Memory Culture and the Contemporary City: Building Sites*, ed. A. Webber, U. Staiger, and H. Steiner, 106–25 (London: Palgrave Macmillan, 2009).
48. Akiva Eldar, "Jerusalem Opens Muslim Quarter Jewish Site to Prayer, Upsetting Status Quo," *Haaretz*, January 14, 2011, www.haaretz.com/print-edition/news/jerusalem-opens-muslim-quarter-jewish-site-to-prayer-upsetting-status-quo-1.336881
49. Neil Asher Silberman, *Digging for God and Country: Exploration in the Holy Land, 1799–1917* (New York: Doubleday, 1982). On Israel's use of archaeology for national purposes, see Nadia Abu El-Haj, *Facts on the Ground: Archaeological Practice and Territorial Self-Fashioning in Israeli Society* (Chicago: University of Chicago Press, 2001).
50. More specifically on the settlers' use of archaeology, see Raphael Greenberg, "Contested Sites: Archaeology and the Battle for Jerusalem," *Jewish Quarterly*, no. 208 (2007), http://jewishquarterly.org/2007/12/contested-sites/; and Raphael Greenberg, "Extreme Exposure: Archaeology in Jerusalem," *Conservation and Management of Archaeological Sites* 11, no. 3-4 (2009): 262–81. See also Abu el-Haj, *Facts on the Ground*.
51. James Hider, "Settlers Dig Tunnels Around Jerusalem," *Timesonline*, March 1, 2008, http://www.timesonline.co.uk/tol/news/world/middle_east/article3463264.ece.

52. The following is derived in part from my own visits in 2008, 2009, and 2011; see also Abu El-Haj's insightful analysis in *Facts on the Ground*, 201–38.
53. From the northern gate, the street cut diagonally across the city and then followed the edge of the temple compound. For reconstructions, see Meir Ben-Dov, *Historical Atlas of Jerusalem* (New York: Continuum, 2002), 109–10, 113.
54. Yehoshua Ben-Arieh, *Jerusalem in the Nineteenth Century: The Old City* (Jerusalem: Ben Zvi Institute; and New York: St. Martin's Press, 1984), 379.
55. Matthew Wagner, "'Lost' Synagogue Reopens in Jerusalem's Muslim Quarter," *Jerusalem Post*, October 15, 2008, http://www.jpost.com/Jewish-World/Jewish-News/Lost-synagogue-reopens-in-Jerusalems-Muslim-Quarter.
56. One of the aims of the settler organizations is to reclaim Jewish property in the Muslim Quarter lost before 1948; no similar claims by Palestinians have been allowed in pre-1967 Jewish areas of the city.
57. The foundation runs an extensive website: http://english.thekotel.org/; its home page displays the shield of the State of Israel and has close links to the settler organizations.
58. Abu El-Haj, *Facts on the Ground*, 220.
59. Khaldoun Samman, *Cities of God and Nationalism: Mecca, Jerusalem and Rome as Contested World Cities* (Boulder, CO: Paradigm, 2007), 4.
60. Tamar Mayer, "Jerusalem In and Out of Focus: The City in Zionist Ideology," in *Jerusalem*, ed. Tamar Mayer and Suleiman Mourad (New York: Routledge, 2008), 224–44.
61. Ibid., 238.
62. Hannah Arendt, *Eichmann in Jerusalem: A Report on the Banality of Evil* (New York: Viking Press, 1963).
63. Billig, *Banal Nationalism*, 7.
64. Dalibor Vesely, *Architecture in the Age of Divided Representation: The Question of Creativity in the Shadow of Production* (Cambridge, MA: MIT Press, 2004), 322.
65. Ibid.
66. Ibid., 323.
67. Judaism distinguishes between a place of prayer—that is, a synagogue (in Hebrew, *beit knesset*, literally, "a meeting house")—and the temple, which, as a place of sacrifice and the dwelling place of God, was a sacred place.
68. When asked about the stones facing what is believed to be the burial place of the Holy of Holies, the tour guide spoke of the connecting power of the earth.
69. Zygmunt Bauman, *Culture as Praxis*, rev. ed. (London: Sage, 1999), 101–3.
70. Abu El-Haj, *Facts on the Ground*.
71. Hassner, *War on Sacred Grounds*.
72. For further discussion of this phenomenon, see Pullan, "Frontier Urbanism."

6

THE POLITICS OF OWNERSHIP

STATE, GOVERNANCE, AND THE STATUS QUO
IN THE CHURCH OF THE ANASTASIS
(HOLY SEPULCHRE)

GLENN BOWMAN

RECENT DISCUSSIONS OF shared holy places naturalize situations of either antagonistic dispute or syncretistic mixing. Although each respectively recognizes more or less extended periods of sharing or of conflict, there seems in each formulation to be an underlying logic—either temporal or spatial—of "antagonistic tolerance" or of "syncretistic sharing." This essay, partially ethnographic and partially historical, focuses on the Holy Sepulchre or Church of the Anastasis (resurrection, in Greek), the "mother church" of Christianity, in an attempt to shift the analytic logic away from the identities of communities that cohabit sites toward institutions that attempt to own, or at least control, those sites. A multitude of Christian sects claim the Anastasis as their own, but such claims are always mediated through structures of state power, and these shape choreographies of conflict or of sharing.

Pilgrims and celebrants in Jerusalem's holy places come to the places as guests; the Anastasis, like all of the other sites falling under the regimen of the status quo agreements, is not a parish church and hence has neither parishioners nor parochial duties.[1] Local communities whose members come to these holy places for either calendrical ceremonies or individual prayers have their own parish churches in which local versions of the central rituals are carried out, as are communal services such as baptisms, christenings, marriages, and funerals. Similarly, pilgrims who have left home parishes to travel to the Holy Land and the holy places expect to find something different from what their local churches proffer. When locals and pilgrims come to the Anastasis, the Tomb of the Virgin, the Chapel of the Ascension, the Dar es-Sultan, or Bethlehem's Church of the Nativity, they come to sites over which patriarchates rather than local congregations hold possessory rights. This means, in effect, that these sites are under the immediate jurisdiction of the highest ranking bishops of the respective churches and this, for pilgrims and visitors, associates the places with religion in general far more than religion in the context of the everyday. Furthermore, the resonance of these places with the focal and originary moments of Christian history abstracts them from the local and temporal, associating them far more with the sacred and the universal than with the secular and the quotidian. Local worshippers and pilgrims do not, other than in the most rarefied theological sense, imagine themselves as in any way owning the sacred sites.

The situation is very different for the clergy—almost exclusively monks—affiliated with the monasteries of the authorities who hold possessory rights over the status quo holy places. These monks do not see themselves as custodians of the sites, maintaining them for the usage of Christendom generally, but as literal owners of the places: "The three major communities within the Church of the Holy Sepulchre—the Greek Orthodox, the Latin Franciscans, and the Armenian Orthodox—all claim exclusive *praedominium* to [preeminence over] the places they believe they own."[2] Unlike local worshippers and pilgrims who visit the holy sites, these "keepers" are resident in or near the places and spend much of their time there carrying out liturgies and guarding and maintaining the condition of places they see as their property. The dominant churches of the Holy Land all seek to assert final ownership of the domains sacralized by the Christian narratives that they revere and that ground their authority. During a visit to the Holy Sepulchre in 1927, Nikos Kazantzakis was told by a Greek monk that "this entire church belongs to us, the

Orthodox. All the sacred shrines are ours. . . . We're going to throw the Armenians out. . . . Whatever the Latins tell you is a lie. All their shrines are fakes."[3]

Outside the most sacred sites, these claims rarely give rise to conflict. Although each church has founded shrines and monasteries at sites they assert are the settings of sacred events, these either commemorate the same events at different places, as with the multiple "Shepherds' Fields" (two Latin and one Greek Orthodox) scattered around the town of Beit Sahour or the three "Prisons of Christ" of Jerusalem's Old City, or they focus on different aspects of the same moment in the same locale, as do the Latin Church of the Transfiguration and the Orthodox Church of St. Elias on the bifurcated peak of Jebel et-Tur or Tabor.[4] There are no grounds for dispute as long as the clerics and the pilgrims recognize their churches' claims to the authenticity of these sites, and see those of the other churches as fallacious. Liturgical and pilgrim movements through these commemorative sites are choreographed to ensure that, although they may occasionally run next to, or even across, the paths of other groups, they neither intermingle nor conflict with them.

However, when the churches agree on the sites where core events in the histories of the central figures of Christianity occurred, the question of ownership can come violently to the fore. Lionel Cust notes that

> a remarkable feature . . . of the Moslem domination is the tolerance displayed on all but very rare occasions towards the Christians. . . . In strong contrast is the rivalry of the Christian Churches and Powers. The history of the holy places is one long story of bitter animosities and contentions, in which outside influences take part in an increasing degree, until the scenes of Our Lord's life on earth become a political shuttlecock, and eventually the cause of international conflict.[5]

It is important to note his use of the term "increasing": the early history of the holy places is far less riven by intra-Christian conflict than the period following the Ottoman-French Capitulations of the sixteenth century, and is certainly not as conflictual as the situation in the early twentieth century after the British accession to the Mandate for Palestine.[6]

The present-day Anastasis took shape during the Crusade-established Latin Kingdom of Jerusalem.[7] Despite Catholic ownership during the Latin Kingdom, the Greek Orthodox and Armenians maintained chapels, and "most of the Eastern Churches celebrated their services under the roof of the Holy Sepulchre."[8] After the fall of the Kingdom (Jerusalem surrendered in 1187, Acre in 1291), Latin supremacy was diluted while, under the Ayyubid dynasty, first the Georgians and then the Armenians became the paramount church followed by, under the Ottomans, the Greek Orthodox. Nonetheless, throughout this long period the Anastasis seems to be relatively unproblematically shared. Ludolph of Sudheim reports, in 1348, that although the Georgians are the "Custodians of the Keys of the Holy Sepulchre" there are seven communities in residence, including the Nestorians. Francesco Suriano, in 1485, notes the presence of ten communities in the church while Pietro Casola, nine years later, claims that ownership of the Anastasis is shared by the Latins, Greeks, Georgians, Armenians, Abyssinians, Syrians, Maronites, Jacobites, and Copts (he does not list a Nestorian representation).[9]

Although it is not clear from the extant pilgrim narratives how the churches' sharing of the Anastasis and other mutually revered holy places was choreographed, it appears likely that the pecuniary interests of the rulers of the city and of the Jerusalem district were the preeminent influences. A leitmotif of outrage at the taxes collected by authorities from pilgrims at ports, passes, the gates of cities, and the doorways to the holy places themselves runs through pilgrim narratives, stretching from Jerusalem's fall to Salah ad-Din to its surrender to Gen. Edmund Allenby 730 years later. In addition to these taxes on pilgrims, substantial payments were demanded from religious authorities resident in Jerusalem and from the holy places to maintain their residence and their hold on those sites. Pilgrimage was clearly good business for the local authorities, and allowing and fostering the presence of a diversity of churches ensured the most expansive and, hence, lucrative catchment area for the pilgrimage. Encouraging competition between the churches over access to and control of sites was even more lucrative, as it ensured a continuous flow of bribes and bids for influence. This was as true for the Abbasids and Mamluks as it was later for the Ottomans:[10] "The Christians were a source of revenue to the Turk, and were, therefore, encouraged. . . . As the number of pilgrims increased, so did the number of holy places, both within and without the Church of the Holy Sepulchre. . . . The Turk looked on in derision, and extracted tribute from all inhabitants of Jerusalem with unrelenting vigor."[11]

International developments in the mid-sixteenth century brought the influence of European states into the ecclesiastical politics of Jerusalem and the holy places, with a significant impact on conceptions of sacred property. The Ottoman Empire, seeking allies against the incursions into Hungary by the Hapsburgs under Ferdinand I, opened relations with France and, in 1536, negotiated a series of trade agreements (capitulations) with King Françoise I that meant, in effect, that over the following decades of burgeoning international trade "all European merchants wishing to trade in the Empire had to do so under the French flag."[12] France's consequent influence on the Sublime Porte was manifest in, among other things, diplomatic championing of the cause of the Catholic Church in the holy places as an almost national crusade. This was firmly opposed by the ecumenical patriarch of the Greek Orthodox Church, who was not only resident within the Ottoman capital of Constantinople but who also represented a substantial internal population of the empire.

In 1604 Henry IV negotiated the insertion of clauses in the capitulations of May 20 offering free access to the holy places to subjects and "friends" of France, as well as protection and rights for "the religious" (i.e., Franciscans) living in and serving the Anastasis. The Greek Orthodox response was rapid, and in 1605 Sultan Ahmet I issued a *firman* (decree) restricting Latin rights and substantially expanding the territories within the Church over which the Greeks had *praedominium* (preeminence). Over the following 153 years this struggle for relative hegemony escalated, as did the exactions of the local and imperial authorities. As a result, many of the churches that had shared the Anastasis and the holy places either withdrew altogether (the Nestorians in 1614 and the Georgians in 1644), substantially reduced their holdings (the Abyssinians retreating to the Dar es-Sultan around 1670), or took shelter under the dominion of the more powerful churches (as did, for instance, the Maronites and other Uniate churches under the Latins and the Syrian Orthodox under the Armenians).[13] Control over the holy places, and particularly those within the Anastasis, was in continuous flux with the *praedominium* over the central sites at one moment in Latin hands and the next in Orthodox. Between 1630 and 1637 an effective bidding war went on between the Greek Orthodox and the Latins under the gavel of Sultan Murad IV: "In this brief period the right of pre-eminence [*praedominium*] in the Holy Places principally concerned, namely, the Holy Sepulchre, the Church of the Tomb of the Virgin near Gethsemane and the Basilica of the Nativity at Bethlehem, alternated no fewer than six times between the two protagonists."[14]

The translation of rights of usage, or even custodianship, into effective ownership through fierce and pecuniary contestation impoverished the holy places by stripping away the heterodoxy of communities worshipping there and elevated property rights therein to an absolute value. Increasingly, foreign concerns were drawn into struggles over ownership, and the Sublime Porte was forced to intervene more and more authoritatively in those struggles. Escalating financial and political relations between the Ottoman Porte and the French state led to the signing of the Nointel capitulations in 1673 which, in 1690, handed the entirety of the Anastasis into the control of the Latins. For the next sixty-seven years, only Catholics could perform liturgies therein (this *praedominium* was extended in 1740 to the Church of the Nativity and the Tomb of the Virgin), and increasingly the Anastasis became an enclave of Italian and Spanish Franciscans. Such exclusionary policies tend to rebound, and in 1757 a crowd of local and pilgrim Orthodox attacked the church and threw the Catholics out. Subsequently, Sultan Mustafa III, recognizing the strength of Orthodox feeling, issued a *firman* giving the Greek

Orthodox control over the greater part of the Anastasis—guardianship of the Edicule (tomb) itself as well as possession of the Katholikon, the Chapel of Adam, the Seven Arches of the Virgin, the Prison of Christ, and the northern half of Calvary—and, outside the Anastasis, *praedominium* over the Tomb of the Virgin and the Church of the Nativity.[15] The Catholics were granted some limited *praedominium*, some rights of access, and some cleaning responsibilities that accorded right of possession over what they maintained.[16]

Subsequent developments—saliently, the French Revolution, the Napoleonic Wars, the Greek War of Independence, and the burgeoning power of the Russian Empire—produced instabilities in the forces working on the Sublime Porte not unlike those refracted in the changing ownership of the holy places. While Catholic (and particularly French) pilgrimage waned between the eighteenth and mid-nineteenth centuries under the impact of secularism and revolution, Russian pilgrimage increased exponentially, backed with largesse by the Russian state and Russian Orthodox church.[17] The Russian Empire, already threatening the Ottoman Empire along shared borders, had taken the mantle of "protector of Orthodox interests" from the Greek Orthodox patriarchate when the latter fell out of the good favor of the Sublime Porte as a result of the Greek War of Independence (the Ottomans lynched Patriarch Gregorios in front of the Patriarchal Cathedral Church of St. George [Aya Yorgi] in Constantinople in 1821, the first year of the revolt, because of his failure to control the Rûm [Roman] *millet*). Yet by the mid-1840s Russia's very substantial involvement in Palestine and the holy places began to be countered by that of French Ultramontanes, who reinvigorated Latin monasteries and schools and pressed Pope Pius IX into reestablishing the Latin patriarchate in Jerusalem. Like the Russian Empire, the Second French Republic (about to be declared the Second French Empire) strengthened its claims to popular legitimacy by taking on the role of protector of the holy places. Louis-Napoléon Bonaparte, elected French president in 1848 after the overthrow of the Bourbon monarchy, played the imperial chauvinist card and courted Catholic support (perhaps in anticipation of his well-planned coup d'état of 1851) by directing Gen.

Jacques Aupick, the French representative at the Sublime Porte, to demand of Sultan Abdulmecid in 1850 that he reinstate the near full control of the holy places that the Franciscans had enjoyed after 1740. The Russians objected, and in 1852, after hearing the report of an imperial commission on the sites, the Sultan announced that the *firman* of 1757 was effectively inviolate. A series of threats and counterthreats followed, with the French placing warships off Constantinople and in the Bay of Tripoli (prompted the Sultan to give the keys to the Church of the Nativity and access to the Tomb of the Virgin to the French) and the Russians placing troops along the Turkish border and beginning military preparations on the Black Sea (which initiated an unsuccessful flurry of international negotiations, drawing in the British and the Austrians). The result of the internationalization of the struggle for property rights over the holy places was the Crimean War and, with its conclusion after three bloody years, the Treaty of Paris (1856). The treaty, recognizing the dangers residing in juridical unfixity around the holy places, accepted the *firman* of 1852, a position affirmed in 1878 by the Congress of Berlin in the Status Quo Ante Bellum, Article 62 of the Treaty of Berlin.

I have focused at length on the complex history of negotiations and conflicts leading up to the instatement of the current status quo over the holy places in order to illustrate the increasing involvement of external parties in the governance of day-to-day relations in the holy places. The competition over control of the Anastasis and the other holy places cleared the field of all but representatives of the Catholic, Greek Orthodox, and Armenian Orthodox churches.[18] In effect, however, the real players were anything but local; not only had Sultan Abdulmecid, in 1853, abolished potential local interference in the governance of the holy places by placing all authority to resolve disputes in the hands of the Sublime Porte, but the national patrons of the three contesting churches, most notably France, Russia, and Britain, also treated relations within the holy places as matters of international import. In accepting Sultan Abdulmecid's post–Crimean War ratification of the *firman* of 1757, they authorized what Chad Emmett refers to as "an interlocking system of scattered sovereignty," producing on the terrain of the Anastasis and the other key shared holy sites a simulacra of the international order that, by an effective treaty, enforced "specific schedules coordinat[ing] very complex orders of procession and prayer."[19]

These regulations operated in accord with very particular conceptions of property. During the Ottoman period, as under earlier Islamic regimes, the holy places of the "Religions of the Book" (Judaism, Christianity, and Islam) fell under the remit of sharia law, which considered them *awqaf*, "inalienable religious endowment[s], not *mulk*, private property."[20] Formally they could be said to belong to God and, although the sovereign had custody of them and could thus grant rights of usage to the sites as well as retract such rights and bequeath them to other users, "Moslem law did not allow, and in the words of Sir Anton Bertram, 'viewed with horror,' the alienation of any property devoted to religious purposes."[21] One consequence of this is the long—and still-maintained—practice of having the keys to the door of the Anastasis kept by a member of a prestigious Muslim family, the Nuseibehs, who opens and shuts the church morning and night.

When the British took control of Palestine from the defeated Ottomans after the First World War, they were committed to maintaining the status quo not by sharia but by international law (the Treaty of Berlin) and by a desire to promote good relations with the communities brought under the Mandate. General Allenby, entering Jerusalem on December 9, 1917, announced that "every sacred building, monument, holy spot, shrine, traditional site, endowment, pious bequest, or customary place of prayer of whatsoever form of the three religions will be maintained and protected according to the existing customs and beliefs of those to whose faith they are sacred."[22]

Under what was effectively the secular rule of the Mandate authorities, this commendable but inevitably unfulfilled aspiration had two consequences. One was the extension of the domain covered by the status quo to take in a much wider field of holy places (encompassing a number of Jewish and Muslim sites and adding further Christian sites). The other was the replacing of what had, under the Ottomans, effectively been a theologically legitimated state protectorate over inalienable religious sites with a legislative authority meant to be distinct from the state, which would determine rights and privileges. The new protectorate was initially a religious organization, then an international body, and finally a holy places commission.[23] As we will see, the latter has made the holy places a tinderbox prone to bursting into intercommunal violence while providing incentive for religious authorities to find ways of circumventing, if not seeking to abolish, the status quo regulations that impede their aspirations.

Lionel Cust opens his 1929 *The Status Quo and the Holy Places* with two introductory statements:

> Article 13 of the Mandate for Palestine lays on the Mandatory Power the responsibility of preserving existing rights in the Holy Places.
>   Article 14 provides for the constitution of a special Commission to study, define and determine the rights and claims in connexion with the Holy Places. This Commission has never yet been formed, and in consequence, the Government of Palestine is still under the obligation to maintain the *Status Quo* in every respect.[24]

The Holy Places Commission, not yet formed in 1929, was still inchoate when the British withdrew from Palestine, which meant that, between 1917 and 1948, controversies between communities were dealt with neither by local courts nor by the high commissioner but solely in terms of the rules of the status quo as worked out on the ground by the parties (with mediation by government authorities).[25] Insofar as the status quo, whether of 1767 or of 1852, related to customary usages, one of the first things the British did in order to provide what James Scott calls "legibility" was attempt to assess and record what those usages were.[26] Although this effectively meant the inscription of the status quo operative at the moment when the British took power, Ottoman records kept in Jerusalem had been lost or destroyed at the time of the 1917 retreat. Cust, a district engineer under the Mandate authority, sought to compile as close a record as possible to the contemporary state of play with the assistance of Abdullah Effendi Kardus, a former Ottoman official then district officer for Bethlehem.[27] Harry Luke, chief secretary to the government of Palestine, called their attempt "a succinct account of modern practice ... [that] cannot fail to be a valuable *vade mecum* to those charged with the delicate duty of applying one of the most fluid and imprecise codes in the world";[28] it was, however, never fully accepted by the churches, which continue to this day to contest its accuracy.

Cust's text largely attended to the Anastasis, but it also treated other traditional status quo sites (the Sanctuary of the Ascension, the Virgin's Tomb, the Dar es-Sultan, and the Church of the Nativity) as well as new Jewish sites, such as Rachel's Tomb and the Wailing Wall. The volume provides a history of the relations of the religious communities around the holy sites and with the Ottoman rulers. This culminates in the establishment of the British Mandate for Palestine and its commitment to maintaining the status quo arrangements until replaced by "a solution satisfactory to all parties."[29] Until then,

> the arrangements existing in 1852 which corresponded to the *Status Quo* of 1757 as to the rights and privileges of the Christian communities officiating in the Holy Places have to be most meticulously observed, and what each rite practised at that time in the way of public worship, decorations of altars and shrines, use of lamps, candelabra, tapestry and pictures, and in the exercise of the most minute acts of ownership and usage has to remain unaltered. Moreover, the *Status Quo* applies also to the nature of the officiants. . . . The three Patriarchates of Jerusalem alone are considered as having possessory rights in the Church with the exception of the small Chapel in the possession of the Copts. They alone have the right to require the entrance door to be opened on their behalf, to enter in religious procession and to officiate regularly at their will.[30]

This linkage of maintenance to possessory rights was an extension into secular regulation of Islamic judicial principals that possession was linked to physical maintenance.[31]

Cust's text carefully maps rights and privileges to areas within the churches, attending particularly to common areas, areas under the exclusive jurisdiction of single rites, areas claimed by one rite but censed or visited by other rites during their offices, and sites for which ownership is disputed. Distinct choreographies of engagement are specified for each of these involving both temporal and spatial restrictions. A good example is the following:

> The steps leading up to the Chapel of St. Mary's Agony are Latin property. The question as to who was to clean the lowest step, which is barely above the level of the Courtyard, was in 1901 the cause of a sanguinary encounter between the Latin and Orthodox monks. The position now is that the Latins brush it daily at dawn, and the Orthodox at times together with the rest of the Parvis.[32]

Issues devolving from Ottoman customs pertaining to repair and ownership as well as to usage and precedent led to further restrictions and constraints:

> Authority to repair a roof or floor implies the right to an exclusive possession on the part of the restorers. . . .[33] The right to hang a lamp or picture or to change a lamp or picture is a recognition of exclusive possession of a pillar or wall. The right of other communities to cense at a chapel implies that the ownership is not absolute.[34]

Although the *firman* of 1757, restated by that of 1852, seemed to give the Greek Orthodox *praedominium* over most of the Anastasis (including guardianship of the Edicule) as well as over both the Tomb of the Virgin and the Church of the Nativity, modifications of practice had been effected between those dates and the period of Cust's compilation.

Thus, for instance, Cust's text indicates that "the Edicule is the common property of all three rites," a point reiterated in a working paper titled "The Holy Places" issued by the United Nations Conciliation Commission for Palestine in April 1949.[35] In the Edicule itself, sections are variously parsed between the three dominant communities, and the forty-three lamps over the marble slab in the inner sanctum are owned by all four communities (thirteen each for the Orthodox, Latins, and Armenians and four for the Copts). Although the Orthodox were granted guardianship of the Edicule, it is used by the Armenians for liturgies between 2:30 a.m. and 4:30 a.m., by the Latins between 4:30 a.m. and 8:00 a.m., and by the Orthodox between 8 a.m. and 7 p.m., when the church is formally closed. Throughout this time there is an Orthodox monk within the Edicule who guards the site except at 4:30 p.m. each day, when he leaves the Edicule and allows a procession of Latins to enter (the Armenians also process into the tomb three times a week, but during these times the Greek monk stays in place).[36] Similar variations, about which no consensus on origins exists between the churches, mean that the Church of the Nativity (particularly the Grotto, where the Altar of the Manger is under Latin jurisdiction while the Altar of the Nativity is shared by Armenians and Orthodox and officiated at by Copts and Syrians) and the Tomb of the Virgin (which is under the status quo jurisdiction of the Orthodox and Armenians and where the Syrians and Copts are able to hold liturgies) are no longer as completely under Orthodox *praedominium* as the 1767 *firman* implied.

Despite the attempts of Cust and later successors to spatially and temporally map the detailed workings of the status quo, the only real record of its operation is the operation itself. Each of the communities has its own records of rights, its own grievances about how these have been violated by subsequent developments, and its own awareness of a pressure working on the bounds of quotidian practice and seeking to push the limits and "regain" territories and rights lost to the other(s). Sensitivity to this pressure is amplified by the fact that there is no higher authority to refer to than the status quo regulations, which, in addition to being frequently indeterminate, themselves suggest, through negative examples, guidelines for changing the rules—"authority to repair a roof or floor implies the right to an exclusive possession. . . . The right to hang a lamp or picture or to change a lamp or picture is a recognition of exclusive possession of a pillar or wall. The right of other communities to cense at a chapel implies that the ownership is not absolute."[37]

Despite—or perhaps because of—the status quo agreements, violence frequently broke out and continues to break out between Greek Orthodox, Armenian Orthodox, and Franciscan clergy. While in the Ottoman past such violence had been a productive means of drawing the attention, and intervention, of the authorities, after 1917 and in the absence of an authoritative commission for the holy places, such violence became a reactive response to the assumption that others were trying to seize one's own possessory rights.[38] In other words, this violence was reactive: a response to an expropriative drive sensed in the other, which in fact was a refraction of one's own community's frustrated will to expand and drive that other out. Although formal mediation was provided during both the British Mandate period and the subsequent period of Jordanian rule (1948–1967), this rarely if ever led either to changes in rights and schedules or to the resolution of conflict; the status quo as formalized by Cust effectively remained in aspic, as did the antagonistic structuring of relations between the churches' representatives.

On December 31, 1984, I encountered a group of Greek Orthodox monks, members of the Brotherhood of the Holy Sepulchre, walking down Greek Orthodox Patriarchate Road. Two days earlier Greek, Armenian, and Latin monks had engaged in the annual cleaning of Bethlehem's Church of the Nativity, which traditionally serves as an occasion for the three communities to mark out their areas of the church by dusting and sweeping them. In 1984 a Greek monk, attempting to dust the archway of the northern entrance to the Grotto of the Nativity, had perched on a wooden beam designated by the status quo as Armenian. According to the report I'd read the previous day in the *Jerusalem Post*, Armenian monks had knocked his ladder out from under him, leaving him stranded twenty feet above the stone floor while Greek and Armenian monks, clearly already prepared for battle, pulled clubs and knives from under their robes and attacked each other, leaving at least one monk badly injured. The fight was broken up by Israeli police who had evidently themselves come prepared for a fracas. In my field notes from that day, I wrote, "I asked one of the monks, Brother Philadelphus, if he'd been in Bethlehem during the event and he brightened immediately saying that day was the best of his life. He realized during the fighting what has always eluded him, the precise meaning of his presence in the holy places. With the fight came the awareness of the concreteness of the term 'defenders of the holy places.'"[39]

A whole series of incidents of violence in the holy places, now and in the past, can be explained by this "defensive violence." Cohen writes of several of these, citing, for instance, a 1951 attack by Greek monks armed with clubs on a group of French pilgrims who had moved some benches into the parvis in order to set up a photograph, a series of bloody fights between Greek and Latin monks in Bethlehem in 1955 prompted by attempts to replace some old chairs, and a 1975 struggle involving pickaxes between Copts (who continue to hold minimal rights in the Anastasis under the status quo) and Armenians prompted by the kicking of a misplaced Coptic lectionary by an Armenian bishop.[40] Such struggles over the regimen legislated by the status quo continue to the present day. In August 2003 the Greeks changed the locks to the Church of the Nativity (locks to which all three communities held keys) because the Franciscans, attempting to remove the bodies of Palestinian militants killed by Israeli forces during the 2002 siege and unable to lay hands on their own keys while the church was under attack, had borrowed keys from the Armenians and opened doors for which the Greeks (who had fled the church when the siege began) had the right to first opening.[41] During the Orthodox Holy Cross celebrations on September 27, 2004, Greek and

Russian Orthodox monks fought with Catholics over the impropriety of a door to a Franciscan section of the church being left open while the Orthodox processed past it.[42]

In 1967, when Israel took control of East Jerusalem, the West Bank, Gaza, and the Golan Heights, other grounds for disputation and inter-sect violence were established. Israel declined to commit itself to maintaining the status quo agreements per se; Gen. Chaim Herzog, military governor of the West Bank, announced to the heads of Christian Churches on June 8, 1967, that "the State of Israel will . . . protect the Holy Places of all religions . . . [but that] arrangements for protecting the Holy Places would be made by the religious leaders themselves, each in the places revered by his own religion."[43] This meant that "the internal administration of the sites and the measures to be taken for their management would be left entirely to the spiritual heads concerned."[44] Israel adopted from the British and Jordanian governments the role of policing the holy sites so as to prevent public disorder but refused to take on the role of mediating controversies between the churches over the application of the status quo regulations. Cohen makes clear the implications of this refusal: "disputes . . . were now negotiated directly and not settled by an umpire. . . . In the past . . . the Jordanian governor was there to help in the event of a deadlock in the talks. Now there was no governor to fall back on."[45] This, Benvenisti notes, was "extremely problematical [as i]t was, after all, the very inability of the Christian communities to solve the problems of internal administration of the Holy Places that led to the *status quo* being instituted."[46]

In practice, this has come to mean that in any situation where a lack of clarity exists in the status quo legislation, or where there is no solid consensus over the application of the existing legislation, confrontations flare up that can only be quenched, if at all, by drawn-out and aggravated negotiations. Whereas under Ottoman rule clashes served to test the waters (both local and international) to assess whether changes in *praedominium* might be effected, and under British and Jordanian rule confrontations served more to vent spleen than as a strategy for changing the status quo (since, when mediation proved ineffectual, the status quo was simply confirmed), under Israeli rule there was—at least formally—no overarching (state) power to either change the status quo or reassert it in the wake of dispute. Struggles can go on in perpetuity in the expectation that one side or the other might succumb to violent pressure. A classic instance that has led to repeated clashes in and around the Edicule itself has to do with a dispute between the Greek Orthodox and the Armenians over guardianship of the Tomb of Christ. A specific group of monks associated with the Greek patriarchate and resident in the Monastery of Saints Helena and Constantine is designated as "guards of the Holy Sepulchre." There should, according to the patriarchate's reading of its guardianship of the Edicule, be one of these monks present within the antechamber of the Tomb of Christ (the Chapel of the Angel) whenever the Anastasis is open. Status quo regulations have it that the Greek Orthodox guardian of the Edicule leaves the Chapel of the Angel each day at 4:30 p.m. when a specific Catholic procession enters; he does not, however, leave when, three times a week, Armenian processions enter. This discrepancy has given rise to a vehement dispute between the two communities, which comes to a head during religious feasts when the fervor of clerics is at a peak and an audience of coreligionists is present. Thus, twice in 2008 alone, during the Orthodox Palm Sunday celebrations (April 20) and those linked to the Armenian Feast of the Discovery of the Cross (November 9), violent confrontations broke out when Armenian clerics attempted to force the Greek guardian from the Edicule.[47] Insofar as state agencies disavow any role other than carrying out "law and order functions"—that is, breaking up fights and arresting violent monks—such confrontations must continue until an agreement is reached between all parties to effect a change in the status quo.[48] In the absence of an authority willing to, as in the past, cap the trouble and reinstate the status quo, it is in the interest of the party that wishes to change current practices to continue to provoke confrontation until the situation becomes intolerable for the other parties. In light of the strengths of the

Greek investment in its guardianship and the Armenian desire to instate its right, one can imagine that Greek–Armenian bloodshed around the Edicule will continue as a ritualized occurrence.

There is, however, another means by which contestants in the struggle over rights to the holy places have been able to anticipate achieving victory over competitors. Israel's formal abnegation of its role in maintaining the status quo in 1967 left local decisions (i.e., those pertaining to the governance of the holy places) to be worked out between church authorities, but Israel also legally absolved itself of any need to respect the status quo, thus placing the state in a position analogous to that of the Ottoman authorities before they fixed the legislation in 1852 (and were held to that stabilization by the Treaties of Paris and Berlin).[49] After taking control of Jerusalem and the West Bank (the regions in which all the status quo sites are located), Israel assumed the legal right to reallocate permissions and privileges, and even to hand holy place *praedominium* over to one of the contesting parties. Under Mandate Law, established by the British and maintained by the Jordanians, "substantive" disputes—those dealing with rights of ownership, worship and possession—would be investigated by the high commissioner who, if unable to resolve them through consultation, would dismiss them and insist on the maintenance of the status quo; under Israeli law such "non-justiciable" cases are decided by the government, which "has become the supreme authority in whom the ultimate power of adjudicating matters on the Holy Places is vested."[50] Although this sovereignty has not been formally asserted to date, most likely because of fears of international repercussions, it has heightened tensions between the communities because, as Eordegian indicates, "assigning such judicial powers over the Holy Places to the government is an innovation with regard to the Mandatory law that may indicate the politicization of the matter."[51] Even without formal application, such a power of adjudication over rights and privileges considerably increases the influence of the state over the churches and the communities, local and international, in which they are embedded.

The long-standing dispute between the Ethiopian Orthodox and Coptic Orthodox churches over the Dar es-Sultan illustrates this politicization saliently. The Dar es-Sultan is a monastic compound of huts and narrow passageways perched on the roof of the St. Helena Chapel and currently in the possession of the Ethiopian Orthodox patriarchate. A narrow stairway, off which are both the Chapel of the Four Living Creatures and that of St. Michael, runs from the courtyard of the Dar es-Sultan to the parvis of the Anastasis and connects both the monastery and the Coptic patriarchate beyond to the main church. A long dispute over ownership and usage of the site has run since the sixteenth century, when the Ethiopian community, then in possession of the Dar es-Sultan and other sites within the Anastasis, was impoverished by the loss of support from its homeland and increasingly "could not find means to pay the taxes and bribes demanded by the new Ottoman rulers."[52] In 1640 the Ethiopians became clients of the Monophysite Armenians and in 1656 were forced to surrender to the Greeks their rights to properties and ritual permissions within the main body of the Anastasis.[53] The Ethiopians (frequently referred to in contemporary work as "Abyssinians") nonetheless retained their hold on the rooftop, the stairway, and the two chapels until 1838, when the Jerusalem community was effectively wiped out by plague, and the Copts, formally the mother church of the Ethiopians in the Oriental Orthodox Communion, pressed Ibrahim Pasha, son of Egypt's *wali* (governor) Muhammad Ali and himself governor of Syria, to grant them the keys of and control over the site.[54] When the Ethiopians later sought to reestablish themselves on the site, they were forced to do as guests of the Copts.

The two communities continued to dispute possession of the site over the following decades, and Cust's compendium of status quo rights leaves its *praedominium* indeterminate, saying that the Dar es-Sultan is "occupied by Abyssinian monks under a Coptic guardian" before entering into a history of the complex disputation and of British attempts to ascertain rights.[55] The Jordanian government, considering the status quo indeterminate, convened committees—as had the British before it—to investigate the situation and in late February 1961 determined that the Ethiopians should be granted control over the site. This decision, however, was suspended five weeks later, allegedly under pressure from the Nasserite regime, and the preexisting status quo was reestablished.[56]

After midnight on April 13, 1970, while the Coptic patriarch and monks were celebrating Easter at their chapel in the Anastasis, it was reported to them that Ethiopian monks had changed the locks at both ends of the stairway connecting the Dar es-Sultan to the Anastasis.[57] When the Copts attempted to approach the doors from either end, they were blocked by Israeli police, and eventually the patriarch and his party were forced to return to their monastery through the streets of the Old City. Two weeks later the Ethiopian archbishop announced that the Ethiopians had regained their rights over the Dar es-Sultan. The Copts subsequently petitioned the Israeli Supreme Court for the removal of the locks and the return of the monastery and chapels. Although the Supreme Court returned a decision that the changing of the locks was illicit, that the police had acted wrongly in preventing the Copts from approaching the doorways, and that the stairway, the chapels, and the Dar es-Sultan should be returned to the guardianship of the Copts, it also delayed implementation of its decision for a year so the government could consider the "substantive" or "non-justiciable" issue of possession. The government announced that a consultative committee would be established but that, until that committee reached its conclusions, "the present status quo would remain."[58] The operative term is "present." The status quo had been changed by violent action in the course of which police participation evidenced state collusion. The state's decision ex post facto not to intervene before the decision of a committee that has still—forty-two years later—not made any announcement but to instead insist on the maintenance of the newly imposed status quo meant authorization of a radical change under the guise of noninterference. Cohen notes that this "effectively annulled the decision of the high court, which now declined to get involved in an area that came under government jurisdiction."⁵⁹ The Ethiopians today retain possession of the Dar es-Sultan, the two chapels, and the stairway.

Richard Hecht, who interviewed participants in the dispute in the mid-eighties, contends that

> geopolitics help explain why the committee froze the situation through inaction. . . . Yisrael Lippel, who was then the director of the Ministry of Religious Affairs, gave some insight into the government's position. First, the Jordanian committee had ruled in favor of the Ethiopians in 1961, and the Israeli committee could simply defer to the earlier position. Second, the Israeli government was interested in gaining the support of the Ethiopian government for the emigration of the Falasha Jews. Third, the Israel government wanted access to Ethiopian airspace for its commercial airline routes to sub-Saharan Africa. Fourth, diplomatic recognition of Israel by the Ethiopian government would further Israel's foreign policy towards the African nations.⁶⁰

Cohen, researching the matter more recently and with access to archival materials Hecht had not seen, narrates an even more complex set of events and negotiations, originating in a promise made to the head of the Ethiopian church by the Israeli prime minister soon after the 1967 conquest of the Old City that the monastery and staircase would be given to the Ethiopians. This promise—in return for which Israel expected (in addition to what Hecht cites) a security alliance with Ethiopia against Nasserite Egypt and the opening of an Ethiopian embassy in Jerusalem—initiated complex and legalistic discussions within the Foreign Ministry and the Ministry of Religious Affairs as well as in the prime minister's chambers about how effectively to violate the status quo without raising substantial international condemnation.⁶¹ The changing of the locks, which Cohen suggests was in fact carried out by the Israeli police, and the perennial stalling of any decision on the legitimacy of the Ethiopian takeover were the solution to the question.⁶²

The Dar es-Sultan has remained a focus of political negotiations between states rather than simply between religious communities. Ethiopia failed in what Israel saw as its promised alliance, never opening an embassy in Jerusalem, sponsoring in 1971 a UN resolution hostile to Israel, and breaking off diplomatic relations in the wake of the 1973 Yom Kippur War. In the context of the Begin–Sadat negotiations and the signing of a peace treaty between Israel and Egypt, Israel mooted returning the Dar es-Sultan to Egypt, first in return for normalization of relations after the diplomatic rupture brought about by the First Lebanon War (1982) and subsequently as a concession in the 1986 negotiations over Taba. Moves in that direction were initially stalled by the necessity of appeasing the Ethiopian government during Operation Moses (1984–1985), the covert mass emigration of Falasha Jews out of Ethiopia, as well as by anxiety about losing access to Ethiopian air space. The Taba offer was perhaps not acted upon because of, as Hecht chillingly notes in his account of the dispute, a warning during those negotiations by the secretary of the National Council for Ethiopian Jews in Israel that Jews remaining in Ethiopia might be put at risk if Israel were to offend the Ethiopian government by returning the Dar es-Sultan to the Copts.[63] Thus, as in the 1850s, the politicization of disputes over communal property rights in the holy places rapidly escalated those struggles, bringing in states as players and producing unsettling effects far beyond the bounds of the Holy Land.

Israel's willingness to use the holy places for political gain and its de jure disavowal of both the status quo and the Treaties of Paris and Berlin has also weakened the churches' political stances vis-à-vis Israel. It has influenced their hierarchies' decisions to collude with the state because of the possibility that Israeli might be convinced to make a bilateral settlement in favor of one or the other of them. This latter assumption gains credence from the negotiations that have gone on between the Catholic Church and the Israeli state since the founding of the state. On the one hand, the UN Conciliation Commission for Palestine eventually gave up on its proposal to put the holy places of former Palestine under UN protection in response to Israel's insistence that the term "holy places" and the protection to be guaranteed them would apply solely to those sites that came under the status quo arrangements.[64] On the other hand, the Catholic Church, through the Vatican, retained its commitment to the internationalization of a "Greater Jerusalem," including Bethlehem. In secret negotiations that took place at the same time as Israel and the UN debated the latter's proposal for internationalization, Israel unsuccessfully offered the Vatican "a separate agreement . . . bestowing additional rights on the Catholic church" if it were to drop its support for internationalizing the Holy City.[65] After the Six-Day War, which delivered the holy places from Jordanian to Israeli control, the Catholic Church publicly maintained its call for internationalization while engaging in secret negotiations to abandon it. Yaakov Herzog, director of the prime minister's office, offered "proposals [that] included changing the *status quo* by giving the Catholics senior status as the expense of the Eastern communities; by recognizing the Pope as the representative of all the Christian groups; and by granting diplomatic status to the Holy Places."[66] Although the Vatican turned down the offer because it felt it could not formally recognize Israel's sovereignty over Jerusalem and the rest of the Occupied Territories by entering into a bilateral agreement with the state, it "agreed to 'accept with its blessing' a unilateral Israeli declaration promising priority status to the Catholic Church."[67]

Israel, snubbed by the refusal, retracted the offer, but the two parties continued over subsequent years to keep diplomatic channels open. At the end of December 1993 this resulted in the bilateral signing of the *Fundamental Agreement Between the Holy See and Israel,* which claimed to respect the status quo (Article 4) while, in Article 12, noting that "the Holy See and Israel will continue to negotiate for a solution to those questions [of extraterritorial status for the Holy Places] agreed upon in the agenda of July 15, 1992."[68] This assertion, aggravated by the claims of Metropolitan Christodoulos that "according to unnamed Middle Eastern sources an agreement between Israel and the Palestinians was imminent . . . provid[ing] for Saudi control over the Muslim Holy Places and Vatican control over the Christian Holy Places," gave rise to significant anxiety among Orthodox Christians and non–Roman Catholics in general.[69] Sotiris Roussos, reporting on Greek responses to the *Fundamental Agreement*, noted that "there was a widespread view within the Greek press that Israel had come to some sort of arrangement with the Holy See that would be detrimental to the dominant status of the Greek Orthodox Patriarchate in the Holy Land."[70]

Anxiety about collusion between churches and the Israeli state and its proxies has led the authorities of the three major churches to seek to accommodate Israeli wishes, often at their own and their parishioners' expense in order to retain strength in bargaining. These anxieties are exacerbated by Israel's ostentatious interference in church affairs and are manifest in such practices as delays in, or refusals of, the granting of visas to priests and nuns or attempts at influencing or refusing to recognize the appointment of senior clergy such as patriarchs.[71] Such interference has become more open and commonplace in the wake of the 1977 Likud victory in national elections and was amplified when Ehud Olmert was elected as Jerusalem's mayor in 1993. Appointments were made then, and since then, to the ministries of justice, religious affairs, housing, and the Israel Land Administration, which entrenched policies of "ensuring Israeli Jewish dominance over East Jerusalem" at the expense of earlier more politic relations with the churches.[72] In 1997 Shmuel Evyatar, a settler who had played a significant role in the occupation of St. John's Hospice, was appointed as Olmert's advisor on Christian communities.[73] This increasingly hostile environment has tended to radically worsen interchurch relations rather than pushing the churches into defensive solidarity around the holy places.

Sotiris Roussos notes that the Greek patriarchate's policy of "cooperating closely with state policy in Israel in order to maintain its prevailing position in the Holy Places" continues an earlier practice under Islamic rule of cooperating with the state "in the political, social and economic spheres in exchange for Church autonomy in its internal matters."[74] Certainly since the creation of the Israeli state the Brotherhood of the Holy Sepulchre has not only opposed itself to the Greek state's initially critical position on Israel but also obliged Israeli agencies by facilitating the selling off, permanent leasing, and alleged confiscation of the considerable properties it holds either straightforwardly or as trusts (*waqf*) in Israel, Jerusalem, and the Occupied Territories.[75] In a context in which the recent Israeli drive to expand Jewish settlement and land ownership is matched by increased dissatisfaction among the lay populace with the failure of the churches to defend local rights, both Christian and Muslim, such accommodation is more visible than it had been in the past. In March 2005 Patriarch Irenaios I was implicated in a number of land deals made with Israeli companies with purported links to the settler association Ateret Cohanim. In response to pressure from the Christian Palestinian population, the Palestinian National Authority, and the Orthodox Church outside of Israel/Palestine, Irenaios was deposed in May of that year and replaced by Theophilus III, whose installation was blocked until December 2007 by the Israeli government.[76] In a 2006 interview with a Greek newspaper, "Theophilus complained of Israeli 'blackmail,' the purpose of which he said was 'to ratify the agreements for the purchase and sale of property signed by our predecessors.'"[77] However, in the wake of Theophilus's approved installation, the aforementioned lease of the land linking the Gilo and Har Homa settlements (and thus closing another gap in the settlement encirclement of Jerusalem) suggests to some in the Palestinian community that recognition came at a price. Marwan Toubasi said, "I think the continued leasing of land was a condition by Israel [to grant him recognition]."[78]

The relations of the Armenian patriarchate of Jerusalem with the Israeli state and particularly with the Israel Lands Administration have tended to attract less attention from national and international media than do those of the Greek Orthodox Church. However, as Dumper points out, the patriarchate is not only "reputed to be the largest landowner in the Old City and one of the largest in Jerusalem" but has also shown "willingness to sell land and property to the Israel Lands Administration."[79] That "willingness" generated a major scandal when Archbishop Karekian Kazanjian, appointed from Australia in 1981 as grand sacristan (protector of the Armenian holy places in Jerusalem) by the catholicos of the Armenian Church in Etchmiadzin, discovered that Archbishop Shahe Ajamian, who was serving as superintendent of the estate of the Armenian patriarchate, chancellor, and chief aide to Patriarch Yeghishe Derderian, and who Israeli officials considered "a special friend of Israel," had not only been stealing and selling ancient manuscripts from the patriarchate library but more importantly selling Armenian lands in Jerusalem and the West Bank to Israeli land developers.[80] Ajamian was deposed and expelled from the St. James Monastery, sparking a violent feud between Derderian and Ajamian, the latter claiming that Derderian was scapegoating him for his own crimes.[81] Further investigation implicated Derderian in land sales and misappropriations of church funds. The King of Jordan (the Jordanian monarch was recognized by the church as the only legitimate secular authority over the Jerusalem patriarchate) pressured His Holiness Vazken I, catholicos of the Armenian church, to instruct the St. James Brotherhood (the Armenian equivalent of the Brotherhood of the Holy Sepulchre) to investigate Derderian as a means to deposing him. Derderian, however, purged that governing body of unsupportive prelates (made up of the entirety of the membership serving outside of Israel/Palestine) and had the remainder refuse to vote for an investigation.[82] He stayed in power until his death in 1990, when Shahe Ajamian, supported by armed guards, barricaded himself within his reappropriated flat in the monastery while apparently waiting for an anticipated popular demand for his installation to be raised.[83] There was little if any support for such a move, especially in the context of the Palestinian intifada, which, while directly involving few Armenians, nonetheless had given rise to a general fury among the lay populace against ecclesiastical corruption and collaboration with what was increasingly perceived as a hostile state. Instead, Torkom Manoogian, an Iraqi by birth who had served for twenty-four years as primate of the Eastern Diocese of America and had earlier been appointed by the catholicos as an investigator of the Ajamian affair, was elected patriarch and, until his collapse into a coma on January 19, 2012, was a vocal defender of the positions of both Armenians and Palestinians in the Holy Land.

Power shifts and although for a substantial period it looked as though the Israeli state was favoring the Vatican, with its influence on international politics, it recently appears as though the Greek Orthodox patriarchate is in the ascendant. It is likely that this has to do both with the successive Catholic appointment as Jerusalem patriarch of two outspokenly political ethnic Palestinians (the first, Michel Sabbah, an Israeli Arab who served from 1987–2008, the second, Fouad Twal, a Jordanian appointed in 2008) as well as with the Armenian decision to appoint as patriarch an outsider who, lacking the close ties with the state of his predecessor, has been far less amenable to Israeli demands for concessions and collaboration. Certainly the Greek assertions of rights in both the Anastasis and, more saliently, the Church of the Nativity—where a concerted effort was made to force the Catholics and the Armenians out of the Grotto by exploiting claims that they had supported the Palestinians during the siege of 2002 and violated the status quo in the course of so doing—suggest that the Greek patriarchate feels itself to be negotiating from a position of power. Sossie Andezian, an anthropologist of religion who has been carrying out fieldwork around holy places in Israel/Palestine, has noted that on the Jordan River, particularly around the sites of the baptism, the Greeks are developing monasteries and holy places on the Israeli side of the Jordanian border while the Catholics (and to a lesser degree the Armenians) are instead building holy places on the Jordanian side. She notes that "the Latins are building new holy sites in Jordan, leaving Jerusalem to the Greeks. And the Armenians are very uncomfortable with this."[84]

It initially appears as though the Israeli state's relation to the churches and the holy places is effectively analogous to that of the Ottoman Empire before the international agreement in 1856 to institutionalize the *firman* of 1757. Before then the perceived strategic interests of the sultanate could lead to the unrestrained granting or retraction of rights and privileges in the central Christian shrines.[85] After the Treaty of Paris, the status quo was rendered far more stable and far less vulnerable to local, imperial, or international interference. With the collapse of Ottoman rule over Palestine and the establishment of the British Mandate, the purview of the status quo was expanded to take in significant Jewish and Muslim sites while the rationale for protecting them was secularized. Under the Mandate's status quo regime, one adopted by the subsequent Jordanian government, the autonomy of the churches involved in the status quo was protected by systems of mediation and oversight, which ensured that any change in the status quo could only be effected with the agreement of the ecclesiastical parties; unsettled issues (such as that of the Dar es-Sultan) would be transparently investigated and adjudged. In the wake of the Israeli conquest of Jerusalem and the West Bank (the territories in which all the status quo properties were located) the state, while asserting that it would "protect the holy places," repudiated any role in enforcing the status quo. By placing itself over the status quo, and thus in a position to redistribute rights and privileges, it was able to set in play bidding wars between churches anxious to garner favor (wars in which the churches' competitive desire for privileged status in the holy places prompted both the selling of ecclesiastical properties and the covert granting of international influence). Although in most cases the state was able to gather considerable benefit without changing the status quo, it could also actually effect reversals in the status quo in order to pay for alliances and activities promised by states serving as patrons to particular ecclesiastical parties, as the state's role in transferring possession of the Dar es-Sultan from the Copts to the Ethiopians demonstrated.

There are significant differences between the relations of state and status quo in the Ottoman Empire before 1856 and in Israel post-1967 that reflect the difference between a multicommunal empire and an ethnonational state. Perhaps most significant is the responsibility of the state to indigenous populations. The Ottoman Rûm *millet* was substantial and widespread, made up of Christians of the Chalcedonian persuasion (Greeks, Bulgarians, Albanians, Vlachs, Macedonian Slavs, Georgians, Arabs, Romanians, and Serbs) while the smaller Armenian millet was constituted out of non-Chalcedonian Armenian, Syrian, and Coptic Orthodox. Only the Catholic Church lacked a notable population within the empire. Its privileges within the holy places depended on the Sublime Porte's international relations with extraterritorial European powers (in particular France), while those granted to the churches representing the Rûm and Armenian *millets* appeased internal populations and their ethnarchs in Istanbul. Israel, on taking control of Jerusalem and the West Bank in 1967, discontinued Britain's and Jordan's policies of supporting indigenous Christians in their struggles for rights with the foreign churches and dealt with the three patriarchates as representatives of foreign powers.[86] The massive diaspora of Palestinians—Christian and Muslim alike—out of Israel and the territories conquered in 1967 had substantially reduced the size of the indigenous Christian populations.[87] Israel, which represented itself to itself and to the outside world as a Jewish state, effectively disenfranchised remaining indigenous non-Jewish populations (made up now of all the communities previously encompassed within the Armenian and Rûm *millets* as well as Catholics and some Protestants), leaving them as minorities to be controlled while it focused on appeasing and alluring Christians outside the Holy Land through granting privileges in the holy places to foreign clergy and promoting international pilgrimage.

The Porte was forced (see the events of 1757 described earlier) to favor the indigenous Greek Orthodox over the foreign Catholics by the presence within its territories of an influential lay and clerical population and to recognize and reward the lesser but not insignificant power of the empire's Armenian community. Israel, to the contrary, can ignore its reduced and weakened Palestinian Christians while using foreign Christian concern—popular, ecclesiastical, and governmental—with the holy places as means of gaining influence and support. Palestinian Christians have been increasingly marginalized and alienated, contributing to their accelerating exodus into diaspora, while the churches—mirroring the development of the Franciscan enclave of the Holy Sepulchre in the period leading up to the riot of 1757—have grown increasingly foreign in their personnel and increasingly distant from local congregations.[88]

The seeming increase in the power of the foreign churches comes at a substantial price, particularly for those (the Greek Orthodox and the Armenian Orthodox) whose long-term inhabitance of the Holy Land has resulted in extensive land holdings. Whereas the Catholic Church, with a massive international following, has been able to use its influence over international opinion and foreign governments to negotiate with the Israeli state and the Ministry of Religious Affairs, the Greek and Armenian churches, with much smaller demographic footprints and more restricted political influence, have bought their rights through the sale of lands.[89] Such sales, which involve the direct property of the churches as well as *waqf* (inalienable religious endowments) given by families and communities into the keeping of the churches, fuel local Christian anger toward the clergy as well as diminish what the churches will be able to exchange for the perpetuation of their privileges in the future.

It may be that the Armenian and Catholic Churches, by retracting from their dependency on Israel and Israeli territory by developing Jordanian holy sites, and simultaneously courting the Palestinian and Arab "street" by appointing patriarchs less likely to bend to Israeli demands, are preparing for a future in which the capital they have to trade with the State of Israel will be expended and new allies will be needed to support their continued presence in the Middle East. However, the Greek Orthodox Brotherhood of the Holy Sepulchre seems to be making no such moves; it is likely that it, with the largest portfolio of properties in the holy places, assumes it will be able to hold on to what it thinks it owns. That was an appropriate strategy for a period in which the status quo ensured that its only competition came from other Christian churches; now, with an ethnonational state ruling over the territory and according no allegiance to that regime, that strategy may be somewhat shortsighted.

NOTES

1. In 1757 Sultan Mustafa III announced a *firman* (decree) establishing rites and relations between Christian communities in focal holy places; this, after the Crimean War and the Treaty of Paris, was accepted by the major European pow-

ers as binding. It "granted the various religious communities shared rights in the holy places, demarcating which areas came under whose control and establishing time schedules for officiating in areas shared by more than one religious group." Chad Emmett, "The Status Quo Solution for Jerusalem," *Journal of Palestine Studies* 26, no. 2 (1997): 16–28, at 19; and Lionel George Arthur Cust, *The Status Quo in the Holy Places* (London: HMSO, 1929).

2. Richard Hecht, "The Construction and Management of Sacred Time and Space: 'Sabta Nur' in the Church of the Holy Sepulcher," in *Now Here: Space, Time and Modernity*, ed. R. Friedland and D. Boden, 181–235 (Berkeley: University of California Press, 1995), 190.

3. Nikos Kazantzakis, *Journeying: Travels in Italy, Egypt, Sinai, Jerusalem and Cyprus*, trans. Themi Vasils and Theodora Vasils (1961; repr., Boston: Little, Brown, 1973), 153.

4. The first is dedicated to the initial moment of transfiguration and the latter to the subsequent appearance of Elijah (Matt. 17:1–9; Mark 9:2–8; Luke 9:28–36).

5. Cust, *The Status Quo*, 3–4.

6. The capitulations were bilateral commercial agreements between the Ottoman sultanate (the "Sublime Porte") and France that allowed Europeans rights of residence and trade under the protection of France and extending to Europeans resident in the empire (and to members of sectarian communities taken under France's protection) the protection of that state's extraterritorial jurisdiction. See Bruce Masters, *Christians and Jews in the Ottoman Arab World: The Roots of Sectarianism*, Cambridge Studies in Islamic Civilization (Cambridge: Cambridge University Press. 2001); and Alexander de Groot, "The Historical Development of the Capitulary Regime in the Ottoman Middle East from the Fifteenth to the Nineteenth Centuries," *Oriente Moderno* 83, no. 3 (2003): 575–604. Further capitulations were later negotiated with other European states and even companies.

7. Previously, except for two periods of destruction at the hands of the Persians (614) and the Khalif Hakim (1009), the church had been under the control of the patriarch of Jerusalem, albeit, as of 800, with Western European patronage initiated by Charlemagne. From the sixteenth century on, this patronage retrospectively grounded French claims to be the rightful protectors of the holy places.

8. Harry C. Luke, "The Christian Communities in the Holy Sepulchre," in *Jerusalem 1920–22: Being the Records of the Pro-Jerusalem Council During the First Two Years of the Civil Administration*, ed. C. R. Ashbee, 46–56 (London: John Murray, 1924).

9. Ibid., 48, 50–51.
10. Saul Colbi, *Christianity in the Holy Land: Past and Present* (Tel Aviv: Am Hassefer Publishers, 1969), 60–61.
11. Lionel George Arthur Cust, *Jerusalem: A Historical Sketch* (London: A&C Black Ltd, 1924), 180.
12. Suraiya Faroqhi, *The Ottoman Empire and the World Around It* (London: I. B. Tauris, 2006), 145.
13. Otto Meinhardus, "A Note on the Nestorians in Jerusalem," *Oriens Christianus* 51 (1967): 124; and Luke, "The Christian Communities," 54.
14. Luke, "The Christian Communities," 53.
15. Raymond Cohen, *Saving the Holy Sepulchre: How Rival Christians Came Together to Rescue Their Holiest Shrine* (New York: Oxford University Press, 2008), 7.
16. Charles Frazee, *Catholics and Sultans: The Church and the Ottoman Empire 1453–1923* (Cambridge: Cambridge University Press, 1983), 215.
17. Stephen Graham, *With the Russian Pilgrims to Jerusalem* (London: Macmillan, 1916); and Derek Hopwood, *The Russian Presence in Syria and Palestine 1843–1914: Church and Politics in the Near East* (Oxford: Clarendon Press, 1969).
18. Armenian retention of rights over a small purview of the holy places reflects the fact that the Armenian Orthodox patriarchate represented a substantial population resident within the bounds of the Ottoman Empire, subsuming other Christian groups that did not easily fit into the Orthodox category, such as the Monophysites of Syria and Egypt, the Bogomils of Bosnia, and the Copts, all of whom it was better to appease than antagonize. See Karen Barkey, *Empire of Difference: The Ottomans in Comparative Perspective* (Cambridge: Cambridge University Press, 2008).
19. Emmett, "The Status Quo Solution for Jerusalem," 16, 21.
20. Cohen, *Saving the Holy Sepulchre*, 7.
21. Walter Zander, "On the Settlement of Disputes About the Christian Holy Places," *Israel Law Review* 8, no. 3 (1973): 357.
22. Edmund Allenby, "Official Proclamation Following the Fall of Jerusalem, 9 December 1917," in *Source Records of the Great War*, vol. 5, ed. Charles F. Horne (New York: National Alumni Press, 1923), 417.
23. See Marlen Eordegian, "British and Israeli Maintenance of the Status Quo in the Holy Places of Jerusalem," *International Journal of Middle East Studies* 35 (2003): 307–28; and Zander, "On the Settlement."
24. Cust, *The Status Quo*, 2.
25. Cust's text reads, "Any dispute that now arises is submitted to the government. If the government's decision is not accepted, a formal protest is made and the fact is recorded that no change in the *status quo* is held to have occurred." Ibid.,

11. This was also the case during Jordanian rule over Jerusalem and the West Bank, from 1948 to 1967. See Meron Benvenisti, *Jerusalem: The Torn City* (Jerusalem: Isratypeset, 1976); Cohen, *Saving the Holy Sepulchre*, 86; and Eordegian, "British and Israeli Maintenance," 311.

26. James Scott, *Seeing Like a State: How Certain Schemes to Improve the Human Condition Have Failed* (New Haven, CT: Yale University Press, 1998), 2.

27. Cust gave little or no credence to the documents possessed by the respective patriarchates struggling over control of the sites: "The Orthodox and Franciscan archives contain many *firmans* and *hojjets* (i.e., decisions of the Sharia Court at Jerusalem) and other documents of this period quoted in support of their claims; they cannot however be considered of much value except as an indication of the nature of the struggle and of the profit that must have flowed into the coffers of the Turk." See Cust, *The Status Quo*, 8.

28. Harry C. Luke, "Introductory Note," in *The Status Quo in the Holy Places* (London: HMSO, 1929), 1. See also Michael Dumper, *The Politics of Sacred Space: The Old City of Jerusalem in the Middle East Conflict* (Boulder, CO: Lynne Rienner, 2001), 110.

29. Cust, *The Status Quo*, 11.

30. Ibid., 11, 14.

31. Frazee, *Catholics and Sultans*, 215.

32. Cust, *The Status Quo*, 16.

33. The rules on repair produced an impasse on necessary structural repairs to dome of the rotunda, which was severely damaged in the earthquake of 1927. The impasse, as Raymond Cohen chronicles in his *Saving the Holy Sepulchre*, was broken only in 1949 when an offer by the Jordanian monarch to carry out the work drove the three patriarchates to begin to negotiate about collaborating in the face of the threat that, in line with the Ottoman law that one who repairs the roof of a house owns the house, "the Hashemite kingdom intended to assume direct responsibility for the church." See Kimberly Katz, "Building Jordanian Legitimacy: Renovating Jerusalem's Holy Places," *Muslim World* 93, no. 2 (2003): 211–32; Cohen, *Saving the Holy Sepulchre*, 94.

34. Cust, *The Status Quo*, 12.

35. Ibid., 22; and United Nations Secretariat, *The Holy Places* (United Nations Conciliation Commission for Palestine, Committee on Jerusalem, April 8, 1949), available at *MidEastWeb*, http://www.mideastweb.org/un_palestine_holy_places_1.htm. Accessed November 26, 2009.

36. I am grateful to Raymond Cohen, who provided this information in private correspondence.

37. Cust, *The Status Quo*, 12.

38. For example, the overturning of the Latin hegemony granted by the treaty of 1740 came about in the wake of an Orthodox provoked riot in the Anastasis in 1757.
39. On December 27, 2007, a clash broke out between Greek and Armenians over the same section of wall involving stones and broomsticks and leaving four monks and two Israeli police injured; see "Broom Scuffle in Bethlehem's Church of the Nativity," Youtube video, http://www.youtube.com/watch?v=WjogvDivTRM, accessed August 10, 2012.
40. Cohen, *Saving the Holy Sepulchre*, 88, 113, 212–13.
41. Ross Dunn, "Row Seethes in Bethlehem Over Keys to the Birthplace of Jesus," *Christianity Today*, August 1, 2003, http://www.christianitytoday.com/ct/2003/augustweb-only/8-11-43.0.html.
42. Allyn Fisher-Ilan, "Dozens Hurt as Clerics Clash in Jerusalem Church," *AlertNet*, Reuters Foundation, September 27, 2004.
43. Quoted in Benvenisti, *Jerusalem*, 272.
44. Colbi, *Christianity in the Holy Land*, 159.
45. Cohen, *Saving the Holy Sepulchre*, 211.
46. Benvenisti, *Jerusalem*, 263–64.
47. See "Church of the Unholy Punch Up: Holy Shame," *Nation News Agency*, November 10, 2008, Youtube video, http://www.youtube.com/watch?v=A_fRGFbQ5Oo&feature=player_detailpage.
48. Cohen, *Saving the Holy Sepulchre*, 211.
49. After 1967 the government was "entirely satisfied that it had absolutely no legal obligation to honor any of the *status quo* rights." David-Maria Jaeger, quoted in Eordegian, "British and Israeli," 319.
50. Ibid., 321.
51. Ibid.
52. Anthony O'Mahony, "Pilgrims, Politics and Holy Places: The Ethiopian Community in Jerusalem Until ca. 1650," in *Jerusalem: Its Sanctity and Centrality to Judaism, Christianity and Islam*, ed. L. Levine, 476–81 (New York: Continuum, 1999).
53. Ibid., 477.
54. Cust, *The Status Quo*, 27; and Kristen Pedersen, "Deir Es-Sultan: The Ethiopian Monastery in Jerusalem." *Quaderni di Studi Etiopici* 8–9 (1987–88): 40.
55. Cust, *The Status Quo*, 30–33.
56. Hecht, "Construction and Management," 196. See also Cohen, *Saving the Holy Sepulchre*, 193–94.
57. Hecht, "Construction and Management," 194–98; and Cohen, *Saving the Holy Sepulchre*, 194–201.

58. Quoted in Benvenisti, *Jerusalem*, 235.
59. Cohen, *Saving the Holy Sepulchre*, 195.
60. Hecht, "Construction and Management," 197.
61. Cohen, *Saving the Holy Sepulchre*, 197.
62. Ibid., 200.
63. Hecht, "Construction and Management," 198.
64. Doing so would not only substantially reduce the number of sites listed in the UN Conciliation Commission for Palestine in April 1949 (Secretariat 1949), ensuring that the only ones to fall under jurisdiction were sited in Jordanian controlled territory but would also loose sites other than Christian ones from international protection. On the subsequent expropriation and nationalization of Muslim sites, see Michael Dumper, "Muslim Institutions and the Israeli State: Muslim Religious Endowments (*waqfs*) in Israel and the Occupied Territories, 1948–1987" (Ph.D. diss., University of Exeter, 1991); and Yitzhak Reiter, *Islamic Institutions in Jerusalem: Palestinian Muslim Organization Under Jordanian and Israeli Rule* (Amsterdam: Kluwer Law International, Amsterdam, 1997).
65. Eordegian, "British and Israeli Maintenance," 318.
66. Benvenisti, *Jerusalem*, 268.
67. Ibid.
68. Charalambos Papasthathis, "A New Status for Jerusalem? An Eastern Orthodox Viewpoint," *Catholic University Law Review* 45 (1995–96): 729–30.
69. Quoted in Sotiris Roussos, "The Patriarchate of Jerusalem in the Greek-Palestinian-Israeli Triangle: Is There a Place for It?" *One in Christ* 39, no. 3 (2004): 18.
70. Ibid.
71. See Dumper, *The Politics of Sacred Space*; and Roussos, "The Patriarchate."
72. Dumper, *The Politics of Sacred Space*, 53.
73. Ibid.
74. Roussos, "The Patriarchate," 15.
75. Amikam Nachmani, "So Near and Yet So Far: Greco-Israeli Relations," in *Israel, Turkey and Greece: Uneasy Relations in the East Mediterranean* (London: Frank Cass, 1987). On Christian use of the Muslim *waqf* system, see Ron Shaham, "Christian and Jewish 'Waqf' in Palestine during the Late Ottoman Period." *Bulletin of the School of Oriental and African Studies* 54, no. 3 (1991): 460–72.
76. After the death of Diodoros I, Irenaios (elected patriarch in August 2001) was similarly blocked for sixteen months by the refusal of the government of Ariel Sharon to recognize his election. After the provocation of the state backed Easter Week takeover by Jewish settlers of the Christian Quarter's St. John's Monastery in 1990, Diodoros had irritated Israeli authorities by organizing local and international protests. After his death, the Israeli government attempted to "fix"

the list of candidates for the patriarchate and, when local and international protests forced a withdrawal, simply refused to allow Irenaios to take office until certain promises were made. See Roussos, "The Patriarchate"; "Jerusalem Patriarch in Sharon Pact: Report of Land for Recognition," *Kathimerini* (English ed.), December 27, 2002; and Donald Macintyre, "Patriarchs, Property and Politics in Jerusalem," *Independent*, November 6, 2007.
77. Macintyre, "Patriarchs, Property and Politics."
78. Quoted in Omar Karmi, "West Bank Land Sales by Church Spur Uproar," *National*, January 13, 2010.
79. Dumper, *The Politics of Sacred Space*, 65.
80. Haim Shapiro, "Quest for New Jerusalem Patriarch Set in Motion," *Jerusalem Post*, March 7, 1990.
81. William Claiborne, "Orthodox Armenians in Holy Land Split in Bitter Feud Over Leaders," *Ottawa Citizen*, June 14, 1986.
82. Kay Bird and Max Holland, "Dispatches: Armenia—the Renegade Patriarch," *Nation*, March 2, 1985.
83. Shapiro, "Quest for New Jerusalem." 10.
84. Personal communication, December 23, 2009.
85. Prior to 1853, when the sultan abolished local interference in the governance of holy places, such changes were also effected in response to the pecuniary interests of local and regional authorities.
86. Particularly notable was Mandate British, and subsequent Jordanian, support for the Arab Orthodox Society's struggle with the Greek Orthodox Patriarchate for greater representation within the Church and an increased say in its decision making processes. See Sir Anton Bertram and J. W. A. Young, *The Orthodox Patriarchate of Jerusalem: Report of the Commission Appointed by the Government of Palestine to Inquire and Report Upon Certain Controversies Between the Orthodox Patriarchate of Jerusalem and the Arab Orthodox Community* (London: Humphrey Milford, 1926); and Itamar Katz and Ruth Kark, "The Greek Orthodox Patriarchate of Jerusalem and Its Congregation: Dissent Over Real Estate," *International Journal of Middle East Studies* 37, no. 4 (2005): 509–34. For Jordanian support more generally, see Katz, "Building Jordanian Legitimacy."
87. Bernard Sabella, "Palestinian Christians: Challenges and Hopes," *al-Bushra*, 1996, http://www.al-bushra.org/holyland/sabella.htm.
88. Michael Dumper, *The Politics of Jerusalem Since 1967*, The Institute for Palestine Studies Series (New York: Columbia University Press, 1997), 180–96.
89. See Katz and Kark, "Greek Orthodox Patriarchate"; and Katz, "Building Jordanian Legitimacy."

7

CHOREOGRAPHING UPHEAVAL

THE POLITICS OF SACRED SITES IN THE WEST BANK

ELAZAR BARKAN

WHO ORGANIZES AND who benefits from religious strife? This chapter explores several political riots in Jerusalem and the West Bank surrounding religious sites and the role played by the state in creating space for the riot and in responding to it. It argues that the riots serve a larger political agenda of aggravating the Israeli/Palestinian conflict and are intentionally manipulated by the political entities that have the capacity to either inflame or contain the level of violence. It further claims that popular religious violence serves as an informal political tool that is used by formal governing bodies. The goal of this violence is both strategic and domestic politics. While prevention is harder to measure, this essay explores at least one successful case of prevention as an example of the government's ability to control religious violence when it contradicts the government's larger agenda. I show that while the violence revolves around religious sites, and sacredness and religious sentiments are central to the conflict, the violence itself has immediate political goals, and the religious rhetoric is often a manipulation by various parties to further their political agenda. This is not to say that religious beliefs are insincere. On the contrary, religious beliefs are central to the protagonists' worldview and are the driving force of their actions. However, the choice of how to manifest religious beliefs in sacred spaces of conflict is chiefly political and is shaped by the actions of political actors, primarily the governments. This also applies to religious authorities and individuals whose power stems from their religious standing, although they are often constrained by government policies. The protagonists' relative autonomy stems from government indecision and less from a religious/secular divide. Here the argument goes against the notion that religious violence is structurally different from political violence, that it is somewhat more ingrained and is therefore harder to control. Instead this suggests that in the Israeli/Palestinian conflict, religion is a political ideology and religious violence is a byproduct of politics. While religion simmers continuously and focuses on terminology and spaces of the sacred, religious violence is incited (or encouraged) to achieve short-term political goals and should be treated as such by national and international conflict resolution experts and politicians.

The notion at the heart of the present inquiry is that shared religious sites are focal conflagration points subject to manipulation. There is a general expectation that religious sites that have been a place of political violence once are doomed to be subject to repeated eruptions.[1] This collides with the global commitment to prevent violence, including the solemn responsibility to protect religious sites endorsed by so many governments around the world.[2] It is therefore imperative to look at the structure of religious violence to develop a framework to anticipate forthcoming violence as a first measure of prevention. We may ask: How are we to understand the sources of religious violence frequented upon these sites? Whose responsibility is it? Can these spurts of violence be anticipated at a level of specificity that has political implications? Is prevention possible? Who controls the discourse and shapes the politics surrounding those sites?

I explore the choreography of cases of upheaval in Jerusalem and the West Bank, and in particular at two sites in Hebron/al-Khalil and Nablus. In Jerusalem, I look specifically at three incidents instigated by Israeli government action, two of which created a backlash that led to major violence while the third case, which had all the makings of comparable violence, averted a similar outcome. These involve the opening of the 1996

Temple Mount tunnels, the 2000 "visit" by Ariel Sharon to the al-Aqsa, and the inclusion of three sites located in the occupied West Bank and Jerusalem in the Israeli heritage sites in 2010.[3] In each instance in response to Israeli action and Palestinian backlash, political violence erupted that caught the Israeli government and security forces unprepared. In the first two cases the violence led to significant political consequences, but in the third it was controlled.

In the West Bank there are four major "joint" religious sites and numerous minor ones. The four major sites are divided into two that are more significant, Cave of the Patriarchs (Hebron) and Rachel's Tomb (Bethlehem), and two that are of lesser religious centrality, Joseph Tomb's (Nablus) and Nebi Samuel (north of Jerusalem). Only the last one has not been a site of violence and consequently has not been built into a fortress. The other three have been the object of repeated and intense violence. I address the question of the role of religion in the violence relative to the politics of the sites. Based on these cases and analyzing the role of the various stakeholders, I propose several tentative conclusions about prevention and underscore the malleability of political myopia, official incompetence, and the need for governmental vigilance in the face of nationalist extremism.

The role that a shared religious site plays in a conflict depends on several variables, and the outcome is unpredictable. Clearly physical and religious centralities are important; each is shaped by the actions of stakeholders and political authorities. But the inverse is also true: violence bestows greater religious centrality to a site. One repeated factor for many sites is the presence of a concerted effort to turn it into a space of confrontation in order to claim greater possession of it. When religious extremists conduct a sustained campaign for control, it becomes difficult to stem the tide and at times nearly gives radical stakeholders a monopoly in determining the outcome. Yet, under more or less diligent governmental control, such violence can be averted or minimized. For example, decades of activism by extremist Jews to incite conflict on the Temple Mount has largely failed. The violence that has been instigated repeatedly by the Temple Mount Faithful movement over the years has largely been controlled, as opposed to conflict instigated by more specific political motivations that have used religious symbols and sites to frame the violence (discussed later). This may be changing. More Jews are allowed under police protection to the Haram al-Sharif/Temple Mount plaza, and an increasing number are praying there despite police prohibition for non-Muslims to do so. Slowly, this is becoming a new controversial reality.[4]

Unilateral swaggering actions aimed at the symbolic heritage of specific sacred space have been used both as a provocative act against the other and perhaps even more often as a trump card for domestic politics. On the Arab side, religious rhetoric has often served to reject all negotiations with Israel. Yet the expansive and prolonged peace process shows the limited overall impact of rigid Islamist rejection politics; nonetheless, in times of crisis it is used to justify all uncompromising positions. For its part, Israel has declared Jerusalem (a space with infinitely malleable borders) to be its undivided eternal capital numerous times in laws, parliamentary declarations, and political statements. These provide prime examples of employing religious rhetoric as justification for political acts, anchoring this rhetoric of persuasion in religious heritage. This has become a conventional political tool; primarily when the Israeli government is criticized domestically for being "soft" toward the Palestinians in peace talks, the state raises the flag of the "undivided eternal city" and often authorizes additional building in the expanded municipal borders. The notion of the undivided Holy City—which has expanded geographically threefold since it was occupied in 1967—includes large areas that the rest of the world sees as part of the West Bank. In Israel's treatment of Jerusalem, we see a prime example of the state using religious symbols of the Holy City to incite nationalist political emotions.[5] Shared sites have to be understood as conveying multiple spatial meanings. Jerusalem is a site that is an amalgam of multiple specific sites. The Holy Land itself is both a site and a space, at once sacred as well as secular. For believers, the distinction does not really exist. For society at large, the two are delineated, and this is particularly true for politicians. In Hebron, for example, when the settlers attempt to expand their foothold within the

Holy City, they occupy specific structures that are not sacred but are part of a larger religious space. The question of indivisibility is particularly complicated when it refers beyond specific sites to larger spaces such as cities or the country.

JERUSALEM

Interfaith violence has been a repeated phenomenon in Jerusalem over millennia, though long periods of cohabitation are perhaps even more characteristic of the city. Here I refer to three minor events that, in and of themselves, illustrate the dominance of politics over religion even though the language and the substance of the disputes concerned religious sites. The first, in 1996, is the opening of the tunnels under in the Old City, running from the Western Wall to the Via Dolorosa; the second is the visit by Ariel Sharon in 2000 to the Temple Mount/Haram al-Sharif, which was the explosive event (and one of the causes) that led to the Second Intifada; and the third event, in 2010, took place when several sites that Palestinians see as their own were declared national heritage sites by Israel. In this last case the media were bracing for violence that never erupted.

OPENING THE TUNNELS

On September 23, 1996, Israel opened an exit to an archaeological tunnel in East Jerusalem running from under the Western Wall to the Muslim Quarter of Jerusalem's Old City. When fighting between Israeli soldiers and Palestinian police exploded into several days of mass violence, almost a hundred people died and hundreds more were wounded. The violence soon subsided, and the semblance of a peace process was renewed. It led nowhere, but neither did calls to inflame the conflict further. Indeed, in prayers held the following Friday, religious leaders in the Haram publicly and actively urged an end to violence. On Friday, September 27, 1996, Israeli security responded to Palestinian stone throwing by invading the Haram and shooting into the crowd, killing three. In the following week both sides tried to avoid violence as the Palestinian leadership calmed the crowd and the Israeli forces kept out of the Haram compound. The relatively short eruption became the most violent Palestinian–Israeli collision during the period between the Oslo agreement and the failed Camp David summit.

The tunnel along the ancient Herodian road outside the wall of the Old City had been rediscovered by Charles Warren in the nineteenth century, and Israel has been excavating the site since the late 1960s. While some stages have been completed, the archaeological excavation is ongoing. These excavations have been continuously criticized by Palestinians, and the archaeological value of the site has been overshadowed by its political implications. There was great deal of suspicion during the time the tunnel was closed to the public, and rumors had it that the tunnel was dug under the Haram al-Sharif.[6] Many Palestinians see it as part of a plan to undermine Islam's sacred site. The tunnel was originally opened to the public in 1990, with one entrance next to the Western Wall. Plans to open a second exit for the tunnel in the Muslim Quarter were shelved as a result of international pressure. Israel's Labor government, which was engaged in the peace process with the Palestinians, delayed the opening once the work was completed. This changed after Benjamin Netanyahu (Likud) won the 1996 election and formed a right-wing government. Netanyahu declared the tunnel would be beneficial for both Jews and Palestinians, with increased tourism and economic activity. From the Palestinian side, Yasser Arafat described it as "'extremely dangerous' and said they were part of a campaign to 'change the characteristics of the city' and to appropriate Muslim sites."[7]

Benjamin Netanyahu's actions displayed a lack of confidence in his immediate response to the opening of the tunnel when he sought to create a distance between himself and the political upheaval by immediately leaving for Europe. The decision to open the new exit to the tunnel was made in the face of warnings that violence would follow, yet seemingly few precautions were taken. The decision to open the new exit reversed the policy of the three previous governments, including the right-wing government of Yitzhak Shamir, which, on the advice of the security establishment, had avoided opening the tunnel. The policy change was done despite reservations from the defense minister and without consulting the army. It explicitly excluded any coordination with the Palestinians to counter anticipated violence. The week before the opening, Sheikh Mohammed Hussein, director of al-Aqsa Mosque, warned that Israel "has declared war against the entire Islamic world by opening a new gate."[8] Despite the anticipated opposition, the government was seemingly not ready, and it took its time to counter the eruption. The "secret" opening took place at night and with only a few municipal workers present. The Israeli government presented the affair as a nonissue, feigning surprise at the opposition to such a minor affair. Yet in the context of rejecting Palestinian demands in the peace negotiations, the explosive atmosphere was evident.

In the wake of the tunnel crisis, the Institute for Palestine Studies held a meeting with some of the most prominent Palestinian intellectuals to analyze the causes and consequences of the violence.[9] Most notable, perhaps, was the little attention paid to the religious aspects of the violence. Emphasizing that the immediate cause (opening of the tunnel) was only a trigger, the focus was on the general oppressive conditions of the occupation and the hopelessness of the peace process. The report attributed the Palestinian's success in capturing public opinion to their ability to connect the issue with the Haram, which made it impossible for the Arab states "which frequently remain silent about Israeli abuses of Palestinians" to ignore the violence.[10] Furthermore, the tension enhanced the leadership of Arafat, who had been weakened previously when his calls for demonstrations at the Haram were ignored. Similarly, Palestinians viewed it as a choice by Netanyahu to stage the confrontation over the religious site, testing his support both within Israel and internationally. Israel did so as part of its policy to determine the future of East Jerusalem, a decision over which had been anticipated to take place as part of peace negotiations the following year. The violence was a proxy war. While religion was at the heart of the confrontation, the particular conflict over the tunnel opening was a projection of accumulated frustration, and it became a controversy both sides welcomed and tried to leverage for farther-reaching political goals.

SHARON'S VISIT—BRINGING ON ARMAGEDDON

The next major violence surrounding the site took place in the wake of Ariel Sharon's reckless visit to the Haram al-Sharif/Temple Mount on September 28, 2000. His visit was a political provocation on a sacred site that used religious symbolism to incite public emotions on both sides. Mounted in the immediate aftermath of the failed peace process at Camp David and against a background of ongoing demonstrations, frustration, accusations, political instability, and fearmongering, Sharon's visit aimed directly at influencing domestic politics and even more specifically was part of a party leadership struggle. Sharon was accompanied by more than one thousand security officers, which for the Palestinians appeared as a "major military operation"; the "excessive use of force" was intended as "a message to the Palestinians about their intentions to declare statehood."[11]

Two months after the failed intense peace negotiations at Camp David, which took place toward the end of Bill Clinton's presidency, the political atmosphere was at a boiling point. Violence had been increasing, pressuring politicians and the public alike. As Clinton's term was coming to an end, everyone imagined momentous impending decisions, which increased the fear factor dramatically. Every action was viewed not for its substance but as an indication of foretelling the outcome of the peace agreement and, hence, eternity. The violence in the spring of 2000 over transferring authority from Israel to Palestinians in three villages around Jerusalem and the subsequent intense political pressure within Israel underscored the way religious space represented the rhetoric of identity beyond any specific religious site: the villages came to symbolize Jerusalem. The pent-up pressure at Camp David was infused with fear and was not an atmosphere conducive to negotiation. Accusations followed the failed summit, and the public was primed for a political explosion. The political leadership both in Palestine and among Israel's right-wing opposition further inflamed the public with doomsday scenarios.

The violence was expected.[12] Ra'anan Gissin, Sharon's spokesperson, acknowledged that "Sharon knew he was playing into their [Palestinians] hands, but he went in a clear-headed manner to prove that he wouldn't compromise on Jerusalem and that Israel would stand up for its rights."[13] His political struggle was aimed directly at then prime minister Ehud Barak and at his upcoming leadership struggle within the Likud against former prime minister Netanyahu. Sharon's spokesman characterized the visit to the compound as "the definitive move to capture the premiership."[14] The site was secondary. Sharon claimed that he decided to go because the "Temple Mount is the holiest place for the Jewish people—the remains of the Temple are there. It is not only my right but my duty to go there."[15] But the official Jewish orthodox religious view forbids entering the site because of the area's special sanctity under Jewish law and the risk of sacrilege, and Sharon's evasiveness is indicative of the provocation. The question was of timing, not of rights. Similarly, the Palestinians justified their response as a result of the risk to the holy sanctuary. The violence quickly escalated, the Israeli government under pressure called for elections, and Sharon's ascendency to power shortly thereafter was seen as a successful strategic move. The difficulty posed by this analysis is that events spun out of the control of any of the players, leading to the worst violence the West Bank had witnessed, which lasted for several years. Yet, for conflicting reasons, various stakeholders claimed to have acted according to principles; in truth, badly planned actions led to unforeseen consequences.

The debate has focused on whether Sharon's visit was a cause of the violence, or merely provided an opportunity for the Palestinians to instigate the violence. Either way, the political conflagration resulted from inciting political extremism that was grounded in strong religious sentiments. There is clear evidence that the Palestinians prepared to demonstrate against Sharon as part of the battle over Jerusalem and its religious significance, which was at the heart of the peace process. They were prepared to use some violence. The question remains the extent of the anticipated violence. A follow-up investigation led by George J. Mitchell concluded that "the Sharon visit did not cause the 'Al Aksa intifada,'" but added that "it was poorly timed, and the provocative effect should have been foreseen." Mitchell's conclusion was diplomatic. In May 2001 Bill Clinton was reported to have said that Sharon did provoke the intifada.[16] The provocation was intended, not unforeseen, and amplified when filtered through religious symbolism. But one can only surmise that probably neither side expected a new intifada that would lead to almost six thousand fatalities, including the deaths of almost five thousand Palestinians and over a thousand Israelis. Initially Arafat gained political capital both among the Palestinians and internationally (including in the Arab world), as did Sharon, who promptly became prime minister. Yet the violence expanded beyond any religious context, and eventually the losses overshadowed any perceived immediate political advantage.

Asserting Israeli presence and rejecting "dividing Jerusalem," are conventional mantras in Israeli politics. The provocation, however, did not have to take place. The Israeli government could easily have either stopped Sharon or not responded with excessive violence to the demonstrations.[17] Israel is able to control Jewish violence when it wants to; for example, the Israeli police have shut access to the Temple Mount to non-Muslims for long periods during tension or on specific religious holidays. This often has gone hand-in-hand with limiting Muslim access to men over forty to forty-five years old (the age varies on different occasions), thereby diminishing points of contact.[18] Internal Israeli political posturing clearly provided motivation for Sharon. Was the region ripe for conflict, one that would have occurred regardless? Probably. This at least became the official Israeli position. Sharon's provocation was more of a pretext than the cause, but whether Palestinian anger would have erupted or not remains speculative. It is clear, though, that the violence was not over the religiosity of the space as such; rather, it was an expression of the political disagreements over symbolic national spaces, which in this case was a sacred space. The "al-Aqsa intifada" was a violent four years sparked by Sharon's maneuvers to gain political power and the framing of it as a battle over the future sovereignty of the Temple Mount. Religion was and remains in this sense a tool, not the goal.

A MUTED CONFRONTATION: THE NATIONAL HERITAGE PLAN OF 2010

As was shown earlier, managing controversial religious sites is constitutive of the physical coexistence of the two communities, and it is also relatively easy to upset any balance that exists by unilateral action, especially a tense equilibrium. This seemed as if it would be the case when the Israeli government announced that it would include two West Bank religious shrines as part of a larger list of Israeli national heritage sites. The national heritage plan called for the investment of $100 million to improve heritage infrastructure, most of it within the pre-1967 border. It was the inclusion of Rachel's Tomb (Bilal Mosque) in Bethlehem and the Tomb of the Patriarchs (Ibrahimi Mosque) in Hebron—both Palestinian cities with histories that include Jewish heritage—that created the conflagration.

The declaration instigated an immediate confrontation in which about one hundred protesters pelted stones and burned tires in the West Bank city of Hebron. Others declared a general strike in the city. CNN reported:

> The Palestinian reaction after the announcement was fast and furious. A statement by the Revolutionary Council of Fatah, the political faction in charge of the Palestinian Authority, called the Israeli plan a move to "consolidate the occupation" and an effort at "judaizing" Palestinian land. Dr. Hamdan Taha, an official at the Palestinian Authority's Ministry of Tourism, said the two sites were "an integral part of Palestinian culture" and that if the Israeli government persisted in its efforts, "Palestinians will feel free to nominate sites inside the green line in their heritage list.[19]

Robert H. Serry, the United Nations special coordinator for the Middle East peace process, also expressed concern: "These sites are in occupied

Palestinian territory and are of historical and religious significance not only to Judaism but also to Islam, and to Christianity as well."[20]

The Palestinian Authority warned that the decision would "wreck" peace efforts. Once again the process that had gone nowhere for two decades was "stalled." Religious sites have the capacity to bring out self-righteousness and animosity on both sides, though in this case it was unilateral, with the Palestinians responding to a provocation. The Israeli government acted under pressure from right-wing parties in Israel, which see this as a first step for the inclusion of more West Bank religious sites on the heritage list, and as a step toward annexing the territories. To exclude the West Bank would also have made a statement, one the right-wing government declined. "This is another symbol of the people of Israel's connection to these areas, which cannot be cut off," declared Knesset member Uri Ariel during a tour of the Cave of the Patriarchs with the Land of Israel lobby the day before the government announced its decision: "One day additional areas, like Sebastia and Kfar Etzion, which were the beginning of the Jewish settlement in Judea and Samaria [West Bank], will also become national heritage sites."[21] The two religious sites were the top priority for the settlers. The Israeli left-wing opposition criticized the government for trying to efface the distinction between Israel and the Palestinian territories. Regardless of the political perspectives, all stakeholders recognized that the goal and the rationale for the government action was creeping annexation.

While the long-term goal was undisputed, the government's immediate policy was not carefully formulated but rather was a last-minute concession to right-wing pressure. In this regard the choreography is illuminating, as the tension between politics and religious identity is managed by political pressure and a lack of strategic thinking. The metaperspectives of identity—in this case, Jewish heritage in the Land of Israel (which includes the Occupied Territories)—shape political action even against what would be the better judgment of the politicians. One would imagine that this is not a negligible issue that may or may not have been thought about previously. Yet the last-minute action as though it was a response to external pressure rather than an initiative exposes the deep structure of Israeli politics and its privileging of religious persuasion.

Thus, the terminology of "Judaizing" the land, which is a critique of Israeli action when voiced by the Palestinians, is the self-designation by Israel for its actions of increasing Jewish presence in both pre- and post-1967 territories. Here again the Palestinian critique and the Israeli self-affirmation are shared. Judaizing is deeply influenced by religious motivation, inseparable from nationalist manifestations, and expands the notion of sites to the land at large.

The government decision was taken at a meeting held in Tel Hai in the Upper Galilee on the anniversary of an earlier Zionist confrontation with local Palestinians in 1920.[22] The occasion was not a religious celebration but a national declaration. Although heritage projects are validated globally and often viewed as noncontroversial, when given a particularistic spin they can turn from a validation of self-identity to a mark of expansionist policy. The heritage that was underscored in this case, both from the site of commemoration and the confrontational content of the list, was one of a conflict, not of coexistence, although only the (religious) sites in the West Bank were controversial. There is plenty in the heritage that could have been celebrated to underscore culture, pluralism, or peace. The choice, while perhaps not self-conscious, was distressfully illuminating.

Israeli violence is either structural—employing state institutions, including the security forces—or instigated by settlers who demonstrate against the government's "restraint" in its anti-Palestinian policies. (The Temple Mount Faithful is one example, discussed earlier. More examples follow). In contrast, Palestinians express their anger and politics through street violence (including, sometimes, terror) and peaceful demonstrations. In designating the shared religious sites as Jewish heritage, the extreme right wing pushed the government to carry its "creeping annexation" policy through state mechanisms. If the religious "essence" of the dispute was the driving force, one might have expected a Palestinian response similar to the violence surrounding the 1996 tunnel opening.

However, international and regional political considerations, including the internal Palestinian divisions between the Palestine Liberation Organization and Hamas and the memory of earlier violence that led to great Palestinian suffering, minimized physical confrontations beyond rhetorical claims and a few demonstrations. This is a clear indication of the way political context determines the response to violating equilibrium at shared sacred sites when religious rhetoric plays a complex but secondary role and the interests of the parties are to maintain tension but avoid violent conflict.

THE WEST BANK

Of the four major shared religious sites in the West Bank, the Cave of the Patriarchs in Hebron and Rachel's Tomb in Bethlehem are more significant than Joseph's Tomb and Nebi Samuel. Hebron has been the site of much more political violence than Bethlehem, and Joseph's Tomb attracts more extremism and violence than Nebi Samuel. This would suggest that religious centrality of a site in and of itself is a partial, variable explanation. Nebi Samuel continues to be a relatively peaceful shared site and has not been the target of particular efforts to disrupt it. In contrast, Joseph's Tomb has been a flash point for three decades, monopolized by radicals. Joseph's Tomb is situated in Nablus, in the midst of a dense Palestinian population. Following the Oslo Accords, it was placed under Palestinian control and specifically recognized as a religious site that was to be respected and allowed freedom of worship and protection. But it did not take long for Joseph's Tomb to become embroiled in the general violence of the West Bank, especially early during the Second Intifada (2000–2006). The tomb has become a favorite space for Jewish radical nationalists—primarily a specific group of orthodox extremists (Breslov)—to trigger repeated conflicts with the Palestinian Authority. For a host of reasons, the Israeli government is pleased to maintain the visible conflict while containing the flames of the skirmishes. Its "inability" to control the Breslov orthodox serves its wider interests, both geopolitically vis-à-vis the Palestinian Authority and in its coalition calculations with the most extreme nationalists. The Palestinian Authority's actions illuminate its limitations, highlighting its inability to provide protection to religious sites and testifying to its (lack of) authority, which also serves Israeli interests.

The choreography and politics of control over religious sites, which are viewed as places of national heritage by the less formally religious governments, both left and right wing, have been consistent: a confrontation instigated by settlers paves the way for the permanent occupation of a site. The pattern was initiated by the first settlers in Hebron, who initially entered the Park Hotel in 1968 ostensibly to celebrate Passover in the city of the patriarchs. They soon became illegal squatters but received protection from the military, which eventually led to the establishment of a Kiryat Arba (a Jewish settlement just outside Hebron, which, from the settlers' view, was a suburb of the city) and later to a settlement in the former Hadassah building in the middle of Hebron. Several of these confrontations played out as an extension of internal politics within the government when the settlers were supported by various politicians—including, famously, Shimon Peres—who were competing with their colleagues for public approval. What was an exception in Elon Moreh in 1974—the first confrontation between the settlers and the government over establishing a settlement next to Nablus[23]—became the norm in later years.

All settlements in the occupied West Bank are considered illegal by international law. In contrast, the Israeli designation of "illegal" covers only a settlement made without the approval of the government. The language of illegal settlements established in the public discourse and government politics became increasingly central to peace negotiations over the last two decades as Palestinians demanded that Israel evict the settlements that it recognizes as illegal. Given the overwhelming might of Israel security forces, the existence of illegal settlements is a political decision, not an indication of inability by the government to impose its own law. Indeed, in rare occasions the settlers were removed from a few illegal settlements only to return with greater force and with little or no government opposition. This designation of certain settlements as illegal means other settlements are supposedly legal. This has become a useful tactic for international negotiations, which attracts attention to these illegal marginal settlements and allows Israel to postpone addressing the larger phenomenon of dispossession. The appearance of a rule of law plays into Israel's self-image while allowing the settlers to advance their nationalist agenda. Both appearance and substance are served. The government pursues a policy that is viewed domestically as legal; the settlers operate in the legal space while maintaining an aura of adventurous and national sacrifice.

HEBRON

The most confrontational religious site in the West Bank is at the heart of Hebron's Old City, at the Ibrahimi Mosque/Ma'arat HaMachpela (Cave of the Patriarchs), a two-millennia-old shrine that is revered by the three monotheistic religions where the three patriarchs (and matriarchs) are reputedly buried. The religious role of the patriarchs differs for each religion, but the site is the second most important religious site both for Judaism and for Islam in Palestine (fourth rank overall for Islam). It is of relatively less importance to Christianity. It had been a church during the Crusades and became exclusively a mosque under Muslim rule, when Jews had no, or very limited, access. Despite the constrained access, the city had a Jewish minority between the sixteenth century and 1929. After the 1967 war, Jewish settlers reentered the city and have been living in and around it (Kiryat Arba) ever since. The area has become an ongoing focus for conflict, with the Jewish presence gradually growing. Some of the most extreme Jewish nationalists live in the area, and they see a Jewish presence in the city as the heart of their campaign to annex the West Bank to Israel. Over the years, the army has managed to control some of the more provocative actions, but it has largely avoided confrontation with the settlers. Similarly, politicians have refrained from evicting them, which has kept the city a political cauldron of conflict.

The conflict is best illustrated by the polarized views of the concept of the "massacre in Hebron," which dominates both sides' perspectives. In

Jewish memory, "the massacre" refers to August 1929, when the Palestinian killing of sixty-seven Jews signaled the end of Jewish presence in the city until 1967. This symbolizes for Israel the rationale and the legitimacy for its domination of the region and use of force, and justifies the distrust toward the Palestinians. For Palestinians, however, "the massacre" refers to February 1994, when a Jewish settler, Baruch Goldstein, killed twenty-nine Muslim worshippers in Ibrahimi Mosque and wounded many others. This was the height of Jewish extremism, part of a wave of violence in the wake of the Oslo peace negotiations, which was followed by the assassination of Prime Minister Rabin a year later.[24]

The Israeli commission that investigated the crime found that Goldstein had acted alone, but others saw a conspiracy. The massacre shocked the Israeli mainstream who distanced themselves and viewed it as an abomination. Regarding the massacre as criminal and as counter to Israeli policy meant that, as a state, Israel was not responsible for it. Although the settlers had ostensibly been acting against government policies, this was part of a larger wave of violence against which the government did not react. In contrast, increasing number of settlers came to revere the murderer who became a right-wing hero, commemorated and celebrated widely. The massacre led to demands in the wider Israeli political discourse to evict the settlers from Hebron. This would have been in line with the (at the time) ongoing peace negotiations with the Palestinians. It would also have corresponded to the long-terms plans, which called for Palestinian control in the area. The demands were ignored, as the Rabin government refused to act against the settlers. This unchecked political extremism led eventually to the murder of Rabin. A new policy at the site led to segregating Muslims and Jews, with visitors and worshippers undergoing severe security checks. As an active religious site, it has become a military fortress. The 1994 massacre signaled the beginning of a period of mass and political violence, in particular Hamas terror, which derailed the peace negotiations and brought an Israeli right-wing government into power.

Hebron is at the heart of the conflict. The area is now home to permanent Israeli settlers, a large army presence, and after the 1994 massacre, international observers.[25] There have been several local conflagrations over the years, a continuous oppressive occupation that includes control of the center of the city, and frequent curfews, lack of services, and continuous daily collisions. Jews in Hebron include the most violent among the settlers, including a large part of the Kach (Jewish Defense League) movement (of which Goldstein was a member). Against this background, one possible conclusion is to understand the relative control by the government over the decades and the violence as exceptional. While I would agree that the violence is largely under control, the symbiosis of the settlers and the government can best be described as an antagonistic collaboration. This relationship can be illustrated through a less central site in Nablus.

JOSEPH'S TOMB: EXTREMISTS' AGENDA

Joseph's Tomb is a sacred site for both Jews and Muslims. The conventional Jewish narrative is that Joseph, Jacob's son, was buried in Shechem (Nablus) on property purchased by his father. (Joshua 24:32). The current site near Nablus (now within the city) has been recognized for hundreds of years. This may convey its antiquity or, more likely, its imaginary nature—its invented tradition—since its first identification came thousands of years following the reputed burial at the site. The historical veracity of the site is at best impossible to ascertain, and this is critically important for the way the site is politically manipulated. The traditions associated with the tomb vary, but they have been in existence long enough to create their own historical reality.

The Muslims have two traditions regarding Joseph's burial location: one at the site in Nablus, the other in Hebron. The Jewish nationalist perspective tries to undermine the Muslim attachment to the site by privileging one Muslim tradition over another. The Jewish narrative exploits this duality in the Muslim tradition and privileges the version that sees the location of Joseph's Tomb in the Cave of the Patriarchs in Hebron. It emphasizes the Nablus location as a site to commemorate the death of Sheikh Yusuf Dukat, a figure of lesser importance. Muslims revere Joseph and, while believing that Joseph is buried in Hebron, see the site Nablus as sacred in his memory. Israelis who reject the political and religious significance of the tomb emphasize the mythical nature of the Jewish tradition of the site, the impossibility of verification, and the site's designation as a sheikh burial site.[26] The official Israeli narrative is that Jews made "frequent pilgrimages" to the site before 1948, and they returned in 1967 when Israel occupied the West Bank. There is evidence of neither frequent pilgrimages nor a return in 1967. Indeed, it was only in the 1980s that the site began to receive any significant attention. While there had been pilgrimages to the site, these were more touristic than religious per se, and there was no Jewish presence at the site. To undermine the Jewish narrative of the site, Hamas argued in 2000 that Joseph was buried in Egypt.[27]

The site emerged on the political scene as a result of radical Jewish settlers' activism to expand the Jewish presence into Nablus during the early 1980s. These political developments bear repeating as they illustrate the secondary, or dependent, role religion played in the violence that enveloped it. Force and violence rule supreme in the politics of the site; they are exercised with the aim of controlling the site and the area. Soldiers guarding the site reported to journalists that "controlling Joseph's Tomb isn't all that important to most of the settlers. Off the record, their leaders admit that they only declare the place a holy historic site in order to make a point vis-à-vis the government."[28]

A Jewish settlement a few miles outside the urban population had been established earlier (1974), but the tomb itself did not come into public focus until 1982, when the expansion of Jewish settlements across the West Bank (under the protection of the Israeli Army) collided with Arab resentment "that occasionally flares into violence." It was at this time that "Orthodox Jews [began] to make daily visits to Joseph's Tomb and to discuss the establishment of a yeshiva" near a Palestinian refugee camp next to Nablus.[29]

While the government's explicit goal was to establish new permanent Jewish settlements, the priorities of specific settlements were shaped greatly by activists. One of the more vocal and extreme leaders, Rabbi

Moshe Levinger, declared that "the will of the settlers was what would decide the government's policies."[30] In 1983, in a move similar to their previous invasion of Hebron and using the tomb as a launching point, settlers from across the West Bank rallied to demand a settlement within the city of Nablus. The demonstrators—as is the rule in the West Bank—were protected by hundreds of Israeli security personnel who "erected roadblocks to prevent Arab residents from entering the market during the march." The protest ended "without violence."[31] This Israeli practice of nonviolence is one in which the settlers are protected by the very government and army against which they are demonstrating while the Arabs are kept at bay.

The demonstrators succeeded in their first aim of establishing a beachhead—that is, in shifting the debate from whether they had a right to be there to an internal Israeli dispute around whether the settlers had a right to stay permanently (overnight) in the tomb or only during the day. Gradually the government prohibition on a permanent Jewish presence eroded. The duality of the government's position—consisting of domestic support for settlements while internationally repudiating excesses—translated into a local political power play as the settlers felt morally superior to the government and entitled to confront its policies. Initial declarations by the defense minister and by the chief of staff on the illegality of the settlers' actions and the prohibition of a permanent stay in the tomb were not matched by action. Although during these early days the settlers declared that they would cooperate with an eviction (a posture that changed very radically later), they rhetorically tussled with the government, reminding them of their commitment to settle every part of the land. The disputes were largely a political show aimed at the external community. Indeed, domestic declarations by then prime minister Shamir and by Sharon—who embodied expansionist policies and would be a future prime minister—only amplified the settlers' convictions and confidence. The support was personally and consistently exemplified by Sharon in 1984, when he remarked: "I visited Joseph's tomb on numerous occasions . . . in my eyes Joseph's tomb was the first step of Jews entering Nablus, and Jews ought to live in Nablus."[32] This was a clear political statement that had little to do with religion. During the mid-eighties the army attempted to control the Jewish presence in the tomb and faced settlers who resisted in the belief that they had government support. Both the public and the settlers believed that, notwithstanding occasional international pressure that demanded governmental rebuke, the clear policy was to support the settlers.

The violence was integral to the policy of expansion, even if at the local level the army/police and the settlers seemed locked in confrontation. One case of vandalism and violence, which led to the murder of a thirteen-year-old Palestinian girl in 1989, exemplified the power relations among the settlers, the Palestinians, and the security forces: "The Police report stated that some 30 people entered the Palestinian village 'in a planned and organized operation . . . firing in all directions.' They destroyed hay and trees by fire, smashed windows and fired into solar heaters. At the center of the village, they 'murdered 13-year-old Ibtissam Boudhieh by gunshot and attempted to murder Ghassan Mohammed Said Salah and wounding him in the stomach.'"[33]

Settlers from the Joseph's Tomb yeshiva were arrested, but the combination of Palestinian fear—they quickly buried the body and did not cooperate with the police investigation—and settlers' pressure led to a dismissal of the case. There was no accountability for any violence. The settlers' ideology of violence was explicated by the yeshiva's rabbi, Yitzchak Ginsburg, who asserted "that Jewish blood and a goy's blood are not . . . equal" and Jews can kill Arabs without punishment.[34] Noam Livnat, the coordinator of the yeshiva, denied responsibility for the murder not because the violence was wrong but because the suspects were not "stupid enough to commit such crimes in broad daylight."[35] He would be killed twenty-two years later during a violent night infiltration of the tomb and collision with Palestinian security. Ginsburg's declaration that killing non-Jews is "legitimate" was mostly rebuked in Israel in the late 1980s and was advocated only by the most marginal fringe. Over the years, however, this view has become more widespread and acceptable among settlers.[36] For three decades Ginsburg has been the spiritual leader of the yeshiva in Joseph's Tomb but, as is clear from his violent rhetoric against goyim, his vitriol is not site-specific. The focus on Joseph's Tomb is a spearhead to dominate the whole Land of Israel. In this, the site is differently constructed by the various protagonists. If in 1989 the mainstream settlers' leaders criticized the extremism of the Joseph's Tomb yeshiva and the violence and rampage through Palestinian towns and villages, a decade later it became the norm.

The geographic location of Joseph's Tomb yeshiva, which was likely to involve confrontation with Palestinians, attracted from the beginning primarily people who were inclined to violence. This became self-fulfilling situation. In contrast, in the Israeli discourse the extremism was explained away as a response by the settlers to the First Intifada and the rising violence that infected the region despite the chronology of the violence that preceded the intifada. The settlers saw the army as ineffective, and they were challenging the government. The Palestinians viewed the Israeli government and the settlers as two facets of one colonial occupation force.

Following the Oslo agreement, the peace negotiations between 1993 and 1995 created an appearance of cooperation between Israel and the Palestinian Authority. The indeterminate situation led to the postponement of every possible decision pending a final agreement, encouraging intransigence on both sides for fear of looking weak in public. In December 1995 the control of Nablus, and with it the surrounding of Joseph's Tomb and the yeshiva, was transferred from Israel to the Palestinian Authority. Under the Oslo agreement, Palestinian police were to secure the parameters of the site, and Israeli security officers its inside. A joint Palestinian–Israeli force patrols the access routes to the tomb. One could have seen it as a form of cooperation—Israel controlled the security, the Palestinians the commercial and tourist aspects of the site—but this is neither how the public perceived it nor how it turned out. Israel demanded to maintain its control of Joseph's Tomb even after the Palestinian Authority became responsible for the area in general. The divided authority faced continuous hostility from both Palestinian and Israeli nationalists, which led to a series of collisions, intermittent access, extensive Israel presence in the midst of Palestinian urban population, and repeated confrontations. While the form of violence by the nationalists from each side differed depending on available force and legitimacy, their goals were similar: to scuttle any possible agreement and to undermine the possibility of coexistence.

For three decades, the routine interaction between the settlers and the army at the tomb has been one of settlers attempting to infiltrate (i.e., visit, with or without permission) the site and to expand the Jewish presence (such as building a ritual bath without a permit, which the army demolished) and the army trying to minimize the friction with Palestinians by restricting access. The story repeated itself numerous times as it ebbed and flowed according to the general security situation.[37] The settlers dismissed the Muslim claims for ownership by challenging the site's religious significance; ergo, the two sides' claims were similar. This competition of who spiritually owns the place, and to which side the site is more important, is characteristic of contested sites. In this regard, Nebi Samuel is the exception while Hebron, Nablus, and Bethlehem are more representative.

The next major conflagration at Joseph's Tomb was in response to the opening of the tunnels in Jerusalem in 1996 (discussed earlier) as part of the general mass demonstrations and violence across the Occupied Territories. The Palestinian protesters and militia assaulted Joseph's Tomb, an attack that led to the death of six Israeli soldiers and two Palestinians. The eruption was violent, but local cooperation between the Palestinian and Israeli security forces enabled containment, and the Palestinians even provided an ambulance to evacuate a wounded Israeli soldier, and a new cease-fire was negotiated. The clash showed the ambivalence of the Palestinian position; while the crowd attacked the tomb, the Palestinian security forces initially participated in the assault but at a certain point began to protect the sieged Israelis. The policies had little to do with religion. The negotiations for settling the conflict were focused on political issues as each side played to its home audience. The Israelis refused to evacuate the site and remained there ringed by Palestinian police with a Palestinian flag flying over them.[38]

The geography of the site in Nablus manifested the complexity of a shared site under conflict. The settlers' outpost is surrounded by a

Palestinian urban area, and its protection is dependent on the Palestinian police. When violence breaks out, even if it begins as a demonstration, the context and memory of previous times when weapons were used quickly leads to escalation and reciprocal recriminations of who started the violence.[39] The radical settlers continuously evoke the myth of the weak persecuted Jew and referred to the attack in 1996 as a pogrom, although this does not account for the context of the provocation of the violence (the opening of the tunnels) or for the overall occupation. Controlling the local violence once it erupts takes time, and its legacy becomes a permanent feature of the history of the contested place. During the intifada, as in 1996, the violence was neither more nor less intense in religious sites relative to other settlements, such as in Gaza. The critical variable was how isolated the Jewish post was within Palestinian population: the smaller the outpost, the more vulnerable.

Following the 1996 violence, the combustible religious nationalist militant site remained with a few settlers (students) guarded by the military. Jews were not allowed to stay overnight in the site and instead were daily escorted by the army in and out. Over the next few years, whenever the tension escalated, such as a result of the expansion of settlements (e.g., Har Homa in Jerusalem, March 1997), or on dates of commemoration (e.g., Land Day), the tomb was closed to avoid clashes. The army choreographed a period of nonconfrontation. Rebuilding after the burning of the site in 1996 was done slowly and with a view for securing the site during violent clashes, not with a civilian or religious goal. This form of conflict control worked to a degree. But the militants were conducting a long-term attrition struggle and at times were able to enlarge their foothold as a result of external circumstances. Every violent encounter against Jewish settlers in the region (e.g., August 1998) provided an excuse to expand their presence in the tomb, to which the Palestinians would retaliate with tit-for-tat actions, leading the Israelis to back down.[40]

The fighting that erupted in October 2000 proved the most violent over the last twenty years. At the start of the Second Intifada, after a few days of the siege and the killing of an Israeli soldier and up to eighteen

Palestinians, Israel withdrew from Joseph's Tomb. The Palestinian crowd ransacked much of the tomb, and although the Palestinian police helped the evacuation of the Israeli soldiers and protected them, the public and the media in Israel focused exclusively on the burning of the site.[41] While the Palestinians celebrated the liberation of the shrine and hoped to build a mosque, the media reported little religious talk but a large dose of national rhetoric.

Indeed, despite pressure from Hamas, the Palestinian Authority rejected turning the site into a mosque and worked hard to minimize the destruction and then rebuild the place. Israelis were more eager to underscore the damage. The larger context became a struggle over future memory and the question of the ability to allow free access to religious sites. If Joseph's Tomb is under Palestinian control, is it accessible to Jews? Is it safe and respected? It may well have been in the Israeli interest to lose access in 2000.

The settlers were adamant to sustain the conflict and the pressure on the Palestinians. Within three weeks they organized an expedition to the area with the army's support. The expedition led to a collision, a firefight, and casualties. The dynamics of the clash, including the army permit, which was described by high officials as a mistake, exemplified the dynamics between the nationalists and the government/army. While the government is presented as giving in to pressure, thereby maintaining a façade of political responsibility, it allowed the extremists to set the agenda. In the years following 2000 there were several religious excursions to the site, each of which involved a major security operation. This incited the local Palestinian population, which turned around and attacked the site after the army cleared the area. The destruction was all the fodder the settlers needed to prove their demand for control over the site. These collisions occurred despite the extensive cooperation between the army and the Palestinians, especially as the security situation in the West Bank improved overall. The settlers looked particularly askance at the growing general coexistence that they tried to disrupt.

Most violent were the illegal excursions by Breslov Hassidim to enter Joseph's Tomb as they collided with both Israeli and Palestinian security forces. But having the political support—at least a third of the Parliament members signed petitions on their behalf—meant that the army provided protection even when the action was directed against it. Gradually the infiltrators regularized the exchanges, and although violence was always in the air (potential and sometimes real), the notion that these kinds of visits were "business as usual" meant that the extremists had defined the arena according to their wishes.

Since 2007 the number of participants in the excursions increased, as did the pressure on the army to allow more frequent and bigger groups. A critical aspect of the events is the representation in the international media of the Breslovs' perspective. Using terminology of devotion and renewal, of risky and perilous night visits, the Breslovs' infiltration into the Palestinian territory without either Palestinian or Israeli permits is presented as religious action, which ignores the political goal of the action, their intention of inciting conflict, and that the activities are altogether illegal. There is little doubt that the Breslov activists do not distinguish their religious beliefs from political goals; however, for the international media to buy in, accepting the religious construction over presenting it as political extremism, is a different matter. An Arab report of these events is expectedly different: "Palestinian sources reported that dozens of settlers stormed the so called 'Joseph's Tomb' east of the city and performed religious rites before they withdrew under a large military protection."[42] As political pressure increased, the army found it necessary to negotiate with the Breslov rabbi, to work out a modus vivendi that gave the actions increased political legitimacy. By 2011 the number of visitors taking part in these night excursions had increased to over a thousand, who were accompanied by a similar number of soldiers. The excursions have become an intense ritual of religious effervescence. Will these new practices elevate the centrality of the tomb religiously? Will this political confrontation become a new religious practice? This will be likely shaped politically, but in the meantime the surrounding Palestinian population of tens of thousands is placed under unofficial curfew during these night excursion rituals.[43]

NEBI SAMUEL

From an external perspective Nebi Samuel is a unique and peaceful holy site for the three monotheistic religions. It is a mosque built on the ruins of a medieval church, below which is a cave that operates as a synagogue. Muslim and Jewish worshippers overlap, especially on Friday afternoons, and for the impartial observer the situation seems one of peaceful coexistence.[44] Obviously it is coexistence under occupation taking place in a liminal space that does not belong to the West Bank and is not under Palestinian Authority. It is not formally part of Jerusalem, and the Palestinian inhabitants in the village bordering the site are isolated both from Israel (they have West Bank identification cards) and physically from the West Bank by being on the western side of the separation wall. They are truly in a marginal undetermined situation.[45] Palestinians who wish to visit the site face security constraints as they must go through checkpoints and searches, and the possibility of denial at times. Nonetheless, these obstacles do not deter a steady stream of visitors.

The site had been archaeologically excavated extensively during Israeli rule and under Israeli management. The work limited the villagers' space, especially their ability to build; their land was confiscated for a national park that has been designated on the mountain, and their travel was confined to minimal public transportation. A few of the villagers make their living from tourism, but most are poor and find their lives very constrained. For Israelis and international tourists from the Jerusalem side, the situation is much simpler: they can drive to the site without any limitations. Notwithstanding the intensive and close interaction between the two groups, the site has not been subject to political violence or religious extremism, no radical nationalist group has turned the site into a contentious space so far, and the cohabitation (under Israeli supremacy) is exemplary, given the context. The contrast with Joseph's Tomb underscores politics over religion. Since Nebi Samuel is within Israel's uncontested control and surrounded with nearby settlements—Jerusalem suburbs, in official Israeli perspective—it has not been the target of attempted Jewish radical domination. This underscores the religious fervor in Joseph's Tomb as politically motivated. The geography of Nebi Samuel's relative isolation meant that it was not likely to be the site for mass popular movements from the Palestinians, as are the other three major sites in the West Bank. The geography might have made it easier for Israel to dispossess the local Palestinians, and the lack of political competition kept the religious fervor of both sides low.

CONCLUSION

The West Bank and Jerusalem have been at the center of religious coexistence and confrontation between Jews and Arabs for almost half a century. Over this period the area has probably received more global attention than any other religious conflict. The discussion in this chapter suggests several conclusions regarding the main questions raised by this volume. Perhaps the most important observation concerns the issue of whether shared sites are more likely to be flash points than national or religious sites in general. Do religious sites revered by conflicting parties attract more contentious, violent, and continuous conflict than other disputed spaces? Because this discussion addressed only shared religious sites, there is little data here to substantiate or refute this proposition. However, given the variability of violent conflicts, I suggest that the violence is primarily political, although it is often instigated by protagonists whose politics is motivated by religious beliefs, or by secular politicians who are happy to align with religious sentiments. There is no evidence to suggest that religious violence is any less political than other forms. Religion as such can lead to different policy choices, but the choice between them is political. Indeed, the frequent violence in the West Bank surrounding the separation wall and various army checkpoints suggests that the volatility of the space is determined by the encounter itself, not by its religious characteristic. Where there is rationale to incite conflict as a way to achieve political gains, shared religious sites provide a good flash point.

What about the religious centrality of sites? It is true that much ongoing violence takes place surrounding central religious space, especially the Haram al-Sharif/Temple Mount. Yet the increased role of Joseph's Tomb, which has become central because of political nationalist manipulation of religious arguments, suggests the malleability of religious centrality as a fixed category. Indeed, for a few Jews the religious importance of Joseph's Tomb has increased as a result of the violence. This also points to the role of stakeholders in inflaming the conflict vis-à-vis the government, which, as the discussion in this chapter shows, has been repeated time and again from Hebron to Joseph's Tomb to Sharon's instigating the 2000 Second Intifada. The ability and willingness of the political authorities to control or use violence to further strategic or short-term political goals is central to understanding the conflict, and as such the causality can be understood more through political lenses than religious framework.

Indeed, the question of centrality is subject to reevaluation in light of political action. The subjective historical and religious narrative involved in claiming a legacy to a place often depends on the desire for conflict. Religion is part of a larger story in this case. The ellipses in the national historical narrative construct a reality that incites the other side to focus on distortion and conflict. This is evident in the Israeli refusal to acknowledge the expulsion of Palestinians in 1948, or the Palestinians consistently ignoring their (and the Arab states) role in the 1948 war.[46] It is particularly notable when it comes to religious sites and the reciprocal refusal by both sides to acknowledge alternative narratives. Joseph's Tomb is a clear example. On the Haram/Temple Mount, there has been interreligious agreement over the narrative since the seventh century, but Palestinians refuse to publicly discuss Jewish tradition and attachment to the site that dates back even earlier, seventeen hundred years prior to Muhammad. The disagreement does not stem from religious disputes but is political, and it has been growing more contentious. Muslim religious pronouncements that deny Jewish tradition encounter angry Israeli responses.[47] There had been extensive Islamic literature that recognized the Jewish attachment to the site, but that has become somewhat taboo with the increased political disputes, and with the fear over the future control of Jerusalem.

The malleability of shared sacred spaces—sites and regions—contradicts decisive conclusions about whether shared sites are either more or less subject to violence than other flash points. What would the category of "shared sites" best be compared to: alternative national sites, exclusive religious sites, any sites of previous conflict (repeated violence)? How many sites fall in each category? Is the question primarily whether there is a greater likelihood or propensity for conflict? One may stipulate that the memory of conflict and fear of impending conflict may provide a likely variable, perhaps more than the sacredness of a site. We lack comprehensive data to examine such a proposition. Indeed, the Nebi Samuel example shows that there are places where a sacred site can remain shared even in the midst of an intense political conflict. The political context suggests a low priority for manufacturing conflict. The considerations are political, not religious. Where the geopolitical situation differs, such as Joseph's Tomb, a new tradition was successfully invented to incite a conflict, and the political narrative pushes the origin of the conflict to a much older time than recorded historically. The case studies presented here suggest that the category of shared sacred sites is fluid and heterogeneous (site, city, and region).Given the political context, it provides a space that is prone to incitement framed by religious rhetoric, but not necessarily more than other points of contact/friction. This would suggest that prevention, while difficult, lies more in the political sphere and less within religious discourse.

Control over religious sites is not in and of itself a religious requirement. Indeed, in 2000 on the eve of the Camp David summit and as the Israeli government was preparing its public opinion, it solicited the opinion of the chief rabbis in Israel, who said that "they would not oppose transfer of control over Rachel's Tomb, Joseph's Tomb and even the Tomb of the Patriarchs, to the Palestinians, as long as appropriate measures were taken to guarantee access, prayer rights and security for Jews at the sites. Neither the halakha nor tradition, they said, requires Jewish sovereignty over graves, including the graves of the religious pantheon."[48]

The Chief Rabbinate is not a government tool; once elected, the two rabbis are often at odds with the government. It was never a clear case that religious imperatives drove the political process. It was a political choice to demand control of territories in the name of religion, for both Muslim and Jews. There was less religious wiggle room over the Haram/Temple Mount, but here the challenge was to give a formal political formulation to maintain the status quo rather than change it. The Jewish religious prohibition to enter the site before the Messiah arrives and the Muslim control of the site fulfilled the desire of both sides, as long as neither ceded their sovereignty. The religious dispute can be resolved on the terms that are agreed to by both sides; it is the political conflict that is protracted. The 2000 intifada fortified the Israeli nationalists in their belief that force and occupation were the only solution, and the wide disillusionment in Israel from the peace talks reassured them. The widespread belief among Jews that the Palestinians were unreasonable in their rejection of the deal offered, and that they always only waited for an excuse to reignite the violence, led to the resurgence of hard-liners and the end of the peace movement in Israel. Religious sites were the focal point of the conflagration, but the fire was started by nationalist—not religious—concerns.

NOTES

1. See introduction to this volume. Hayden speaks about "antagonistic tolerance," and Hassner focuses on the centrality and indivisibility of shared sites, and both see religious conflicts as significantly distinct from political conflicts.
2. For example, UNESCO World Heritage Convention, "Initiative on Heritage of Religious Interest," http://whc.unesco.org/en/religious-sacred-heritage/.
3. "Jerusalem Day" (May 20, 2012) had all the markings of a new violent conflict over a sacred site, the old city. Israeli right-wingers marched through the old city inflaming sentiments and facing counterdemonstrations from the Palestinians, but a conflagration was averted because of police control.
4. Edmund Sanders, "More Jews Praying on Site Also Sacred to Muslims," *Los Angeles Times*, October 28, 2012. For a rebuttal, see Tamar Sternthal, "'The Los Angeles Times' and Temple Mount Provocations," *CAMERA*, October 28, 2012.

5. The examples are numerous. See Akiva Eldar, "Provocative Timing/Bibi's Latest Card," *Haaretz*, October 25, 2010. On the criticism by Arab politicians, see Avraham Sela, "Politics, Identity and Peacemaking: The Arab Discourse on Peace with Israel in the 1990s," *Israel Studies* 10, no. 2 (2005): 15–72.
6. In 1990 "rumors of plans by the extremist Jewish group, the Temple Mount Faithful, to put up a cornerstone for a new Temple on the Temple Mount sparked riots, in which police shot and killed some 17 Palestinians." Bill Hutman, "Darkness at the End of the Tunnel," *Jerusalem Post*, September 27, 1996.
7. Barton Gellman, "Israelis, in Nighttime Move, Open Temple Mount Tunnel," *Washington Post*, September 25, 1996.
8. Hutman, "Darkness at the End of the Tunnel."
9. "The Tunnel Crisis" *Journal of Palestine Studies* 26, no. 2 (Winter 1997): 95–101.
10. Ibid.
11. "Mr. Sharon entered as a police helicopter clattered overheard and a thousand armed policemen were positioned in and around the Temple Mount, including antiterror squads and ranks of riot officers carrying clubs, helmets and plastic shields. Throughout the tour, Mr. Sharon was ringed tightly by agents of the Shin Bet security service." Joel Greenberg, "Sharon Touches a Nerve, and Jerusalem Explodes," *New York Times*, September 29, 2000; and Khalil Shikaki, a leading Palestinian political scientist and director of Ramallah's Palestinian Center for Policy and Survey Research, quoted in Larry Derfner, "The Martyrs of Haram a-Sharif," *Jerusalem Post*, October 13, 2000.
12. Etgar Lefkovits, "Sharon's Planned Visit to Temple Mount Angers Palestinians," *Jerusalem Post*, September 27, 2000.
13. Gil Hoffman, "Ten Years After Temple Mount Visit, R'a'anan Gissin Tells 'Post': Sharon Knew Palestinians Were Planning Violence, but Wanted to Show He Wouldn't Compromise on J'lem," *Jerusalem Post*, September 29, 2010.
14. Ibid.
15. Quoted in "Q&A: Ariel Sharon; My Visit Didn't Cause the Violence," *Washington Post*, October 8, 2000.
16. "Clinton: Sharon Provoked Intifada," *Jerusalem Post*, May 18, 2001; and Herb Keinon, "Mitchell Committee Report: Sharon Is Not to Blame for Intifada," *Jerusalem Post*, May 6, 2001.
17. When Sharon was in power, for example, he could stop similar Israeli provocations. In 2005, in a rematch for the Likud leadership, Landau backed down from a similar goading. "Landau Cancels Temple Mt. Visit," *Jerusalem Post*, October 3, 2005.
18. Steven Erlanger and Greg Myre, "Huge Police Force Bars Israeli Rightist Rally at Jerusalem Holy Site," *New York Times*, April 11, 2005.

19. "Clashes Erupt over West Bank Religious Shrines," *CNN*, February 22, 2010, http://www.cnn.com/2010/WORLD/meast/02/22/israel.palestinians.clashes/index.html.
20. Quoted in "UN Coordinator Slams PM's Heritage Plan," *Jerusalem Post*, February 22, 2010.
21. Hagai Einav, "Cave of Patriarchs Included in National Heritage Plan," *Ynetnews*, February 21, 2010.
22. This first "battle" has become a foundational event in Zionist nationalism, symbolizing heroism and willing national sacrifice. The leader of the group, Joseph Trumpeldor, became a national hero and a symbol for self defense.
23. The confrontation was internal to the government, part of the internal Israeli political struggle; Prime Minister Rabin opposed the settlers, while Defense Minister Peres provided subterfuge support.
24. Ehud Sprinzak, "Extremism and Violence in Israel: The Crisis of Messianic," *Annals of the American Academy of Political and Social Science* 555, no. 1 (1998): 114–26.
25. Karin Aggestam, "TIPH: Preventing Conflict Escalation in Hebron?" *Civil Wars* 6, no. 3 (2003): 51–69; Justus R. Weiner, "The Temporary International Presence in the City of Hebron ('TIPH'): A Unique Approach to Peacekeeping," *Wisconsin International Law Journal* 16 (1997): 281–351.
26. Avraham Burg calls the establishment of the yeshiva "paganism and an act of idolatry." Under the pretense of a love of the land, the act contradicted Jewish tradition. See Avraham Burg, *The Holocaust Is Over; We Must Rise from Its Ashes* (New York: Palgrave Macmillan, 2008), 179. Communications Minister Shulamit Aloni (1992) emphasized it as a tomb of a sheikh, which caused appropriate public commotion as sacrilege in Israel. Others underscored the non-Jewish character of the place historically, and of Shechem, as a place the Talmud says is divinely "designated for disasters." Gershom Gorenberg, "Guide to the Perplexed: The Other Tora." *Jerusalem Post*, June 12, 1989.
27. "Mideast: Hamas Issues Statement on Seizure of Joseph's Tomb," *BBC Worldwide Monitoring*, October 8, 2000.
28. "Soldiers in Joseph's Tomb Were 'Cannon Fodder,' Reservists Warned," *Ha'aretz*, October 3, 2000.
29. David Levy, Israel's deputy prime minister and a relative moderate in a right-wing government, quoted in Edward Walsh, "Neighbors Are Foes in Hebron," *Washington Post*, November 5, 1982.
30. Quoted in "Jewish Settlers' Moves to Create New Settlement in Nablus," *Israel Home Service*, November 29, 1983.
31. Ibid.

32. Quoted in "Sharon on Need for More Jewish Settlements," *Israel Home Service*, March 6, 1984.
33. Joshua Brilliant, "20 Still at Large After Kifl Harith Shooting. Yeshiva Men Suspected of Murder, Arson," *Jerusalem Post*, June 2, 1989.
34. Joshua Brilliant, "Jew's and Goy's Blood Not the Same," *Jerusalem Post*, June 4, 1989.
35. Brilliant, "20 Still at Large."
36. In 2011 Ginsburg's view received validation from a book coauthored by two rabbis and supported by several others. A political turmoil followed, including demands to indict all for incitement for violence, which the attorney general declined in May 2012.
37. A characteristic report: "Several hundred participants in the 'Samaria March' of solidarity with Nablus area Jewish settlers refused to obey an IDF ban on their entry into Nablus on foot, instead of in buses. The marchers swarmed through a roadblock and army commanders decided to escort them through the city to Joseph's Tomb." *Jerusalem Post*, May 19, 1995.
38. Serge Schmemann, "Middle East Conflict: The Overview; 50 Are Killed as Clashes Widen from West Bank to Gaza Strip," *New York Times*, September 27, 1996.
39. Joel Greenberg, "Violence Forces Israeli Army to Rethink Strategy," *New York Times*, October 6, 1996.
40. The killing of two settlers elsewhere led to a demand to allow settlers to mourn the dead, and to do so around the clock, which raised Palestinian opposition and caused security concerns, which led to new closure of the site (in August 1998). The agreement between the Israelis and Palestinians allowed for the settlers to stay there for thirty days of mourning.
41. Benny Morris, *Righteous Victims: A History of the Zionist-Arab Conflict* (New York: Vintage, 2001), 664; and Joel Greenberg, "Whose Holy Land? At the Shrine; Palestinians Destroy Israeli Site That Was Scene of Many Clashes," *New York Times*, October 8, 2000. Eighteen is the number of Palestinian casualties given by the Palestinian police chief for Nablus.
42. "Israeli Settlers Break Into the Eastern Region of Nablus," Petra News Agency Headline, reported by the *BBC Worldwide Monitoring*, October 19, 2010.
43. Anshel Pfeffer, "Turning Joseph Into a Jewish Fanatic," *Haaretz*, July 8, 2011.
44. Yusuf Natsheh, Yitzhak Reiter, Wasfi Kailani, and Galit Hazan, "Guide to the Tomb of Samuel" (unpublished ms. 2009).
45. Joharah Baker, "The Silent Steel Resistance of Nabi Samuel," *MIFTAH*, August 1, 2011.

46. One recent exception was by Abbas in an interview aimed at the Israeli public, not Palestinian. See Khaled Abu Toameh and Tovah Lazaroff, "Abbas: Arabs Erred in Rejecting 1947 Partition Plan," *Reuters*, October 30, 2011.
47. Isabel Kershner, "Western Wall Feud Heightens Israeli–Palestinian Tensions," *New York Times*, November 25, 2010.
48. Amir Oren, "Chief Rabbis Prepared to Forgo Control of Certain 'Holy Places,'" *Haaretz*, July 12, 2000.

8

THE IMPACT OF CONFLICTS OVER HOLY SITES ON CITY IMAGES AND LANDSCAPES

THE CASE OF NAZARETH

RASSEM KHAMAISI

As CITIES UNDERGO dynamic changes, including demographic, geopolitical, sociocultural, and economic transitions, the desire of ethnonational and religious groups to build new holy places—or to rebuild or repurpose existing holy sites—can create tension that has the potential to escalate into physical violence. This chapter focuses on the city of Nazareth in order to illustrate the theoretical and practical implications of ethnoreligious conflict among Arab Palestinian citizens in Israel that arises out of competing claims over the nature, essence, and representation of a holy place. In the case of Nazareth, a city that is subject to multiple faiths' claims on its holy places, changes to status quo relations at holy sites are framed as a challenge to tradition, regardless of how new these claims to religious ownership may be. This essay argues that conflict over holy sites is a manifestation of stakeholder competition over political power and socioeconomic resources. As we will see, multifaceted conflicts between stakeholders impact the ethnoreligious development of the city by overdetermining its character and the way in which it is perceived at local, national, and international levels.

This essay begins with a discussion of the theoretical role that holy sites play in shaping the sociocultural imagery, political structure, and representational function of cities, followed by a general historical review of the Nazareth region. It then describes how conflict over holy sites contributes to the deterioration of relations between different ethnic and religious minority groups in the city. This is followed by a discussion of the role of outsiders (national and international stakeholders) in aggravating a conflict and the ways in which the locals (domestic stakeholders) benefit from the conflict. The essay is based on scholarly literature, media coverage, and twelve open interviews with persons involved in the religious conflict in the city. In addition, the essay relies on the researcher's daily monitoring of developments at the Shihab al-Deen site, including events surrounding the 2007 conflict over the site, and careful review of the development plan for Nazareth, 2007–2012.[1] The conclusion critically reevaluates the various components of the conflict.

DEFINING URBAN HOLY SITES

Holy sites carry physical and symbolic dimensions that are geographically and historically determined and have significance for one or more religious communities, all of which attribute to the sites extraordinary religious significance or consider the sites to be their object of divine consecration.[2] Entry to or worship inside holy sites may be related to the rights or duties of certain members of a community or may be otherwise circumscribed, thus allowing specific groups entrance while prohibiting others. Change or alteration of these sites—particularly as it relates to admission—may lead to opposition, resistance, and even violence. Moreover, holy places are often of intra- and interstate juridical importance, even as the entry of the secular authority to sacred holy places may be restricted.[3] Before turning to the specifics of historical and political developments in Nazareth, it is helpful to summarize the role of holy places with regard to socio- and geopolitical transitions:

- Holy places function as landmarks of space and time. They orient us in the urban space. A holy place is a landmark in space; a historical event is a landmark in time.

- The significance of holy sites is ranked by religious adherents, who attribute a hierarchy of value to sites located in different cities and within the same city. These hierarchical rankings have a direct impact on the ways the sites and cities are perceived both by the group's own members and by outsiders.[4]
- In the aftermath of the Industrial Revolution and the Renaissance, the status of holy places in cities decreased. This decline was met by the growth of new cities and urban centers where such growth was based on the emergence of new economies and services.
- Cities undergo dynamic changes (demographic, political, sociocultural, and economic) while sites generally continue to belong to one group sharing the same beliefs. As cities continue to change and their holy places remain static, conflict can result from competing claims to define the specific nature of the city.
- In secular and modern cultures, holy objects and holy historic places are often disguised as sentimental landmarks, cultural monuments, and tourist attractions, all of which contribute to the economic growth of the cities.
- Like the more official shrines of institutional religions, holy objects and places can fill a need for physical, psychological, and cosmic orientation and can mediate individuals' contact with the larger universe. They may provide a center for identity formation and offer believers a place in which, momentarily transcending their usual selves, they merge with the past and the future.

Generally speaking, cities that develop around ancient holy places continue to be traditional and conservative and therefore less attractive to modern and global activities. The dominant culture of the world and the global economy is secular. As is the case with Nazareth, traditional cities and their holy places may not create an appropriate environment for competing global economic activities; instead, they establish and develop services for pilgrims and cultural activities at the city's holy sites, which can be of less economic value and impact that other nonreligious economic activities.[5] Therefore, developing cities where religious and national conflicts over holy places are deeply rooted face many structural challenges.

Cities that are undergoing organic or planned changes, coupled with transitions in relation to the role and size of holy places, are often characterized by conflict. Gerard van der Leeuw identifies four dynamisms that relate to holy places:

- The dynamism of location or position; namely, every established holy place is a conquest of space that could be used by others, thereby leading to a politics of position.
- The dynamism of property, whereby a holy place is appropriated, possessed, and owned.[6] Its sacredness is maintained through claims and counterclaims to its ownership.
- The dynamism of exile, which takes the form of modern loss of, or nostalgia for the holy past.
- The dynamism of exclusion, which means that the sanctity of the holy place is preserved by maintaining boundaries.

These four components have a direct impact on the cultural geography and hierarchical power relations surrounding holy sites.[7] In addition to their functional uses, holy places play a significant role in the exercise of the majority religion's power, which may strive to impose its cultural and religious dominance over minority faiths residing in the same communities. It comes as no surprise, then, that many cities' sociocultural landscapes are shaped by the configuration of holy sites because mosques, churches, synagogues, and temples are subject to disputes that encompass other aspects of communal life. Such is the case regarding the building of mosques near the World Trade Center "Ground Zero" in New York City, the raising of mosques' minarets in Switzerland, and the erection of a Coptic church in the Aswan district of Southern Egypt.

Similar to believers in most urbanized and modern cities, the heterogeneous religious residents of Nazareth feel deeply connected to the sacred sites located within their city. Yet their affiliations are impacted by chronic tension and instability as regional developments stimulate an increase in identity based politics and outsider involvement. This essay illustrates the aforementioned characteristics and political trends by focusing on the conflict over Nazareth's holy sites, which is part of a larger struggle for control over regional political power and socioeconomic resources. Moreover, Nazareth's significance for Christian Arabs in Israel, as well as for Christians all over the world, endows this struggle with both national and international significance.

TRANSFORMATION OF CONTROL OVER THE HOLY LAND

A clear understanding of the historical development of Nazareth's holy sites can be obtained by examining the background of the ethnonational and religious conflicts that characterize the region. Unique to Palestine is the birth and spread of the three monotheistic religions.[8] While some of the region's holy sites are exclusive to one religion, others are shared by all three; in many cases, this is manifested through a dialectical relationship between ethnonational and religious conflicts.[9] The cities of the Holy Land, such as Jerusalem, Bethlehem, Nazareth, and al-Khalil (Hebron) are traditional religious centers for Muslims, Jews, and Christians. The key holy places located in these cities attract pilgrims, visitors, and tourists and generate income that feeds into the local economy, which is based on services that capitalize on local culture and religion.

The British Mandate for Palestine's (BMP) geopolitical domination over the country and ethnonational relations directly impacted the transformation of holy places in the region. This domination paved the way for the establishment of the State of Israel, and it strengthened the status of Christians in the Holy Land. These circumstances led to an intense geopolitical and ethnonational conflict that eventually culminated in the war of 1948, when Israel was established on approximately 78 percent of the area allocated by the League of Nations to the former BMP. More than 750,000 Arab Palestinians became outsider refugees in neighboring countries.[10] Approximately one-third of the Palestinian population in the newly established State of Israel became internally displaced persons or refugees in their own country. Some of these internal refugees were absorbed by localities such as Nazareth.

The 1948 and 1967 wars caused displacements and the scattering of the Palestinian people. Palestinians ended up comprising three basic groups:

- Arab citizens of Israel, who total approximately 1.3 million. They continue to live in their former villages and towns (e.g., Nazareth) as indigenous communities and are today citizens of Israel.[11]
- Palestinian residents of the West Bank, East Jerusalem, and the Gaza Strip (the so-called Palestinian Territories), who number approximately 3.8 million.
- The Palestinian diaspora (El-Shatate), comprising residents in other countries of the Middle East and elsewhere, numbering about 5 million.[12]

Arab Palestinians therefore became a minority in the new State of Israel, which was established in 1948. They constituted approximately 14 percent of the total population of the new state, which had a population of 873,000, including 156,000 Arabs. Today the number of Arab Palestinian citizens has grown to about 17.5 percent (1,300,000) of the total citizen population of Israel (7,419,000).[13]

The Arab minority in Israel is further divided into three ethnoreligious groups: Muslims account for 81 percent; Christians, for 10 percent; and the remaining 9 percent of the population identifies as Druze. The Christian population dropped from 22 percent in 1949 to 10 percent in 2010.[14] This decline was due to a decrease in natural growth and an increase in migration.[15] The decrease that occurred among the Arab Christian population on the national level was especially marked on the local level in Nazareth, as I will explain later.

The struggle of Arab citizens to gain recognition as a national minority and to be treated as equal and full citizens in Israel has not yet been successful. The State of Israel deals with the Arab community as ethnonational subgroups—not as one national minority group—and often ignores the narrative shared by Christian and Muslim Arab Israelis. Most of the Palestinian diaspora is united by a tenacious, albeit thus far unsuccessful, demand to secure their right to return to a sovereign Palestinian state in the West Bank, which would include East Jerusalem and the Gaza Strip under Palestinian rule, and entail living side by side with the State of Israel. Although these three Palestinian subgroups all consider themselves part of a common Palestinian people consisting of Muslims, Christians, and Druze, they tend to evince differing attitudes about the region's geopolitical issues, rights to a homeland, and self-determination. Though this essay concentrates on the first group—Palestinian citizens of Israel, particularly in Nazareth—other Palestinian groups have different attitudes and are directly and indirectly involved in the conflict, as explained later.

THE CONFLICT WITH AND WITHIN ARAB PALESTINIAN CITIZENS IN ISRAEL AND THE HOLY PLACES

The State of Israel, with a Jewish majority and an Arab minority, is engaged in a protracted conflict with Palestinians outside Israel and with various states in the Arab world.[16] Cities with holy places, such as Nazareth, are strongly affected by the geopolitical conflict between the Jewish majority of the Israeli state and the Arab Palestinian minority. As a result, the cities of the Holy Land suffer from two kinds of conflicts: outsider geopolitical/ethnonational (between Arabs and Jews) and internal ethnoreligious (between Christians and Muslim Arabs). These conflicts take shape through processes of landscape transformation and Judaization due to territorial displacements, the building of Jewish settlements, and Arab exclusion from public spaces.[17] The deep ethnoreligious conflict also includes skirmishes over holy places such as mosques, churches, and cemeteries as well as Islamic *waqf*—land and building endowments. Arab Palestinians collectively resist attacks on their holy places that arise from these conflicts.[18]

The second type of conflict is a silent ethnoreligious struggle in the cities. It is a subterranean conflict characterized by hidden tensions generated from localized feelings of discrimination on the part of some ethnoreligious groups within the Arab community. Some of these ethnoreligious groups want to secure domination over the area, emphasizing their historical narrative and images of belonging to a city or a village. This internal conflict between Arab subgroups, particularly between Christians and Muslims, is clearly present in Nazareth and Tura'an Village. In places such as Muqhar, the conflict is present between Christians and Druze. The conflict in Nazareth is unique because it is manifested over a holy place.

Since 1948 Nazareth has become the largest Arab Palestinian city in Israel; Haifa and Jaffa have evolved into cities with Jewish majorities. Thus, Nazareth is largest and the capital city for Arab Israelis, who are sensitive to its developments. Its uniqueness for Christians all over the world has contributed to its prominence locally, and until the 1960s Nazareth had an Arab Palestinian Christian majority. This has changed gradually, and Christians now constitute less than one-third of the city's inhabitants, with the Muslim population composing the majority. Similar to many other cases, the international geopolitical conflict aggravates the domestic conflict in Nazareth by influencing various coalitions and alignments of players and stakeholders. In the following sections we will see how local, national, and international actors have become involved in the conflict over holy places in Nazareth and have contributed to the creation of ethnoreligious tension in the city.

NAZARETH FROM PERIPHERY TO CENTER

Nazareth's importance stems from its prominent place in Christianity. Nazareth means "Little Root," and it was a small, insignificant village during the time of Jesus. Nonetheless, it has become the starting point for Christian pilgrimages because Nazareth was the remarkable place where Jesus spent most of his life and from where he started his public ministry.[19] It was here that the angel Gabriel proclaimed to the Virgin:

"Hail, highly favored one!" However, this small, peripheral village, transformed over time into a town, never functioned as a national urban center. Nazareth gained initial importance when the missionary Franciscan churches were built and developed during the late eighteenth and nineteenth centuries. In 1875 the Ottoman rulers established a municipality to manage the growing town.[20] At this time Nazareth began to develop as a subdistrict center, which included a market, a courthouse, and a police station. Different Christian denominations began to build churches, convents, and schools in the area.

In 1785 the first mosque to ever be built in Nazareth was constructed without a minaret. Known today as the White Mosque, it received a minaret in 1799. An additional room was built onto the White Mosque in 1804, which functioned as a school for the Muslim community.[21] Four *maqams* (shrines), Nabe-Seian, al-Shikh Amer, Abed al-Samad, and Shihab al-Deen, were built in addition to the White Mosque.[22] The second mosque to be built in Nazareth, al-Salam Mosque, was constructed during the 1960s. Fourteen more mosques have been built in Nazareth since the 1980s. These mosques are all small and were built in the different neighborhoods to serve the religious requirements of the city's growing Muslim community. Nazareth also has twenty-four Christian churches, schools, and convents. Most of the churches are located in the center of the city and visually dominate the surrounding landscape, as does the Basilica of the Annunciation, which has become a landmark in Nazareth.

The modern history of Nazareth is characterized by three main factors. First, the Nakba and its aftermath (the catastrophe of the Palestinian people in 1948) transformed Nazareth into the largest Arab town in Israel. Nazareth is the regional center and national core of the Arab minority in Israel. In addition to its natural growth, Nazareth absorbed about five thousand internal refugees from the surrounding villages after the war of 1948. Most of the refugees were Muslims who had lived on the periphery of the town and created a belt of neighborhoods. Second, because of its importance to the Christian world, the largest concentration of Christians within the Holy Land can be found today in Nazareth. The population of Nazareth today is 73,000, of whom about 30 percent are Christian and 70 percent are Muslim.[23] Nazareth is still considered a small town by national and international standards; however, its status belies its small size. Third, the Israeli government was interested in granting Nazareth special status as a way to appeal to Christian Western countries, particularly after Bethlehem and East Jerusalem, which are important to Christians, fell under Jordanian rule between 1948 and 1967. We should therefore understand that Israel's interest in serving the Christian minority's needs has been in the service of improving its relationship with the Christian world.

In the early 1960s the Israeli government gave permission for the construction of the new Basilica of the Annunciation in Nazareth built over the remains of Byzantine and Crusader churches.[24] The new church opened to the public and pilgrims in 1969. Currently the Basilica of the Annunciation is the biggest church in the Holy Land and a focal point for Catholic and Protestant believers and pilgrims. The church was built with the help of the Israeli government in order to strengthen the Christian status of Nazareth for a number of reasons, including the desire to attract Christian visitors and pilgrims to Israel when Bethlehem and East Jerusalem, including the Old City, were under Jordanian rule. The immediate impetus for building the church was Israel's desire to prepare for the impending visit of Pope Paul VI to Nazareth on January 5, 1964. Other driving factors were largely socioeconomic and included a desire to compensate Nazareth for the building of the Nazareth Illit (Jewish Upper Nazareth, which is the twin town to Nazareth and was founded in 1957 as part of Judiziation of the Galilee region) by solving the city's high rate of unemployment (especially among Arab Christians).

THE SUBTERRANEAN CONFLICT

The hidden tension between Christians and Muslims in Nazareth surfaces in local politics, municipal governmental institutions, and in resource allocation.[25] These antagonistic eruptions are the outcome of several factors. The first relates to the demographic structure of the city.

In 1912 Christian residents constituted approximately 74 percent of the population of Nazareth. Almost a century later the Christian population dropped to about 30 percent. Moreover, the drop in the size of the Christian population of Nazareth continues. This decrease is the result of a drop in natural growth, which totaled 1.15 percent among Christians compared to 2.53 percent among the Muslim population of the city in 2010.[26] The drop in the numbers of the Christian population in Nazareth can also be attributed to foreign migration and domestic relocation as Christians have moved to adjacent localities such as Upper Nazareth. At the same time, the increase in the Muslim population of Nazareth can be attributed to the city's absorption of internal refugees in the aftermath of the 1948 Nakba, when most of the displaced were Muslims. These demographic changes have created a phobia among some of the city's Christian residents, particularly in the aftermath of the Islamic Movement's emergence as a local political power that could compete in local elections.[27] This situation was explained by some of the Christian residents of Nazareth as a threat to tolerance and coexistence between Muslims and Christians in the city.

Second, there has been an increase in the number of educated people in the Muslim community and a consequent reduction in education disparities between Christian and Muslim inhabitants of the city. This has created greater competition for jobs among the middle class. Previously, Nazareth's Christians were better educated because they benefited from private and missionary schools that were built and operated by churches to primarily serve the Christian community. The people who were educated by the missionary schools became an elite class occupying professional positions in government offices (e.g., the social security and income tax offices) and becoming doctors, teachers, and public servants in the municipality. In an interview, a Christian resident of Nazareth illustrated the disparity, stating, "What further proof do you need? Muslims of Nazareth were born in a Christian hospital, mostly by the assistance of Christian doctors, and they go to Christian schools where most of the teachers and principals are Christian. The municipality is dominantly operated by Christian staff. The mayor is Christian. The employees of public offices are mostly Christians. This situation causes envy and tensions."[28] Rising levels of education among Muslims in Nazareth has raised the possibility of open competition and the potential waning of Christian domination in the public services.

Third, the internal refugees absorbed in Nazareth mostly reside in separate neighborhoods at the periphery of the city. The second and third generations of this community were born and live in Nazareth, they feel part of the city, and they want to practice their rights and duties. The feeling of alienation in the city and development of a sociocultural geography—where Christians in powerful positions benefit from more resources while Muslim refugees on the periphery have difficulty obtaining resources—has contributed to rising tensions. Lastly, some Muslims feel that the Israeli government supports and prefers Christians, and the governmental policy of dealing with Arabs as sub-ethnoreligious groups contributes to the silent tension between Muslims and Christians at local and municipal levels.[29]

KEEPING THE CONFLICT SIZZLING

The centrality of Nazareth grew when the Israeli government began to prepare for events celebrating the beginning of the third millennium. The Israeli government and the Nazareth municipality authorized a project called Nazareth 2000 to prepare the city to host a large number of Christian visitors and pilgrims, including Pope John Paul II, who visited Nazareth on March 25, 2000. The Nazareth 2000 project was implemented parallel to the Palestinian Authority's Bethlehem 2000 project.[30] Furthermore, the two projects were implemented during a period of peacemaking and in an atmosphere of concession making. Negotiations between the Palestinian Liberation Organization and the government of Israel seemed as if they might succeed in establishing a Palestinian state that would include Bethlehem and East Jerusalem while Nazareth would remain in Israel. Consequently, national and municipal efforts joined forces to develop Nazareth in preparation for the coming of the new millennium.

The development of the Nazareth 2000 project provided the city with infrastructure and secured its image as a center for the Christian religion.[31] At the end of May 1995 a steering committee consisting of municipal and governmental representatives was established to oversee the implementation of the project. The Nazareth 2000 project's aims were as follows:

- Establish appropriate infrastructure in preparation for expected visitors and pilgrims.
- Ensure comfort for the visitor of today and during the expected wave of visitors in the year 2000.
- Enable all Christian communities to have access to the holy places.
- Highlight the aesthetic value of Nazareth, and develop points of interest including long and varied touring routes.
- Raise the standard of living for residents of Nazareth by developing sources of employment, increasing options for tourist accommodations and services in the city, and creating conditions for investment in the tourist industry.[32]

In the beginning both Christian and Muslim residents of the city welcomed the project and development of the city; they considered it an opportunity to gain leverage and change the face of the city, which suffered from government discrimination as an Arab town.[33]

The silent tension in Nazareth erupted into open conflict in the summer of 1997. As part of Nazareth 2000, the municipality decided to implement an old plan, which was drafted in the 1960s as part of the building of the Basilica of Annunciation and included the creation of a large plaza close to the main road. The plaza was to be named the Plaza of Paul IV and was to connect to the basilica through large steps two hundred meters long. The plan was supported by government offices such as the Tourists Office, the Construction and Housing Office, and Israel Land

Authority (ILA). However, an Ottoman-era school and a small mosque built around the tomb of Shihab al-Deen were located in the area of the plaza plan. Shihab al-Deen was the nephew of Saladin, who defeated the Third Crusade, which was led by Richard the Lionheart in 1191–1192 at the Battle of Hattin.[34] The relationship between Saladin and Shihab al-Deen evokes a much longer legacy of conflict between Muslims and Christians around the history of the Crusades. Both Muslim and Christian Arabs generally avoid explicitly reviving the history of the Crusades in discussions of contemporary Arab identity. But among a few members of both groups there is an attempt to implicitly connect contemporary ethnoreligious disputes to some sort of crusade.

The mosque of Shihab al-Deen and the Al-Rashedia School are defined as Muslim *waqf* (endowment) land. However, in accordance with the 1950 Absentees' Property Law, the school and mosque area are defined by the Israeli government as absentees' land.[35] The law also defines the High Islamic Council, which was established in 1922 during the British Mandate over Palestine, as an entity that serves the Muslim community. This council registered and managed the *waqf* land, including mosques and Islamic schools; however, the ILA, an arm of the Israeli government, now administers Islamic *waqf* land and buildings. These multiple authorities and definitions of the legal standing of the properties cause confusion and create conflictual interpretations.

The municipality of Nazareth did not officially recognize the area surrounding the basilica as *waqf* land, so it obtained a permit from the ILA to build a plaza on the site. One proposal for the land included building a large mosque with four high minarets that could compete with the Basilica of the Annunciation as a landmark in Nazareth.[36] The work was to begin with the demolition of the Al-Rashedia School, the only Islamic school in Nazareth, which was built by Asa'ad Afandy, the district governor, in 1886 during the Ottoman rule. The school also included a room where prayers were held. The Islamic Movement representative was against the demolition of the Al-Rashedia School and the use of the Islamic *waqf* land for the plaza. However, the municipality continued with its plan to demolish the school. The local representatives of the Muslim *waqf* stated that the demolition constituted a serious threat to the Shihab al-Deen Mosque, which was renovated by the Islamic community in 1971. In any case, municipal politicians ignored the issue and various interest groups became involved. The dispute quickly transformed into an open conflict that involved physical violence between the Muslim and Christian communities of Nazareth. The conflict led to a disagreement over who was authorized to decide what to do with the land and called into question how Nazareth 2000 would impact the nature of Nazareth. In turn, these conflicts led to a broader dispute over how to reorganize and restructure relations between the Muslim and Christian communities of Nazareth.

On December 21, 1997, a group of Muslim activists, supported by the local *waqf* committee and the Islamic Movement, erected a tent on the area. While ostensibly used for prayers, the tent's primary purpose was to physically prevent the plaza from being built. Local Muslim representatives claimed that all the land was *waqf* land and supported the construction of a central mosque on the disputed site.[37] In 1998 the municipal local elections in Nazareth put the topic of Shihab al-Deen Mosque and the building of the main urban plaza on the campaign agendas of the two candidates running for Nazareth mayor: Salman Abu Ahmad, the Islamic Movement candidate, and Ramiz Jarayse, the incumbent mayor who was running for reelection. Jarayse was a member of Al Jabha (the Front), which was a coalition supported by the Christian community of Nazareth and a number of secular Muslims. The dispute intensified and on April 3 and 4, 1999, physical confrontations and riots broke out between Muslims and Christians. The deterioration of the situation forced the Israeli government to directly intervene to put an end to the violence.[38]

On April 18, 1999, the Katsav committee, which was formed during Benjamin Netanyahu's government, decided to build a mosque within the disputed area. The proposed mosque was to occupy 450 square meters of the 1,955-square-meter area. The same year brought national elections in Israel, with Ehud Barak winning more votes than Netanyahu in the run for Israeli premiership. In September 1999 the Ben-Ami committee, which was formed by the new Barak government, proposed building a mosque with an area of about 700 square meters. The Israeli government financed an international architecture competition for the plans of the new mosque, appointed a professional steering committee to join the process of planning, and issued the building permit. On November 23, 1999, the Islamic local *waqf* committee began to build the mosque, which led to a dispute with the district planning committees, the ILA, and other parties. The district planning committee and the district governor and presenters of ILA managed to convince the district court in Nazareth Illit to rule on halting building activities. In March 2002 the court order led the governmental committee—the Sharansky Commission—to recommend discontinuing the construction of the mosque.

The Sharansky Commission was formed during Ariel Sharon's government, in the shadow of the September 11, 2001, terrorist attacks on the United States. September 11 had profound ramifications for the West's attitudes toward Muslims and the Middle East, and it brought Samuel Huntington's theory of an impending "clash of civilizations" to the forefront of international relations and led to changes in Israeli government policies.[39] The attacks also led to increased pressure and involvement in the region from the United States under President George Bush's administration as well as pressure from the Vatican, as evidenced by the papal spokesman's declaration on March 4, 2002, that "a provocative initiative" had been stopped when the Israeli government decided to demolish the foundation of the mosque.[40]

The attacks also had an impact on the political and public activities of different stakeholders and on the brewing tension in Nazareth. The Shihab al-Deen Mosque issue was brought before an Upper Nazareth court on March 6, 2003, and the court ordered the demolition of the foundations of the mosque. The Israeli government implemented the court order on July 1, 2003, and demolished the mosque's foundations. However, the demolition of the foundations did not end the dispute. The government offices led by the Ministry of Construction and Housing closed the Shihab al-Deen area and continued to build and develop the plaza after amending the original plan. In 2005 the government completed the development of the central tourist square and opened it to the public. Since then Muslims continue to hold Friday prayers in the square, which today functions as open space that is close to the old, small Shihab al-Deen, which has undergone renovation. Since the demolition of the mosque's foundation and the building of the public square, tension between the communities persists but without violence

LOCAL AND GLOBAL CONSEQUENCES

This short chronology of the development of the Shihab al-Deen Mosque in Nazareth shows the conflict over a holy site from national and local political perspectives as well as how various local, national, and international stakeholders were involved in and affected by the conflict. At the local level, stakeholders sought to gain more benefits, more power, more resources, and functional or symbolic representation in the landscape and fabric of the city. The plurality of ideological and political identities in the region created conflicting narratives and discourses of ownership and belonging. Competition in local elections between the Islamic Movement (mainly supported by Muslims) and Al Jabha (a coalition of the Communist party, Christians, and secular Muslims) further polarized the city as the ascendant Islamic Movement threatened to disrupt Nazareth's political status quo.

Before the eruption of the dispute over the *waqf* land and the Shihab al-Deen Mosque, the local discourse primarily focused on the Israeli government's discriminatory policies toward Nazareth. From 1975 on, Al Jabha had won local elections. The emergence of the Islamic Movement in the beginning of the 1990s threatened the political dominance of Al Jabha by exerting political power at the municipal and national levels. These polarized political parties used the sensitive topic of holy places to attract voters and supporters. Moreover, at the same time, communities in Nazareth were undergoing a process of urbanization. This led to changes in traditional roles, orders, and relationships both within and between stable, organic, and veteran Christian and Muslim families. A new order was established in which the traditional sociocultural structure lost power, and immigrants, internal refugees, and Bedouins (Muslims) who settled in Nazareth began to request the right to take part in sociopolitical processes. These changes contributed to the instability of the city of Nazareth.

Israel is dominated by a Jewish majority, and its involvement in settling conflicts over holy places between Christians and Muslim is sensitive, especially due to the state's history of discriminatory actions and policies toward the Palestinians and its conflictual relationship to holy places such as Jerusalem, Hebron, and other locations. The Israeli state played dual political roles as it attempted to appease both national and international stakeholders. The conflict in Nazareth is unique because the Jewish Israeli government has no religious stake in disputes between Christian and Muslim Arab communities apart from seeking to maintain control over the Arab community as a whole. Israel was therefore required to balance a different set of considerations that involved ethnoreligious majority and minority relations as well as local political competition between the Islamic Movement and Al Jabha. In the beginning, the Israeli government gave its permission for the construction of a mosque in Nazareth, a step that was favorable to the Muslim population. However, subsequent Israeli governments had a change of heart and Sharon's government finally decided to demolish the new mosque's foundation, which had been green-lighted by previous Israeli governments. In the end, the Israeli government backed the court's decision to halt construction activities, which Muslims had begun to carry out without a permit, and later demolished the structure.

The second Palestinian intifada, which was known as the Al-Aqsa Intifada, broke out in late September 2000. Israel responded with military incursions into Palestinian towns under the control of the Palestinian Authority. Violence also broke out in Israel proper in support of the intifada, leading to the killing of thirteen Arab Israeli citizens in October 2000. One of those killed was a citizen of Nazareth. The October violence intensified local tensions between Arabs and the Jewish Israeli government as well as the Jewish community. While some Jewish citizens called for a boycott of the Arab localities, the government intensified control over

Arab citizens and reduced the number of governmental resources allocated to them.[41]

The Israeli government's decision to stop the construction of the Shihab al-Deen Mosque was also influenced by the Vatican, which opposed the construction of a mosque in the vicinity of the Basilica of the Annunciation. From the Israeli government's point of view, Israel's interest was to secure the status quo relationship between Muslims and Christians in Nazareth. With an eye to influencing the West's position on Jerusalem, Israel also sought to convince Christians and the Western world that it was capable of maintaining law and order at its holy sites and could provide secure access to them.

The Arab world and the Palestinian Authority tried to intervene in the dispute both on the national and international level. The local Muslim *waqf* committee received support for building a mosque on Shihab al-Deen *waqf* land by gaining a fatwa (religious decree) from different Muslim sheikhs, such as Dr. Ekrema Sabri (Palestine), Prof. Mahmoud Sartawi (Jordan), Dr. Osama Alrefae, Sekhe Ahmad Kaftwe, and Dr. Mohamad Ramadan Alboty (Syria).[42] In contrast, the former Palestinian president Yasser Arafat objected to the construction of the mosque at the disputed site and instead advocated building a mosque in a different location in Nazareth with the support of a representative of Saudi Arabia. The attitude of the Palestinian leader was influenced by the position of Western governments, including the government of the United States, and by the Vatican, by the Palestinian Christian population, and by fears of damaging Palestinian claims of ownership over East Jerusalem.[43]

The conflict over the construction of the Shihab al-Deen Mosque gave rise to a dispute among Palestinian Arabs because some supported the construction while others opposed it. Moreover, for some of the people, the whole issue was viewed as a *fitnah*, or an incitement between the Muslim and Christian communities of the city. It would seem that Israel has a vested interest in fostering these types of conflicts because they support the state's claim that Arabs are divided into ethnoreligious groups and cannot be recognized as a national minority in Israel. Members of the Muslim and Christian communities share an explicit national discourse that asserts the need to secure an ethnonational affiliation and common interest of Arab Palestinians citizens as a national minority within Israel. Nonetheless, there are some who continue to resist ethnonational belonging and instead ascribe more importance to ethnoreligious affiliation and representations of diversity, which contributes to the production of local tension. This tension manifested on the ground during local municipal elections and in relation to concerns over the building of mosques and churches as well as providing land for housing needs, which is still mostly segregated according to ethnoreligious identification.

CONCLUSION

It is difficult to understand the conflict over sacred sites such as in Nazareth without considering the dispute in the local, national, and international contexts. The conflict is, in fact, not just about sacred sites; it is part of a wider power struggle that has significant sociocultural and geographical repercussions. Since the European invasion of the Holy Land in the beginning of the eighteenth century, Nazareth's face and landscape have become more clearly Christian.[44] The changes include the construction of churches, convents, and missionary schools, which began to be seen clearly in the landscape of the town. The construction of new churches and the reconstruction of existing small ones are related to Nazareth's status as a holy place of value for pilgrims. Although Arab Christians have become a minority in Nazareth over the last five decades, their influence is disproportionate and equivalent to that of a majority group as a result of the nature and the appearance of the city, which is deeply intertwined with the more than 1.5 billion believers of the Christian faith.

The conflict over the image and the nature of the city of Nazareth lies at the root of the dispute over Shihab al-Deen, which serves as both a catalyst and prism for other political and socioeconomic conflicts. Despite the religious façade of the conflict, the competition between Christians and Muslims over the image of the city and for control over its resources is largely political. The mayor of Nazareth is Christian even though two-thirds of the city inhabitants are Muslims. Relative to their percent in the population, Christians hold disproportionate power. However, an analogous if reversed situation took place surrounding the building of the Omar Ibn al-Khattab Mosque in Bethlehem in 1954, while the city was under the rule of King Hussein, the former king of the Hashemite Kingdom of Jordan. The site adjacent to the Church of Nativity was donated by the Orthodox Patriarchate Church. This historic event represents a different, albeit ambiguous, example of religious tolerance that has been promoted and sustained by central and local governments. Here we can identify a complex relationship between the Defender of the Faith (the king) who headed an authoritarian regime but nonetheless promoted toleration. This obviously complicates the belief in any sort of one-to-one relationship between democracies and toleration.

In both instances, the power and legitimacy of the central government vis-à-vis various religious groups has a direct impact on the nature and representation of the town and its holy places. In some cases, the defense of holy places and faith is carried out in conjunction with ethnoreligious groups, and in other cases it is imposed on the groups. Both depend on the role played by the central government and the willingness of the communities to tolerate coexistence. The municipal government is very much subjected to external constraints and forces that often delegitimize the local government. The tension between the government at the state and municipal levels shapes the policies governing freedom of religion as well as those that protect holy places and govern religious conflict over holy places. These conflicts permeate the interreligious politics of Nazareth's interested groups, affecting municipal politics, the Arab community in and beyond the city, and Israeli party politics (largely Jewish). These multiple stakeholders and interests manipulate the conflict over holy places, resulting in further political polarization. The conflict over the Shihab al-Deen Mosque aggravated the internal polarization of Nazareth, which was itself impacted by the increasing visibility of religion in political public life as parties (on the national or municipal levels) became more religiously homogenous and provided a mark of community affiliation and belonging. This trend seems to be ascendant, with disputes over the holy places forming the core of a conflict that has come to envelop the city and toleration is becoming increasingly constrained and diminished.

The national geopolitical conflict between the Israelis and the Palestinians to control holy places in Jerusalem, in addition to the international involvement of the United States and the Vatican, show that the conflict over holy places is not just a local issue but also a global one. The conflict over significant cities from a religious point of view leads to direct and indirect involvement from outside, which in the national and global world benefit from the local conflict over holy places.

Holy places contribute to the creation of multiple mechanisms for development along traditional and cultural lines. Development brought forth by globalization occurs more in cities with fewer traditional and religious holy sites because such places may become obstacles for development. Global and regional immigration gives rise not only to the growth of multicultural and multireligious groups within cities but also to structural changes in sociocultural and religious fabric of urban areas as they reflect more and more diversity. From the point of view of urban development, this sociocultural and religious pluralism demands the creation of a new ideology of tolerance that possesses the potential to integrate traditional cultural practices with modern global developments. It must also recognize the importance of preserving and constructing holy sites for multiple religious groups. Further politicization of holy places and their use as instruments of conflict should be avoided. We need to look for ways for conciliation and coexistence to secure development in the holy cities. Today the development of events in one city does not remain within its boundaries; it spills over and impacts the relationships between ethnonational and religious groups in other locations, as we have seen with the case of the mosque in Nazareth.

NOTES

1. Rassem Khamaisi and Elan Oren, "Fifth Year General Physical and Social Development Plan for the City of Nazareth 2007–2011," submitted to Ministry of Construction and Housing and Nazareth Municipality, R. A. B Engineering Ltd., Kafer Kanna, 2007.

2. Catherine Brace, Adrian Bailey, and David Harvey, "Religion, Place and Space: A Framework for Investigating Historical Geography of Religious Identities and Communities," *Progress in Human Geography*, no. 30 (2006): 28–43.
3. Christian Rumpf, "Holy Places," in *Encyclopedia of Public International Law*, ed. Rudolf Bernhardt, vol. 2, *East African Community to Italy–United States Air Transport Arbitration (1965)* (Amsterdam: Elsevier, 1995), 863–66.
4. As an illustration of this point, for Christians, the hierarchy of holy places includes Bethlehem, Jerusalem, Nazareth, and Rome. A cathedral for Christian people and a main mosque or *jamea* are of foremost significance for the religious and urban fabric of a city. Muslim communities' ethnoreligious affiliations are organized around mosques that develop geographically in a sociocultural and economic context. Holy places' size, centrality, architecture, and functional and symbolic components establish their landmark and images in the landscape of the city. Holy places also grant a hierarchy of importance, which ranks the cities that embosom them. For instance, the Muslim hierarchy is based a the saying of Prophet Mohammad: "A travel of worship is only worthwhile to three mosques; the Haram (sacred) Mosque in Mecca, Al Aqsa Mosque [in Jerusalem], and My Mosque (the Prophet's Mosque in Medina)."
5. Rassem Khamaisi, "Holy Places in Urban Space: Foci of Confrontation or Catalyst for Development?," in *Holy Places in the Israeli Palestinian Conflict: Confrontation and Co-Existence*, ed. Marshall Breger, Yitzhak Reiter, and Leonard Hammer, 128–44 (New York: Routledge, 2010).
6. Gerard van der Leeuw, *Religion in Essence and Manifestation* (Princeton, NJ: Princeton University Press, 1986).
7. David Chidester and E. T. Linenthal, eds., *American Sacred Space* (Bloomington: Indiana University Press, 1995), 1–42.
8. Shukri Arraf, *Tabaqat al-Anbiyya w-al-Salihin fi al-Ard al-Muqadssa* (Tarshiha: Matbaat al-IkhqanMakul, 1993); and Meron Benvenisti, *Sacred Landscape: The Buried History of the Holy Land Since 1948* (Berkeley: University of California University, 2000).
9. Mustafa al-Dbag, *Beladona Falestine* [Palestine our country], vol. 1 (Koffer Karea: Dar Elshafac, 1988).
10. Janet L. Abu-Lughod, "The Demographic Transformation of Palestine," in *The Transformation of Palestine: Essays on the Origin and Development of the Arab-Israeli Conflict*, ed. Ibrahim Abu-Lughod, 139–63 (Evanston, IL: Northwestern University Press, 1971).
11. Central Bureau of Statistics, *Statistical Abstract of Israel 2010*, no. 62 (Jerusalem: Printiv, 2011).
12. PCBS (Palestinian Central Bureau of Statistics), "Population, Housing and Establishment Census 2007. Main Indicators by Locality Type" (Ramallah, Pales-

tine: Palestinian Central Bureau of Statistics, January 2009). http://www.pcbs.gov.ps/Portals/_PCBS/Downloads/book1529.pdf.
13. Central Bureau of Statistics, *Statistical Abstract.*
14. Ibid., 87–88.
15. Khamaisi, "Holy Places in Urban Space."
16. Dan Rabinowitz, "Strife Over Nazareth: Struggles Over the Religious Meaning of Place," *Ethnography* 2 (2001): 93–113.
17. Ibid.
18. Marshall Berger, Yitzhak Reiter, and Leonard Hammer, eds., *Holy Places in the Israeli–Palestinian Conflict: Confrontation and Co-Existence* (New York: Routledge, 2010).
19. Asa'ad Mansor, *Tarich Alnaserah* [History of Nazareth] (Cairo: Dar Alhelal).
20. NohaZorob Keawar, *Tarich Al-Naserah* [History of Nazareth] (Nazareth: Vinos, 2000); and Al-Dbag, *Beladona Falestine.*
21. Interview with Atef Alfahome, mutawaly-manager of the White Mosque, July 1, 2011.
22. Keawar, *Tarich Al-Naserah*, 318–20.
23. Central Bureau of Statistics, *Statistical Abstract*, 131.
24. Masha Halevi, "The Politics Behind the Construction of the Modern Church of the Annunciation in Nazareth," *Catholic Historical Review* 96, no. 1 (2010): 27–55.
25. Chad F. Emmett, *The Christian and Muslim Communities and Quarters of the Arab City of Nazareth* (Chicago: University of Chicago Press, 1991); and Chad F. Emmett, *Beyond the Basilica: Christians and Muslims in Nazareth* (Chicago: University of Chicago Press, 1995).
26. Central Bureau of Statistics, *Statistical Abstract*, 176–77; and Rafael Israeli, *Green Crescent Over Nazareth: The Displacement of Christians by Muslims in the Holy Land* (London: Frank Cass, 2002).
27. Emmett, *The Christian and Muslim Communities.*
28. Interview with an educated Christian person, July 20, 2007.
29. Israeli, *Green Crescent Over Nazareth.*
30. Mitri Raheb and Fred Strickert, *Bethlehem 2000* (Heidelberg, Ger.: Palmyra, 1998).
31. Kobi Cohen-Hattab and Noam Shoval, "Tourism Development and Cultural Conflict: The Case of 'Nazareth 2000,'" *Social & Cultural Geography* 8 (2007): 701–17.
32. Ibid.; and Khamaisi, "Holy Places in Urban Space."
33. Dan Rabinowitz, *Overlooking Nazareth: The Ethnography of Exclusion in Galilee*, Cambridge Studies in Social and Cultural Anthropology (Cambridge: Cambridge University Press, 2000); and Rabinowitz, "Strife Over Nazareth; and

Rabinowitz, "The Palestinian Citizens of Israel, the Concept of Trapped Minority and the Discourse of Transnationalism in Anthropology," *Ethnic and Racial Studies* 24, no. 1 (2001): 64–85.

34. Arraf, *Tabaqat al-Anbiyya*; and Peter Holt, *The Age of the Crusades* (London: Longman, 1986).
35. Yitzhak Reiter, "The Waqf in Israel Since 1965: The Case of Acre Reconsidered," in *Holy Places in the Israeli–Palestinian Conflict: Confrontation and Co-Existence*, ed. Marshall Breger, Yitzhak Reiter, and Leonard Hammer, 104–27 (New York: Routledge, 2010).
36. Uriely, Israeli, and Reichel, "Identity and Residents' Attitudes."
37. Tsimhoni, "The Shihab Al-DIN Mosque Affair."
38. Tsimhoni, "The Shihab Al-DIN Mosque Affair."
39. Huntington, *The Clash of Civilizations*; and Amaney Jamal and Nadine Naber, eds. *Race and Arab Americans Before and After 9/11: From Invisible Citizens to Visible Subjects* (Syracuse, NY: Syracuse University Press, 2008).
40. Ahmad Askar, *Altadmer Althate: Nazareth as Example* [in Arabic] (Ramallah: Markez Al Aamel, 2002); and Alshark Alawst, July 23, 2003 [in Arabic], http://www.aawsat.com/details.asp?article=178673&issueno=8977. On March 4, 2002, in Rome, papal spokesman Joaquín Navarro-Valls issued a formal statement saying that the final decision was an important step on "re-establishing legality, respect of the holy places, and consideration for the respective communities of believers." He pointed out that the decision was not directed against the Muslims of the region since most Muslim leaders had opposed the effort by a militant group to build a mosque on that site. He expressed relief that "a provocative initiative" had been stopped, and hope "that the traditional harmonious coexistence between Muslims and Christians" could be restored in Nazareth. Archbishop Pietro Sambi, the papal nuncio in the Holy Land, said that government had made "a wise decision, which reflects respect for the holy places." The Vatican envoy told the Fides news service that he hoped to see a restoration of "the atmosphere of coexistence that existed previously, and was ruined by the project for the mosque on this site." Christian groups had bitterly protested that decision and complained that, even in the early stages of the construction process, pilgrims visiting the Annunciation basilica were facing intimidation and abuse. Christian leaders—with the backing of most Muslim officials—had recommended the construction of a new mosque on another site in Nazareth. Archbishop Sambi, while welcoming the government's resolution of the dispute, reminded Israeli officials that they would need to be vigilant in preventing new conflicts in Nazareth in the wake of their weekend decision." "Final Bar in Controversial Nazareth Mosque," *Catholic Culture*, March 4, 2002, http://www.catholicculture.org/news/features/index.cfm?recnum=17590.

41. Sara Ozacky-Lazar and Ghanem Asa'd, eds., *The Orr Commission Testimonies* (in Hebrew) (Jerusalem: Ketter, 2003).
42. For details, see "Pictures and Documents from Shebab Aldeen-Nazareth," http://www.geocities.ws/shhabaden/indexshhabpic.htm.
43. Askar, *Altadmer Althate*; and Seham Gnam-Fahom, *Tahadiat and Taquorat fe Tarekh Alnasera: Alolakat almasehya al islamia* [Challenges and changes in Nazareth history: The Islamic–Christian relations] (Nazareth: Alnhada Publishing, 2003).
44. Mansor, *Tarich Alnaserah*.

MUSEUMS

9

TOLERANCE VERSUS HOLINESS

THE JERUSALEM MUSEUM OF TOLERANCE
AND THE MAMILLA MUSLIM CEMETERY

YITZHAK REITER

THE PROPOSED MUSEUM of Tolerance (MOT) in Jerusalem, an initiative of the Simon Wiesenthal Museum of Tolerance in Los Angeles, was planned, beginning in 1999, to occupy a portion of Mamilla Cemetery, an important Muslim cemetery that had been removed from use, rezoned for construction, and covered by a parking lot many years before. In 2006 a dispute over the museum suddenly erupted. The arguments advanced for and against the museum's placement provide us with an opportunity to examine the choreography of sacred spaces around notions of sharing that are somewhat removed from the kinds of sharing encountered in sites where competing religious organizations make claims on a site for their present religious practices. On the one hand, the notion of tolerance embraced by the museum's organizers, with the support of the State of Israel, allows them to promote a human and universal value that transcends religious and ethnic identities. It envisions sharing as living together in society under a regime of mutually satisfactory justice and fairness. As a human value, this kind of tolerance would seem to be beyond all objection, and yet the construction of the museum threatened to violate that ideal directly through what some portion of the Muslim minority in Jerusalem, and in Israel more broadly, as well as some Jewish personalities and organizations in Israel and in general perceived as blatant insensitivity to its history. On the other hand, the actors involved in the case make competing claims about the conditions under which the dead identified with one religion may be made to share their space to meet the purposes of the living, where the holiness of the site would protect them from any kind of present-day encroachment. The conflicts over these claims emerge as much within any one religious identity as they do between identities. When does a cemetery cease to be a sacred space?

I analyze the case of the MOT from the perspective of conflict resolution. In terms of choreography, I will examine the history of the dispute by paying close attention to the specific legal regime, the combinations of religious and civil courts under the British Mandate, and the Israeli justice system. Thus far this legal regime has provided the range of venues in which the claims associated with a politics of identity—through which minority status in the State of Israel has become intimately entangled with questions of religious identity—are adjudicated according to an objective legality that makes its own claims on the abstract values of tolerance, justice, and fairness that provide the ideological foundation for the museum itself.[1] Within this legal regime, the actual content of the rights claimed for the Arab Muslim minority vis-à-vis the majority in the State of Israel—the right to representation in the public domain and the landscape, the right to equal treatment by the state regarding heritage sites and holy places, and the right to administer holy properties (*waqf*) according to religious law and the rulings of religious (sharia) courts—is determined. Since the question of the appropriate venue for dealing with conflicts over holy places inevitably arises, I will also pay close attention to the moments in this history when various actors attempt to gain advantages through "scale shift" by moving the conflict into a higher legal arena where they expect to gain a more satisfactory hearing for their own identity claims.[2] At the time of writing, Israeli Muslim actors are presenting their case to international organizations, so the process of scale shift in this history continues to reveal new stages of articulation in the network of institutions involved in choreographing the use of this particular site.

STAGES IN THE DEBATE OVER USING THE TERRITORY OF MAMILLA CEMETERY

The disputed plot of land in Mamilla (sometimes called Ma'man Allah, meaning "Allah's safe haven" in Arabic) that was assigned by the Jerusalem Municipality for building the MOT had been part of the important cemetery described by the sixteenth-century Jerusalemite Muslim historian Mujir al-Din (d. 1521): "The Mamilla Cemetery west of Jerusalem's walls is the largest cemetery of the city, containing the graves of notables, *ulama'*, righteous people, and slain people."[3]

The southern part of the Mamilla Cemetery was already designated for building in the nineteenth century, during the last years of Ottoman rule, and a stone wall was constructed to protect the rest of the cemetery.[4] Under the British Mandate in Palestine (1920–1948), the cemetery was diminished to only 134 *dunums* (about 33 acres), included in the 1938 land registry as a *waqf* property overseen by the director of the General Waqf (administration of Islamic endowments) of Jerusalem. The land south of Gaza Road was designated for building.

The first major controversy over the cemetery's new designation broke out in 1925, when Haj Amin al-Husayni, the president of the Supreme Muslim Council and the grand mufti of Jerusalem and Palestine, initiated construction of a hotel as a real estate investment that would yield fruits to the *waqf* administration he headed.[5] The controversy focused on the moral and sharia question of whether it was appropriate to build on a plot that had previously served as part of the cemetery, despite being rezoned in modern Jerusalem for urban development. Although the land had been extracted from the cemetery under Ottoman rule, many Muslims during the 1920s and 1930s still perceived the land as part of the cemetery.[6] Following is the account of the subcontractor of the hotel, a Jew named Baruch Katinka:

> The hotel is located exactly opposite to the old Muslim cemetery. When we dug three meters down we found old Graves with human remains. I

was afraid that the Arab workers would tell the Mufti that we desecrated graves; therefore, I came to the Mufti and told him about the whole issue. To my surprise, he instructed me not to publicize this affair, and to keep it as a secret between the two of us. He said that he will make sure that the Arab workers will keep it quiet. He asked me to collect all of the bones and at the end of the digging work, to secretly relocate them to another grave.[7]

While Katinka asserts that the building site was located outside the (officially zoned) cemetery, he nevertheless found human remains. No wonder that the mufti's Palestinian opponents used his hotel project to criticize his violation of Islamic law and traditions. In any event, a contemporary Palestinian-Jordanian historian Kamil Jamil al-Asali viewed the mufti's action as improper. He tells us that the Palace Hotel was built in 1930 inside the cemetery, above the remains of al-Zawiya al-Qalandariyya.[8]

The actions of the Supreme Muslim Council during the British Mandate period have a significant impact on current Israeli attitudes to Muslim complaints about building over other parts of the same historical cemetery. Because the Palace Hotel project was initiated by a Muslim official, the MOT entrepreneurs have used it as a precedent within Muslim practice for allowing development on a former cemetery. The High Court of Israel was convinced that Muslim religious adjudicators interpret the sharia flexibly enough to recognize practical needs and issue building permits for cemetery property when the public interest justifies it. In fact, the mufti's attorney, Ahmad Raghib, arguing before the Sharia Court in 1927, did not refute that the hotel was being constructed in the cemetery. On the contrary, he defended the mufti's action by arguing that "there is a debate between Shari'a jurists regarding the question whether cemeteries could be rendered for construction and graves permitted to be excavated or not. Some jurists prohibit it completely, while others ultimately permit it," and cited the sources that permit building over cemeteries.[9] These previous Muslim building initiatives lead present-day courts to suspect that current complaints are primarily political.

In 1931 the Palace Hotel hosted the All-Muslim Congress, for which Islamic leaders came from all over the world. These visiting Muslim leaders ignored local Palestinian criticism against the mufti for reutilizing cemeteries and passed a resolution to build a Muslim university in Jerusalem (after the opening of Hebrew University) to be named the al-Aqsa University. They did not mention a particular location to build the university, but David Kroyanker has found photographic evidence of a sketch prepared by an Egyptian architect for planning the Islamic university over the Mamilla Cemetery.[10] In the mid-1940s, when Amin Abd al-Hadi was president of the Supreme Muslim Council, a housing project was approved over what remained of the cemetery.[11]

Several further instances that touched on the status of the cemetery followed the division of Jerusalem in 1948 between Jordanian al-Quds (East) and Israeli Yerushalayim (West).The Mamilla Cemetery was included in a central part of downtown West Jerusalem and gained new symbolic significance in the accusations over damaged cemeteries exchanged between Israel and Jordan. In 1950 the government of Jordan protested officially and in the Arab press against "Israeli damage to the Mamilla Cemetery."[12] Israeli authorities reacted by cleaning and protecting the cemetery. A complementary controversy occurred in the early 1960s, when the government of Jordan endorsed the construction of a hotel on the Mount of Olives (East). A road leading to the hotel ran through the middle of the old Jewish Har HaZeitim Cemetery, damaging many gravestones. Most of the graves themselves were not damaged, but it was said that some of the gravestones were used as a foundation for the road.[13]

In 1964 the mayor of Jerusalem asked the senior *qadi* (Sharia Court judge) of Israel, Sheikh Tahir Hammad, to issue a fatwa (legal opinion of a sharia sage) to remove the sacred character from most of the Mamilla Cemetery so that the cemetery could become a public park. Hammad approved the park (but did not permit building), reserving a small cemetery plot as a heritage site. Hammad was the most highly trained expert on Islamic law in Israel; he had not only studied but also taught at al-Azhar University. Apparently, under the martial rule on Israeli Arabs

(1948–1966), Hammad wanted to satisfy the Jewish establishment. He titled the permit, with significant consequences, *qarar fatwa*, giving the impression that the document should be treated not only as his opinion (fatwa), but also as a judicial decision (*qarar*). His permit was based, aside from sharia sources, on accepting at face value the mayor's citation of records from the British Mandate period that declared the Mamilla Cemetery *mundaris* (extinct) because no one had been buried there for a certain period of time, thus making it available for other uses.

Beginning in the 1960s the Jerusalem Municipality approved a series of urban plans to develop the Mamilla Cemetery for housing, business, and public facilities, including Independence Park, the Experimental School, the Engineer's House, the Agron House, and other projects. In 1979 the plot later allocated for the MOT was set aside for a parking lot (completed in 1986). Two Jordanian ministers, the minister of foreign affairs and the minister of *awqaf* (the East Jerusalem Waqf Authority continued to be affiliated with Jordan even under Israeli rule) complained on January 28, 1986, to the general director of UNESCO that the Israeli authorities were harassing and plotting against the Ma'man Allah Cemetery, and were causing damage to the graves of important Muslim dignitaries.[14] In November 1986 the Palestine Liberation Organization (PLO) observer to the United Nations, Omar Massalha, sent another complaint to UNESCO claiming that municipality bulldozers had dug in the cemetery to put down a sewage pipe. Waqf administration representatives reported that many human remains had been exposed during this process.[15] Israel denied the accusations and said that the work exposed very few bones.

Upon completion in 1986 the municipal parking lot constructed in the northern part of the cemetery served the city's residents, including many Muslims, and complaints that it had been constructed over a historic cemetery ceased. In the late 1990s the Jerusalem Municipality led by Ehud Olmert offered the parking lot as a venue for the MOT, changing its zoning status to "business zone," instead of another plot of land that the museum entrepreneurs had located at the French Hill. Shortly afterward, in 2000, the Municipality approved further construction, in the compound of the former cemetery, including two additional stories on the Engineer's House and two new buildings.

Plans for the MOT proceeded without protest over the next several years. Architect Frank Gehry had been engaged in 1999 to design the complex, and the MOT plan was advertised in four newspapers (two in Hebrew, *Mariv* and *Yerushalayim*, and two in Arabic, *al-Ittihad* and *al-Quds*) as well as in the *Official Gazette*.[16] The plan was finally approved in March of 2002.

An unveiling ceremony for the museum's model took place on November 24, 2002, at the residence of Israeli president Moshe Katsav, and the model was subsequently displayed to the general public in the main hall of the Jerusalem Municipality. The cornerstone ceremony took place on May 2, 2005, in the presence of high-ranking Israeli officials, including President Katsav, Deputy Prime Minister and Minister of Industry and Trade Ehud Olmert, Minister of Foreign Affairs Silvan Shalom, and Minister of Defense Shaul Mofaz as well as California governor Arnold Schwarzenegger. The building permit for the MOT in Mamilla had been issued in 2004 and the museum corporation had begun work in late 2005 by digging the area intended for the building's foundation. As soon as human remains were unearthed during this work, the Authority of Antiquities (IAA) came in to conduct excavations, during which some four hundred graves were discovered and archaeological artifacts were exposed. At this point the IAA determined that, from an historical-archaeological point of view, there was no obstacle to prevent the MOT building from being erected on its main designated plot, with some restrictions aimed at preserving the small part of the site that still contained human remains.

THE DISPUTE

After several years without incident, a dispute erupted in late December 2005 when three activists from the NIM in Israel appeared at the construction site of the planned foundation for the MOT. They were received as respected guests and invited to participate in a committee that would be responsible for removing and respectfully reburying bones from the site in the part of the cemetery still visible above ground. The Islamic Movement has claimed that they were responding in part to speeches delivered at the cornerstone ceremony in which a connection was drawn between the establishment of the museum and the rebuilding of Solomon's Temple (there is no evidence that such speeches were actually given). The Movement also claimed retroactively in an Arabic publication that the Islamic institutions in Jerusalem had already denounced building the museum project in a cemetery.[17] I could not find any record to support this claim.

While the symbolism of the two last claims only highlights the politics of identity at work in the renewed dispute over the Mamilla site, a simultaneous action in the Israeli courts demonstrated the NIM's attempt to enlist the Israeli legal system in its cause by, on the one hand, forcing the court to confront the validity of decisions in religious courts, and, on the other, appealing to the notion of tolerance that supposedly gave the museum its reason for being. On December 28, 2005, the al-Aqsa Association for the Development of the Assets of the Muslim Waqf in the Land of Israel Ltd. (affiliated with the NIM in Israel) petitioned the High Court (HCJ 52/06) against eight defendants: the Simon Wiesenthal Center Museum Corporation in both Israel and Los Angeles, three Israeli governmental authorities (the Israel Land Administration, the District Planning and Building Committee for Jerusalem, and the Israel Antiquities Authority), and three municipal authorities (the Jerusalem Municipality, the local Jerusalem Planning and Building Committee, and Moriyah for Developing Jerusalem). This case wasn't the first attempt by the NIM to preserve abandoned Muslim holy places. NIM leaders were involved in activities by the Palestinian Intifada and Hama in the 1990s to preserve remnants of Muslim cemeteries and other abandoned Muslim holy places inside Israel as a political action to rejuvenate the identity and landscape of the land to its past Arab and Muslim character.

Advocate Muhammad Sulayman Arghbariya, representing the al-Aqsa Association, claimed in his case to the High Court that the digging was being conducted within the actual boundaries of the Ma'man Allah Cemetery.[18] According to him, "Throughout history the entire cemetery was completely preserved" and had been registered under the name of the Islamic Waqf of Jerusalem. Against this background he claimed that the museum construction was "an additional and significant damage to what remained of the Cemetery." The al-Aqsa Association further argued that according to sharia law, "it is ultimately impermissible to dig or rummage inside a grave, or to unearth graves or to cause harm of any kind to the sacredness of dead people."[19] This claim was backed by two fatwas, one issued in 1991 by Qadi Tawfiq Asaliya, former president of the Sharia Court of Israel, and the second in 2004 by Qadi Ahmad Natour, who succeeded him as president of the Sharia Court. Despite the fact that senior muftis and other religious establishment officials in Muslim countries have approved development in cemeteries for the benefit of the community, Natour held that building the MOT over the Muslim cemetery cannot be justified from a sharia point of view because the project does not benefit the Muslim community.

In addition, the Muslim plaintiffs argued that the purpose of the museum as it was presented by museum sponsors—to act "for promoting amicability between the different peoples in the Holy Land"—could never be realized through actions that damaged dead bodies and offended the sentiments of the Muslim community in the country and around the globe. They appealed not only to the decisions of religious courts that could potentially be dismissed for being tied too closely to the politics of identity but also to a level of universal human values that could transcend religious identities. The digging and construction, according to their petition, were a severe violation of the law of human dignity and freedom that has been enshrined in the values of the officially Jewish and democratic State of Israel—and so they are a violation of the principles of Judaism itself.[20]

When a few weeks passed without an order by the High Court to stop the construction work, three Muslims from notable East Jerusalem families, Muhammad Khayr al-Dajani, Muhammad Zaki Nusseibeh, and Muhammad Badr al-Zayn, represented by Karama Association, an Israeli

Arab organization for human rights, filed a case in the Sharia Court, asking the *qadi* to issue a temporary decree to cease work at the museum compound. This complaint aimed to transfer decision-making powers from the High Court to the Sharia Court, which was the Muslims' hometown judicial court. The Israeli *qadi* of Jerusalem, Muhammad Zibde, issued the requested decree, but the police refused to enforce it. The plaintiffs reacted by filing another petition in the High Court, asking it to compel the police to enforce the decree issued by the Sharia Court.[21] In a parallel move, the museum entrepreneurs and the relevant state authorities moved to take advantage of the entangled legal jurisdictions by filing another case in the High Court against six defendants: the Sharia Court of Jerusalem, the three above-cited Muslim dignitaries, and two government authorities—the Custodian of Absentees' Properties at the Ministry of Finance and the Development Authority, an organ of the Israel Land Authority.[22] The Development Authority holds all absentee properties handed over to it by the custodian organizations, including the Mamilla Cemetery after its sacred status had been removed. The entrepreneurs requested that the Sharia Court decrees be declared null and void, claiming that this court had no authority regarding land not possessed by the Waqf administration.[23]

The first gesture toward moving the conflict out of strictly legal jurisdictions and into the broader public sphere was made while the High Court hearing was in its final stages in April 2007. A group of some seventy senior Israeli academics, headed by Shimon Shamir and including five Israel Prize laureates as well as seven civil and human rights organizations that objected to the construction of the museum in Mamilla, applied to the High Court asking to join the legal case as "Friends of the Court." Their opposition to the location of the museum was explained on yet another set of grounds: they stressed the consequences of the project on relationships between state institutions, and between Jews in Israel and the Arab Muslim minority as well as with other Arab and Muslim countries, and the consequences regarding preserving Jewish cemeteries abroad. The High Court decided not to accept them as an official party to the legal suit. However, the judges agreed that the group would have the right to voice its opinion during the hearing procedure and to submit reports by experts that could challenge reports submitted by the MOT corporation. Although the application to the court adhered to the established rules for the legal process, it clearly contained a threat to take the conflict into the broader court of public opinion. The museum, on its own behalf, reacted accordingly by organizing an alternative group of senior academics and public figures headed by a former head of Mossad, Shabtai Shavit, and with the participation of 182 members who would be capable of meeting that threat in defense of the museum. This group also submitted expert reports to counter those submitted by the museum's opponents.

During the hearing of the three cases, the High Court issued three provisional decrees. The first ordered digging in the compound to cease until the case could be adjudicated. The second prohibited the Sharia Court from taking any parallel procedures regarding the museum. When the High Court realized that the digging in two out of three subsections of the land designated for the museum had already been completed, it issued a third decree to cease work only in the third plot, containing 12 percent of the entire space designated for construction of the museum. This section was numbered 3 and painted purple on the map submitted to the court, and therefore was referred to as the "purple section," where, according to the archaeological report, most of the human remains could be found. The decree ordered the museum entrepreneurs and the state authorities to explain to the High Court why they should not be required to change the building plan to remove the purple section.

The High Court first handed the suit over for mediation to Justice Meir Shamgar (a former president of the High Court). The mediation process lasted seven months and failed. The Muslim plaintiffs refused any compromise that would allow construction of the museum in Mamilla. Following this, the museum entrepreneurs were asked by the High Court to suggest a technical solution to the problem regarding the purple section. They presented two alternatives to the court. First, they could remove the human remains at their own expense and rebury them in another Muslim cemetery. They suggested that this transfer would "be conducted in a professional, respectful and proper way, according to Muslim religious guidelines, and under the supervision of Muslim clerics." They also suggested different technical ways to remove the human remains without causing damage to the graves themselves. The second alternative was to build over the purple section, but to refrain from digging deep in the earth in order to minimize damage to the graves. The entrepreneurs also indicated to the court that they would build a floating floor over this section to preserve a space between the ground surface and the building itself, preventing physical contact between the two.

In December 2008, three years after the petition was submitted to the High Court, the verdict that was finally issued rejected the claim of al-Aqsa Association and enabled the museum entrepreneurs to resume the building project under the condition that they take measures to respectfully treat the human remains found in part of the land designated for the museum (which, according to the estimate of the IAA archaeologist, may contain about six hundred graves, even after four hundred bodies were already removed from the major area designated for the museum). The court permitted the entrepreneurs to choose an alternative that they themselves had proposed. They could relocate all of the graves and rebury them elsewhere. Following the relocation, they would be permitted to build an underground parking lot for the museum, but they would have to submit a change to the plan. Alternatively, they could conduct minimal digging in this part of the building site to position columns to carry a floating floor for the museum, in order to keep the estimated remaining six hundred bodies intact.

Once the official legal dispute had ended, the academics and civil organizations who had applied for Friend of the Court status made good on the implied threat in their original application by attempting to act against the museum in the public sphere. Their efforts, however, failed to stir up a significant public campaign within Israeli society. Palestinian civil organizations initiated a parallel international campaign by presenting the Mamilla dispute as one facet of an Israeli policy intended to erase Muslim cultural heritage sites. Still another development in August 2010 showed that the conflict had not been satisfactorily resolved despite the

High Court's verdict. Islamic activists erected three hundred new tombstones in order to "thicken" the Muslim character of the preserved portion of the Mamilla Cemetery by filling in open spaces between graves. When the Israeli authorities discovered their initiative, they removed the new tombstones.[24]

There is indirect evidence that, despite the overall failure of the public campaign to create a visible movement within Israeli society to oppose the museum's location in Mamilla, its protests did have some impact after all, particularly on potential donors and those who had already committed funds to the museum. I draw this conclusion because, not long after the public protests, museum entrepreneurs ordered a new, less ambitious and costly design, possibly contributing (although he has denied it) to architect Frank Gehry's decision to resign from the museum project in early 2010. The result of the new project competition, won in September 2010 by the Israeli architectural firm of Chyutin from Givatayim, anticipated a complex of 46,000 square meters, composed of three stories underground and three above, and including a theater, an academic center, and an exhibition hall, to be completed in 2015 at an estimated cost of $100 million, significantly reduced from the $250 million projected for the original plan.[25]

The Mamilla affair, despite the official legal ruling in favor of the museum's construction, has also cast a shadow over further, previously uncontroversial construction plans for the territory of the former cemetery. In 2009 the government intended to integrate Jerusalem's local and magistrate courts by erecting the Jerusalem Courts' Compound (Heikhal HaMishpat) over an adjacent plot of the same historical cemetery where the Experimental School now stands. The Israeli press revealed that the president of the High Court at the time, Justice Dorit Beinisch, hesitated over the appropriate location of this project in Jerusalem, presumably as a result of the court's experience with the Mamilla MOT case.[26] As I write these words, I have been told that the authorities have decided to withdraw from this location and that perhaps the Hebrew publication of my book on this topic contributed to the decision.

312 | MUSEUMS

FIGURE 9.1 MUSLIM GRAVES ABUTTING THE MUSEUM OF TOLERANCE WALL.

(Photograph by author)

ARGUMENTS AND RESPONSES

Although I emphasized, in my account of the controversy over the Mamilla Cemetery and the MOT, the character of the various arguments introduced by actors on both sides as well as the specific venues in which those actors chose to advance them, I would like to step back and analyze the three main arguments that the opponents to the MOT presented to the High Court within the framework proposed in my introduction.

REPRESENTATION IN THE SYMBOLIC LANDSCAPE

The proposal to build the MOT in Mamilla raises the major question of a minority population's right to represent its heritage landmarks in the landscape of a city like Jerusalem. The landscape in Israel and particularly in Jerusalem has taken shape over thousands of years under the imprint of different civilizations and cultural entities. Since 1948 the processes of shaping the landscape have been influenced mostly by the Jewish Zionist hegemonic majority in Israel and entail the erasure and exclusion of past landscapes, particularly those representing the country's Arab and Islamic past.[27] Saree Makdisi even referred to the Mamilla MOT project as "the second erasure" and "denying the denial."[28] Hence, the Arab Muslim minority in Israel strives to preserve and establish in the public landscape the spaces associated with their own particular activity, such as mosques, saints' tombs, and, most importantly for our case, cemeteries. These physical spaces represent resistance to the majority's hegemony as well as the struggle to be represented politically in public space.[29] Because Palestinian identity is so deeply entangled with religious identity, holy places inevitably play an important role in strategies of resistance to Jewish hegemony.[30]

The MOT project in the center of Jerusalem has a strong symbolic meaning. The museum's message of tolerance is already more partial than the universal human values it invokes. In fact, the museum, in its local setting, embodies the Zionist project and even reinforces the Zionist paradigm of Jerusalem as a reunited city where two national peoples who adhere to three religions live side by side in peace and toleration. The initiators from the Simon Wiesenthal Center state:

> The Simon Wiesenthal Center's new Israel Project—The Center for Human Dignity in Jerusalem—attempts to give institutional substance to the popular injunction that we should "think globally, but act locally." The Center will take the broad lessons about tolerance promotion that we have learned over the past decade in the United States and tailor them to the distinctive realities of a diverse Israel and the Middle East values crucible . . . a moral, an ethical beacon light for three of the worlds' great religions. Jerusalem is the contested ground where a shared faith in the sacredness of human dignity took shape, and where common ground in shared values of human rights must be reclaimed. Our ultimate hope is that The Center for Human Dignity, Museum of Tolerance, Jerusalem, will develop into a global hub that will promote civility and mutual respect

among the multiplicity of peoples of the Middle East as well as international visitors of all faiths and origins.[31]

The High Court justices, in their response to the suit brought by the al-Aqsa Association, chose to adopt the narrative presented by the museum's entrepreneurs rather than the plaintiff's own attempt to place the value of tolerance within a competing narrative that accused the museum itself of violating the universal (but also Jewish) values it claimed to promote precisely by doing harm to the physical traces of minority heritage in the Jerusalem landscape. In a sense, in adjudicating the case, the court was faced with accommodating the value of tolerance to local circumstances. But because the court considers itself to be a venue free of the politics of identity, its ruling in favor of the universal human value of tolerance became particularly susceptible to merely repeating one of the particular narratives produced within that politics of identity and approving the particular way that narrative perceives the value of tolerance embodied in the landscape. It should be noted that while there were many reasons for the court to adopt the defendant's narrative, in my personal opinion the court's attitude toward the plaintiff's claims for tolerance might have been more favorable if the suit had been filed by a more moderate Muslim organization. Since al-Aqsa Association had a reputation for political extremism, the court was more likely to stigmatize its claims as identity politics. In the words of the High Court:

> The Museum of Tolerance embodies the idea of establishing a spiritual center from which a message will spread of human tolerance among peoples, among population sectors, and among individuals. The construction of the museum can make an important national contribution to the entire state, which to date has had no center whose purpose is to deal with the substance of tolerance in its various aspects and to act to disseminate this value amidst the general public. This center ought to serve as a point of reference both within Israel and with respect to the states of the entire world. It ought to attract visitors from all over the country and the world

who while visiting will have the special architectural and artistic experience that the museum provides. There is a special significance to the location of the museum in the center of Jerusalem, a city that has a special valuable meaning for three religions as well as a long history and a special place in human civilization. The existence of the Museum of Tolerance in the capital of Israel, against the background of the ongoing Israeli-Palestinian conflict, also has special weight regarding the dynamics of dialogue and efforts to bridge between the conflicting parties. The construction of the Museum in the center of the city of Jerusalem is aimed at making an important contribution to the development of Jerusalem as the capital of Israel and to advance the urban development of the center of the town as a city center that has an important significance both in the local and national realms. . . . To restore Jerusalem's ancient crown, which it has lost over the years.[32]

The seemingly neutral emphasis on urban development in the last quoted sentences from the High Court's decision highlights the way in which the struggle over representation in the landscape could also be swayed by engaging internationally renowned architect Frank Gehry, an American Jew whose projects are often the most striking features in their environments and frequently become visual symbols for the values of the institutions housed within. In other words, the MOT entrepreneurs intended for the museum to dominate its surrounding so thoroughly as to take over the space of the former cemetery not only physically but also symbolically. The association between the value of tolerance and the image of the museum itself, according to the Muslim opponents, may reach the point of erasing traces of Mamilla in memory (with the exception of a small part of the original graveyard south of the MOT plot).

Through its association with the Wiesenthal Center, the museum became, for the court, not only a conduit for future aspirations (toward a tolerant society and a developed urban center) but also a means of symbolizing the memory of the Holocaust and of Jewish heritage in the Jerusalem landscape. This is the way that Justice Ayalah Procaccia began her verdict:

> The idea of forming the Center of Tolerance in Jerusalem was envisioned by the late Simon Wiesenthal, who belongs to the generation of the Holocaust of the Jews in Europe. In his special and individual way, he instilled the lessons of the Holocaust by detecting Nazi criminals all over the world and taking care to punish them through the courts; in the framework of this commitment, the late Simon Wiesenthal wanted to establish a spiritual center dedicated in its content and activity to transmitting the message of tolerance to humankind. No wonder, then, that he chose Jerusalem, the capital of Israel and the Jewish people, which is also a world center of the three great religions of humanity, to implement this idea. The Museum of Tolerance was planned to reflect the lessons of the past and to disseminate these lessons into the values of tolerance and amicability for the future. It ought to link past, present, and future by promoting the basic rights of the individual as a supreme human value and as a supreme value in the regimes of peoples and states.[33]

The discourse that the initiator of the museum project used, which was entirely adopted by the Supreme Court justices, is a Jewish national narrative centered around "Jerusalem as the capital of Israel and the Jewish people" and "center to the three great religions of humanity." This narrative ignores entirely the city's Palestinian residents, who hold an opposing vision, and the reality of a socially and politically divided city. The mission of the MOT advances the image of Jerusalem not as politically divided but as a city of interfaith tolerance under Israeli control.

Another expression of the symbolic nature of the MOT project is what the Wiesenthal Center described among the purposes of the Jerusalem MOT:

> [It will be] a social laboratory that speaks to the world and confronts today's important issues—like global antisemitism, terrorism and hate. A place that will reminds *us* that greater than any external threat is the internal divide that separates *us*. A place that will reinforce the idea that Jewish unity is not a slogan but an essential recipe for survival in the 21st century.[34]

Viewing the Mamilla dispute in these terms, as a struggle over the character of and symbolic representation in public space and, consequently, as a competition between the power of the state and the power of the minority helps us to understand the controversy better.[35] Henri Lefebvre, who wrote about the shaping of urban spaces, noted that anyone who is discriminated against and excluded from urban space will find a legitimate response in actions of resistance.[36]

The MOT project in Mamilla also has a symbolic aspect from an Islamic and Arab point of view. The NIM, headed by Sheikh Raed Salah, confronted the Jewish Zionist landscape of Jerusalem by underlining its own vision of the past Muslim Arab al-Quds. Salah and his followers have been active over the last two decades in an effort to expose, preserve, rebuild, and reinstitute Muslim cemeteries and monuments within the country's landscape; their focus is on those mosques, saints' tombs, and Muslim cemeteries that were obliterated and abandoned during the 1948 war. Interestingly, Kamil Jamil al-Asali, a contemporary Palestinian-Jordanian historian, notes that the Islamic Movement as well as current Palestinian campaigners have erased from their historical texts any reference pertaining to the importance of the cemetery's Christian origins. This unexplained erasure takes place in spite of the fact that this piece of history could provide a possible basis for collaboration with the Christian world institutions.[37]

A close reading of the High Court's verdict leaves no doubt that the discourse on identity moved the justices and that they self-identify with the Zionist goals that the museum aims to symbolize. This inclination is seen not only in the way the judges have cited the assertions of the parties favorable to the museum but also in the way they described the importance of the MOT project in relation to the center of the city of Jerusalem and not elsewhere. The symbolic weight of locating the museum in Jerusalem was so strong that the court also rejected moving the future museum to another spot outside the center of Jerusalem, a proposal that had been suggested by a group of academics and civil organizations. The High Court made its stance clear: "[Such a move] will damage the chance to establish such a center in Jerusalem with all its symbolic meaning."[38]

The Mamilla dispute embodies, even in a very literal way for the court, the struggle over the symbolic landscape of Jerusalem.

As I suggested earlier, the High Court hewed very closely to the identity claims presented by the museum's proponents, holding them as equivalents to the universal value of tolerance. The three Palestinian East Jerusalemites involved in the lawsuit and their own identity interests received no attention at all in the court's written decision, even when they were presented as equivalents to the universal value of tolerance. Their reaction to the verdict, expressed by Advocate Durgham Sayf, was: "The verdict is political and biased in favor of the Jews. Another tribunal with non-Jewish judges would decide in favor of us."[39]

IS A CEMETERY A HOLY PLACE?

One avenue for dismissing the plaintiff's claims on tolerance, then, led to identifying the universal value of tolerance with a narrative that had been, in fact, formed through the Israeli Jewish "politics of identity." It would also have been possible to dismiss the plaintiff's suit if it could be shown that the Mamilla Cemetery could not legitimately be claimed as a heritage site, so another debate in the High Court centered on the question of whether, according to Islamic law and tradition, a grave or a cemetery is eternally holy or whether it is possible to release cemetery land for development once the buried human remains have decomposed.

The al-Aqsa Association submitted to the court a report by an expert on sharia, Professor Hussam al-Din Afana.[40] Afana cited a hadith that emphasizes the holiness of the dead and of graves. He also quoted a fatwa by the former chief mufti of Saudi Arabia, Sheikh Muhammad ibn Ibrahim Aal al-Sheikh, which holds that cemeteries are holy and should be preserved from any violation because a grave is the house of the human person after his death and should not be harmed, just as the house of a living person should not be touched. The Saudi mufti added that the location of old cemeteries within the center of a city does not justify their violation, even for paving roads or expanding the width of an existing road, because roads can be planned to circumvent cemeteries. The court was also provided, as I mentioned in my account of the dispute, with the opinion of the highest ranking Muslim cleric in Israel, Qadi Ahmad Natour, president of the Sharia Court of Appeals. Natour claimed that, according to sharia, Muslim cemeteries are holy until the Day of Judgment and should not be used for anything but human burial.

The adjudication of muftis and sages over treatment of graves and the practice in such matters has always been a matter determined by political context. Muslim tradition and legal interpretation, as Qadi Natour noted, has permitted reopening graves and transferring remains under certain circumstances, provided that the body has decomposed and that the purpose of the project is publicly important to Muslims. According to Qadi Natour, however, the two principal legal justifications for permitting unearthing graves—*maslaha* (interest of the public) and *darura* (necessity) were lacking in the disputed case of Mamilla. The public interest, from the sharia point of view, should be the interest of the Muslim community alone and not the interest of Jewish state authorities and a Jewish corporation.

The museum entrepreneurs, for their part, submitted expert reports written by professors of Islamic law to counter those submitted by the Muslim plaintiffs. The professors claimed that the sharia is flexible, and that it also includes opinions to support building over an old cemetery that is no longer used for burial and where the human remains have already decomposed in the earth. The strongest report was written by Wael Hallaq of Columbia University.[41] Hallaq wrote (apparently without knowing that his report was requested for a case in Israel) that the holiness of graves and other land emanates from the holiness of the human body. Therefore, when the remains of the body have decomposed in the soil, the holiness of the soil in which it was buried is also depleted. Once only the central skeleton of the buried body remained, the land could be used for different purposes, including agricultural development or real estate, among others. According to Hallaq, al-Shafi'i stated that it is prohibited to rummage in a new grave only for one year.[42] But other jurists from the Hanafi and Hanbali schools permitted digging even in a new grave.[43] Hallaq also added that the practice of transferring graves to another location is anchored in the Hadith.

The MOT entrepreneurs also submitted a long list of cases in which Muslim cemeteries in Israel and in Muslim countries had been transformed (as in the case of the Palace Hotel, discussed earlier), and demonstrated that these transformations had been approved by Muslim sages in order to accommodate the Islamic law to the reality of modern urban development.

After examining the court's attitude toward issues of symbolic representation in the Jerusalem landscape, it comes as no surprise that the evaluations submitted by academic experts impressed the judges of the High Court more than the opinion of the president of the Sharia Court of Appeals. After all, the evidence presented in favor of considering Mamilla a heritage site to be protected was tied to a religious, and thus particularistic, court and rested entirely on authorities recognized only among Muslims and therefore easily dismissed as internal to a politics of identity. The academic experts spoke directly to the court's interest in both urban development and its symbolic aspiration to attain a universal perspective on the problem, unconstrained by particular religious views. Justice Procaccia concluded the dispute over the sharia standing on the inviolability of cemeteries with following:

> I see no room to address the conceptual debate that was conveyed to us in the different expert reports submitted to the court by clerics and experts regarding the question to what extent Islam is strict in defending cemeteries and to what extent it permits overriding a holy place for the needs of the living, particularly when old burial sites which were hidden underground are considered. There were opinions from each side, and there is no necessity to decide as to this question in its general perspective. . . . In our circumstances it is appropriate to assume only that there is a debate regarding the question, to what extent Islam permits, from the point of view of legal commandments, construction and development, on land under which there are the remains of old graves, and to what extent it al-

lows the transfer and removal of graves to alternative places and makes development possible. We can also say that there is at least one dominant stream of thought in Islam that strives to balance between old and new, even in this sphere. And reality shows that even in Israel there have been construction and development works over Muslim burial compounds in different regions of the country which were not conducted contrary to the position of the Muslim Community.[44]

The religious courts had almost no standing in the High Court's deliberations. The High Court completely overlooked the opinion of the highest authority of sharia in Israel today—Qadi Ahmad Natour—and took advantage of the competing positions available within Islamic tradition, and of the precedents that bolstered the court's interest in urban development, to dismiss the need to make any serious determination of whether a consensus could be reached on the dominant interpretation of the sharia. It eagerly embraced the position of the academic experts, widely quoting their opinions in the verdict to assert that there are different opinions in the sharia on this matter, and then allying itself with the opinion most convenient to its purposes. Aside from the disposition against the politics of identity I have noted earlier in my analysis, the High Court was apparently impressed by the defendants' (museum entrepreneurs and state authorities) explicit argument that Qadi Natour's rulings on issues pertaining to *awqaf* and holy sites have been ideologically and politically driven. I tend to conclude that these reports had an impact on the High Court judges' decision to ignore Natour's opinion and rule against it.

The High Court's treatment of the Sharia Courts and its dismissal of any need to make a determination according to sharia became issues among the group of academics and social organizations who joined the High Court hearing against the construction of the MOT in Mamilla. They argued, invoking another version of the notion of tolerance, that the matter of whether the cemetery is holy or not should be left to the decision of the Sharia Court, saying, "In the same way that Halachic questions are being determined by Rabbis and not by researchers of Halacha, so the High Court should respect the religious autonomy of the Muslim believers community in Israel and the adjudications of their religious leaders."[45] They meant that the High Court should respect the position of the president of the Sharia Court of Appeals, Qadi Ahmad Natour, in the same way that it respects the decisions of rabbis, rather than experts on Jewish law, regarding Jewish cemeteries in Israel. The court, apparently, did not find that this objection to their practice merited any response whatsoever.

The position taken by Natour and the Sharia Court created a turning point in the Mamilla affair and put the jurisdiction of the Sharia Court under High Court examination. The jurisdiction of the Sharia Court as a quasi-autonomous institution of the Muslim minority in Israel was tested.

It should be remembered that Israel left under the jurisdiction of the Sharia Court the same authorities granted by article 52 of the 1922 British Mandate Order-in-Council. The 1961 Qadis Law clarifies that the *qadis* are subjected to the state laws.[46] The High Court has the authority to override Sharia Court rulings, but in practice such cases are rare and equate with the situation regarding rabbinical court decisions. The High Court interferes in religious courts only when this intervention is essential to safeguard the basic values of society.[47]

The mere fact that state authorities and Jewish enterprises used to ask *qadis* to issue a fatwa permitting the sale of old abandoned Muslim cemeteries for development purposes compelled Qadi Natour to conclude that determining the holiness of a cemetery or the removal of its sacredness is under the exclusive jurisdiction of the Sharia Court. Moreover, in many cases, Israeli civil courts validated fatwas of Sharia Court *qadis* by respecting the *qadis*' opinions regarding Muslim holy places in disputes about the sale or use of *waqf* properties and holy sites without questioning the *qadis*' legal authority to issue a *fatwa*. The *qadis* (as well as the Muslim plaintiffs) believed that, according to a version of religious tolerance that had been operative within the Israeli legal system for years, they were the authentic representatives of Islamic law in Israel. They believed that they would be able to convince the High Court justices that only formal religious clerics should be authorized to adjudicate whether a plot of land that contains hundreds of Muslim graves is holy and inalienable or not. Apparently they believed that the High Court, which according to Israeli Jewish public opinion generally solidifies liberal values in its rulings and refrains as much as possible from intervening in the affairs of religious courts, would also refrain in the Mamilla case. However, their opinion was found to be wrong.

The plaintiffs, most likely aware of the High Court's dispositions, had also attempted to gain an advantage by raising a larger dispute over venue and jurisdiction. Another claim for the holy status of a Muslim cemetery depended on its legal status as a *waqf* property under the sole jurisdiction of the Sharia Court, the very court so blatantly disrespected by the High Court. Israel had enacted in 1965 an amendment to the Absentees' Properties Law that emptied the General Waqf properties of their *waqf* status and handed them over to a government custodian. The Sharia Court of West Jerusalem attempted to disregard the civil law and to treat the disputed land in Mamilla as if it were still a *waqf* property under its jurisdiction. By so doing, both the Muslim plaintiffs and the *qadis* challenged the Israeli law in an attempt to use the Mamilla dispute as a precedent for restoring expropriated *waqf* assets. On March 1, 2006, the *qadi* of Jerusalem, Muhammad Zibde, appointed two administrators (*mutawallis*) affiliated with the NIM on "a General *Waqf* asset named the Ma'man Allah Cemetery."[48] He ordered them to take any action necessary to protect the cemetery. This decision and action was overruled by the High Court according to the Absentees' Properties Law.

It should be pointed out that procedural issues internal to the legal system can have an impact as great or greater than ideological dispositions; this might ultimately have been the case regarding the High Court's treatment of the Sharia Court in this particular instance. The High Court was offended to learn that the Sharia Court had intervened in the dispute while the case awaited hearing at its plenum. The appeal to the Sharia Court was considered not to be a good faith action. If the major case submitted by the al-Aqsa Association had been submitted to the Sharia Court first, I doubt whether the High Court would have overruled the decision of a *qadi*. However, filing the case in the Sharia Court was a clear attempt to circumvent the High Court and to create a fait accompli. Hence, the justices ruled that Sharia Courts in Israel have no jurisdiction regarding General Waqf properties that were transferred to the government. The result harshly degraded the Sharia Court apparatus and damaged one of the minority's semiautonomous institutions.

DISCRIMINATION

The importance of tolerance in determining the court's attitude toward the right to symbolic representation in the landscape merges with its interest in establishing the status of unused cemeteries in light of a final consideration: How well does the treatment of Mamilla in the MOT plan compare with the standards set for treating, first of all, cemeteries associated with other religions within Israel and, second, cemeteries in other parts of the world? The issue here is not simply respecting the heritage sites of other religions but one of fairness. The Muslim plaintiffs claimed that Israeli authorities invoke discriminatory policies regarding the preservation of cemeteries. They contended that "in the same way that the utmost protection is given to Jewish cemeteries in Israel and abroad, so too should a Muslim cemetery not be desecrated."[49] The same critical view was expressed by American historian Rashid Khalidi, of Palestinian extraction, who wrote that the Israeli government morally failed to deal with the matter since the government had protested desecration of old Jewish cemeteries when East Jerusalem was under Jordanian rule (1948–1967).[50]

A number of Jewish organizations attempted to influence the stance of the Israeli government by emphasizing the Jewish approach to cemeteries. The Central Conference of American Rabbis (reform congregations) resolved in its annual convention of February 2008 to join a group of one hundred Israeli rabbis (Shomrei Mishpat) and Jewish academics along with civil organizations to strongly object to the construction of the MOT above a Muslim cemetery.[51] In their joint petition to the High Court, the Israeli academics said the following:

> Desecrating tens of thousands of graves in the Mount of Olives between 1948 and 1967 [under Jordanian Rule in East Jerusalem] was deeply engraved in the memory of Jerusalem Jews and in the awareness of Jews worldwide. Anger at the insult and fear of further desecration of the holy affected not only religious believers, and rightly so. Allowing construction over a Muslim cemetery will create strong feelings of a double standard, discrimination, and hypocrisy. Desecrating cemeteries is major ammunition in the arsenal of anti-Semites in both the Christian and Muslim worlds. Non-recognition of the holiness of the Mamilla Cemetery will damage the moral basis of the just battle against anti-Semitism. . . . It will play into the hands of the anti-Semites, to the extent of actual danger of damage to Jewish cemeteries in Europe, in the Muslim world, and in North and South America.[52]

The High Court was fully aware of this critique and gave it serious consideration, as one can conclude from the fact that the verdict contained a long section studying comparative law. The court's motives for producing this section of the verdict are somewhat obscure; perhaps it was apologetic, and perhaps it reflected a genuine fear that ruling in favor of the resumption of construction for the museum in Mamilla would be interpreted as a discriminatory policy legitimize reprisal attacks on Jewish cemeteries around the world.

The court concluded, in line with the disposition we have already noted, that in modern times, both the law and practice of other countries as well as Israel (including cases in which Jewish graves were exposed) allow urban development on old graves. At the same time the Mamilla case differs significantly from all the comparative cases cited by the High Court in ways that merely reintroduce the issues with which the case started. The construction in other cases involved urban development infrastructure, while the case of Mamilla involves a project that aspires to be a symbol of tolerance to the three major monotheistic religions in a city that is holy. Moreover, in all of the comparable examples, there were few graves or excavation of a grave was incidental, while the disputed land in Mamilla, a large and historically important cemetery, is estimated to contain about one thousand graves. In choosing the cases with which to compare Mamilla, the court showed once again that its attempt to avoid the "politics of identity" made it entirely deaf to the issues that brought the plaintiffs to court in the first place.

In conclusion, it seems that the High Court verdict raises the following difficulties:

- The verdict referred to the excavated graves as if they were incidentally exposed and were hidden from view. However, the Mamilla Cemetery is an important historical graveyard and the disputed plot contained about one thousand graves.
- The High Court was not aware of the fact that the fatwa permitting the removal of the cemetery's sanctity did so for the purpose of developing a public park and not for building. Unlike a building, developing a public park does not entail digging down deeply.
- The verdict underlines that the Muslim plaintiffs delayed their objection to the project, but it was not aware of three previous Muslim objections to development works and neglect of the cemetery (a Jordanian complaint from 1950, an Israeli Muslim official from Haifa's complaint of 1958, and petitions to UNESCO by the PLO and Jordanian Waqf of the mid-1980s).
- Unlike most cases of using cemeteries for development purposes of vital infrastructure, the MOT project could be erected in an alternative location.
- One of the main justifications to resume building of the MOT in Mamilla was the particular quasi-sculpture architectural plan that was laid down by Frank Gehry. This argument is invalid after Gehry withdrew from the project in 2010.

THE COURT AS A VENUE FOR RESOLVING A CONFLICT

Petitioning the High Court in the Mamilla case turned out to be disadvantageous for the NIM headed by Sheikh Raed Salah. My personal impression from my conversations with Muslim functionaries during the court hearing was that they believed they had a golden opportunity to challenge an action that was is patently unreasonable, and that the High Court as well as Jewish public opinion would side with them. They believed that the Mamilla dispute was an opportunity to win an important precedent against the Israeli government's policy regarding abandoned Islamic holy places. However, the al-Aqsa Association also took a huge risk because losing a case in the High Court would mean reaffirming the legitimacy of Israeli law and policies and generating a precedent that would block the Islamic Movement from implementing its strategy and from rejuvenating abandoned Muslim holy sites. In fact, this was exactly the result of the High Court verdict.

Referring a dispute over a holy place to be decided by a judicial tribunal such as a civil court or even commission of inquiry is an autocratic method to resolve a conflict that has its pros and cons. For some conflicts, a tribunal would be the most efficient process, while in other cases, a legal framework further complicates the conflict and prolongs its duration. Resorting to the court is an "autocratic" method because once the dispute is turned over to the legal domain, adjudication in the dispute and its consequences are not negotiable but are imposed from above.[53] What makes such a decision autocratic is also the fact that one of the parties, whether a direct party or an indirect ruling authority, determines unilaterally the particular venue of legal procedure. There is always one party upset by the choice of the tribunal, and this dissatisfaction negatively influences its cooperation with compromise options during court hearings. Moreover, even when a process of mediation or even arbitration takes place, the final adjudication will be taken as arbitrary and will not necessarily bring an end to the conflict.[54] This may occur despite the fact that the decision has been made within an accepted framework of law, and regardless of whether the parties to the conflict comply with the rule of law.[55] Another shortcoming to the judicial treatment of a conflict over sacred sites is that a court procedure is usually limited to specific legal questions rather than able to deal with a broad spectrum of relations between the parties; hence, its decision will not solve the conflict from its root.[56]

A judicial hearing on such a dispute restricts the parties to a particular framework of procedures and laws; it frames the boundaries of the conflict, limits the number of directly involved parties, and limits broader public involvement in the process of mitigating the dispute.[57] Conversely, a court ruling can impose a quick solution to a dispute and enable governing authorities to control and enforce law when there is a risk that the dispute will lead to bloodshed or will digress into mass protest and potential violence.[58] In this case, the legal treatment does not pretend to solve every aspect of the dispute, but only to contain the danger of an outbreak of violence.[59]

Another weakness of a legal process is that its efficiency depends on a ruling body to enforce its verdict.[60] In other words, the need for enforcement indicates that an autocratic solution by a legal tribunal does not bring an end to a conflict but is only one stage of it.[61] One could only expect that sometime in the future the original conflict will once again erupt. However, a temporary situation of tranquility resulting from a court verdict may endure for a long period; in this case the legal treatment could be advantageous. Thus, a permanent solution to a conflict over holy places will materialize only when the parties to it arrive at an agreement without the imposition of a solution by a third party. Hence, a judicial decision is part of conflict management and not of conflict resolution.[62]

In conclusion, a court is not an appropriate venue for resolving conflicts over construction in cemeteries because a judicial decision is only a locally applicable determination that does not in fact resolve the conflict. The losing side can still take the struggle to other less comfortable venues, such as the international forum dealing with human and minority rights, and it can also exacerbate its protest actions.

Thus, in conflicts involving symbolic aspects of identity when one party fails to achieve its end on the local level, it may opt to shift the confrontation to a higher level mostly the international arena. In the literature of political science, this process is known as "scale shift" and, in our case, as "upscaling" from the state to the international level.[63] This is, in fact, a development that began in 2010 regarding the Mamilla dispute.

A successful action of shifting the struggle to a more powerful venue was carried out by Palestinian organizations. In 2010 fifteen Palestinian organizations recruited sixty East Jerusalem dignitaries whose families are buried in Mamilla and launched a media campaign via the Internet. Throughout the same year thousands of people signed a petition against the construction in Mamilla. On February 10, 2010, the Palestinian organizations appealed to five senior officers of the United Nations and to the government of Switzerland (in her capacity of trustee on the Fourth Geneva Convention). They demanded an investigation of the issue and an order for Israel to stop the work, preserve the cemetery as a site of antiquities, and rebury the human remains that had been removed from it. One impact of the campaign was that the U.S.-based Center for Constitutional Rights also appealed to the United Nations, demanding the building of the MOT on cemetery land be stopped. Another outcome of the upscaling action was the decision by the UN Human Rights Council dated March 19, 2010, against Israel's actions in the occupied territories that included an article referring to the Mamilla Cemetery; it determined that the construction of the MOT was illegal and called for the government of Israel to stop its construction.[64] This development shows that Israel has paid a high price in the international arena for insisting on building the MOT in Mamilla.

CONCLUSION

The dispute over building the MOT in Mamilla, a holy place, embodies a significant symbolic identity issue within a politics of identity in the wider Israeli–Palestinian conflict. Examining the various debated arguments from the angle of conflict resolution leads to the conclusion that a High Court verdict did not put an end to the conflict, and that an upscaling of the dispute to the international arena instead took place. International organizations should consider this dispute in comparison to similar cases of building over cemeteries, which I summarize in the following paragraphs.

Three aspects distinguish the Mamilla Cemetery dispute from other similar cases of building over Jewish graves in Israel:

1. In all other disputes, the burial sites were intended for development and infrastructure, while the Mamilla enterprise aimed to embody the concept of tolerance. The very fact that a dispute broke out over the Mamilla Cemetery and had to be dealt with in a judicial court casts a shadow over the project and its goal.
2. The comparable cases discussed by the High Court dealt with cemeteries that were neither of significant historical value nor located in cities that are holy and important to the three monotheistic religions.
3. In the other cases of comparison, the number of graves discovered was not as high as in the case of Mamilla, where the human remains of four hundred deceased have already been unearthed and another six hundred are estimated by the IAA archaeologists to remain under an unexcavated part of the museum plot.

On the other hand, the following points that impacted the High Court verdict should also not be overlooked:

1. The Muslim community neglected the cemetery throughout decades and did not protect this site despite the unfortunate political circumstances.
2. The Mamilla affair articulates an identity struggle between ideological groups of a national and a religious minority and the state's hegemonic culture. When a minority provokes the majority on a highly charged sensitive issue, there is no wonder that the majority counter reacts.
3. Senior Muslim clerics themselves contributed to the regression of the Mamilla Cemetery, beginning with the British Mandate Supreme Muslim Council and ending with the president of the Sharia Court of Appeals during the 1960s.
4. The museum project was not the first to inflict upon the plot of land assigned to the MOT. Over the same piece of land there was a parking lot

that the museum building was planning to replace. The construction of the parking lot in the mid-1980s did not raise protest and Muslims did not express public resentment but only registered a complaint with UNESCO.

Backed by the Israeli High Court decision, the construction of the MOT in Jerusalem has already begun and its completion seems inevitable. However, the upscaling of the campaign against this project at international institutions and media outlets may detract the mission of the museum.

NOTES

1. The term "politics of identity" underlines the particularity of different identity groups within a society and aspires to promote the interests of these identity groups. C. Calhoun, ed., *Social Theory and the Politics of Identity* (Oxford: Blackwell, 1994).
2. Sidney Tarrow, *The New Transactional Activism* (Cambridge: Cambridge University Press, 2005), 25; and Charles Tilly and Sidney Tarrow, *Contentious Politics* (Boulder, CO: Paradigm Publishers, 2007), 45.
3. Mujir al-Din, *Al-uns al-jalil bi-ta'rikh al-quds wal-khalil* (Amman: Al-Muhtasib, 1973), 2:63–65.
4. See expert report by Yehoshua Ben-Arieh dated March 20, 2007, submitted to the High Court (High Court Archive, file 52/06).
5. Uri M. Kupferschmidt, *The Supreme Muslim Council: Islam Under the British Mandate for Palestine* (Leiden: E. J. Brill, 1987), 136; and Yitzhak Reiter, *Islamic Endowment in Jerusalem Under British Mandate* (London: Frank Cass, 1996), 195.
6. In 2006 two Israeli leading geographers debated the question of building the Palace hotel over a cemetery. See expert reports by Yehoshua Ben-Arieh and Gideon Biger (High Court Archive, file 52/06). See also *Al-Aqsa Association for the Development of the Assets of the Muslim Waqf in the Land of Israel Ltd. v. Simon Wiesenthal Center Museum Corp*, HCJ 52/06 verdict, articles 60–62.
7. Barukh Katinka, *Me'az Ve-Ad Hayom* (Jerusalem: Kiryat Sefer, 1961), 261.
8. Kamil Jamil al-Asali, *Ajdadna fi Thari Bayt al-Maqdis* (Amman: Royal Council for the Study of Islamic Civilization, 1981), 117–32, 159–96.
9. Al-Quds Shari'a Court, Sijill Ahkam 444, p. 19 # 95. For the printed booklet of the opposition, see Raghib al-Khalidi, Arif Hikmat al-Nashashibi, and Hasan al-Budayri, *Bayan ila al-'alam al-Islami 'ammatan 'an al-amakin al-Muqaddasa*

al-Islamiyya fi Filastin (Jerusalem: Matba'at Bayt al-Maqdis, February 7, 1932). For the responses of the Supreme Muslim Council, see Supreme Muslim Council, *Al-Jami'a al-Arabiyya*, no. 738 (December 1, 1931): 21, Sha'ban 1350h.

10. David Kroyanker, "Museum Is Prohibited and a University Is Permitted?," *Haaretz*, January 10, 2006; and David Kroyanker, *Halom BeHakitz: Yerushalayim HaLo-Bnuya*, (Jerusalem: Migdal David—The Museum for Jerusalem's History, 1993). On the decision to establish a university regardless of its location, see Kupferschmidt, *The Supreme Muslim Council*, 206–18.

11. See the project's sketch at Henry Kendall, *Jerusalem, the City Plan: Preservation and Development During the British Mandate, 1918–1948* (London: H. M. Stationery Office Press and Admiralty Chart Establishment, 1948), 53. For the deliberations, see Yitzhak Reiter, *Allah's Safe Haven?: The Controversy Surrounding the Mamilla Cemetery and the Museum of Tolerance: Contesting Domination Over the Symbolic and Physical Landscapes* [in Hebrew, forthcoming in English] (Jerusalem: Jerusalem Institute for Israel Studies, 2011).

12. Raghib Al-Khalidi, *Filastin*, March 25, 1950.

13. Zeev Vilnai, *Sacred Gravestones in Eretz Israel* (Jerusalem: Ahiever, 1996), 2:329. The hotel was built on land that the government expropriated from the *waqf* of the family of Abd al-Razzaq al-'Alamibelonged to the Intercontinental chain, later called the Seven Arches Hotel.

14. UNESCO Executive Board, 125th Session, "Jerusalem and the Implementation of 23 C/Resolution 11/3." Report 125 EX/15, July 17, 1986, http://unesdoc.unesco.org/images/0006/000695/069594eo.pdf.

15. Ibid.

16. Local zoning plan 8030 was published in the *Official Gazette* 5023, October 16, 2001, after advertisement in *Maariv*, September 16, 2001; *Yerushalayim*, September 21, 2001; and *al-Ittihad* and *al-Quds*, September 2001.

17. This was published on the Northern Islamic Movement's website, www.islamic-aqsa.com, on May 9, 2006, accessed September 8, 2008. The website has since been removed.

18. *Al-Aqsa Association v. Simon Wiesenthal Center Museum*, HCJ 52/06.

19. Ibid.

20. Ibid.

21. *Muhammaed Khayr al-Dajani vs. Israel's Police*, judgment dated February 12, 2006, HCJ 1331/06.

22. *Simon Wiesenthal Center Museum Corp. vs. the Shari'a Court of Jerusalem*, HCJ 1671/06.

23. Ibid.

24. Israeli radio broadcast by Shai Zilber, heard on August 12, 2010, at 9:15 p.m.

25. S. Linde, "Hier: Jerusalem Tolerance Museum in 3 Years," *Jerusalem Post*, June 6, 2012.
26. Doron Bar-Gil, "The Plan to Contact Heikhal HaMishpat in Jerusalem Was Cancelled," NRG website February 1, 2009, http://www.nrg.co.il/online/54/ART1/834/590.html.
27. Meron Benvenisti, *Sacred Landscape: The Buried History of the Holy Land 1948–1998* (Berkeley: University of California Press, 2000), 288–99.
28. Saree Makdisi, "Architecture of Erasure," *Critical Inquiry* 36, no. 3 (Spring 2010): 555.
29. Nimrod Luz, "Metaphors to Live By: Identity Formation and Resistance Among Minority Muslims in Israel," in *Religion and Place: Landscape, Politics and Piety*, ed. Peter Hopkins, Lily Kong, and Elizabeth Olson, 57–74 (Dordrecht: Springer, 2013). Luz cites the following references: James Duncan and Nancy Duncan, "Re(reading) the Landscape," *Environment and Planning D: Society and Space* 6, no. (1988): 117–26; D. Harvey, "'Monument and Myth," *Annals of the Association of American Geographers*" 69 (1979): 362–81; D. Haynes and G. Parkash, "Introduction: The Entanglement of Power and Resistance," in *Contesting Power: Resistance and Everyday Social Relations in South Asia*, ed. D. Haynes and G. Parkash (Delhi: Oxford University Press, 1991), 1–22; L. Kong, "Ideological Hegemony and the Political Symbolism of Religious Buildings in Singapore," *Environment and Planning D: Society and Space* 11 (1993): 23–45; D. Mitchell, *Cultural Geography: A Critical Introduction* (Oxford: Blackwell, 2000); S. Pile, "Introduction: Opposition, Political Identities and Spaces of Resistance," in *Geographies of Resistance*, ed. S. Pile and M. Keith (London: Routledge, 1997), 1–32; J. C. Scott, *Weapons of the Weak* (New Haven, CT: Yale University Press, 1985); and Y. Tuan, "Thought and Landscape," in *The Interpretation of Ordinary Landscape*, ed. D. W. Meinig (New York: Oxford University Press, 1979), 89–102.
30. On the symbolic meaning of sacred landscape within the Israeli–Palestinian conflict, see W. J. T. Mitchell, *Sacred Landscape*, ed. Larry Abramson [in Hebrew] (Tel Aviv: Resling, 2009).
31. Quoted in Reiter, *Allah's Safe Haven*, 30–31.
32. *Al-Aqsa Association v. Simon Wiesenthal Center Museum*, HDJ 52/06 verdict, article 239, translated from Hebrew.
33. Ibid., article 1.
34. Quoted in Makdisi, "Architecture of Erasure," 551.
35. See W. J. T. Mitchell, "Imperial Landscape," in *Landscape and Power*, 2nd ed., ed. W. J. T. Mitchell (Chicago: University of Chicago Press, 2002).
36. H. Lefebvre, *The Production of Space* (Oxford: Basil Blackwell, 1991), 401–16.
37. al-Asali, *Ajdadna fi Thari Bayt al-Maqdis*, 117–32, 159–96.

38. *Al-Aqsa Association v. Simon Wiesenthal Center Museum*, HCJ 52/06 verdict, article 242.
39. Quoted in Neety C. Gross, "Grave Thoughts," *Jerusalem Report*, January 5, 2009, 21–24.
40. The report is dated December 8, 2007. Afana graduated with a PhD in Islamic Law from Umm al-Qura University, Saudi Arabia, and presently teaches at al-Quds University in Jerusalem. Afana has also taught in the Islamic College of Umm al-Fahm (affiliated with the Islamic Movement and not recognized by the state institutions) and other academic institutions.
41. Hallaq, a Christian Arab, was born in Nazareth, Israel. He was graduated from the University of Haifa in Middle East Studies.
42. Muhammad b. Idris al-Shafi'I, *Al-Umm*, 2:316.
43. He referred to the following sources of Islamic jurisprudence: Abd al-Razzaq al-San'ani, *Al-Musannaf*, 3:192; Yahya b. Sharaf al-Din al-Nawawi, *Al-Majmu': Sharh al-Muhadhdhab* (mentioned in the 1964 fatwa of Tahir Hammad), 5:273; and Muhammad b. Habib al-Mawardi, *Al-ahkam al-sultaniyya wal-wilayat al-diniyya: Ibn Qudama al-Maqdisi, Al-Mughni* (Beirut: Dar al-Kitab al-Arabi, 1983), 2:194.
44. *Al-Aqsa Association v. Simon Wiesenthal Center Museum*, HCJ 52/06 verdict, article 245.
45. Affidavit to HCJ 52/06 by Professor Shimon Shamir.
46. Article 9 of the 1961 Qadis Law (amending a previous law of 1953).
47. See Emanuel Nave, "Implementation of Shari'a in 20th Century Civil Courts: A Comparative Study of Adjudication in Personal Status and Waqf Issues of Muslims in a Muslim Country (Egypt) and a Non-Muslim Country (Israel)" (Ph.D. diss., Hebrew University, 1997).
48. *Muhammaed Khayr al-Dajani vs. Israel's Police*, judgment dated February 12, 2006, HCJ 1331/06.
49. File submitted to the High Court 52/06.
50. "Appendix VI: Resolution of the Central Conference of American Rabbis Opposing Construction over the Mamilla Cemetery," http://www.mamillacampaign.org/photos/pdfs/Appendix6.pdf.
51. Central Conference of American Rabbis, "Appendix VI: Resolution of the Central Conference of American Rabbis Opposing Construction Over the Mamilla Cemetary," February 25, 2008, http://www.mamillacampaign.org/photos/pdfs/Appendix6.pdf.
52. Ibid.
53. Manifesto signed by Israeli faculty experts in Middle East studies.

54. Stepehn LaTour, Pauline Houlden, Laurens Walker, and John Thibaut, "Some Determinants of Preference for Modes of Conflict Resolution," *Journal of Conflict Resolution* 20, no 2 (1976): 320; and Y. Maley, "From Adjudication to Mediation: Third Party Discourse in Conflict Resolution," *Journal of Pragmatics* 23, no. 1 (1995): 96, 101.
55. Alan Tidwell, *Conflict Resolved?* (New York: Pinter Press, 1998), 22.
56. Ibid.; and M. Hudson, *International Tribunals, Past and Future* (Concord, NH: Rumford Press, 1994), 236.
57. Maley, "From Adjudication to Mediation," 92–100.
58. LaTour et al., "Some Determinants," 320; and Hudson, *International Tribunals*, 236.
59. Hudson, *International Tribunals*, 238.
60. C. R. Mitchell, *The Structure of International Conflict* (New York: St. Martin's Press, 1989), 276.
61. L. Kriesberg, *Constructive Conflict: From Escalation to Resolution* (Lanham, MD: Rowman & Littlefield, 1998), 323.
62. Mitchell, *The Structure of International Conflict*, 276.
63. B. Hill, "An Analysis of Conflict Resolution Techniques: From Problem-Solving Workshops to Theory," *Journal of Conflict Resolution* 26, no. 1 (1982): 115.
64. UNHRC 13th session, agenda item 7, document GE 10-12403, March 19, 2010, http://unispal.un.org/UNISPAL.NSF/0/272537975C97EAD1852576F100 4EBB0A.

10

SECULARIZING THE UNSECULARIZABLE

A COMPARATIVE STUDY OF THE HACI BEKTAŞ AND MEVLANA MUSEUMS IN TURKEY

RABIA HARMANŞAH, TUĞBA TANYERI-ERDEMIR, AND ROBERT M. HAYDEN

SACRED SITES THAT are shared by members of differing religious communities create interesting dilemmas for analysis since they may often be seen as flashpoints of conflict but may equally well be perceived as places in which religious tolerance is exhibited, if not, perhaps, always with great enthusiasm by the parties involved. When de facto shared sites are also the focus of latent conflict and sometimes more open strife, there are practical problems of trying to provide systems of management that can make a site open to members of all communities who claim the right to be able to use it. One way to facilitate access by multiple communities while denying ultimate control over a site to any one of them might be to turn it into a museum, run by museum professionals employed by the state rather than by religious officials, a course of action that may appear promising as a way to end competing claims on the site by granting access to all.

For almost a century, however, writers from viewpoints as far removed as phenomenology, on the one hand, and fieldwork-based archaeology, on the other, have noted that sacred space is tied to secular power.[1] If that is the case, transforming religious sites into putatively state ones will not guarantee the neutralization of sacred sites since it is likely—indeed, almost certain—that the standardized practices of the museum professionals running the site will reflect the ideological stance of the state's policy toward religion. In fact, a museumification process itself is a political statement about a sacred site, asserting state control over religious practice. Such control might be that of a secular state claiming the right to regulate not religious belief but religious "actions which were in violation of social duties or subversive of good order," in the classic phrasing of the U.S. Supreme Court's approval of a legal ban on the social practices of a religious group;[2] but it might also be that of a sectarian state that explicitly favors one religion over others, even if it claims to tolerate other faiths.

Turkey presents interesting possibilities for studying the museumification of sacred sites. Since the founding of the republic in 1923, modern Turkey has been officially a secular state, although Turkish secularism is widely seen as being under strong pressure since the 1990s.[3] Since the Republic replaced a religiously grounded regime, there was a strong effort to weaken the power of Muslim religious institutions in the early Republican period and at various times since then. These efforts included closing important religious sites, including the subjects of this paper, for periods of years.[4] Thus, part of the story of Turkish secularism is one of competition between the state and religious authorities, competition played out at times in religious sites.

Yet there is another, more subtle facet of the politics of religion in Turkey that is also played out at key religious sites. In fact, the constitutionally secular Turkish state now favors Sunni Islam, although a substantial percentage of the population are not Sunnis but rather Alevi-Bektaşi or other forms of so-called heterodox Islam.[5] We claim in this essay that this dynamic secularization, imposed and administered by the Turkish state, actually structures competition over the use of key religious sites to favor the Sunni practices it tacitly supports and to obstruct Alevi-Bektaşi practices.

In seeing the matter this way, we are also demonstrating the utility of the theoretical model of antagonistic tolerance (AT) that we have been developing through comparative research in Bulgaria, India, and Portugal as well as in Turkey. The AT model was presented first in a 2002 article by Robert Hayden on competitive sharing of religious sites in India and the Balkans. That original model is criticized in some of the other chapters in this volume and elsewhere, though it is not always presented accurately by the critics and has in any event been much more thoroughly developed since its 2002 introduction.[6] The AT model is applicable in situations in which two communities that distinguish themselves consistently as "Self" and "Other," primarily on the basis of differing religions, live intermingled but rarely intermarrying over long periods of time. In such cases there is inherent competition between the communities, and dominance of one group over the other is indicated by control over primary religious sites, which are generally appropriated and transformed when domination changes. Thus, the predominant indicators of the religious affiliation of a site (from structural features through iconography) will change to reflect the appropriation of it by actors serving differing religions as they become dominant. Well-known changes of the kind we are considering would include the transformation of the Hagia Sophia church in Constantinople into a mosque in 1453, or the transformation of the great mosque of Cordoba into the cathedral there, but the process is common in widely varying geographical and historical contexts.

AT analysis requires consideration of the cultural forms of a site in any given ethnographic present in the context of the trajectories of development that have produced those specific forms at that moment (and when possible, those that come after). Another necessary context for analysis is that of the networks of other sites of the several competing religious communities. These networks are seen as religioscapes, which are composed of structures associated with particular religions, each site comprising a node of the religioscape in question.[7] Comparing changes in religioscapes through time allows us to evaluate changes in patterns of dominance of one group over another, as revealed by the changes in the physical and symbolic components of the nodes of the intersecting religioscapes. The model anticipates that when one group is dominant, or when both groups are subordinated to a higher political power, such as an imperial government, interactions will be peaceful and syncretism may well be found, but when dominance is threatened or overturned, violence occurs as a key site is appropriated or even destroyed. The model is thus one of punctuated equilibrium, anticipating long periods of peaceful but competitive interaction interspersed with periods of violence.

For the present chapter, the important point about the AT model is that it holds that when members of more than one religious community use a sacred site, we should anticipate competition over control of that site, or of aspects of it (e.g., exclusive or preferred use of particular locations within it, or of access at specific times, or of shares in the proceeds of contributions made to the shrine). Indeed, another term for the AT model is "competitive sharing." The AT model thus resolves the apparent analytical dichotomy between sharing a site and engaging in conflict over it by envisioning competition between the groups involved as a constant condition manifested in varying ways, usually peaceful but occasionally violent.

In the terms of the AT model, efforts by a secular state to control religious sites constitute competition over those sites between the state and its agencies, on the one hand, and religious practitioners and their leaders, on the other. Indeed, secularism may in some cases be an ideological form comparable to that of religion, but in an inverted form; an example is the aggressive atheism of the early Soviet Union with its museums of atheism, many of which were built in church structures, most notably the Museum of Scientific Atheism in what had been (and is again) St. Isaac's Cathedral in Leningrad (now again St. Petersburg).[8]

Viewing secularism as a competing model of religious belief lets us understand why turning a sacred site into a museum cannot be acceptable to a body of believers who continue to see the site as sacred. If the museumification of the site hinders their access to it or obstructs their ability to make use of the site as they wish to do for religious observances, denying the sacredness of the place in the name of secularism is no less disruptive to believers than would be a manifestation of control over it by another overtly religious group. It is for this reason that we see government attempts to turn sacred sites into museums as trying to secularize the unsecularizeable.

The sites in Turkey on which we focus are the shrine complexes of Hacı Bektaş Veli in Hacıbektaş and Mevlana Jalal ad-Din Rumi in Konya. Both sites were major focal points of so-called heterodox or Sufi practices during the Ottoman period, both were closed by the early Republican government in 1925, and both were later reopened as museums, albeit at different times, the Konya site already in 1926, and the one in Hacıbektaş not until 1964. Despite their current institutional labels and functions as museums, these shrines are still among the most frequently visited sacred sites in Turkey. The meaning and functions of these sites are continually transformed by contestations and negotiations between the state, the visitors, and the museum staff. Based on fieldwork we have conducted in the summers of 2008 and 2009, we present a comparative study of these sites, which are visited as sacred shrine complexes by believers but institutionalized as museums by the state. In our conclusion, however, we turn to wider implications of seeing museumification of religious sites in Turkey as an effort to transform buildings from nodes of religioscapes to nodes of secularscapes, as we note the efforts of the Turkish government since about 2010 to turn museums into mosques. In these cases, as in those of the Hacı Bektaş and Mevlana museums, the nominally secular Turkish state seems to be imposing a Sunni religioscape on what are nominally secular institutions, thus displacing nodes of the secularscape with the forms of a Sunni religioscape.

HISTORICAL BACKGROUND: HETERODOX SAINTS AND THE OTTOMAN STATE

Both the Hacı Bektaş and Mevlana museums are formed around the dervish lodges of thirteenth-century Anatolian mystics and share common structural, historical, ritual, and affective features. Their conversions from sacred sites into museums in the last century, as well as their current use by visitors, also reveal important parallels. However, there are differences in the institutional practices that are indicative of the secular Turkish state's inconsistent ideological stances toward different faiths and practices.

Hacı Bektaş Veli was a thirteenth-century Anatolian mystic, and eponym of the Bektaşi Order.[9] The order was established following his death and became widespread as one of the most popular Sufi orders in Anatolia and the Balkans. The order was institutionalized and gained its present characteristics through the efforts of a later figure, Balım Sultan. The Bektaşi Order played a significant role in the integration of the newly conquered areas into the Ottoman Empire. According to Svante Cornell and Ingvar Svanberg, "in particular, the Bektaşi order was responsible for the religious education of the Christian-born children raised to serve in the Ottoman bureaucracy through the devshirme ['blood-tax'] system."[10]

Despite their close connections to the ruling elite and important institutional roles within the empire, Bektaşis' relations with the Sunni Muslim majority and the predominantly Sunni political authorities were uneasy and remain so today. According to John A. Norton, "doubts about their political loyalty plus their disregard for standard Islamic observances, while at the same time indulging in heretical practices, often led to their being persecuted."[11] Mahmud II suppressed the Bektaşi Order in 1826 and executed or exiled many Bektaşi leaders, and the order's possessions were either razed or handed over to the Nakşibendi, one of the most widespread and influential Sufi orders in Turkey, which adhered to the orthodox Sunni interpretation of Islam and the Shariat.[12] Importantly, "this brotherhood [Nakşibendi] has continually exercised a certain power in the administration of Turkey's government, as well as in commercial and industrial life generally."[13] In 1826 a mosque was built within the dervish lodge and shrine complex of Hacı Bektaş as a clear marker of the sectarian transition of the site. This mosque still stands and is part of the story that follows.

The general teachings of the Bektaşi Order are closely associated with rural and non-Sunni practitioners of Islam, in particular Alevism.[14] Very broadly, Alevism can be defined as following the path of Ali, the cousin and son-in-law of the Prophet Muhammad. However, the term "Alevi" is used and perceived variously to refer to a religious, cultural, or ethnic identity distinct from Sunni or Shia Muslims. Both Alevis and Bektaşis, neither of which group follows orthodox Sunni observances, were oppressed by the political authorities for their interpretation of Islam. However, these communities have very different historical experiences.[15]

Despite these differences, the shrine of Hacı Bektaş has traditionally been considered a holy pilgrimage site for Alevis and is still venerated as one of the most holy places of the Alevi faith today.

Mevlana Jalal ad-Din Rumi, for his part, was also a thirteenth-century mystic, poet, and philosopher.[16] He was born in the city of Balkh, Khorasan, which is located in what is now northern Afghanistan, and he moved to Konya with his family to escape the Mongol invasion of Central Asia. Rumi wrote the majority of his works in Persian, the most prominent being *Masnavi Man'avi* (Spiritual couplets), *Divan-i Kabir* (Great work), *Fihi Ma Fihi* (In it what's in it), *Majalis-i Saba* (Seven sessions), and *Maktubat* (The letters). After his death, a mausoleum and a shrine were built over his grave, and this complex became one of the most important pilgrimage sites for many people. His son Sultan Veled and his disciples founded the Mevlevi Order, which is now popularly known as the "Whirling Dervishes." This order was supported by the sultans to balance the special relationship between the Bektaşis and the Janissaries. The order attracted the elite and urban population of the Ottoman Empire, including disciples from among the top-ranking officers. Unlike the Bektaşi Order, the Mevlevi Order was never openly suppressed by the Ottoman state.

SAINTS' SHRINES AND THE CREATION OF THE SECULAR REPUBLIC

The transition from the Ottoman Empire to the Turkish Republic was an important and significant historical juncture in terms of restructuring religious orders and sites in Anatolia. The fundamental change was in the attitude of the ruling government: in 1923 the political structure changed from a religiously defined Sunni-centric empire and the seat of the caliph to a secular republic. As part of the secularizing reform program, the Grand National Assembly of the Turkish Republic passed Law No. 677 on November 30, 1925, closing all dervish lodges. All religious orders were prohibited from operating, and their assets were confiscated. The tombs of the sultans and dervish lodges were closed. In his public speech in Kastamonu on August 30, 1925, Mustafa Kemal Atatürk stated, "The Turkish Republic cannot be a country of sheikhs, dervishes, disciples and lay brothers. The truest and the most authentic *tarikat* is that of civilization."[17] Despite their different historical backgrounds and relations to the Ottoman state, the shrines and dervish lodge complexes of Hacı Bektaş Veli and Mevlana both fell within the scope of the legislation.[18]

Both complexes were eventually reopened as museums under the jurisdiction of the Ministry of Culture. The Mevlana complex was opened in 1926 as the Konya Asar-ı Atika Müzesi (Konya Museum of Ancient Artifacts). The structure was refurbished in 1954 and assumed the name Mevlana Müzesi (Mevlana Museum). The Mevlevi Order's main dervish lodge, the first such institution to be converted into a museum, reopened after only two years, whereas the Hacı Bektaş complex reopened as a museum only in 1964, after almost forty years. The Hacı Bektaş complex remained completely closed during that time. Until they were closed in 1925, both shrines had been the headquarters of their respective religious orders, and today they are among the most visited museums of Turkey. Key differences in their historical backgrounds, especially regarding their relations with the state establishment in the Ottoman Empire, seem to have influenced the way both the Mevlevi and Bektaşi orders are currently understood. This historical background also sheds light on the different stances that the state has taken toward the present institutional organization of each complex.

REPUBLICAN CELEBRATION OF SAINTLY TOLERANCE

Despite the hostility toward the heterodox orders in the early Republican period, the secular republic has moved to commemorate Hacı Bektaş and Mevlana as early proponents of tolerance. As Refika Sarıönder claims, "due to the fact that their tolerant teachings do not represent any threat to secularist republican state issues, both thinkers are also celebrated at

[the] state level."[19] The universality and tolerance of Mevlana and his philosophy have been explicitly embraced and promoted by the Turkish state. Hacı Bektaş Veli has also been portrayed as a "great Turkish personality." The annual festivals organized in the names of Mevlana and Hacı Bektaş have been attended by state officials and supported by state institutions. However, it should be noted that the Mevlevi Order has enjoyed a privileged position since the Ottoman Empire period.

One reason for this attitude toward the Mevlevi may be the order's aesthetic grounding in music, *sema*, and poems.[20] Always more than religious centers, Mevlevi lodges also functioned as cultural and art centers and housed important artists.[21] According to Klaus Kreiser, the Turkish government never rejected the Mevlevi Order's cultural legacy in literature, music, and art.[22] Both secular leftists and conservatives acknowledge the Mevlevi Order's contribution to an elegant and humanist tradition that is compatible with modern life.[23] Further, the humanist and modern philosophy of Rumi has been embraced by people from various backgrounds and increasingly celebrated internationally. Moreover, as Sarıönder claims, "the preference for Mevlevism above any other order was most likely influenced by the fact that the Mevlevis were always very passive when it came to politics."[24] In contrast, Sunni authorities have never been comfortable with the unorthodox nature of the Bektaşi Order and have always harbored doubts about its political loyalty. Bektaşis have often been considered suspect for the eclectic character of their belief system, which includes Sufi practices and supposedly Shiite tendencies.

THE INSERTION OF MOSQUES INTO NON-SUNNI SACRED SPACES

The communal ritual practices of Mevlevi and Bektaşi orders, *sema* and *semah* ceremonies, respectively, are not performed in mosques.[25] Thus, neither order considers mosques to be the primary ritual space for their practices. The Hacı Bektaş and Mevlana shrine and dervish lodge complexes encompass spaces that are or have been dedicated to communal worship. In the Konya site, a partitioned rectangular hall was added in the sixteenth or seventeenth century next to the shrine of Mevlana. On one side of the partition was the *masjid*, a small mosque, with a minaret, and on the other was a *semahane*, the space in which whirling dervishes conducted their ceremonial ritual dances. A monumental mosque outside the walled compound was built by Sultan Selim in the sixteenth century. In the Hacı Bektaş compound, two areas were built for communal worship: the Meydan Evi for the *cem* ceremonies, the primary communal worship of the Alevi-Bektaşi faith; and the Tekke Mosque, which was added to the complex in the nineteenth century by Sultan Mahmud II.

These structural complexes have gradually evolved and been augmented with new buildings. For our purposes, the manner in which mosques were first inserted into both complexes indicates, historically, how the fundamentally different imperial attitudes toward the Mevlevi and Bektaşi sects changed according to shifting sociopolitical contexts. Paying attention to the ways the mosques operate in the present-day museum complexes also helps us to understand what is at stake in some of the current debates and conflicts over the use of these spaces. The mosque was built next to the dervish lodge and shrine of Mevlana in the sixteenth century as an imperial favor, a good deed to recognize the importance and legitimacy of the Mevlevi sect. The mosque in Hacı Bektaş, by contrast, was spectacularly imposed to seal the suppression of the Bektaşi faith in the nineteenth century. Sultan Mahmud II, who abolished the Yeniçeri troops, was also keen on suppressing the Bektaşi sect. The Ottoman state had entrusted the Bektaşi Order with the task of converting the *devshirme*, the main manpower of the Yeniçeri troops, to Islam. Suppressing the Bektaşi faith went hand in hand with abolishing the Yeniçeri troops and sent a powerful message to practitioners of the Alevi-Bektaşi faith. Alevi-Bektaşi practitioners do not include *namaz* (prayer) as their primary form of worship, so the construction of a mosque on the most sacred ground for Alevi-Bektaşi believers was, and remains, problematic.[26]

The Selimiye Mosque in Konya is located adjacent to the dervish lodge of Mevlana but situated outside the walled compound.[27] Although the two institutions have in the past existed somewhat symbiotically, the Mevlana Museum is physically and conceptually separated from the functioning mosque. The Selimiye Mosque is a separate entity, administered under the Directorate of Religious Affairs (Diyanet İşleri Başkanlığı). Visitors to the Mevlana Museum occasionally also visit this nearby mosque. But from the perspective of museum personnel, the mosque has nothing to do with the museum that they run.

The case is different at the Hacı Bektaş Museum. The Tekke Mosque, although located on museum grounds, is a functioning mosque with its own appointed imam. The call to prayer is announced from the minaret, and the mosque hosts communal *namaz* worship five times a day. We have been told, however, that very few people attend the *namaz* in this predominantly Alevi town. Furthermore, the mosque is open for night and early morning prayers, during hours when the museum is officially closed. This situation presents a challenge for museum security.

The addition of this mosque in the nineteenth century during the reign of Mahmud II, as part of a suppressive policy against the Bektaşi Order, is perhaps partially responsible for the negative image of the mosque. Almost all the people of Alevi-Bektaşi background that we have encountered during our fieldwork expressed some level of discomfort with the presence of an operating mosque on the premises. Many thought that the mosque represented a continuation of the centuries-old Sunni-centric policy of assimilating Alevis, a policy adopted by both the religious Ottoman Empire and the secular Turkish Republic. One visitor remarked that when people perform *namaz* toward Mecca, they turn their back to Hacı Bektaş Veli's tomb, and this practice, he thought, was deliberately devised by the state to offend Alevis. It is certainly true, in spatial terms, that when people in the mosque face toward *qibla*, the tomb of Hacı Bektaş, located to the north, is behind them.[28]

Alevis also find it offensive that some of their practices (lighting candles, tying cloths, bowing when entering the tombs, touching tombs with face and hands, expecting healing) have been listed on the wall of the mosque under the categories of *bid'at* (innovation in religion, regarded as a sin) and *hurafe* (superstition), which are said to be "absolutely forbidden" by Islam.

SECULARIZING THE SACRED: THE HACI BEKTAŞ AND MEVLANA COMPLEXES AS MUSEUMS

Despite the state's efforts to run these sites as secular institutions, many visitors continue to treat the museums as important and emotionally charged pilgrimage sites. Sunni Muslims, Alevis-Bektaşis, and non-Muslims visit both museums. Belief in the supernatural powers of the saints may underpin the popularity of these sites. Visitors come for many reasons: to request favors from the saints, to pray about temporal or spiritual matters, and to invoke the saints' healing powers. For people seeking such intercessions, the specific confessional or sectarian origin of the saint does not always matter much; many religious sites are frequented in search of benefits or blessings by people from different sects and different religions.[29]

Since both complexes were erected in the thirteenth and fourteenth centuries, it is no surprise that they exhibit similar architectural styles and structural layouts. As museums, the settings of the displays and the movement of visitors within these complexes are now defined by the transformation of elements of the original architectural features of the structures. Both complexes were built as dervish lodges that formed around the burial places of many venerated people, not only those of the saints Hacı Bektaş and Mevlana but also of others associated with them. The complexes included spaces devoted to various functions. Some rooms were reserved for daily activities, others for secluded sacred ritual enactments. Monumental tombs were erected among the other buildings. Both complexes are surrounded by courtyard walls that define the perimeters of the lodges. The burial grounds of the eponymous saints have always been the most sacred spaces in both complexes and seem to remain so for many visitors to the museums. The Alevi practices of worship at saints'

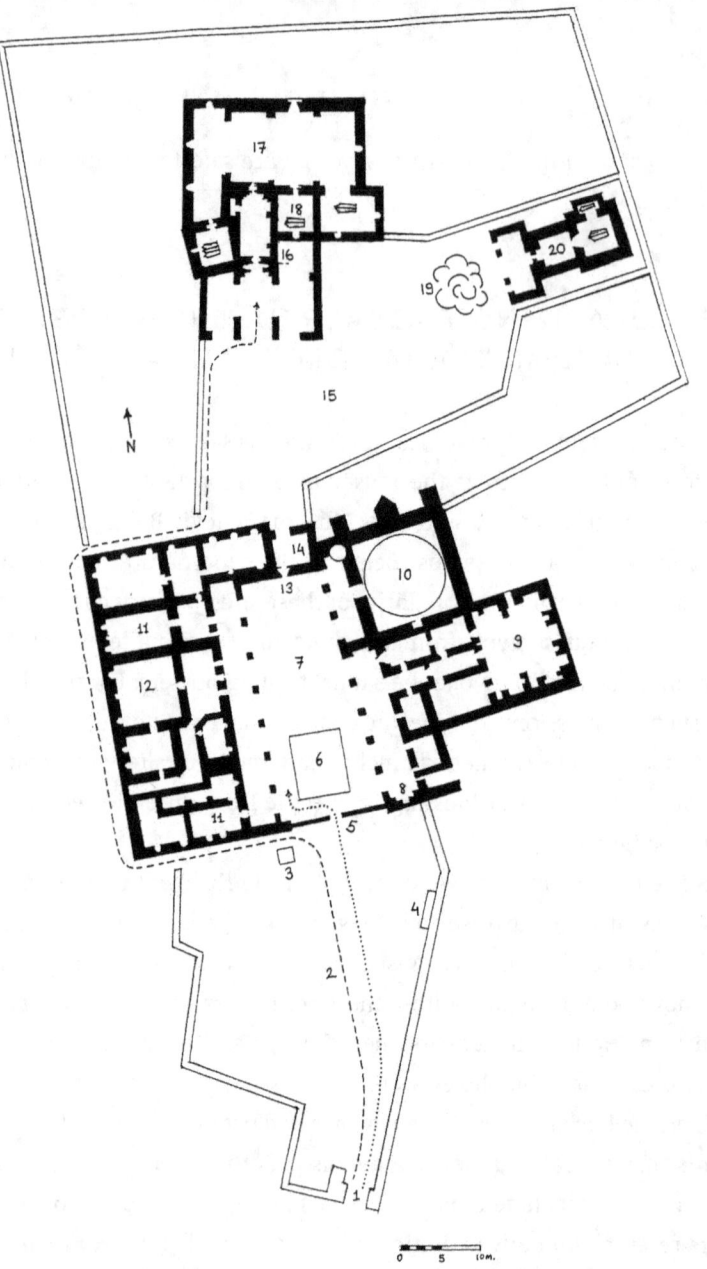

FIGURE 10.1 PLAN OF THE HACI BEKTAŞ MUSEUM COMPLEX. (1) MAIN ENTRYWAY TO THE COMPLEX; (2) FIRST COURTYARD; (3) TICKET BOOTH; (4) ÜÇLER ÇEŞMESI; (5) ENTRANCE TO THE MUSEUM GROUNDS; (6) POOL; (7) SECOND COURTYARD; (8) ARSLANLI ÇEŞME; (9) KITCHEN; (10) TEKKE MOSQUE; (11) EXHIBIT HALLS; (12) MEYDAN EVI; (13) TICKET CONTROL; (14) ATATÜRK'S SCULPTURE; (15) THIRD COURTYARD; (16) ÇILEHANE; (17) KIRKLAR MEYDANI; (18) TOMB OF HACI BEKTAŞ; (19) MULBERRY TREE; 20) TOMB OF BALIM SULTAN. THE DASHED LINE INDICATES THE ROUTE OF ENTRY AND VISITATION DURING HACI BEKTAŞ FESTIVALS IN AUGUST. THE DOTTED LINE INDICATES THE ROUTE OF ENTRY DURING THE REST OF THE YEAR.

(Plan by Tuğba Tanyeri-Erdemir)

shrines that we discuss later require believers to be in close proximity to the tomb. The current use of space in these museums tellingly prevents visitors from gaining this proximity to the tomb of Mevlana and discourages it at the tomb of Hacı Bektaş.

We turn now to the specific features of the complexes as we saw them in 2008–2009.[30] The Hacı Bektaş Museum complex is structured around three courtyards. The ticket counter and Üçler Çeşmesi (Üçler Fountain) are located in the first courtyard, which is entered through a monumental gate structure. In the second courtyard there is a square-shaped pool, Arslanlı Çeşme (Lion Fountain). This second courtyard is surrounded by a columned portico, and a number of rooms and living spaces open into it. Before the complex was closed in 1923, this section of the site served mainly as the living quarters for the Bektaşi dervishes. The kitchen, warehouses, guest house, and the living quarters of the *dedebaba* (the head dervish of the lodge) are located here and marked as museum exhibits.[31] The Meydan Evi, which functioned as the main ritual space of the complex, opens into this courtyard. In 1826 a mosque was added to the complex, next to the kitchens in the second courtyard. Except for the functioning mosque, the spaces around the second courtyard form the museum's major display areas. The museum offices are located in the former mansion of the *dedebaba*, and the rooms reserved for the daily functions of the dervishes are designated as exhibition rooms.

The third courtyard is entered through a narrow gate, where visitors meet a statue of Mustafa Kemal Atatürk, depicting his visit to Hacıbektaş in the 1920s.[32] The third courtyard, defined structurally by the mausoleum of Hacı Bektaş Veli, marks the most sacred area of the complex. Several other tombs and ritual spaces are associated with the tomb of Hacı Bektaş. The Çilehane (the seclusion space for dervishes) is located at the entry to the tomb. The monumental tomb complex also includes a large central hall, Kırklar Meydanı (the courtyard of the Forty Saints). The tomb structure of Balım Sultan, who institutionalized the order after the passing of Hacı Bektaş, is located nearby in the cemetery of dervishes who served in this complex through the centuries. The interior spaces of both the Hacı Bektaş and Balım Sultan mausoleums are used

FIGURE 10.2 THE SHRINE COMPLEX AND THE MAUSOLEUM OF MEVLANA JALAL AD-DIN RUMI (THE SHORTER TOWER ON LEFT), MEVLANA MUSEUM, KONYA; VIEW FROM THE ROSE GARDEN LOCATED TO THE EAST OF THE COMPLEX.

(Rabia Harmanşah, 2008)

for displaying objects, such as candleholders, manuscripts, examples of *teslim taşı* (symbolic twelve-sided stones), *kamberiye* (belts used by Bektaşis), and silk carpets, among many other things.

The Mevlana Museum is similar to that of Hacı Bektaş in the general layout of the complex. Visitors also enter the museum through a monumental gate, where the ticket office is located, and which opens into a marble courtyard. Small domed rooms, formerly the dervishes' living quarters, line the western edge of this open space. The kitchen and the dervishes' training areas are located across the courtyard. A large hall next to the kitchen currently serves as the director's office. Several funerary monuments, including the Hürrem Paşa tomb, are also situated in the courtyard, along with fountains for ablutions.[33]

Unlike the complex of Hacı Bektaş, the Mevlana Museum is organized within a single large courtyard. The mausoleum of Mevlana Jalal ad-Din Rumi is placed at the center of this marble courtyard. Like the Hacı Bektaş complex, the burial place of Rumi and the spaces around it were—and for many people still are, the most sacred area of the architectural complex. The main entrance to the tomb leads into a small domed room, called the Tilavet Room, where the dervishes used to read Qur'an. This room now has been arranged for exhibits of calligraphy. One enters the mausoleum itself through a silver door. On the left side stand six coffins arranged in rows of three and containing the relics of the dervishes who accompanied Mevlana and his family from Belkh. Opposite to them, on a raised platform, stand the cenotaphs belonging to descendants of the Mevlana family and some high-ranking members of the Mevlevi Order.

The monumental sarcophagus of Mevlana is placed under a green octagonal dome. The adjoining small mosque (*masjid*) is now used to exhibit a collection of manuscripts and valuable prayer rugs. The *semahane*, where Mevlevi dervishes performed their ritual dance, *sema*, stands to the north of the green mausoleum. Today visitors can view musical instruments, lecterns, candlesticks, lamps, and Mevlana's clothes in this hall.

Two aspects of museum administration in these two structurally and historically similar dervish lodge and shrine complexes most cogently reveal the ongoing struggle over the meaning of the sites and how they ought, consequently, to be used. First, despite the ostensibly open, secular stance taken by museum authorities, ticketing policies control access to the complexes in ways that subtly favor visitors who adhere to tacitly sanctioned Sunni interpretations of Islam. Second, security policies regulate visitors' behavior on the museum grounds to discourage ritual practices, though some flexibility is shown as long as the practices are not threatening the artifacts and buildings. Visitors to the museums are keenly aware that these policies are, in effect, anything but religiously neutral, and they continue to devise ways to circumvent the rules in order to carry out their cherished but proscribed rituals as far as possible.

TICKETING THE SACRED

The transformation of ritually important sacred sites into museums requires both conceptual and architectural restructuring. One of the requirements for such a transition is the control of access to these sites and restrictions on mobility within them. Both the Hacı Bektaş and Mevlana dervish lodges were already walled-in, composite structural complexes, so presumably ways of controlling access to them when they were dervish lodges had evolved over centuries of use. At the time of their transformation into museums in 1964 and 1926, respectively, the existing perimeters of the complexes were used to define the grounds of the newly established institutions. Access became controlled in a new way: in each case entrance to the museums is ticketed, and the ticket revenue is assigned to the state. Thus, instead of access being controlled by the religious orders, and presumably open to those who sought or seek the blessings of the saints, entrance is conditioned on visitors' ability (and willingness) to pay the state. In our fieldwork in 2008 and 2009, we saw that buying a ticket in order to enter a holy site was an important issue for many visitors of both museums, not only as a financial burden but, more importantly, because it was regarded as improper to pay for entering a holy place, which should be accessible to everyone free of charge.

There appears, however, to be a difference in the current visitor profiles for the two sites. Due to Rumi's international fame, the Mevlana Museum receives very many international visitors each year and caters to a fairly diverse audience. Indeed, in 2007 UNESCO organized a major international commemoration of the eight-hundredth anniversary of Rumi's birth, signs from which (and souvenirs as well) were prominent in Konya during our 2008 visits. Most of the visitors to the Hacı Bektaş Museum, by contrast, arrive from within Turkey, many during the annual Hacı Bektaş Festival from August 16 to 18. These different visitor profiles have an impact on the varying ticketing practices in the sites. In both cases, however, the ticketing practices serve as a barrier to visitors who wish to engage in non-Sunni forms of worship at the sites but not to visitors who wish to engage in orthodox Sunni religious practices at them.

At the Mevlana Museum, ticketing is very strictly controlled and enforced by the museum staff and is not open to negotiation. The large international tourist groups and individual domestic visitors alike must purchase tickets at the entrance. A sign above the ticket counter, however, lists "exceptional" categories of people who can enter without a ticket, such as veterans or visitors over and under a certain age.

Ticketing practices at the Hacı Bektaş Museum are more complicated. We have encountered numerous instances in which visitors negotiated with the Hacı Bektaş Museum staff in a ways that we never observed at the Mevlana Museum. In some cases the museum staff allowed visitors in without a ticket. Furthermore, during the annual Hacı Bektaş Festival in August thousands of people, most of them practitioners of the Alevi-Bektaşi faith, visit each day. The museum traditionally does not issue tickets during the month of August, but this suspension of normal ticketing policy is probably functionally unavoidable because the museum staff is simply too small to operate ticket offices and control the tickets during festival time, even if they wished to do so. Relaxing this control may also have the additional benefit of reducing the potential for confrontations and contestations over buying tickets during this ritually important and very busy period.

Ticketing practices at the Hacı Bektaş Museum also reveal the differing policies of the museum, and of the state, toward religious activities associated with Sunni and non-Sunni forms of Islam. As noted earlier, a functioning mosque stands on the museum grounds in the second courtyard. The mosque is open for prayer throughout the day, and the five daily Sunni prayers are regularly held under the guidance of the imam. Yet, even though this mosque is within the grounds of the museum and after the ticket booth at the entrance to the second courtyard, Sunni practitioners who wish to use the mosque do not have to pay the entry fee. No formal rule exempts them from paying, but they are simply never asked to produce a ticket since tickets are collected only at the entrance to the third courtyard.

Even more remarkably, this arrangement means that all of the museum except for the tomb complexes of Hacı Bektaş and his close followers is also effectively free, since the main displays are located, like the mosque, in the second courtyard. Visitors can pass through the exhibits in the dervishes' living quarters and drink water from the Arslanlı fountain without paying. Anyone who wishes, however, to visit the tombs of Hacıbektaş and Balım Sultan, or the cemetery needs to purchase a ticket. These areas are, of course, precisely the parts of the shrine that pilgrims wish most to visit and that constitute the most sacred part of the complex, especially for Alevi-Bektaşi practitioners. In practice, then, it is the tombs that are ticketed, not the museum, or at least not those parts of the museum that are not key to the religious practices of Alevi-Bektaşis. When we asked a museum official why the ticketing was set up this way, he tellingly stated that some people were coming here just to pray in the mosque or to get water from the fountain, and that the museum could not ask for money for these practices. Clearly, however, the museum can ask for money for access to spaces where the key Alevi-Bektaşi practices take place.

We did not encounter any complaints about ticketing policy at the Mevlana Museum. Some visitors who did not want to pay for a ticket simply prayed at the gate and left. In the Hacı Bektaş Museum, however, buying a ticket to gain access seemed unacceptable for many people who visit the site for ritual and religious purposes.[34] Visitors often argued that this was a tomb of a holy person and thus should not be ticketed under any circumstances. Some visitors complained not about the tickets themselves but about what was done with the revenue they generated. They criticized the lack of proper investment in the site in particular and, more generally, in the town of Hacıbektaş. One of them exclaimed, "What did the government do for Hacıbektaş that they are asking for money!" Others, however, felt that the museum could legitimately collect money at the entrance in order to pay for maintaining the complex.

RITUAL PRACTICES IN THE MUSEUM GROUNDS

Visits to both shrines are distinguished from those to traditional museums by the possibility of undertaking a number of ritual activities within the architectural complexes. Some of these ritual acts are accommodated by the museum staff but others are discouraged or even expressly prohibited. However, both categories of practices and performances create a myriad of situations in which conflicts and negotiations over the use and control of these spaces arise.

For the great majority of visitors to the Hacı Bektaş Museum, going to the shrine is itself a ritual act.[35] Each route through the complex encompasses a variety of ritual performances. One of the most common of these is paying respect at the gateways, of which there are more than thirty. The thresholds are considered holy by Bektaşis and Alevis, and some visitors get down on their knees to kiss the jambs, especially those at the entryways of the saints' tombs. Occasionally, visitors murmur prayers while they engage in this act.

For many visitors these tombs are the main object of their ritual observance. The Hacı Bektaş complex includes a large number of graves of the saint's followers who have been buried in the lodge throughout the centuries. In addition to the cemetery of dervishes, which is located in the third courtyard of the complex, there are a large number of intramural burials scattered around in different buildings. Most museum visitors consider these burials to be holy even though the deceased may not be of any special significance and, in some cases, their identities may even be unknown. Certain rituals are commonly enacted at or around these tombs, especially those placed in intramural contexts and in association with other holy figures. Visitors kiss the tombstones and try to touch the textiles covering the sarcophagi. Sometimes they try to lie down on the tombs in an attempt to maximize bodily contact with them. Most of the time the museum staff allow the visitors to touch the tombs, but guards occasionally interrupt the visitors, especially if they try to lie down on top of a burial ground. Such interventions are usually done politely, avoiding open conflict with the visitors.

In the Hacı Bektaş complex, the most sacred space is the shrine of Hacı Bektaş himself. His sarcophagus is located at the center of a square room, has a headstone, and is covered with a brightly colored green textile.

Upon entering the room through a relatively narrow gate made of white marble, the visitors turn right and slowly circulate around the sarcophagus. A great majority of the visitors murmur prayers as they do so and try to place their hands on the sarcophagus. Visitors frequently try to tie a piece of textile or headscarf around the headstone of Hacı Bektaş. Although this practice is not openly opposed by the museum staff, the textiles tied to the headstone are quickly removed by the officials. We were told that the green textile covering the sarcophagus is replaced regularly by the members of the Ulusoy family living in Hacıbektaş, who were responsible for the dervish lodge before it was closed in the 1920s. Visitors try to touch the headstone with both of their hands while they say their prayers. Almost all of them try to kiss the headstone.

A number of rituals are also enacted around water within the site. Two fountains, Üçler Çeşmesi and Arslanlı Çeşme, are considered sacred, and the water flowing from them is believed to have healing powers. Visitors try to drink and collect water from these fountains. *Lokma*, edible offerings, are distributed throughout the complex. The museum staff almost always allow these practices as long as visitors do not pose a significant threat to displays or endanger themselves.

Yet there are some other practices that are not commonly permitted in the Hacı Bektaş Museum. For example, a mulberry tree in front of the tomb of Balım Sultan is thought to be holy, and visitors used to tie pieces of cloth to its branches and make wishes. During the Hacı Bektaş Festival in 2001, for instance, the tree was covered in shredded textiles. By 2008, however, this practice had been almost completely prohibited in order, according to the museum staff, to prevent the ancient tree from dying. In response to the new rules, a large number of visitors began praying under the tree's branches instead of tying pieces of cloth onto them. This practice was allowed.

A wall with several niches stands to the right of Balım Sultan's tomb. There are signs of scorching in the niches and congealed white wax drips out of them. Many visitors try to make wishes by placing and lighting votive candles within these niches. The museum staff does its best to stop visitors from lighting candles, and guards intervene whenever they catch anyone in the act. Almost all Alevi-Bektaşi visitors to the site perform these individual, rather than collective, rituals.

Forms of communal worship are also enacted on the museum grounds. A group commonly called Perşembeciler (Thursday worshippers) frequents the site every Thursday at 10:00 a.m. to perform what they call a *cem* ceremony at three different locations within the complex. In each location they sit in a circle and pray together. Upon completing their rituals, they distribute *lokma* in front of the tomb of Balım Sultan. Museum personnel allowed these rituals in 2008 and 2009 because they do not take long and they cause minimal disruption, and from a distance the rituals look similar to Sunni communal prayers. Museum staff may also feel comfortable granting permission for the rituals because they are not considered a proper *cem*—namely, they do not include performances, like *semah*—and so technically do not definitively fall into the category of discouraged practices. It should be noted, however, that no museum staff explicitly made such a claim; certainly, from the perspective of the Perşembeciler, the performance is a legitimate *cem*.

Some communal rituals, to be sure, are strictly prohibited within the museum. Alevi communal worship, the proper *cem* ceremony, is not allowed.[36] The Ministry of Culture has appointed a group of folk dancers to perform a folkloric version of the *cem* ceremony within the museum grounds every weekend. The stage actors and dancers present a strictly theatrical performance aimed at giving visitors an idea of what the ritual looks and sounds like. The actors maintain their distance from the ritual by periodically pausing during their enactment to explain to viewers what they are doing. For Alevi-Bektaşi practitioners, the prohibition of *cem* within their most sacred site is a major source of discontent.

Perhaps in response to this discontent, museum authorities occasionally permit *semah*, the actual ritual dance associated with the *cem* ceremony, within the museum grounds. During the Hacı Bektaş Festivals of 2009, an Istanbul-based Alevi organization requested oral permission to perform a *semah* in the second courtyard of the complex. The museum officials treated it as a theatrical performance, like the regular exhibitions by the dancers of the Ministry of Culture. The practitioners and a majority of the audience, by contrast, gave the *semah* its full value as a ritual act, performed within what for them was the sacred ground of the Hacı Bektaş complex. The oral negotiation, by avoiding official written documentation for the performance, made it easier for each side to interpret the ritual in the way it preferred.

At the Mevlana Museum complex, rituals are regulated in a similar fashion. Individual visitors, like those to the Hacı Bektaş Museum, regularly enact rituals in an ad hoc manner as they move through the complex, but communal practices, because they are easier to control, are allowed only under certain conditions. Visitors are permitted, for example, to throw coins into the pool in front of the mausoleum and to make wishes by tying pieces of cloth to trees in the complex. A practice more unique to the Mevlana Museum involves a large oval monolithic stone situated among the tombs of the dervishes in the courtyard behind the mausoleum of Mevlana. According to local legend, the stone was given to the complex by a German (a fascinating attribution about which, unfortunately, we could obtain no further information). Visitors believe that if a woman sits on the stone, it has the power to make her more fertile. This practice is allowed by the museum staff.

The most holy space within the Mevlana Museum is also the tomb of the saint Mevlana. Although the museum is considered a secular establishment, the museum staff has placed a bin full of head scarves at the entrance of the tomb structure so that female visitors can, if they wish, put on a scarf to cover their heads. Many women bring their own scarves to cover their heads, an act motivated by religious belief that would not normally be expected in a museum. Moreover, visitors to the tomb structure are provided with plastic coverings for their shoes. This is common practice in functioning mosques that host large numbers of tourist visitors, such as the Blue Mosque in Istanbul, but not in museums, even those that were formerly sacred sites, such as the Hagia Sofia Museum in Istanbul.

The sarcophagus of Mevlana itself is not as accessible to visitors as is that of Hacı Bektaş. It is raised up on a dais and separated from visitors by a marble barrier to prevent them from laying clothes on it or touching it in the same way that Alevis-Bektaşis do at the tomb of Hacı Bektaş. It is common for many visitors to hold their hands up in a praying position and pray in front of the tomb, a typically Sunni gesture. Museum officials allow these actions as long as the visitors do not touch the tomb and do not pose an obstacle to the circulation of visitors inside the chamber. Museum officials told us, however, that some visitors also wanted to perform *namaz* in front of Mevlana's tomb, either individually or in groups, but since *namaz* requires the performance of several bodily gestures, including bowing, prostration, and sitting on the floor, the museum staff intervenes and orients people toward the mosque next to the complex. We also witnessed a slightly different response on the part of museum staff to some visitors who performed *namaz* inside the tomb. The museum staff did not interfere with their *namaz* performance once it started, but they gently warned them after their prayer was over.

The whirling dervishes regularly use the Mevlana Museum for ritual performances. These ceremonies are performed with the support of the government every year during the week of December 10–17 to commemorate Rumi's death. The ceremony's name, Şeb-i Arus, which means "wedding night," recalls the term Rumi used in a ghazal to define death as reunion with the Divine.[37] Top-level state officials, including the prime minister, have attended the ceremonies, and they draw both domestic and international tourists to the museum. During Şeb-i Arus, *sema* rituals are performed, passages from *Mathnawi* and *Divan-i Shams* are read, and lectures on the life and teachings of Rumi are given.

Sema is the Mevlevis' particular form of worship, along with *dhikr*.[38] Mevlevis believe that *sema* represents a mystical journey to one's own spirit; it is "a state of unconsciousness due to excessive ecstasy."[39] The clothes that dervishes wear during *sema* represent death in general: a white gown symbolizing the shroud, a black cloak symbolizing the grave, and a high brown cap symbolizing the tombstone.

Postnişin (Mevlevi sheikh) Fahri Özçakıl, who was leading the *sema* ceremonies organized by the Ministry of Culture, told us that *sema* performed within the museum is especially important for Mevlevis, thanks to the impressive atmosphere of the space. He said that "the complex should not be seen as a museum, it is a lodge for Mevlevis." Özçakıl did not seem to be disturbed by performing *sema* for touristic purposes, since it has become part of the Turkish culture for him; he underlined, however, that these performances are "*gerçek zikr*" (real invocation) for Mevlevis.[40]

Although the Mevlana Museum staff always emphasize that the place is a museum, they know that it is not just an ordinary museum. The manager claims that the site is subject to the laws and regulations for all museums, but many practices there are not normally encountered in museums. In contrast, the staff with whom we spoke at the Hacı Bektaş museum in 2008 and 2009 considered the complex to be a sacred site, although they also attempted to act in accordance with the rules and regulations governing museums. This difference between the two museums can probably be explained by the fact that most of the museum staff in Hacı Bektaş, with the exception of the museum director, were Bektaşis or Alevis. We were told that the Ministry of Culture never appoints an Alevi or Bektaşi to be the museum's director.

CONCLUSION

From the observations we have made, it seems clear that the transformation of the Hacı Bektaş and Mevlana sites into museums actually manifests several forms of control by the state. In certain ways the state protects and preserves the complexes, but in others it limits and even prohibits the ritual use of the shrines by non-Sunni Muslims while subtly facilitating Sunni practices within them. Further, despite the professed intentions of the state to run these sites as secular institutions, to most visitors the museums continue to be important and emotionally charged pilgrimage and ritual sites. Thus, the conversion of such sites into museums and the state's attempts to underline the saints' transcommunal character and to reconstruct their images in a modern, secular, and aesthetic way is actually not a neutral solution to the contestation over the meanings and uses of these sites. Our ethnographic research clearly shows that members of the communities of the original users of the sites, who still consider the museums to be the sacred shrines of religious figures, feel deprived of their heritage and, consequently, challenge the regulations by trying to impose their own interpretations of these places in various creative ways. The Mevlana Museum, with its more diverse visitor profile, allows this challenge to proceed with minimal conflict partly because its portrayal as a Sunni site does not bring those who wish to worship into conflict with the unspoken religious preferences of the state. At the Hacı Bektaş Veli Museum, the contest over how to use the museum space emerges much more forcefully because it also remains an arena in which the secular state undeniably reveals its tacit alliances in the conflict between the dominant Sunni Islam and Alevism-Bektaşism.

We believe that these two cases illustrate the advantages of analyzing shared sites by using the model of competitive sharing that we call "antagonistic tolerance." Just as that model predicts, the actions of even the secular Turkish state actually favor the practices of the majority Sunni Muslims over the minority Alevis and Bektaşis. But we must note that, in doing so, the Turkish government of the second decade of the twenty-first century is reversing the efforts of that of the early republic, ninety years earlier. Atatürk's government had converted shrines into museums, most prominently major former Byzantine churches that had been converted into mosques by the Ottomans, thus reducing in many places the prominence of the museum religioscapes while developing prominent nodes in a local and nationwide secularscape. Our analysis has shown that the AKP (Justice and Development Party) government has acted to reincorporate Alevi-Bektaşi shrines into a Sunni religioscape, but we must also note recent efforts by the AKP-led government to reconvert into mosques prominent structures that had been built as Byzantine churches, converted into mosques by the Ottomans, and then converted into museums in the early Republican reforms. Where Atatürk had turned nodes of the

Muslim religioscapes into nodes of secularscapes, the Erdoğan government is displacing nodes of the secularscape with a purely Sunni religioscape, which has also incorporated parts of the Alevi-Bektaşi religioscapes. The courts in Turkey have reportedly accepted the argument that once a mosque has been established in a building, the structure cannot be used for other purposes, in essence claiming that mosques are not secularizeable.[41] The Hagia Sophia museums of Iznik and Trabzon were thus reconverted into mosques in 2011 and 2013, respectively, and there is international concern that the Hagia Sophia in Istanbul might be next.[42]

We should note that Turkey is not unique as a secular republic that facilitates majority control over religious sites also claimed by minority religious communities, or manipulating nominally secular museumification to achieve sectarian goals. We have observed similar situations in India in 1990 and in Bulgaria in 2008. For example, the *türbe* (shrine) and *tekke* (dervish lodge) of Ak Yazili Baba at Obrochishte, one of the best preserved *türbes* in Bulgaria, is undergoing a slow transformation from a museum into a monastery and tomb of the Christian saint Atanas, which is particularly notable as the state is now a part of the European Union.[43] From the normative perspective of both the rights of religious minorities and the proper management of museums, such transformations are not appropriate. That they are taking place anyway, even in such nominally secular states as Bulgaria, India, and Turkey is, we think, evidence of the impossibility of secularizing the unsecularizable.

NOTES

The research reported here was supported by the Wenner-Gren Foundation for Anthropological Research and the National Science Foundation, but the findings are those solely of the authors and may not be seen as being endorsed or otherwise supported by either of the funding agencies. We thank Dr. Aykan Erdemir and Dr. Milica Bakić-Hayden for their assistance at various stages of the research, and Meral Salman for her assistance in conducting further fieldwork at Hacıbektaş in 2009.

1. Gerard van der Leeuw, *Religion in Essence and Manifestation*, vol. 2. (1933; repr., New York: Harper & Row, 1963); and F. W. Hasluck, *Christianity and Islam Under the Sultans* (Oxford: Clarendon Press, 1929).

2. *Reynolds v. United States*, 98 U.S. 145 (1878).
3. See Jenny B. White, *Islamist Mobilization in Turkey* (Seattle: University of Washington Press, 2002); and Esra Özyürek, *Nostalgia for the Modern: State Secularism and Everyday Politics in Turkey* (Durham, NC: Duke University Press, 2006).
4. See, for example, Gotthard Jäschke, *Yeni Türkiye'de İslamlık* (Ankara: Bilgi Yayınevi, 1972); David Shankland, *Islam and Society in Turkey* (Huntingdon, UK: Eothen Press, 1999); and Bernard Lewis, *Modern Türkiye'nin doğuşu* (Ankara: Türk Tarih Kurumu, 2004).
5. John Kingsley Birge, *The Bektashi Order of Dervishes* (London: Luzac, 1965); Tord Olsson, Elisabeth Özdalga, and Catharina Raudvere, eds., *Alevi Identity: Cultural, Religious and Social Perspectives* (Istanbul: Swedish Research Institute, 1998); David Shankland, *The Alevis in Turkey: The Emergence of a Secular Islamic Tradition* (London: Routledge, 2003); and Paul J. White and Joost Jongerden, eds., *Turarkey's Alevi Enigma* (Leiden: Brill, 2003).
6. For criticisms of AT, see Dionigi Albera, "Why Are You Mixing What Cannot Be Mixed? Shared Devotions in the Monotheisms," *History and Anthropology* 19 (2008): 37–59; and Glenn Bowman, "Orthodox–Muslim Interactions at 'Mixed Shrines' in Macedonia," in *Eastern Christianity: Anthropological Perspectives*, ed. C. Hann and H. Goltz, 163–83 (Berkeley: University of California Press, 2009). For further development of AT, see Robert M. Hayden, Hande Sözer, Tuğba Tanyeri-Erdemir, and Aykan Erdemir, "The Byzantine Mosque at Trilye: A Processual Analysis of Dominance, Sharing, Transformation and Tolerance," *History & Anthropology* 22, no. 1 (2011): 1–17; and Robert M. Hayden and Timothy D. Walker, "Intersecting Religioscapes: A Comparative Approach to Trajectories of Change, Scale and Competitive Sharing of Religious Spaces," *Journal of the American Academy of Religion* 81, no. 2 (2013): 399–426.
7. Hayden and Walker, "Intersecting Religoscapes."
8. See Crispin Paine, "Militant Atheist Objects: Anti-Religious Museums in the Soviet Union," *Present Pasts* 1 (2009): 61–76.
9. Rabia Harmanşah and Aykan Erdemir, "Hacı Bektaş Veli," in *The Oxford Encyclopedia of Islamic World*, vol. 2, ed. John L. Esposito, 345–46 (Oxford: Oxford University Press, 2009).
10. Svante Cornell and Ingvar Svanberg, "Turkey," in *Islam Outside the Arab World*, ed. David Westerlund and Ingvar Svanberg (Richmond, Surrey: Curzon, 1999), 140. See also J. D. Norton, "Bektashis in Turkey," in *Islam in the Modern World*, ed. Denis Mac Eoin and Ahmed Al-Shahi, 73–87 (New York: St. Martin's Press, 1983); and Albert Doja, "A Political History of Bektashism from Ottoman Anatolia to Contemporary Turkey," *Journal of Church & State* 48, no. 2 (2006): 423–50.

11. Norton, "Bektashis in Turkey", 73-87.
12. See Şerif Mardin, "The Naksibendi Order in Turkish History," in *Islam in Modern Turkey: Religion, Politics and Literature in a Secular State*, ed. Richard Tapper (London: I. B. Tauris, 1991), 121-42.
13. Niyazi Öktem, "Religion in Turkey," *Brigham Young University Law Review*, no. 2 (2002): 371-403, http://digitalcommons.law.byu.edu/lawreview/vol2002/iss2/10.
14. Ahmet Karamustafa, "Hacı Bektaş Veli ve Anadolu'da Müslümanlık," in *Hacı Bektaş Veli: Güneşte Zerresinden, Deryada Katresinden*, ed. Pınar Ecevitoğlu, Ali Murat Irat, Ayhan Yalçınkaya, Proceedings of the International Hacı Bektaş Veli Symposium. Dipnot Yayınları (2010), 42-48; and Aykan Erdemir and Ali Yaman, *Alevism-Bektashism: A Brief Introduction*. Trans. Rabia Harmanşah and Kaan Evren Başaran (London: Alevi Cultural Centre, 2006).
15. Irène Mélikoff, "Bektashi/Kızılbas: Historical Bipartition and Its Consequences," in *Alevi Identity: Cultural, Religious and Social Perspectives*, ed. Tord Olsson, Elisabeth Özdalga, and Catharina Raudvere, 1-7 (Istanbul: Swedish Research Institute, 1996); and Hülya Küçük, *The Role of the Bektashis in Turkey's National Struggle* (Leiden: Brill, 2002), 26-32. Also see Birge, *The Bektashi Order of Dervishes*, 211-12; and Shankland, *Islam and Society in Turkey*, 18-19.
16. William C. Chittik, *The Sufi Path of Love: The Spritiual Teachings of Rumi* (Albany: State University of New York Press, 1983); Abdülbâki Gölpınarlı, *Mevlânâ'dan Sonra Mevlevilik* (İstanbul: İnkılâp and Aka, 1983); and Annemarie Schimmel, *I am Wind, You Are Fire: The Life and Works of Rumi* (Boston: Shambala, 1992).
17. Atatürk refers here to both the general ("way, path") and specific ("religious order") meanings of the word "*tarikat*." Quoted in Arı İnan, *Düşünceleriyle Atatürk* (Ankara: Türk Tarih Kurumu, 1983), 262.
18. Rabia Harmanşah, "Facts, Meanings, and Cosmologies: Bektashi Responses to the Abolition of Religious Orders in 1925" (Master's thesis, Middle East Technical University, 2006).
19. Refika Sarıönder, "Mevlana Celaleddin Rumi and Haci Bektas Veli: Two Faces of Turkish Islam: Encounters, Orders, Politics," in *On Archaeology of Sainthood and Local Spirituality in Islam: Past and Present Crossroads of Events and Ideas (Yearbook of the Sociology of Islam 5)*, ed. Georg Stauth (Bielefeld: Transcript Verlag, 2004), 57.
20. Füruzan Hüsrev Tökin, "Mevlevîlik: Mevlâna ve Sema," *Türk Düşüncesi* 7, no 4 (1957): 28. *Sema* is Mevlevi religious ceremony, including performances of whirling, singing, playing instruments, reciting poetry and prayers.

21. Ömer Tuğrul İnançer, "Mevlevi Musikisi ve Sema," in *Dünden Bugüne İstanbul Ansiklopedisi*, vol. 5 (İstanbul: T. C. Kültür Bakanlığı, Tarih Vakfı, 1994), 420–22.
22. Klaus Kreiser, "Türkiye'de Tarikatların Mevcut Durumu ve Geçmisi Hakkında Notlar," in *İslâm Dünyasında Tarikatlar*, ed. Alexandre Popovic and Gilles Veinstein (İstanbul: Sûf Yayınları, 2004), 99.
23. Cemal Kafadar, "The New Visibility of Sufism in Turkish Studies and Cultural Life," in *The Dervish Lodge: Architecture, Art and Sufism in Ottoman Turkey*, ed. Raymond Lifchez (Berkeley: University of California Press, 1992), 312.
24. See Sarıönder, "Mevlana Celaleddin," 65. See also Rabia Harmanşah, "Tarikatların Yasaklanması ve Sonrasında Mevleviler," paper presented at the International Symposium on Mawlana Jalaladdin Rumi in Thought and Art, Çanakkale Onsekiz Mart University, Faculty of Theology, Gelibolu, Turkey, May 25–28, 2006.
25. *Semah* is the ritual dance performed during the Alevi-Bektaşi cem ceremony.
26. *Namaz* is considered one of the five pillars of Sunni Islam. It is a ritual worship that involves the recitation of the verses of Qur'an and the rhythmic exercise of certain bodily movements.
27. Rudolph M. Riefstahl, "Selimiyeh in Konya," *Art Bulletin* 12, no. 4 (1930): 311–19.
28. *Qibla* is the direction that should be faced during prayer, toward the Kaaba in Mecca.
29. See Hasluck, *Christianity and Islam*, 70–71.
30. For a detailed study of the architectural transformations of the Hacı Bektaş shrine complex in the fifteenth and sixteenth centuries, see Zeynep Yürekli-Görkay, *Architecture and Hagiography in the Ottoman Empire: The Politics of Bektashi Shrines in the Classical Age*, Birmingham Byzantine and Ottoman Studies (Surrey, UK: Ashgate, 2012).
31. In Bektaşism, *baba* (literally, father) is the spiritual guide, and *dedebaba* is "the *baba* elected to head the whole movement." See Norton, "Bektashis in Turkey," 74.
32. See Mustafa Kara, *Din hayat sanat açısından tekkeler ve zaviyeler* (İstanbul: Dergah Yayınları, 1999): 261–64.
33. Hürrem Paşa was the governor general of the Karaman Province of the Ottoman Empire. The tomb was built during the reign of Süleyman the Magnificient in 1527.
34. During her visit to the Hacıbektaş Festival in 2013, Tuğba Tanyeri-Erdemir encountered several posters hung on the exterior perimeter wall of the Hacıbektaş Museum. The posters had a list of arguments summarizing why the Turkish state should not be ticketing the ritual visit to the tomb of Hacı Bektaş: that this

practice was unfair to those who believed in Alevi faith, and that the money collected was going to a state and was being used to pay the institutions of the Sunni state to build mosques and to employ imams. These posters were prepared by an Alevi citizen who hung them as a form of protest. He had also written numerous complaints to the authorities and stated that he would be continuing his pursuits in this regard in the future.

35. Tuğba Tanyeri-Erdemir, Rabia Harmanşah, and Robert Hayden, "Serçeşme'den Hacıbektaş Müzesi'ne: Kültür mirası olan bir mekanda ritüel ve kurumsal pratikler," in *Hacı Bektaş Veli güneşte zerresinden, deryada katresinden*, ed. Pınar Ecevitoğlu, Ali Murat İrat, and Ayhan Yalçınkaya (Ankara: Dipnot Yayınevi, 2010), 437–43.

36. To the best of our knowledge, the only *cem* ceremony performed in the Hacı Bektaş Museum after it was closed down in 1925 was conducted in October 2009, following the International Hacı Bektaş Veli Symposium, which was sponsored by the Turkish Ministry of Culture. The organizers of the symposium made an official written request to conduct this *cem* ceremony in the Meydan Evi. The official request was initially rejected but was approved later after officials from the Ministry of Culture intervened and explained to the local government that the organizers of the symposium had received permission from the ministry. The *cem* ceremony conducted in 2009 was highly unusual because the participants were not a faith-based group but rather academics working on issues related to Hacı Bektaş. Nevertheless, all the required rituals of the *cem* ceremony were enacted in the presence of an Alevi religious leader, *dede*.

37. A *ghazal* is a poetic form composed of successive rhyming couplets, usually dealing with themes of love.

38. *Dhikr* means invocation, remembrance of God with repetition of his names or certain sacred phrases.

39. Metin And, "The Mevlana Ceremony [Turkey]," *Drama Review* 21, no. 3 (1977): 83–94.

40. Some Mevlevis, however, do criticize performing *sema* as a display for tourists. They consider such performances as a degeneration. For such a critique, see Kudsi Ergüner, *Ayrılık Çeşmesi: Bir Neyzenin Yolculuğu* (İstanbul: İletişim Yayınları, 2002).

41. Andrew Finkel, "Mosque Conversion Raises Alarm," *Art Newspaper*, no. 245 (2013): 15.

42. Tuğba Tanyeri-Erdemir, "A Tale of Three Hagia Sophias: Conversion, Museumification, Contestation," paper delivered at the University of Pittsburgh (April 13, 2013); see also Hayden and Walker, "Intersecting Religioscapes," 418–20, and Andrew Finkel, "From Church to Museum Back to Mosque," *New York Times*,

May 2, 2013, http://latitude.blogs.nytimes.com/2013/05/02/the-cost-of-turning-turkeys-old-churches-and-museums-back-into-mosques/.

43. Robert M. Hayden, "Intersecting Religioscapes in Post-Ottoman Spaces" (paper presented at the conference "Shared Spaces and their Dissolution: Practices of Coexistence in the Post-Ottoman Sphere," Nicosia, Cyprus, October 2011).

BIBLIOGRAPHY

Abu El-Haj, Nadia. *Facts on the Ground: Archaeological Practice and Territorial Self-Fashioning in Israeli Society.* Chicago: University of Chicago Press, 2001.

Abu-Lughod, Janet L. "The Demographic Transformation of Palestine." In *The Transformation of Palestine: Essays on the Origin and Development of the Arab-Israeli Conflict,* ed. Ibrahim Abu-Lughod, 139–63. Evanston, IL: Northwestern University Press, 1971.

Adanir, Fikret. "The Ottoman Peasantries, c.1360–c.1860." In *The Peasantries of Europe from the Fourteenth to the Eighteenth Centuries,* ed. Tom Scott, 269–310. London: Longman, 1998.

Adelman, Howard, and Elazar Barkan. *No Return, No Refuge: Rites and Rights in Minority Repatriation.* New York: Columbia University Press, 2011.

Aggestam, Karin. "TIPH: Preventing Conflict Escalation in Hebron?" *Civil Wars* 6, no. 3 (2003): 51–69.

al-Asali, Kamil Jamil. *Ajdadna fi Thari Bayt al-Maqdis.* Amman: Royal Council for the Study of Islamic Civilization, 1981.

Albera, Dionigi. "Combining Practices and Beliefs: Muslim Pilgrims at Marian Shrines." In *Sharing the Sacra: The Politics and Pragmatics of Inter-Communal Relations Around Holy Places,* ed. Glenn Bowman. Oxford/New York: Berghahn Books, 2012.

———. "La Vierge et l'islam. Mélange de civilisations en Méditerranée." *Le Début,* no. 137 (2005): 134–44.

———. "'Why Are You Mixing What Cannot Be Mixed?' Shared Devotions in the Monotheisms." *History and Anthropology* 19, no. 1 (2008): 37–59.

Albera, Dionigi, and Maria Couroucli, eds. *Religions traversees: Lieux saints partages entre Chretiens, Musulmans et Juifs en Mediterranee.* Arles: Actes Sud, 2009.

———, eds. *Sharing Sacred Spaces in the Mediterranean: Christians, Muslims, and Jews at Shrines and Sanctuaries.* Bloomington: Indiana University Press, 2012.

Albera, Dionigi, and Benoit Fliche. "Les pratiques dévotionelles des musulmans dans les sanctuaires chrétiens: Le cas d'Istanbul." In *Religions traversées: Lieux saints partages entre Chrétiens, Musulmans et Juifs en Méditerranée,* eds. Dionigi Albera and Maria Couroucli, 141–74. Arles, France: Actes Sud, 2009.

Al-Dbag, Mustafa. *Beladona Falestine* [Palestine Our Country], vol. 1. Koffer Karea: Dar Elshafac, 1988.

al-Din, Mujir. *Al-uns al-jalil bi-ta'rikh al-quds wal-khalil,* vol. 2. Amman: Al-Muhtasib, 1973.

Algar, Hamid. "Some Notes on the Naqshbandī Tarīqat in Bosnia." *Die welt des Islams* 13, no. 3–4 (1971):168–203.

al-Khalidi, Raghib, Arif Hikmat al-Nashashibi, and Hasan al-Budayri. *Bayan ila al-'alam al-Islami 'ammatan 'an al-amakin al-Muqaddasa al-Islamiyya fi Filastin.* Jerusaalem: Matba'at Bayt al-Maqdis, February 7, 1932.

Allenby, Edmund. "Official Proclamation Following the Fall of Jerusalem, 9 December 1917." In *Source Records of the Great War,* vol. 5. Ed. Charles F. Horne. New York: National Alumni Press, 1923.

An, Ahmet. *Kıbrıs'ın yetiştirdiği değerler (1782–1899)* [Valuable persons raised in Cyprus, 1782–1899]. Ankara: Akçay Yayınları, 2002.

And, Metin. "The Mevlana Ceremony [Turkey]." *Drama Review* 21, no. 3 (1977): 83–94.

Anderson, Benedict. *Imagined Communities: Reflections on the Origin and Spread of Nationalism,* rev. ed. London, New York: Verso, 2006.

Arendt, Hannah. *Eichmann in Jerusalem: A Report on the Banality of Evil.* New York: Viking Press, 1963.

Arraf, Shukri. *Tabaqat al-Anbiyya w-al-Salihin fi al-Ard al-Muqadssa.* Tarshiha: Matbaat al-IkhqanMakul, 1993.

Askar, Ahmad. *Altadmer Althate: Nazareth as Example* [in Arabic]. Ramallah: Markez Al Aamel, 2002.

Bağışkan, Tuncer. *Ottoman, Islamic and Islamised Monuments in Cyprus.* Nicosia: Cyprus Turkish Education Foundation, 2009.

Baker, Joharah. "The Silent Steel Resistance of Nabi Samuel." *MIFTAH,* August 1, 2011.

Baker, Samuel White. *Cyprus, as I Saw It in 1879.* London: Macmillan, 1879. Available at http://www.gutenberg.net/etext/3656.

Balivet, Michel. "A la maniere de F. W. Hasluck: A Few Reflections on the Byzantine-Turkish Symbiosis in the Middle Ages." In *Archeology, Anthropology and Heritage* in the Balkans and Anatolia: The Life and Times of F. W. Hasluck (1878–1920), ed. David Shankland, 13–30. Istanbul: The ISIS P, 2004.

———. "Aux origines de L'Islamisation des Balkans Ottomans." *La Revue du Monde Musulman et de La Mediterranee* 66 (1992): 11–20.

Barkan, Omer Lufti. "Osmanli Imparatorlugunda bir iskan ve kolonizasyon metodu olarak vakiflar ve temlikler I: Istila devrinin kolonizator Turk dervisleri ve vakfiyeler." *Vakiflar Dergisi* 2 (1942): 283–304.

Barkey, Karen. *Empire of Difference: The Ottomans in Comparative Perspective*. Cambridge: Cambridge University Press, 2008.

Barth, Frederik. "Introduction." In *Ethnic Groups and Boundaries: The Social Organization of Cultural Difference*, ed. Fredrik Barth, 9–38. London: Allen & Unwin, 1969.

Bauman, Zygmunt. *Culture as Praxis*. 1973. Rev. ed., London: Sage, 1999.

Baussant, Michèle. *Pieds-noirs: Mémoires d'exils*. Paris: Stock, 2002.

Beckingham, Charles Fraser. "Islam and Turkish Nationalism in Cyprus." *Die Welt des Islams* 5, no. 1–2 (1957): 65–83. doi:10.1163/157006057X00027.

———. "The Turks of Cyprus." *Journal of the Royal Anthropological Institute of Great Britain and Ireland* 87, no. 2 (1957): 165–74.

Ben-Arieh, Yehoshua. *Jerusalem in the Nineteenth Century: The Old City*. Jerusalem: Ben Zvi Institute; and New York: St Martin's Press, 1984.

Ben-Dov, Meir. *Historical Atlas of Jerusalem*. New York: Continuum, 2002.

Benthall, Jonathan, and Jérôme Bellion-Jourdan. *The Charitable Crescent: Politics of Aid in the Muslim World*. London: I. B. Taurius, 2003.

Benvenisti, Meron. *Jerusalem: The Torn City*. Jerusalem: Isratypeset, 1976.

———. *Sacred Landscape: The Buried History of the Holy Land Since 1948*. Berkeley: University of California University, 2000.

Bertram, Sir Anton, and J. W. A. Young. *The Orthodox Patriarchate of Jerusalem: Report of the Commission Appointed by the Government of Palestine to Inquire and Report Upon Certain Controversies Between the Orthodox Patriarchate of Jerusalem and the Arab Orthodox Community*. London: Humphrey Milford, 1926.

Bielenin-Lenczowska, Karolina. "Visiting of Christian Holy Places by Muslims as a Strategy of Coping with Difference." *Anthropological Notebooks* 15, no 3 (2009): 27–41.

Bigelow, Anna. "Everybody's Baba: Making Space for the Other." In *Sharing the Sacra: The Politics and Pragmatics of Intercommunal Relations around Holy Places*, ed. Glenn Bowman, 25–43. New York: Berghahn Books, 2012.

———. *Sharing the Sacred: Practicing Pluralism in Muslim North India*. Oxford: Oxford University Press, 2010.

Billig, Michael. *Banal Nationalism*. London: Sage, 1995.

Bird, Kay, and Max Holland. "Dispatches: Armenia—the Renegade Patriarch." *Nation*, March 2, 1985.

Birge, John Kingsley. *The Bektashi Order of Dervishes*. London: Luzac, 1965.

Boisson, Didier, and Yves Krumenacker. "La coexistence confessionelle à l'épreuve: Études sur les relations entre protestants et catholiques dans la France moderne." In *Chrétiens et Sociétés, Documents et Mémoires*, no. 9. Rhône-Alpes: Religions, Sociétés et Acculturation du Laboratoire de Recherche Historique, 2009.

Bougarel, Xavier, Elissa Helms, and Ger Duijzings. "Introduction." In *The New Bosnian Mosaic: Identities, Memories and Moral Claims in a Post-War Society*, eds. Xavier Bougarel, Elissa Helms, and Ger Duijzings, 1–35. Aldershot: Ashgate, 2007.

Bowman, Glenn. "Identification and Identity Formations Around Shared Shrines in West Bank Palestine and Western Macedonia" (Processus Identitaires Autour de Quelques Sanctuairs Partages en Palestine et en Macedonia). In *Lieux saints en partage: Explorations anthropologiques dans l'espace méditerranéen*, eds. Dionigi Albera and Maria Couroucli, 27–52. Arles, France: Actes Sud; Canterbury, UK: University of Kent, 2009. http://kar.kent.ac.uk/28168/1/couroucli.pdf.

———. "'In Dubious Battle on the Plains of Heav'n': The Politics of Possession in Jerusalem's Holy Sepulchre." *History and Anthropology* 22, no. 3 (2011): 371–99.

———. "Nationalizing the Sacred: Shrines and Shifting Identities in the Israeli-Occupied Territories." *Man* 28, no. 3 (1993): 431–60.

———. "Orthodox-Muslim Interactions at 'Mixed Shrines' in Macedonia." In *Eastern Christians in Anthropological Perspective*, ed. Chris Hann and Hermann Goltz, 195–219. Berkeley: University of California Press, 2010.

———, ed. *Sharing the Sacra: The Politics and Pragmatics of Inter-communal Relations Around Holy Places*. Oxford: Berghahn, 2012.

Brace, Catherine, Adrian Bailey, and David Harvey. "Religion, Place and Space: A Framework for Investigating Historical Geography of Religious Identities and Communities," *Progress in Human Geography*, no. 30 (2006): 28–43.

Breger, Marshall J., Yitzhak Reiter, and Leonard Hammer, eds. *Holy Places in the Israeli–Palestinian Conflict: Confrontation and Co-Existence*. New York: Routledge, 2010.

Bringa, Tone. *Being Muslim the Bosnian Way: Identity and Community in a Central Bosnian Village*. Princeton, NJ: Princeton University Press, 1995.

Bronner, Ethan. "Mideast's Christians Losing Numbers and Sway." *New York Times*, May 12, 2009.

Brooks, Robert D., ed. *The Wall: Fragmenting the Palestinian Fabric in Jerusalem*. Jerusalem: International Peace and Cooperation Center, 2007.

Brubaker, Rogers. "Ethnicity Without Groups." *Archives Européennes de Sociologie* 43, no. 2 (2002): 163–89.

———. *Nationalism Reframed: Nationhood and the National Question in the New Europe.* Cambridge: Cambridge University Press, 1996.

Bryant, Rebecca. *Imagining the Modern: Cultures of Nationalism in Cyprus.* London: I. B. Tauris, 2004.

Bryer, Anthony. "The Late Byzantine Monastery in Town and Countryside." In *The Church in Town and Countryside,* ed. D. Baker, 219–41. Oxford: Oxford University Press, 1979.

Burg, Avraham. *The Holocaust Is Over: We Must Rise from Its Ashes.* New York: Palgrave Macmillan, 2008.

Burgoyne, Michael Hamilton. *Mamluk Jerusalem: An Architectural Study.* London: British School of Archaeology in Jerusalem and World of Islam Festival Trust, 1987.

Brilliant, Joshua. "Jew's and Goy's Blood Not the Same," *Jerusalem Post,* June 4, 1989.

———. "20 Still at Large After Kifl Harith Shooting: Yeshiva Men Suspected of Murder, Arson." *Jerusalem Post,* June 2, 1989.

Calhoun, Craig, ed. *Social Theory and the Politics of Identity.* Oxford: Blackwell, 1994.

Cameron, Keith, Mark Greengrass, and Penny Roberts, eds. *The Adventure of Religious Pluralism in Early Modern France.* Oxford: Peter Lang, 2000.

Čehajić, D. *Dervišski redovi u Jugoslovenskim zemljama sa posebnim osvrtom na Bosnu I Hercegovinu.* Sarajevo: Orijentalni Institut, 1986.

Ceillier, Jean-Claude. *Histoire des missionnaires d'Afrique, Pères blancs: De la fondation par Mgr Lavigerie à la mort du fondateur, 1868–1892.* Paris: Karthala, 2008.

Central Bureau of Statistics. *Statistical Abstract of Israel 2010,* no. 62. Jerusalem, Israel: Printiv, 2011.

Central Congress of American Rabbis. "Resolution of the Central Conference of American Rabbis opposing construction over the Mamilla Cemetery." February 25, 2008. http://www.mamillacampaign.org/photos/pdfs/Appendix6.pdf.

Certeau, Michel de. *The Practice of Everyday Life.* Berkeley: University of California Press, 1984.

Cesari, Jocelyne. "Mosque Conflict in European Cities: Introduction," *Journal of Ethnic and Migration Studies* 31, no. 6 (2005): 1015–24.

Cetin, Onder. "Mujahidin in Bosnia: From Ally to Challenger." *ISIM Newsletter* 21 (2008):14–15.

Chanoine, Mathieu. *La Vierge de l'Oranie au XIXe siècle: Histoire du pèlerinage de N.-D. du Salut à Santa-Cruz.* Oran: D. Heintz, 1900.

Chidester, David, and E. T. Linenthal, eds. *American Sacred Space.* Bloomington: Indiana University Press, 1995.

Chittik, William C. *The Sufi Path of Love: The Spiritual Teachings of Rumi.* Albany: State University of New York Press, 1983.

Christin, Olivier. *Confesser sa Foi: Conflits confessionnels et identités religieuses dans l'Europe modern*. Seyssel: Champ Vallon, 2009.

——. *La paix de religion: L'autonomisation de la raison politique au XVIe siècle*. Paris: Seuil, 1997.

Claiborne, William. "Orthodox Armenians in Holy Land Split in Bitter Feud Over Leaders." *Ottawa Citizen*, June 14, 1986.

Cohen, Anthony P., ed. *Signifying Identities: Anthropological Perspectives on Boundaries and Contested Values*. London: Routledge, 2000.

Cohen, Hillel. *The Rise and Fall of Arab Jerusalem: Palestinian Politics and the City Since 1967*. London: Routledge, 2011.

Cohen, Raymond. *Saving the Holy Sepulchre: How Rival Christians Came Together to Rescue Their Holiest Shrine*. New York: Oxford University Press, 2008.

Cohen-Hattab, Kobi, and Noam Shoval. "Tourism Development and Cultural Conflict: The Case of 'Nazareth 2000.'" *Social & Cultural Geography* 8 (2007): 701–17.

Colbi, Saul. *Christianity in the Holy Land: Past and Present*. Tel Aviv: Am Hassefer, 1969.

Constantinou, Costas M. "Aporias of Identity: Bicommunalism, Hybridity, and the 'Cyprus Problem.'" *Cooperation and Conflict* 42 (2007): 247.

Constantinou, Costas M., and Mete Hatay. "Cyprus, Ethnic Conflict and Conflicted Heritage." *Ethnic and Racial Studies* 33, no. 9 (2010): 1600–1619.

Couroucli, Maria. "Saint Georges l'Anatolien, maîtres des frontiers." In *Religions traversées: Lieux saints partagés entre chrétiens, musulmans et juifs en Méditerranée*, ed. Dionigi Albera and Maria Couroucli, 175–209. Arles, France: Actes Sud, 2009.

——. "Sharing Nostalgia in Istanbul: Christian and Muslim Pilgrims to St. George's Sanctuary." Paper presented at the Sharing Sacred Space: Religion and Conflict Resolution conference, February 14–15, 2008. Columbia University, New York.

Cornell, Svante, and Ingvar Svanberg. "Turkey." In *Islam Outside the Arab World*, ed. David Westerlund and Ingvar Svanberg, 125–48. Richmond, Surrey: Curzon, 1999.

Crews, Robert D. *For Prophet and Tsar: Islam and Empire in Russia and Central Asia*. Cambridge, MA: Harvard University Press, 2006.

Cuffel, Alexandra. "'Henceforward All Generations Will Call Me Blessed': Medieval Christian Tales of Non-Christian Marian Veneration." *Mediterranean Studies* 12 (2003): 30–67.

Cust, L. G. A. *Jerusalem: A Historical Sketch*. London: A&C Black Ltd., 1924.

——. *The Status Quo in the Holy Places*. 1926. Facsimile of the first edition. Jerusalem: Ariel, 1980.

——. *The Status Quo in the Holy Places*. London: HMSO, 1929.

Dalrymple, William. *From the Holy Mountain: A Journey Among the Christians of the Middle East*. New York: Henry Holt, 1997.

Danişmend, İ. H. "İslam ve Türk tarihinde Kıbrıs." *Türk Düşüncesi* 8, no. 9 (1958): 15-16.

Erdengiz, Ahmet. "Kıbrıslı Türklerin Alevi kimliği." In *Halk bilimi sempozyumları III*, ed. Fatma Kükrer, 240-54. Ankara: KKTC Milli Eğitim ve Kültür Yayınları, 2001.

de Groot, Alexander. "The Historical Development of the Capitulary Regime in the Ottoman Middle East from the Fifteenth to the Nineteenth Centuries." *Oriente Moderno* 83, no. 3 (2003): 575-604.

Derfner, Larry. "The Martyrs of Haram a-Sharif." *Jerusalem Post*, October 13, 2000.

Dermenghem, Émile. *Le culte des saints dans l'islam maghrébin*. Paris: Gallimard, 1954.

Dirèche-Slimani, Karima. *Chrétiens de Kabylie 1873-1954: Une action missionnaire dans l'Algérie coloniale*. Paris: Ed. Bouchène, 2004.

———. "Dolorisme religieux et reconstructions identitaires: Les conversions néo-évangéliques dans l'Algérie contemporaine." *Annales. Economies, Société Civilisations* 5 (2009): 1137-62.

———. "Évangélisation en Algérie: Débats sur la liberté de culte," *L'année du Maghreb* 5 (2009): 275-84.

Dixon, Scott, Dagmar Freist, and Mark Greengrass, eds. *Living with Religious Diversity in Early-Modern Europe*. Surrey, UK: Ashgate, 2009.

Documents relatifs à la position de Mgr Dupuch, ancien et premier Evêque d'Alger. Bordeaux: Henry Faye imprimeur de l'archevêché, 1851.

Doja, Albert. "A Political History of Bektashism from Ottoman Anatolia to Contemporary Turkey." *Journal of Church & State* 48, no. 2 (2006): 423-50.

Donadio, Rachel. "Catholic Bishops Deplore Mideast Christians' Plight." *New York Times*, June 6, 2010.

Dousse, Michel. *Marie la musulmane*. Paris: Albin Michel, 2005.

Dubisch, Jill. *In a Different Place: Pilgrimage, Gender, and Politics at a Greek Island Shrine*. Princeton, NJ: Princeton University Press, 1995.

Duijzings, Ger. "Pilgrimage, Politics and Ethnicity: Joint Pilgrimages of Muslims and Christians and Conflicts over Ambiguous Sanctuaries in Yugoslavia and Albania." In *Power and Prayer: Religious and Political Processes in Past and Present*, ed. M. Bax and A. Koster, 80-91. Amsterdam: VU University Press, 1993.

———. *Religion and the Politics of Identity in Kosovo*. New York: Columbia University Press, 2000.

Dumper, Michael. "The Christian Churches of Jerusalem in the Post-Oslo Period." *Journal of Palestine Studies* 31, no. 2 (2003): 51-65.

———. "Muslim Institutions and the Israeli State: Muslim Religious Endowments (waqfs) in Israel and the Occupied Territories, 1948-1987." Ph.D. diss., University of Exeter, 1991.

———. *The Politics of Jerusalem Since 1967.* The Institute for Palestine Studies Series. New York: Columbia University Press, 1997.

———. *The Politics of Sacred Space: The Old City of Jerusalem in the Middle East Conflict.* Boulder, CO: Lynne Rienner, 2002.

Dumper, Michael, and Craig Larkin. "Political Islam in Contested Jerusalem: The Emerging Role of Islamists from within Israel." *Conflict in Cities*, Working Paper 12, 2009. http://www.conflictincities.org/PDFs/WorkingPaper12_10.11.09.pdf.

Duncan, James. *The City as Text: The Politics of Landscape Interpretation in the Kandyan Kingdom.* Cambridge: Cambridge University Press, 1990.

Duncan, James, and Nancy Duncan. "Re(reading) the Landscape." *Environment and Planning D: Society and Space* 6 (1988): 117–26.

Dunn, Ross. "Row Seethes in Bethlehem Over Keys to the Birthplace of Jesus." *Christianity Today*, August 1, 2003. http://www.christianitytoday.com/ct/2003/augustweb-only/8-11-43.0.html.

Durkheim, Emile. *The Elementary Forms of the Religious Life.* New York: Free Press, 1965.

Eade, John, and Michael J Sallnow, eds. *Contesting the Sacred: The Anthropology of Christian Pilgrimage.* London: Routledge, 1991.

Einav, Hagai. "Cave of Patriarchs Included in National Heritage Plan." *Ynetnews*, February 21, 2010.

Eldar, Akiva. "Jerusalem Opens Muslim Quarter Jewish Site to Prayer, Upsetting Status Quo." *Haaretz*, January 14, 2011. www.haaretz.com/print-edition/news/jerusalem-opens-muslim-quarter-jewish-site-to-prayer-upsetting-status-quo-1.336881.

———. "Provocative Timing / Bibi's Latest Card." *Haaretz*, October 25, 2010.

Eliade, Mircea. *Image and Symbol.* Princeton, NJ: Princeton University Press, 1991.

———. *The Myth of the Eternal Return.* London: Arkana, 1989.

———. *Patterns in Comparative Religion.* London: Sheed and Ward, 1958.

———. *The Sacred and the Profane: The Nature of Religion.* New York: Harcourt, 1959.

Emmett, Chad F. *Beyond the Basilica: Christians and Muslims in Nazareth.* Chicago: University of Chicago Press, 1995.

———. *The Christian and Muslim Communities and Quarters of the Arab City of Nazareth.* Chicago: University of Chicago Press, 1991.

———. "The Siting of Churches and Mosques as an Indicator of Christian–Muslim Relations." *Islamic and Christian–Muslim Relations* 20, no. 4 (2009): 451–76.

———. "The Status Quo Solution for Jerusalem." *Journal of Palestine Studies* 26, no. 2 (1997): 16–28.

Englezakis, Benedict. *Studies on the History of the Church of Cyprus, 4th to 20th Centuries.* Aldershot, UK: Variorum, 1995.

Eordegian, Marlen. "British and Israeli Maintenance of the Status Quo in the Holy Places of Jerusalem." *International Journal of Middle East Studies* 35 (2003): 307–28.

Erdemir, Aykan, and Ali Yaman, *Alevism-Bektashism: A Brief Introduction.* Trans. Rabia Harmanşah and Kaan Evren Başaran. London: Alevi Cultural Centre, 2006.

Ergüner, Kudsi. *Ayrılık Çeşmesi: Bir Neyzenin Yolculuğu,* İstanbul: İletişim Yayınları, 2002.

Erlanger, Steven, and Greg Myre. "Huge Police Force Bars Israeli Rightist Rally at Jerusalem Holy Site." *New York Times,* April 11, 2005.

Evripidou, Stephanos. "Christofias: Solution Will Heal Wounds and Cleanse Souls." *Cyprus Mail,* April 1, 2010.

Faroqhi, Suraiya. *The Ottoman Empire and the World Around It.* London: I. B. Tauris, 2006.

Fearon, James, D. "Bargaining, Enforcement, and International Cooperation." *International Organization* 52, no. 2 (1998): 269–306.

Ficatier, Julie. "La Pentecôte de fraternité des catholiques d'Algérie." *La Croix,* May 13, 2008.

Finkel, Andrew. "From Church to Museum Back to Mosque," *New York Times,* May 2, 2013, http://latitude.blogs.nytimes.com/2013/05/02/the-cost-of-turning-turkeys-old-churches-and-museums-back-into-mosques/

———. "Mosque Conversion Raises Alarm," *Art Newspaper,* no. 245 (2013): 15.

Fisher-Ilan, Allyn. "Dozens Hurt as Clerics Clash in Jerusalem Church." *AlertNet,* Reuters Foundation, September 27, 2004.

Fotic, Aleksander. "The Official Explanations for the Confiscation and Sale of Monasteries (Churches) and Their Estates at the Time of Selim II." *Turcica* 26 (1994): 33–54.

Frazee, Charles. *Catholics and Sultans: The Church and the Ottoman Empire 1453–1923.* Cambridge: Cambridge University Press, 1983.

Frenkel, Yehushua. "Baybars and the Sacred Geography of Bilad al-Sham: A Chapter in the Islamization of Syria's Landscape." *Jerusalem Studies in Arabic and Islam* 25 (2001): 153–70.

Friedland, Roger, and Richard Hecht. "The Bodies of Nations: A Comparative Study of Religious Violence in Jerusalem and Ayodhya." *History of Religions* 38, no. 2 (1998): 101–49.

Friedman, Francine. *The Bosnian Muslims: Denial of a Nation.* Boulder, CO: Westview Press, 1998.

Gadamer, Hans-George. *Truth and Method.* London: Sheed and Ward, 1975.

Gellman, Barton. "Israelis, in Nighttime Move, Open Temple Mount Tunnel." *Washington Post,* September 25, 1996.

Geraci, Robert P., and Michael Khodarkovsky, eds. *Of Religion and Empire: Missions, Conversions and Tolerance in Tsarist Russia*. Ithaca, NY: Cornell University Press, 2001.

Ghodsee, Kristen. *Muslim Lives in Eastern Europe: Gender, Ethnicity, and the Transformation of Islam in Postsocialist Bulgaria*. Princeton, NJ: Princeton University Press, 2010.

Gnam-Fahom, Seham. *Tahadiat and Taquorat fe Tarekh Alnasera: Alolakat almasehya al islamia* (Challenges and changes in Nazareth history: The Islamic–Christian relations). Nazareth: Alnhada Publishing, 2003.

Goddard, Stacie E. "Uncommon Ground: Indivisible Territory and the Politics of Legitimacy." *International Organization* 60, no. 1 (2006): 35–68.

Gölpınarlı, Abdülbâki. *Mevlânâ'dan Sonra Mevlevilik*. İstanbul: İnkılâp and Aka, 1983.

Gorenberg, Gershom. *The End of Days: Fundamentalism and the Struggle for the Temple Mount*. Oxford: Oxford University Press, 2000.

———. "Guide to the Perplexed: The Other Tora." *Jerusalem Post*, June 12, 1989.

Grabar, Oleg, and Benjamin Z. Kedar, eds. *Where Heaven and Earth Meet: Jerusalem's Sacred Esplanade*. Austin: University of Texas Press, 2010.

Gradeva, Rossitsa. "Ottoman Policy Toward Christian Church Buildings." *Etudes Balkaniques*, 4 (1994): 14–36.

Gradeva, Rossitsa, and Svetlana Ivanova. "Researching the Past and Present of Muslim Culture in Bulgaria: The 'Popular' and 'High' Layers." *Islam and Christian-Muslim Relations* 12, no. 3 (2001): 317–37.

Graham, Stephen. *With the Russian Pilgrims to Jerusalem*. London: Macmillan, 1916.

Green, Sarah. *Notes from the Balkans: Locating Marginality and Ambiguity on the Greek-Albanian Border*. Princeton, NJ: Princeton University Press, 2005.

Greenberg, Joel. "Sharon Touches a Nerve, and Jerusalem Explodes." *New York Times*, September 29, 2000.

———. "Violence Forces Israeli Army to Rethink Strategy." *New York Times*, October 6, 1996.

———. "Whose Holy Land? At the Shrine; Palestinians Destroy Israeli Site That Was Scene of Many Clashes." *New York Times*, October 8, 2000.

Greenberg, Raphael. "Contested Sites: Archaeology and the Battle for Jerusalem." *Jewish Quarterly*, no. 208 (2007). http://jewishquarterly.org/2007/12/contested-sites/.

———. "Extreme Exposure: Archaeology in Jerusalem." *Conservation and Management of Archaeological Sites* 11, no. 3–4 (2009): 262–81.

Grell, Ole Peter, and Bob Scribner, eds. *Tolerance and Intolerance in the European Reformation*. Cambridge: Cambridge University Press, 1996.

Gross, Neety C. "Grave Thoughts." *Jerusalem Report*, January 5, 2009.
Guinn, David E. *Protecting Jerusalem's Holy Sites: A Strategy for Negotiating a Sacred Peace*. Cambridge: Cambridge University Press, 2006.
Habib al-Mawardi, Muhammad b. *Al-ahkam al-sultaniyya wal-wilayat al-diniyya: Ibn Qudama al-Maqdisi, Al-Mughni*. Beirut: Dar al-Kitab al-Arabi, 1983.
Hadžijahić, Muhamed. "Sinkretistički elementi u Islamu u Bosni i Hercegovini." *Prilozi zaorijentalnu filologiu* 28–29 (1978): 301–28.
Halevi, Masha. "The Politics Behind the Construction of the Modern Church of the Annunciation in Nazareth." *Catholic Historical Review* 96, no. 1 (2010): 27–55.
Hanlon, Gregory. *Confession and Community in Seventeenth-Century France: Catholic and Protestant Coexistence in Aquitaine*. Philadelphia: University of Pennsylvania Press, 1993.
Harmanşah, Rabia. "Facts, Meanings, and Cosmologies: Bektashi Responses to the Abolition of Religious Orders in 1925." Master's thesis, Middle East Technical University, 2006.
———. "Tarikatların Yasaklanması ve Sonrasında Mevleviler." Paper presented at the International Symposium on Mawlana Jalaladdin Rumi in Thought and Art, Çanakkale Onsekiz Mart University, Faculty of Theology, Gelibolu, Turkey, May 25–28, 2006.
Harmanşah, Rabia, and Aykan Erdemir, "Hacı Bektaş Veli." In *The Oxford Encyclopedia of Islamic World*. 6 vols. Ed., John L. Esposito. Oxford: Oxford University Press, 2009.
Harvey, D. "Monument and Myth." *Annals of the Association of American Geographers* 69 (1979): 362–81.
Hasluck F. W. *Christianity and Islam Under the Sultans*. Oxford: Clarendon Press, 1929.
Hasluck, Frederick William. "Ambiguous Sanctuaries and Bektashi Propaganda," *Annual of the British School at Athens* 20 (1913–1914): 94–119.
———. "Graves of the Arabs in Asia Minor." *Annual of the British School at Athens* 19 (1912–1913): 182–90.
———. "Heterodox Tribes of Asia Minor." *Journal of the Royal Anthropological Institute of Great Britain and Ireland* 51 (1921): 310–42.
Hassner, Ron E. "The Pessimist's Guide to Religious Coexistence." In *Holy Places in the Israeli–Palestinian Conflict: Confrontation and Co-Existence*, ed. Marshall Breger, Yitzhak Reiter, and Leonard Hammer, 145–57. New York: Routledge, 2010.
———. *War on Sacred Grounds*. Ithaca, NY: Cornell University Press, 2009.
Hasson, Nir. "Israeli Reining in Old City Merchants." *Haaretz*, August 21, 2009. www.haaretz.com/hasen/spages/1108762.html.
Hayden, Robert M. "Antagonistic Tolerance: Competitive Sharing of Religious Sites in South Asia and the Balkans." *Current Anthropology* 43, no. 2 (2002): 205–31.

———, "Intersecting Religioscapes in Post-Ottoman Spaces." Paper presented at the conference "Shared Spaces and their Dissolution: Practices of Coexistence in the Post-Ottoman Sphere." Nicosia, Cyprus, October 2011.

Hayden, Robert M., Hande Sozer, Tuğba Tanyeri-Erdemir, and Aydin Erdemir. "The Byzantine Mosque at Trilye: A Processual Analysis of Dominance, Sharing, Transformation and Tolerance." *History and Anthropology* 22, no. 1 (2011): 1–17.

Hayden, Robert M., and Timothy D. Walker. "Intersecting Religioscapes: A Comparative Approach to Trajectories of Change, Scale and Competitive Sharing of Religious Spaces." *Journal of the American Academy of Religion* 81, no. 2 (2013): 399–426.

Haynes, D., and G. Parkash. "Introduction: The Entanglement of Power and Resistance." In *Contesting Power: Resistance and Everyday Social Relations in South Asia*, ed. D. Haynes and G. Parkash, 1–22. Delhi: Oxford University Press, 1991.

Hecht, Richard. "The Construction and Management of Sacred Time and Space: 'Sabta Nur' in the Church of the Holy Sepulcher." In *Now Here: Space, Time and Modernity*, ed. R. Friedland and D. Boden, 181–235. Berkeley: University of California Press, 1995.

Henig, David. "'Knocking on My Neighbour's Door': On Metamorphoses of Sociality in Rural Bosnia." *Critique of Anthropology* 32, no. 1 (2012): 3–19.

———. "'This Is Our Little Hajj': Muslim Holy Sites and Reappropriation of the Sacred Landscape in Contemporary Bosnia." *American Ethnologist* 39, no. 4 (2012): 752–66.

Herbert, Mary Elizabeth. *A Saint in Algeria*. London: Burns and Gates, 1878.

Hider, James. "Settlers Dig Tunnels Around Jerusalem." *Timesonline*, March 1, 2008. http://www.timesonline.co.uk/tol/news/world/middle_east/article3463264.ece.

Hikmetağalar, Hizber. *Eski Lefkoşada semtler ve anılar*, 2nd ed. Istanbul: Fakülteler Matabaası, 2005.

Hill, B. "An Analysis of Conflict Resolution Techniques: From Problem-Solving Workshops to Theory." *Journal of Conflict Resolution* 26, no. 1 (1982): 109–38.

Hoffman, Gil. "Ten Years After Temple Mount Visit, R'a'anan Gissin Tells 'Post': Sharon Knew Palestinians Were Planning Violence, but Wanted to Show He Wouldn't Compromise on J'lem." *Jerusalem Post*, September 29, 2010.

Holt, Peter. *The Age of the Crusades*. London: Longman, 1986.

Hopwood, Derek. *The Russian Presence in Syria and Palestine 1843–1914: Church and Politics in the Near East*. Oxford: Clarendon Press, 1969.

Hopwood, Keith. "Christian–Muslim Symbiosis in Anatolia." In *Archeology, Anthropology and Heritage in the Balkans and Anatolia: The Life and Times of F. W. Hasluck (1878–1920)*, ed. David Shankland, 13–30. Istanbul: Isis, 2004.

———. "The Turkish-Byzantine Frontier." In *Acta Viennensia Ottomanica, Akten des 13*, ed. Markus Kohbach, Gisela Prochazka-Eisl, and Claudia Romer, 153–61. Vienna: Institut für Orientalistik, University of Vienna, 1999.

Hudson, M. *International Tribunals, Past and Future*. Concord, NH: Rumford Press, 1994.

Huntington, Samuel. *The Clash of Civilizations and the Remaking of World Order*. New York: Simon & Schuster, 1996.

Hutman, Bill. "Darkness at the End of the Tunnel." *Jerusalem Post*, September 27, 1996.

İnan, Arı. *Düşünceleriyle Atatürk*. Ankara: Türk Tarih Kurumu, 1983.

İnançer, Ömer Tuğrul. "Mevlevi Musikisi ve Sema." In *Dünden Bugüne İstanbul Ansiklopedisi*, vol. 5. İstanbul: T.C. Kültür Bakanlığı, Tarih Vakfı, 1994.

Israeli, Rafael. *Green Crescent Over Nazareth: The Displacement of Christians by Muslims in the Holy Land*. London: Frank Cass, 2002.

Ivanova, Svetlana. "Muslim Charity Foundations (Vakf) and the Models of Religious Behavior of Ottoman Social Estates in Rumeli (late 15th to 19th Centuries)." *Weiner Zeitschrift zur Geschichte der Neuzeit* 5, no. 2 (2005): 44–68.

Jamal, Amaney and Nadine Naber, eds. *Race and Arab Americans Before and After 9/11: From Invisible Citizens to Visible Subjects*. Syracuse, NY: Syracuse University Press, 2008.

Jäschke, Gotthard. *Yeni Turkiye'de İslamlık*. Ankara: Bilgi Yayınevi, 1972.

Jasmin, Jacques. *La Bièrges, poème dédié à Monseigneur Pavy, évêque d'Alger*. Agen: Imprimerie Prosper Noubel, 1860.

Jeffrey, George. *A Description of the Historic Monuments of Cyprus*. Nicosia: Government Printing Office, 1918.

Jennings, Ronald C. *Christians and Muslims in Ottoman Cyprus and the Mediterranean World 1571–1640*. New York: New York University Press, 1993.

Kadi, Amine. "Les chrétiens d'Algérie sous pression." *La Croix*, April 6, 2008. http://www.la-croix.com/Religion/Actualite/Les-chretiens-d-Algerie-sous-pression-_NG_-2008-04-06-670031.

Kafadar, Cemal. *Between Two Worlds: The Construction of the Ottoman State*. (Berkeley: University of California Press, 1995.

———. "The New Visibility of Sufism in Turkish Studies and Cultural Life." In *The Dervish Lodge: Architecture, Art and Sufism in Ottoman Turkey*, ed. Raymond Lifchez, 307–22. Berkeley: University of California Press, 1992.

Kamrava, Mehran. *The Modern Middle East*. Berkeley: University of California Press, 2005.

Kapferer, Bruce. *Legends of People, Myths of State: Violence, Intolerance, and Political Culture in Sri Lanka and Australia*. Washington, DC: Smithsonian Institute Press, 1988.

Kaplan, Benjamin J. *Divided by Faith: Religious Conflict and the Practice of Toleration in Early Modern Europe*. Cambridge, MA: Harvard University Press, 2007.

Kara, Mustafa. *Din hayat sanat açısından tekkeler ve zaviyeler*. İstanbul: Dergah Yayınları, 1999.

Karamustafa, Ahmet. "Hacı Bektaş Veli ve Anadolu'da Müslümanlık." In *Hacı Bektaş Veli: Güneşte Zerresinden, Deryada Katresinden*, ed. Pınar Ecevitoğlu, Ali Murat Irat, Ayhan Yalçınkaya, 42–48. Proceedings of the International Hacı Bektaş Veli Symposium. Dipnot Yayınları, 2010.

Karčić, Harun. "Islamic Revival in Post-Socialist Bosnia and Herzegovina: International Actors and Activities." *Journal of Muslim Minority Affairs* 30, no. 4 (2010): 519–34.

Karmi, Omar. "West Bank Land Sales by Church Spur Uproar." *National*, January 13, 2010.

Katinka, Barukh. *Me'az Ve-Ad Hayom*. Jerusalem: Kiryat Sefer, 1961.

Katz, Itamar, and Ruth Kark. "The Greek Orthodox Patriarchate of Jerusalem and Its Congregation: Dissent Over Real Estate." *International Journal of Middle East Studies* 37, no. 4 (2005): 509–34.

Katz, Kimberly. "Building Jordanian Legitimacy: Renovating Jerusalem's Holy Places." *Muslim World* 93, no. 2 (2003): 211–32.

Katznelson, Ira, and Gareth Stedman Jones, eds. *Religion and the Political Imagination*. Cambridge: Cambridge University Press, 2010.

Kazantzakis, Nikos. *Journeying: Travels in Italy, Egypt, Sinai, Jerusalem and Cyprus*. Trans. Themi Vasils and Theodora Vasils. 1961. Reprint, Boston: Little, Brown, 1973.

Keawar, Noha Zorob. *Tarich Al-Naserah* [History of Nazareth]. Nazareth: Vinos, 2000.

Keinon, Herb. "Mitchell Committee Report: Sharon Is Not to Blame for Intifada." *Jerusalem Post*, May 6, 2001.

Kendall, Henry. *Jerusalem, the City Plan: Preservation and Development During the British Mandate, 1918–1948*. London: H. M. Stationery Office Press and Admiralty Chart Establishment, 1948.

Kermeli, Eugenia. "Central Administration Versus Provincial Arbitrary Governance: Patmos and Mount Athos Monasteries in the 16th Century." *Byzantine and Modern Greek Studies* 32, no. 2 (2008): 189–202.

Kershner, Isabel. "Western Wall Feud Heightens Israeli-Palestinian Tensions." *New York Times*, November 25, 2010.

Khamaisi, Rassem. "Holy Places in Urban Space: Foci of Confrontation or Catalyst for Development?" In *Holy Places in the Israeli Palestinian Conflict: Confrontation and Co-Existence*, ed. Marshall Breger, Yitzhak Reiter, and Leonard Hammer, 129–45. New York: Routledge, 2010.

Khamaisi, Rassem, and Elan Oren. "Fifth Year General Physical and Social Development Plan for the City of Nazareth 2007-2011." Submitted to Ministry of Construction and Housing and Nazareth Municipality, R. A. B Engineering Ltd., Kafer Kanna, 2007.

Kimhi, Israel, ed. *The Security Fence around Jerusalem: Implications for the City and Its Residents*. Jerusalem: Jerusalem Institute for Israel Studies, 2006.

Kirimtayif, Suleyman. *Converted Byzantine Churches in Istanbul*. Istanbul: Ege Yayinlari, 2001.

Koca, Şefki. *Kıbrıs'ta Bektaşi dergahları*. İstanbul: Cem Dergisi, 2001.

Kong, Lily. "Ideological Hegemony and the Political Symbolism of Religious Buildings in Singapore." *Environment and Planning D: Society and Space* 11 (1993): 23-45.

Kriesberg, L. *Constructive Conflict: From Escalation to Resolution*. Lanham, MD: Rowman & Littlefield, 1998.

Kreiser, Klaus. "Türkiye'de Tarikatların Mevcut Durumu ve Geçmisi Hakkında Notlar." In *İslâm Dünyasında Tarikatlar*, ed. Alexandre Popovic and Gilles Veinstein. İstanbul: Sûf Yayınları, 2004.

Kroyanker, David. *Halom BeHakitz: Yerushalayim HaLo-Bnuya*. Jerusalem: Migdal David—The Museum for Jerusalem's History, 1993.

———. "Museum Is Prohibited and a University Is Permitted?," *Haaretz*, January 10, 2006.

Küçük, Hülya. *The Role of the Bektashis in Turkey's National Struggle*. Leiden: Brill, 2002.

Kupferschmidt, Uri M. *The Supreme Muslim Council: Islam Under the British Mandate for Palestine*. Leiden: E. J. Brill, 1987.

Kyriss, Costas P. *Peaceful Co-Existence in Cyprus Under British Rule (1878-1959) and After Independence*. Nicosia: Public Information Office, 1977.

———. "Symbiotic Elements in the History of the two Communities of Cyprus." In *Proceedings: International Symposium on Political Geography*. Nicosia: Cyprus Geographical Association, 1976.

LaTour, Stephen, Pauline Houlden, Laurens Walker, and John Thibaut. "Some Determinants of Preference for Modes of Conflict Resolution." *Journal of Conflict Resolution* 20, no. 2 (1976): 319-56.

Lavigerie, Charles. *Recueil de lettres publiées par Mgr l'archevêque d'Alger, délégué apostolique du Sahara et du Soudan sur les œuvres et missions africaines*. Paris: Plon, 1869.

Lefebvre, H. *The Production of Space*. Oxford: Basil Blackwell, 1991.

Lefkovits, Etgar. "Sharon's Planned Visit to Temple Mount Angers Palestinians." *Jerusalem Post*, September 27, 2000.

Lewis, Bernard. *Modern Türkiye'nin doğuşu.* Ankara: Türk Tarih Kurumu, 2004.
Linde, S. "Hier: Jerusalem Tolerance Museum in 3 Years." *Jerusalem Post,* June 6, 2012.
Lindley, Dan. "Historical, Tactical, and Strategic Lessons from the Partition of Cyprus." *International Studies Perspectives* 8 (2007): 224-41. http://www3.nd.edu/~dlindley/handouts/CyprusPartition.pdf.
Lory, Bernard. "The Vizier's Dream: 'Seeing St. Dimitar' in Ottoman Bitola." *History and Anthropology* 20, no. 3 (2009): 309-16.
Lotfi, Abdelhamid. "Creating Muslim Space in the USA: Masajid and Islamic Centers." *Islam and Christian-Muslim Relations* 12, no. 2 (2001): 235-53.
Lowry, Heath. "Privilege and Property in Ottoman Macuka in the Opening Decades of Tourkokratia: 1461-1553." In *Continuity and Change in Late Byzantine and Early Ottoman Society,* ed. Anthony Bryer and Heath W. Lowry, 97-128. Birmingham, UK: Dumbarton Oaks, 1986.
Luke, Harry C. "The Christian Communities in the Holy Sepulchre." In *Jerusalem 1920-22: Being the Records of the Pro-Jerusalem Council during the First Two Years of the Civil Administration,* ed. C. R. Ashbee, 46-56. London: John Murray, 1924.
———. *Cyprus: A Portrait and Appreciation.* London: George G. Harrap, 1957.
———. "Introductory Note." In *The Status Quo in the Holy Places.* London: HMSO, 1929.
Luria, Keith P. *Sacred Boundaries: Religious Coexistence and Conflict in Early Modern France.* Washington, DC: Catholic University of America Press, 2005.
Luz, Nimrod. "Metaphors to Live By: Identity Formation and Resistance Among Minority Muslims in Israel." In *Religion and Place: Landscape, Politics and Piety,* ed. Peter Hopkins, Lily Kong, and Elizabeth Olson, 57-74. Dordrecht: Springer, 2013.
———. "The Politics of Sacred Places. Palestinian Identity, Collective Memory, and Resistance in the Hassan Bek Mosque Conflict." *Society and Space: Environment and Planning D* 26, no. 6 (2008): 1036-52.
Lynch, Kevin. *Image of the City.* Cambridge, MA: MIT Press, 1960.
Macintyre, Donald. "Patriarchs, Property and Politics in Jerusalem." *Independent,* November 6, 2007.
Makdisi, Saree. "Architecture of Erasure." *Critical Inquiry* 36, no. 3 (2010): 519-59.
Malcolm, Noel. *Bosnia: A Short History.* London: Macmillan, 1994.
Maley, Y. "From Adjudication to Mediation: Third Party Discourse in Conflict Resolution." *Journal of Pragmatics* 23, no. 1 (1995): 93-110.
Mansor, Asa'ad. *Tarich Alnaserah* [History of Nazareth]. Cairo: Dar Alhelal, 1924.
Maoz, Moshe, and Sari Nusseibeh, eds. *Jerusalem: Points of Friction and Beyond.* The Hague: Kluwer Law International, 2000.
Mardin Şerif. "The Naksibendi Order in Turkish History." In *Islam in Modern Turkey: Religion, Politics and Literature in a Secular State,* ed. Richard Tapper, 121-42. London: I. B.Tauris, 1991.

Margalit, Meir. *Seizing Control of Space in East Jerusalem*. Jerusalem: Sifrei Aliat Gag, 2010.

Marioge, Paul. "Une dévotion mariale populaire en terre d'Islam." *Voix d'Afrique*, no. 74 (2007). http://peres-blancs.cef.fr/devotion_mariale.htm.

Massey, Doreen. *For Space*. Los Angeles: Sage, 2005.

Masters, Bruce. *Christians and Jews in the Ottoman Arab World: The Roots of Sectarianism*. Cambridge Studies in Islamic Civilization. Cambridge: Cambridge University Press, 2001.

Maurier, Henri. "Notre-Dame d'Afrique." *Voix d'Afrique*, no. 45 (1999). http://peres-blancs.cef.fr/hmaurie.htm.

Mayer, Tamar. "Jerusalem In and Out of Focus: The City in Zionist Ideology." In *Jerusalem*, ed. Tamar Mayer and Suleiman Mourad, 224–44. New York: Routledge, 2008.

McGahern, Una. *Palestinian Christians in Israel: State Attitudes Towards Non-Muslims in a Jewish State*. Durham Modern Middle East and Islamic World Series. London: Routledge, 2011.

Meinhardus, Otto. "A Note on the Nestorians in Jerusalem." *Oriens Christianus* 51 (1967): 123–29.

Melcion-D'Arc, Casimir. *Notre-Dame d'Afrique, Vierge libératrice*. Alger: Typographie Duclaux, 1862.

Mélikoff, Irène. "Bektashi/Kızılbas: Historical Bipartition and Its Consequences." In *Alevi Identity: Cultural, Religious and Social Perspectives*, ed. Tord Olsson, Elisabeth Özdalga, and Catharina Raudvere, 1–7. Istanbul: Swedish Research Institute, 1996.

Menocal, Maria Rosa. *The Ornament of the World: How Muslims, Jews, and Christians Created a Culture of Tolerance in Medieval Spain*. New York: Black Bay Books, 2002.

Menon, Nivedita. "The Ayodhya Judgment: What Next?" *Economic & Political Weekly*, July 30, 2011.

Michel, R. L. N. "A Muslim–Christian Sect in Cyprus." *Nineteenth Century Journal*, no. 63 (1908): 751–62.

Mirghani, Osman. "Christians' Fears in the Arab World." *Al-Arabiya News*, March 22, 2012.

Mitchell, C. R. *The Structure of International Conflict*. New York: St. Martin's Press, 1989.

Mitchell, D. *Cultural Geography: A Critical Introduction*. Oxford: Blackwell, 2000.

Mitchell, W. J. T. "Imperial Landscape." In *Landscape and Power*, 2nd ed., ed. W. J. T. Mitchell. Chicago: University of Chicago Press, 2002.

———. *Sacred Landscape* [in Hebrew]. Ed. Larry Abramson. Tel Aviv: Resling, 2009.

Moore, Robert. *The Formation of a Persecuting Society*. Oxford: Blackwell Publishers, 1998.

Morris, Benny. *Righteous Victims: A History of the Zionist-Arab Conflict.* New York: Vintage, 2001.

Mourad, Suleiman Ali. "The Symbolism of Jerusalem in Early Islam." In *Jerusalem: Idea and Reality,* ed. Tamar Mayer and Suleiman A. Mourad, 86–102. London: Routledge, 2008.

"Muhammaed Khayr al-Dajani vs. Israel's Police." Judgment dated February 12, 2006. High Court of Justice, 1331/06.

Mulahalilović, Enver. *Vjerski običaji Muslimana u Bosni i Hercegovini.* Sarajevo: Starješinstvo Islamske Zajednice, 1989.

Nachmani, Amikam. "So Near and Yet So Far: Greco-Israeli Relations." In *Israel, Turkey and Greece: Uneasy Relations in the East Mediterranean.* London: Frank Cass, 1987.

Natsheh, Yusuf, Yitzhak Reiter, Wasfi Kailani, and Galit Hazan. "Guide to the Tomb of Samuel" (unpublished ms. 2009).

Nave, Emanuel. "Implementation of Shari'a in 20th Century Civil Courts: A Comparative Study of Adjudication in Personal Status and Waqf Issues of Muslims in a Muslim Country (Egypt) and a Non-Muslim Country (Israel)." Ph.D. diss., Hebrew University, 1997.

Naylor, Simon, and James Ryan. "The Mosque in the Suburbs: Negotiating Religion and Ethnicity in South London." *Social and Cultural Geography* 3, no. 1 (2002): 39–59.

Necipoğlu, Nevra. "Byzantine Monasteries and Monastic Property in Thessalonike and Constantinople During the Period of Ottoman Conquests (late Fourteenth and Early Fifteenth Centuries)." *Journal of Ottoman Studies* 15 (1995): 122–35.

———. "The Coexistence of Turks and Greeks in Medieval Anatolia (Eleventh–Twelfth Centuries)." *Harvard Middle Eastern and Islamic Review* 5 (1999–2000): 58–76.

Nevzat, Altay. *Nationalism Amongst the Turks of Cyprus: The First Wave.* Oulu, Fin.: Oulu University Press, 2005.

Nevzat, Altay, and Mete Hatay. "Politics, Society and the Decline of Islam in Cyprus: From the Ottoman Era to the 21st Century." *Middle Eastern Studies* 45, no. 6 (2009): 911–33.

Nirenberg, David. *Communities of Violence: Persecution of Minorities in the Middle Ages.* Princeton, NJ: Princeton University Press, 1996.

Norton, J. D. "Bektashis in Turkey." In *Islam in the Modern World,* ed. Denis Mac Eoin and Ahmed Al-Shahi, 73–87. New York: St. Martin's Press, 1983.

Notice sur le pèlerinage de Notre-Dame d'Afrique à Alger, 2e édition revue, corrigée et augmentée avec une préface de Monseigneur Leynaud, Archevêque d'Alger. Alger: Papeterie, Imprimerie E. Gaudet, 1924.

Notre-Dame d'Afrique et l'association de prières pour la conversion des musulmans. Extrait du *Messager du Sacré-Cœur de Jésus.* Le Puy: Imprimerie M.-P. Marchessou, 1862.

Oberman, Heiko. "The Travail of Tolerance: Containing Chaos in early Modern Europe." In *Tolerance and Intolerance in the European Reformation*, eds. Ole Peter Grell and Bob Scribner, 13-31. Cambridge: Cambridge University Press, 1996.

Ocak, A. Yaşar. "XIII-XV Yuzyillarda Anadolu'da Turk-Hiristyan Dini Etkilesimler ve Aya Yorgi (Saint Georges) Kultu." *Belleten* 55 (1991): 661-75.

Ohnefalsch-Richter, Magda H. *Greek Customs and Mores in Cyprus*. Nicosia: Laiki Cultural Centre, 2006.

Oikonomides, N. "Monasteres et moines lors de la conquete ottoman." *Sudost-Forschungen* 35 (1976): 1-10.

Öktem Niyazi. "Religion in Turkey." *Brigham Young University Law Review*, no. 2 (2002): 371-403, http://digitalcommons.law.byu.edu/lawreview/vol2002/iss2/10.

Olsson, Tord, Elisabeth Özdalga, and Catharina Raudvere, eds. *Alevi Identity: Cultural, Religious and Social Perspectives*. Istanbul: Swedish Research Institute, 1998.

O'Mahony, Anthony. "Pilgrims, Politics and Holy Places: The Ethiopian Community in Jerusalem Until ca. 1650." In *Jerusalem: Its Sanctity and Centrality to Judaism, Christianity and Islam*, ed. L. Levine, 476-81. New York: Continuum, 1999.

Oren, Amir. "Chief Rabbis Prepared to Forgo Control of Certain 'Holy Places.'" *Haaretz*, July 12, 2000.

Orhonlu,Cengiz. "The Ottoman Turks Settle in Cyprus." In *The First International Congress of Cypriot Studies: Presentations of the Turkish Delegation*, ed. H. İnalcık, 76-77. Ankara: Institute for the Study of Turkish Culture, 1971.

Ozacky-Lazar, Sara, and Ghanem Asa'd. *The Orr Commission Testimonies* (in Hebrew). Jerusalem: Ketter, 2003.

Özkul, A. E. *Kıbrıs'ın sosyo-ekonomik tarihi 1726-1750*. İstanbul: İletişim, 2005.

Özyürek, Esra. *Nostalgia for the Modern: State Secularism and Everyday Politics in Turkey*. Durham, NC: Duke University Press, 2006.

Paine, Crispin. "Militant Atheist Objects: Anti-Religious Museums in the Soviet Union." *Present Pasts* 1 (2009): 61-76.

Pancaroglu, Ova. "The Itinerant Dragon-Slayer: Forging Paths of Image and Identity in Medieval Anatolia." *Gesta* 43, no. 2 (2004): 151-64.

Papadakis, Yiannis. "Nationalist Imaginings of War in Cyprus." In *War, A Cruel Necessity? The Bases of Institutionalised Violence*, ed. R. Hinde and H. Watson, 54-67. London: I. B. Tauris Academic Studies, 1995.

Papasthathis, Charalambos. "A New Status for Jerusalem? An Eastern Orthodox Viewpoint." *Catholic University Law Review* 45 (1995-96): 723-32.

Pavy, Louis-Antoine-Augustin. *Histoire critique du culte de la sainte Vierge en Afrique, depuis le commencement du christianisme jusqu'à nos jours*. Alger: Bastide Libraire, 1858.

———. *Histoire de Notre-Dame d'Afrique: Appel de Mgr L.-A.-A. Pavy, évêque d'Alger, en faveur de cette chapelle*, 4 vols. Paris: E. Repos Libraire, 1864.

———. "Sur le Mahométisme." In *Collection intégrale et universelle des orateurs sacrés*, ed. Jacques Paul Minge. Paris: Imprimerie catholique du Petit-Montrouge, 1856.

PCBS (Palestinian Central Bureau of Statistics). "Population, Housing and Establishment Census 2007. Main Indicators by Locality Type." Ramallah, Palestine: Palestinian Central Bureau of Statistics, January, 2009. http://www.pcbs.gov.ps/Portals/_PCBS/Downloads/book1529.pdf.

Pedersen, Kirsten. "Deir Es-Sultan: The Ethiopian Monastery in Jerusalem." *Quaderni di Studi Etiopici* 8–9 (1987–88): 33–47.

Peters, F. E. *Jerusalem: The Holy City in the Eyes of Chroniclers, Visitors, Pilgrims and Prophets from the Days of Abraham to the Beginnings of Modern Times*. Princeton, NJ: Princeton University Press, 1985.

Pfeffer, Anshel. "Turning Joseph Into a Jewish Fanatic." *Haaretz*, July 8, 2011.

"Pictures and documents from shehab-aldeen Nazareth," http://www.geocities.ws/shhabaden/indexshhabpic.htm.

Pile, S. "Introduction: Opposition, Political Identities and Spaces of Resistance." In *Geographies of Resistance*, ed. S. Pile and M. Keith 1–32. London: Routledge, 1997.

Popović, Alexandre. "The Contemporary Situation of the Muslim Mystic Orders in Yugoslavia." In *Islamic Dilemmas: Reformers, Nationalities and Industrialisation: The Southern Shore of the Mediterranean*, ed. Ernest Gellner, 240–54. Berlin: Mouton, 1985.

Prats, Jean de. *L'Église africaine ancienne et moderne*. Tours: Alfred Mame et fil, 1892.

Press and Information Office of Cyprus (PIO). *Muslim Places of Worship*. Nicosia: PIO, 2008.

Pullan, Wendy. "Frontier Urbanism: The Periphery at the Centre of Contested Cities." *Journal of Architecture* 16, no. 1 (2011): 15–35.

———. "'Sacred Space' as Mediation." In *The Church in the Industrial Landscape*, ed. Kees Doevendans and Gertjan van der Harst, 247–63. Zoetermeer: Uitgeverij Boekencentrum, 2004.

Pullan, Wendy, and Max Gwiazda. "The Biblical Present in Jerusalem's 'City of David.'" In *Memory Culture and the Contemporary City: Building Sites*, ed. A. Webber, U. Staiger and H. Steiner, 106–25. London: Palgrave Macmillan, 2009.

Pullan, Wendy, Maximilian Sternberg, Lefkos Kyriacou, Craig Larkin, and Michael Dumper. *The Struggle for Jerusalem's Holy Places*. London: Routledge, 2013.

Rabinowitz, Dan. *Overlooking Nazareth: The Ethnography of Exclusion in Galilee*. Cambridge Studies in Social and Cultural Anthropology. Cambridge: Cambridge University Press, 2000.

———. "The Palestinian Citizens of Israel, the Concept of Trapped Minority and the Discourse of Transnationalism in Anthropology." *Ethnic and Racial Studies* 24, no. 1 (2001): 64–85.

———. "Strife Over Nazareth: Struggles Over the Religious Meaning of Place." *Ethnography* 2 (2001): 93–113.
Raheb, Mitri, and Fred Strickert. *Bethlehem 2000*. Heidelberg, Ger.: Palmyra, 1998.
Reiter, Yitzhak. *Allah's Safe Haven? The Controversy Surrounding the Mamilla Cemetery and the Museum of Tolerance: Contesting Domination over the Symbolic and Physical Landscape* [in Hebrew, forthcoming in English]. Jerusalem: Jerusalem Institute for Israeli Studies, 2011.
———. "Contest of Cohabitation in Shared Holy Places?" In *Holy Places in the Israeli-Palestinian Conflict: Confrontation and Co-Existence*, ed. Marshall J. Breger, Yitzak Reiter, and Leonard Hammer, 158–77. New York: Routledge, 2010.
———. *Islamic Endowment in Jerusalem Under British Mandate*. London: Frank Cass, 1996.
———. *Islamic Institutions in Jerusalem: Palestinian Muslim Organization Under Jordanian and Israeli Rule (Arab and Islamic Law)*. Amsterdam: Kluwer Law International, 1997.
———. "The Waqf in Israel Since 1965: The Case of Acre Reconsidered." In *Holy Places in the Israeli Palestinian Conflict: Confrontation and Co-Existence*, ed. Marshall Breger, Yitzhak Reiter, and Leonard Hammer, 104–27. New York: Routledge, 2010.
Reiter, Yitzhak, and Yusef Natsheh. "The Samuel Tomb—Tolerance via Museumization." Paper presented at the Sharing Sacred Space: Religion and Conflict Resolution conference, Columbia University, February 14–15, 2008; abstract available at http://hrcolumbia.org/sacred_spaces/abstracts.htm.
Ricard, Antoine. "La piraterie barbaresque et Notre-Dame-d'Afrique." In *Revue du monde catholique*, vol. 4, 161–71. Paris: Victor Palmé, 1862.
———. *Quelques années en Afrique, souvenirs, par l'abbé H. B.* Toulouse: Cluzon, 1861.
Riefstahl, Rudolf M. "Selimiyeh in Konya." *Art Bulletin* 12, no. 4 (1930): 311–19.
Ritchie, Susan. "The Pasha of Buda and the Edit of Torda: Transylvanian Unitarian/Islamic Ottoman Cultural Enmeshment and the Development of Religious Tolerance." *Journal of Unitarian Universalist History* 30 (2005): 36–54.
Rodrigue, Aron. "Difference and Tolerance in the Ottoman Empire." Interview by Nancy Reynolds. *Stanford Humanities Review* 5, no. 1 (1996): 81–92.
Roussos, Sotiris. "The Patriarchate of Jerusalem in the Greek-Palestinian-Israeli Triangle: Is There a Place for It?" *One in Christ* 39, no. 3 (2004): 15–25.
Rudolph, Lloyd, and Susanne Rudolph. "Modern Hate: How Ancient Animosities Get Invented." *New Republic*, March 22, 1993, 24–29.
Rujanac, Dženita Sarač. "Ajvatovica: A Bridge Between Tradition, National and Religious Identity." *History and Anthropology* 24, no. 1 (2013): 117–36.

Rumpf, Christian. "Holy Places." In *Encyclopedia of Public International Law*. Ed. Rudolf Bernhardt. Vol. 2, *East African Community to Italy–United States Air Transport Arbitration (1965)*, 863–66. Amsterdam: Elsevier, 1995.

Sabella, Bernard. "Palestinian Christians: Challenges and Hopes." *al-Bushra*, 1996. http://www.al-bushra.org/holyland/sabella.htm.

Samman, Khaldoun. *Cities of God and Nationalism: Mecca, Jerusalem and Rome as Contested World Cities*. Boulder, CO: Paradigm, 2007.

Sanders, Edmund. "More Jews Praying on Site Also Sacred to Muslims." *Los Angeles Times*, October 28, 2012.

Sarıönder, Refika. "Mevlana Celaleddin Rumi and Haci Bektas Veli: Two Faces of Turkish Islam: Encounters, Orders, Politics." In *On Archaelogy of Sainthood and Local Spirituality in Islam: Past and Present Crossroads of Events and Ideas (Yearbook of the Sociology of Islam 5)*, ed. Georg Stauth, 57–70. Bielefeld: Transcript Verlag, 2004.

Scott, James C. *Seeing Like a State: How Certain Schemes to Improve the Human Condition Have Failed*. New Haven, CT: Yale University Press, 1998.

———. *Weapons of the Weak*. New Haven, CT: Yale University Press, 1985.

Schabel, Chris. "Religion." In *Cyprus: Society and Culture 1191–1374*, ed. Konnari Nicolaou and C. Schabel, 157–218. Lieden: Brill, 2005.

Schimmel, Annemarie. *I am Wind, You Are Fire: The Life and Works of Rumi*. Boston: Shambala, 1992.

Schmemann, Serge. "Middle East Conflict: The Overview; 50 Are Killed as Clashes Widen from West Bank to Gaza Strip." *New York Times*, September 27, 1996.

Scribner, Bob. "Preconditions of Tolerance and Intolerance in Sixteenth-Century Germany." In *Tolerance and Intolerance in the European Reformation*, ed. Ole Peter Grell and Bob Scribner, 32–47. Cambridge: Cambridge University Press, 1996.

Sela, Avraham. "Politics, Identity and Peacemaking: The Arab Discourse on Peace with Israel in the 1990s." *Israel Studies* 10, no. 2 (2005): 15–72.

Sewell, William H., Jr. "Geertz, Cultural Systems, and History: From Synchrony to Transformation." *Representations*, no. 59 (1997): 42.

Shaham, Ron. "Christian and Jewish 'Waqf' in Palestine during the Late Ottoman Period." *Bulletin of the School of Oriental and African Studies* 54, no. 3 (1991): 460–72.

Shankland, David. *The Alevis in Turkey: The Emergence of a Secular Islamic Tradition*. London: Routledge, 2003.

———. *Islam and Society in Turkey*. Huntingdon, UK: Eothen Press, 1999.

Shapiro, Haim. "Quest for New Jerusalem Patriarch Set in Motion." *Jerusalem Post*, March 7, 1990.

Silberman, Neil Asher. *Digging for God and Country: Exploration in the Holy Land, 1799–1917*. New York: Doubleday, 1982.

Smith, Jonathon Z. *To Take Place: Toward Theory and Ritual*. Chicago: University of Chicago Press, 1987.

——. "The Wobbling Pivot." In *Map Is Not Territory*, 88–103. Leiden: Brill, 1978.

Sorabji, Cornelia. "Bosnian Neighbourhoods Revisited: Tolerance, Commitment and Komšiluk in Sarajevo." In *On the Margins of Religion*, ed. F. Pine and J.Pina-Cabral, 97–112. Oxford: Berghahn, 2008.

——. "Islamic Revival and Marriage in Bosnia." *Journal of the Institute of Muslim Minority Affairs* 9, no. 2 (1988): 331–37.

Sprinzak, Ehud. "Extremism and Violence in Israel: The Crisis of Messianic." *Annals of the American Academy of Political and Social Science* 555, no. 1 (1998): 114–26.

Stepan, Alfred, and Charles Taylor, eds. *Boundaries of Toleration*. New York: Columbia University Press, 2014.

Sternthal, Tamar. "'The Los Angeles Times' And Temple Mount Provocations." *CAMERA*, October 28, 2012.

Stewart, Susan. *On Longing: Narratives of the Miniature, the Gigantic, the Souvenir, the Collection*. Durham, NC: Duke University Press, 1993.

Stoyanov, Yuri. "On Some Parallels Between Anatolian and Balkan Heterodox Islamic and Christian Traditions and the Problem of their Coexistence and Interaction in the Ottoman Period." In *Syncretismes et heresies dans l'Orient seljoukide et ottoman (XIVe–XVIIIe siècle)*, ed. Gilles Veinstein, Collection Turcica 9, 75–178. Paris: Peeters, 2005.

Supreme Muslim Council. *Al-Jami'a al-Arabiyya*, no. 738 (December 1, 1931): 21.

Svensson, Isak. "Fighting with Faith: Religion and Conflict Resolution in Civil Wars." *Journal of Conflict Resolution* 51, no. 6 (2007): 930–47.

Tanyeri-Erdemir, Tuğba. "A Tale of Three Hagia Sophias: Conversion, Museumification, Contestation." Paper delivered at the University of Pittsburgh, April 13, 2013.

Tanyeri-Erdemir, Tuğba, Rabia Harmanşah, and Robert Hayden. "Serçeşme'den Hacıbektaş Müzesi'ne: Kültür mirası olan bir mekanda ritüel ve kurumsal pratikler." In *Hacı Bektaş Veli güneşte zerresinden, deryada katresinden*, eds. Pınar Ecevitoğlu, Ali Murat İrat, and Ayhan Yalçınkaya, 437–43. Ankara: Dipnot Yayınevi, 2010.

Tarrow, Sidney. *The New Transactional Activism*. Cambridge: Cambridge University Press, 2005.

Te Brake, Wayne. "Emblems of Coexistence in a Confessional World." In *Living with Religious Diversity in Early-Modern Europe*, eds. Scott C. Dixon and Mark Greengrass, 53–80. Surrey, UK: Ashgate, 2009.

Tekinalp, V. Macit. "Palace-Churches of the Anatolian Seljuks: Tolerance or Necessity?" *Byzantine and Modern Greek Studies* 33, no. 2 (2009): 148–67.

Teissier, Henri. *Chrétiens en Algérie: Un partage d'espérance.* Paris: Desclée de Brouwer, 2002.

Tidwell, A. *Conflict Resolved?* New York: Pinter Press, 1998.

Tilly, Charles. "Micro, Macro or Megrim." In *Stories, Identities and Political Change,* 69–77. Lanham, MD: Rowman & Littlefield, 2002.

Tilly, Charles, and Sidney Tarrow. *Contentious Politics.* Boulder, CO: Paradigm, 2007.

"The Tunnel Crisis." *Journal of Palestine Studies* 26, no. 2 (Winter 1997): 95–101.

Toameh, Abu Khaled, and Tovah Lazaroff. "Abbas: Arabs Erred in Rejecting 1947 Partition Plan." *Reuters,* October 30, 2011.

Toft, Monica Duffy. "Issue Indivisibility and Time Horizons as Rationalist Explanations for War." *Security Studies* 15, no. 1 (2006): 34–69.

Tökin, Füruzan Hüsrev. "Mevlevîlik: Mevlâna ve Sema." *Türk Düşüncesi* 7, no 4 (1957): 23–28.

Tsimhoni, Dafhne. "The Shihab Al-DIN Mosque affair in Nazareth: A Case Study of Muslim–Christian–Jewish Relations in the State of Israel." In *Holy Places in the Israeli Palestinian Conflict: Confrontation and Co-Existence,* ed. Marshall Breger, Yitzhak Reiter, and Leonard Hammer, 193–230. New York: Routledge, 2010.

Tuan, Y. 1979. "Thought and Landscape." In *The Interpretation of Ordinary Landscape,* ed. D. W. Meinig, 89–102. New York: Oxford University Press.

UNESCO. "Initiative on Heritage of Religious Interest." http://whc.unesco.org/en/religious-sacred-heritage/.

———. "Jerusalem and the Implementation of 23 C/ Resolution 11.3." July 17, 1986. http://unesdoc.unesco.org/images/0006/000695/069594eo.pdf.

UNHRC 13th Session, Agenda item 7, Document GE 10-12403, March 13, 2010.

UN Secretariat. *The Holy Places.* United Nations Conciliation Commission for Palestine, Committee on Jerusalem. April 8, 1949. Available at *MidEastWeb,* http://www.mideastweb.org/un_palestine_holy_places_1.htm. Accessed November 26, 2009.

Uriely, Natan, Aviad Israeli, and Arie Reichel. "Identity and Residents' Attitudes Toward Heritage Tourism Development: The Case of Nazareth." *Journal of Hospitality & Tourism Research* 27, no. 1 (2003): 69–84.

Van der Leeuw, G. *Religion in Essence and Manifestation,* vol. 2. 1933. Repr., New York: Harper & Row, 1963.

———. *Religion in Essence and Manifestation.* Princeton, NJ: Princeton University Press, 1986.

Van der Veer, Peter. *Religious Nationalism: Hindus and Muslims in India.* Berkeley: University of California Press, 1994.

Vesely, Dalibor. *Architecture in the Age of Divided Representation: The Question of Creativity in the Shadow of Production.* Cambridge, MA: MIT Press, 2004.

Vilnai, Zeev. *Sacred Gravestones in Eretz Israel,* vol. 2. Jerusalem: Ahiever, 1996.

Vryonis, Speros. *The Decline of Medieval Hellenism in Asia Minor and the Process of Islamization from the Eleventh Through the Fifteenth Century*. Berkeley: University of California Press, 1986.

Wagner, Matthew. "'Lost' Synagogue Reopens in Jerusalem's Muslim Quarter." *Jerusalem Post*, October 15, 2008. http://www.jpost.com/Jewish-World/Jewish-News/Lost-synagogue-reopens-in-Jerusalems-Muslim-Quarter.

Walsh, Edward. "Neighbors Are Foes in Hebron." *Washington Post*, November 5, 1982.

Weiner, Justin R. "The Temporary International Presence in the City of Hebron ('TIPH'): A Unique Approach to Peacekeeping." *Wisconsin International Law Journal* 16 (1997): 281–351.

Werbner, Pnina. "Essentialising Essentialism, Essentialising Silence: Ambivalence and Multiplicity in the Construction of Racism and Ethnicity." In *Debating Cultural Hybridity: Multi-Cultural Identities and the Politics of Anti-Racism*, ed. P. Werbner and T. Modood, 226–54. London: Zed, 1997.

Werbner, Pnina, and Helene Basu, eds. *Embodying Charisma: Modernity, Locality and the Performance of Emotion in Sufi Cults*. London: Routledge, 1998.

White, Jenny B. *Islamist Mobilization in Turkey*. Seattle: University of Washington Press, 2002.

White, Paul J., and Joost Jongerden, eds. *Turarkey's Alevi Enigma*. Leiden: Brill, 2003.

Wolff, Kurt H., ed. and trans. *The Sociology of Georg Simmel*. New York: Free Press, 1950.

Wolper, Ethel Sara. "Khidr, Elwan Celebi and the Conversion of Sacred Sanctuaries in Anatolia." *Muslim World*, 90 (2000): 309–22.

Yousef, Omar, Rassem Khamaisi, Abdallah Owais, and Rami Nasrallah. *Jerusalem and Its Hinterland*. Jerusalem: International Peace and Cooperation Center, 2008.

Yürekli-Görkay, Zeynep. *Architecture and Hagiography in the Ottoman Empire: The Politics of Bektashi Shrines in the Classical Age*. Birmingham Byzantine and Ottoman Studies. Surrey, UK: Ashgate, 2012.

Zachariadou, Elizabeth. "Notes sur la population de L'Asie Mineure Turque au XIVe siècle." *Byzantinische Forschungen* 12 (1987): 223–31.

Zagorin, Perez. *How the Idea of Religious Toleration Came to the West*. Princeton, NJ: Princeton University Press, 2003.

Zander, Walter. "On the Settlement of Disputes About the Christian Holy Places." *Israel Law Review* 8, no. 3 (1973): 331–66.

Zeidan, David. "The Copts: Equal, Protected or Persecuted? The Impact of Islamization on Muslim–Christian Relation in Modern Egypt." *Islam and Christian Muslim Relations* 10, no. 1 (1999): 53–67.

Zertal, Idith, and Akiva Eldar. *Lords of the Land: The War Over Israel's Settlements in the Occupied Territories 1967–2007*, trans. V. Eden. New York: Nation Books, 2007.

CONTRIBUTORS

EDITORS

Elazar Barkan is professor of international and public affairs at the School of International and Public Affairs, Columbia University, and the director of its Human Rights Concentration as well as the director of the University's Institute for the Study of Human Rights. He was the founding director of the Institute for Historical Justice and Reconciliation (IHJR). His research focuses on human rights, historical redress, conflict resolution, and reconciliation. Professor Barkan's recent books include *The Rites of Return: The Failure of Minority Repatriation* (with Howard Adelman, Columbia University Press, 2011); *The Guilt of Nations: Restitution and Negotiating Historical Injustices* (2000); *Claiming the Stones/Naming the Bones: Cultural Property and the Negotiation of National and Ethnic Identity* (edited with Ronald Bush, 2003); *Taking Wrongs Seriously: Apologies and Reconciliation* (edited with Alexander Karn, 2006); and *Shared History—Divided Memory. Jews and Others in Soviet Occupied Poland, 1939–1941* (edited with Elizabeth A. Cole and Kai Struve, 2008).

Karen Barkey is professor of sociology and history and the director of the Institute for Religion, Culture, and Public Life at Columbia University.

Her book *Empire of Difference* was awarded the 2009 Barrington Moore Award from the Comparative Historical Sociology section at the American Sociology Association and the 2009 J. David Greenstone Book Prize from the Politics and History section at the Political Science Association. She has written extensively about toleration and coexistence in the Ottoman Empire and other similar empires. Her first book, *Bandits and Bureaucrats: The Ottoman Route to State Centralization* (1994), studies Ottoman strategies of control. It won the Allan Sharlin Memorial Award for outstanding book of the year in Social Science History, 1995, Social Science History Association.

AUTHORS

Dionigi Albera is director of research at the French National Center for Scientific Research (CNRS) and director of the Institute of Mediterranean, European, and Comparative Ethnology based in Aix-en-Provence (Aix-Marseille University-CNRS). His research interests include mobility, forms of domestic organization, and interfaith mixing in the context of monotheistic religions. His work on religious mixing in the Mediterranean has been quite influential in the debates on sharing and its antecedents. A recent book edited with Maria Couroucli (*Sharing Sacred Spaces in the Mediterranean: Christians, Muslims, and Jews at Shrines and Sanctuaries*, 2012) also appeared in French, Spanish, and Italian.

Rabia Harmanşah is a Ph.D. candidate in anthropology at the University of Pittsburgh. She did her fieldwork in Cyprus between 2010 and 2012 with the support of Wenner-Gren Foundation and is currently working on her dissertation, "Social Forgetting in a Post-conflict Landscape: The Case of Cyprus." She participated in the research project "Antagonistic Tolerance: A Comparative Analysis of Competitive Sharing of Religious Sites" by Robert M. Hayden and the "Cyprus Critical History Archive Project" at the Association for Historical Dialogue and Research and PRIO Cyprus Center.

CONTRIBUTORS | 397

Robert M. Hayden is professor of anthropology, law, and public and international affairs at the University of Pittsburgh, where he is also director of the Center for Russian and East European Studies. Professor Hayden has done extensive fieldwork in India and the Balkans on various topics in legal and political anthropology, especially on topics of ethno-national conflict and coexistence, ethnographically and traced through long periods of time. Hayden's article, "Antagonistic Tolerance: Competitive Sharing of Religious Sites in South Asia and the Balkans," in *Current Anthropology* (2002) established a paradigm for looking at contested sharing of religious sites through time in widely varying regions and historical periods. At present he is directing an international, multidisciplinary project on "Antagonistic Tolerance: A Comparative Analysis of Competitive Sharing of Religious Sites," funded by the National Science Foundation and the Wenner-Gren Foundation for Anthropological Research, with research conducted in Bulgaria, India, Mexico, Portugal, Turkey, and Peru; for further information see http://www.ucis.pitt.edu/antagonistictolerance/AT_Main_Page.html.

Tuğba Tanyeri-Erdemir is the deputy director of the Center for Science and Society and a lecturer in the graduate program in architectural history at Middle East Technical University, Ankara, Turkey. Her research interests include ethnographic investigations of converted historic religious buildings, cultural heritage management of multilayered sacred sites, and reutilization and museumification of religious heritage. Dr. Tanyeri-Erdemir has participated in numerous international interdisciplinary research projects. Most recently she was a team member of the "Antagonistic Tolerance: A Comparative Analysis of Competitive Sharing of Religious Sites" project funded by Wenner-Gren and National Science Foundation and the leader of the Turkish team of FP7 project "RELIGARE: Religious Diversity and Secular Models in Europe."

Rassem Khamaisi is professor in the Department of Geography and Environmental Studies and head of The Jewish-Arab Center at the University of Haifa. He is an urban and regional planner and geographer, specializing in urban and rural geography. The main focus of his efforts is geography and planning among the Arab Palestinians in Israel and the Palestinians in the Palestinian territory and Jerusalem, concentrating on public administration and participation and urban management. His publications (both singly and coauthored) in the field of policy research on urban planning and development in Jerusalem and among the Arabs in Israel include "The Wall of Annexation and Expansion: Its Impact on the Jerusalem Area" and, "The Impact of the Wall the Arabs in Israel." He managed a planning project funded by the Internal Ministry and Israeli Land Administration Office and the Prime Minister's Office. In addition, he is head of planning and research staff at the International Peace and Cooperation Center (IPCC), Jerusalem, as well as the manager of the private Center for Planning and Studies (CPS), which engages in urban strategy planning and management. He initiated and led a project of doing plans for Palestinian villages and towns in area C in the West Bank.

Glenn Bowman is reader in social anthropology and director of research of the School of Anthropology and Conservation at the University of Kent, Canterbury, UK. His research on the circumstances making for harmony or antagonism between social groups within diverse communities, with particular focus on religious sites, has illuminated the nature of social relations in Israel/Palestine as well as the "former Yugoslavia." His essay, "Orthodox-Muslim Interactions at 'Mixed Shrines' in Macedonia," in the edited volume *Eastern Christians in Anthropological Perspective* (2010) explores the respective attitudes of Christians and Muslims across a range of shared holy religious sites in Macedonia and has been influential in establishing a model for investigating social coexistence and intercommunal relations. His recent edited collection, *Sharing the Sacra* (2013), extends this investigation into regions as diverse as China, Vietnam, Sri Lanka, Nepal, Turkey, Morocco, and Tunisia.

David Henig is lecturer in social anthropology at the School of Anthropology and Conservation, University of Kent. His research, conducted mainly in the Balkans and Central Asia, focuses largely on vernacular

Islam, sacred landscape, and exchange theory. He has coauthored numerous articles on the Islamic dream tradition, dervish orders, Muslim politics in Bosnia-Herzegovina, postsocialism, and anthropological research, including the coedited special issue *Being Muslim in the Balkans: Ethnographies of Identity, Politics and Vernacular Islam in South-East Europe* (2013, *Anthropological Journal of European Cultures*). He is currently coediting the book *Economies of Favour After Socialism* (to be published in 2015).

Wendy Pullan is head of research and director of the Martin Centre for Architectural and Urban Studies in the Department of Architecture at the University of Cambridge. She was principal investigator for "Conflict in Cities and the Contested State," an international and multidisciplinary research project based in the UK and funded by the ESRC's Large Grants Programme, and is now director of the Centre for Urban Conflicts Research. She received the Royal Institute of British Architects' inaugural President's Award for University-Led Research for work on "Conflict in Cities." Dr. Pullan has published widely on Mediterranean and Middle Eastern architecture and cities, especially Jerusalem, and has advised on issues to do with urban uncertainty. Her recent publications include: *Locating Urban Conflicts* (co-edited, 2013) and *The Struggle for Jerusalem's Holy Places* (co-authored, 2013). She is a Fellow of Clare College, Cambridge. Further details: www.conflictincities.org; www.urbanconflicts.arct.cam.ac.uk.

Yitzhak Reiter is a professor of Middle East and Israel studies. He chairs the Department of Land-of-Israel Studies at Ashkelon Academic College. His academic expertise in is modern Middle East politics and history; conflict resolution at sacred sites and holy places; the political history of Palestine, Jordan, and Israel; Islamic law and religious institutions, and comparative perspectives on minority-majority conflict. His recent books include: *A City with a Mosque in Its Heart: Conflict Resolution at Holy Places: The Case of the Beer-Sheva Grand Mosque* (with Lior Lehrs, 2013) (in Hebrew); a chapter in *Sacred Space in Israel and Palestine: Religion and*

Politics, edited by Marshall J. Breger, Yitzhak Reiter, and Leonard Hammer (2012); *War, Peace and International Relations in Islam: Muslim Scholars on Peace Accords with Israel* (2011); *National Minority, Regional Majority: Palestinian Arabs Versus Jews in Israel* (2009); and *Jerusalem and Its Role in Islamic Solidarity* (2008).

Mete Hatay is senior research consultant at the Peace Research Institute Oslo (PRIO) Cyprus Centre, where he works on demography, migration, and Islam in Cyprus. He is the author of numerous articles and reports on identity, displacement, and the politics of demography. For the past two years, he has been conducting research on cultural heritage politics as part of a four-year EU-funded project on conflict and cultural heritage.

INDEX

Italic page numbers refer to illustrations.

Abbas, Mahmoud, 269*n*46
Abbasids, 203
Abdulmecid (sultan of Ottoman Empire), 206–7
Abed al-Samad site, Nazareth, 278
Absentees' Property Law, 283, 323
Abu El-Haj, Nadia, 187
accommodation: of Catholic establishment, 7; in Cyprus, 20; and homogenization process, 3; of imperial states, 4; and interreligious relations, 170; in Jerusalem, 163, 223; legacies of, 19; by minorities, 11; in Ottoman Empire, 34, 35, 47–48, 49, 51; and state policies, 42, 43
Adanir, Fikret, 51
Afana, Hussam al-Din, 318, 334*n*40
Afandy, Asa'ad, 283
Africa, 3
Agioi Saranda, Cyprus, 75, 85, 87
Ahmad, Salman Abu, 284
Ahmet I (sultan of Ottoman Empire), 203
Ajamian, Shahe, 224
Ajvatovica pilgrimage: as all-male pilgrimage, 142, 146; changes in, 144, 145–47; and choreography of shared sacred sites, 141–43, 145–47; and Islamic Community, 141–42, 145–47; Karići pilgrimage compared to, 136, 142, 144, 145, 147; and local dervish communities, 146; media coverage for pilgrimages, 144; multiple actors and discourses of, 156; politicization of, 145; Turkish folk groups invited to, 146
Ajvaz-dedo, 141
Akshardham temple, Gujarat, 18
Ak Yazili Baba, 362
al-Aqsa Association, 196*n*35, 306–7, 310, 314, 318, 323, 327
Al-Aqsa Intifada. *See* Second Intifada (2000–2006)

al-Aqsa Mosque, Jerusalem: Israeli Muslim tourist groups visiting, 177, 178; and Marwani Prayer Hall, 196n39; Muslim narratives of, 12–13, 164, 188, 193n6, 193n7; photographs displayed in al-Wad Street shops, 174; Sharon's visit to, 26, 164, 196n39, 237, 239, 242–45, 263, 266n11; and Western Wall Tunnel, 241

al-Aqsa University, Jerusalem, 303

al-Asali, Kamil Jamil, 302, 317

Albania, 57

Albera, Dionigi: on group identities, 10; on power relations between religious groups, 87; on religious boundaries, 78, 80, 81; on religious mixture, 6–7, 57; on social complexity, 134

Alboty, Mohamad Ramadan, 288

al-Dajani, Muhammad Khayr, 307

Alevi-Bektaşis: assimilation of, 346; and cem ceremonies, 344, 345, 357, 365n25, 366n36; in Cyprus, 94n15; and Hacı Bektaş shrine complex, 342, 353, 354, 357, 359, 360, 365–66n34; religious practices as forbidden, 346–47; religious practices at shrines, 347, 349, 354, 357–58; and state-society relations, 20, 337, 345, 361; teachings of, 341; thresholds as holy to, 355. *See also* Bektaşi Order

Algeria: and African martyrs, 100; Catholic Church in, 10, 23–24, 98–101, 114, 119, 120, 123, 124; continuity between colonial and postcolonial Algeria, 7, 97–98; conversion to Christianity, 107–8, 111–13, 114, 120, 121, 123, 124, 125; conversion to Islam, 100; European settlers in, 99, 123; independence of, 97–98, 114, 125; Islam in, 98, 114–19; jihadist groups' elimination of Christians in, 98; and orphanages for Arab children, 109, 110; peace process and politics of reconciliation, 119–20; reduction of Christian presence in, 114–15, 125; reinvention of African past of Catholic Church, 100, 104, 106, 109, 116, 123; state policies on conditions for non-Muslim worship, 121, 129n47; synagogues in, 113; violence in, 114–15, 116, 117, 125. *See also* Our Lady of Africa (Marian sanctuary), Algiers

al-Hadi, Amin Abd, 303

al-Husayni, Haj Amin, 301–2

Ali, Muhammad, 217

Ali (Muhammad's cousin), 94n13, 341

Ali Faik Efendi (sheikh), 80

al Jabha (the Front), 284, 286, 287

Allenby, Edmund, 202, 207

All-Muslim Congress, 303

Aloni, Shulamit, 267n26

al-Quds University, 174

Al-Rashedia School, Nazareth, 283

Alrefae, Osama, 288

al-Shafi'i, Muhammad b. Idris, 319

al-Shikh Amer site, Nazareth, 278

al-Wad Street, Jerusalem: checkpoint at end of, 179, 180, 182; and Cotton Market, 174–75, 175, 177, 188; as heterogeneous, 166; and identity cards, 172, 195n24; and interreligious relations, 27, 168, 179–80; Islamic content of goods, 173–76, 179, 187, 188, 195n29; and Israeli municipal tax, 173, 195n25; and Israeli Muslim tourists from northern Israel, 177–79, 178, 196n35; and Israeli/Palestin-

ian conflict, 171–72, 195n22; and Israeli separation barrier, 171–72, 177, 195n22; Jewish Israelis visiting, 179–80, 183; and Jewish settlements, 180, 183; location of, 166, 170–71; Mamluk religious structures on cross streets, 171; map showing shops selling Islamic goods, *173*; marketplace expansion in, 27, 172–73; mixed populations of, 170; as Muslims' route to Friday prayers, 171, 176–77, *181*; and permeability of sacred space, 168–70, 191, 192; religio-political identities in, 167, 168, 174, 175–76, 178–79, 183, 187–88, 189, 191–92; as secular market area, 166–68, 188, 195n29; Sharon's home spanning, 180, *181*; and underground sites, 183; views of, *167*, *178*
al-Zawiya al-Qalandariyya, 302
al-Zayn, Muhammad Badr, 307
An, Ahmet, 95n35
Anatolia: and Bektaşi order, 341; Islam in, 74–75; and Ottoman Empire, 47, 48–50, 51, 52, 53, 59, 74, 342; and Seljuk Empire, 50–51, 53, 59; and shared sacred sites, 50; Turkish settlers to Cyprus from, 84
Anderson, Benedict, 167
Andezian, Sossie, 225
Andrew, Saint (Apostolos Andreas), 78, 83–84, 91
antagonistic tolerance (AT): and coexistence, 11, 44–45, 59; and competitive shared sacred sites, 10, 132, 199, 337–39, 361; and conflict and sharing, 133; and contested spaces, 88; context of, 338–39; and group competition, 10–11, 338; and political violence at shared sacred sites, 236, 265n1; and religioscapes, 338, 361–62; and violence, 338–39
Anthony of Padua, Saint, 57
anthropological studies: and essentializing collective identities, 133; and role of agency in social anthropology, 45; of shared sacred sites, 8; of violence, 38. *See also* ethnographies
Apostolos Andreas Monastery, Cyprus, 71, 78, 83–84
Arab Christian villages, 109
Arab Orthodox Society, 234n86
Arab Palestinians: and conflict of Shihab al-Deen Mosque, 288; conflicts between Arab subgroups, 277; diaspora of, 275, 276; in Israel, 270, 274–77, 278, 281, 287, 288–89, 316; and Nabka, 279, 280; in Palestinian Territories, 275
Arab uprising of 1929, 184
Arafat, Yasser, 240, 241, 244, 288
Arendt, Hannah, 188–89
Arghbariya, Muhammas Sulayman, 306–7
Ariel, Uri, 246
Armenian Orthodox Church: and Altar of the Nativity, 211; and Church of the Anastasis, 200, 201, 202, 204, 206, 230n18; and Church of the Nativity, 212–13, 232n39; and Edicule, 211, 215–16; and Israel, 223–25, 227, 228; and Ottoman Empire, 227; and status quo agreements, 211, 212; and Tomb of the Virgin, 211
Arsenije III Carnojevic, 21
Asaliya, Qadi Tawfiq, 307
Asia, 3
Asia Minor, 51, 52

404 | INDEX

assimilation, 3, 11, 41, 50, 76, 346
Atanas, Saint, 362
Atatürk, Mustafa Kemal, 343, 349, 361–62, 364n17
Ateret Cohanim (Jewish settler group), 184, 223
Athos, Saint, 53
Augustine, Saint, 106, 107, 116
Aupick, Jacques, 205–6
Austro-Hungarian Empire, 136–37
Authority of Antiquities (IAA), 305, 310, 330
Ayioi Iliofotoi festival, 89–90
Ayios Therapon, 85
Ayodhya, Uttar Pradesh, India, 17, 130
Ayyubid dynasty, 202

Babri Masjid (mosque), India, 5, 18–19
Bağişkan, Tuncer, 77, 80, 85, 95n40
Balım Sultan, 341, 349, 354, 356, 357
Balivet, Michel, 50–51
Balkans: and Bektaşi order, 341; and conflict in shared sacred sites, 92, 155; ethnic cleansing in, 57; and Great Serbian Migrations, 21; Islamization in, 52–55, 138; and Muslim cult of Virgin Mary, 124; and Ottoman Empire, 47, 51, 52, 53, 59, 131; shared sacred sites in, 1, 26, 57–58, 131, 132–36, 338. *See also specific countries*
Barak, Ehud, 243, 284
Barkan, Elazar, 14, 25, 135, 136
Barkey, Karen, 4, 135, 136
Barth, Fredrik, 42, 48
Battal Ghazi monument, Nakoleia/Seyyit Gazi, 49
Battle of Hattin (1187), 283

Battle of Kosovo (1389), 5
Battle of Manzikert (1071), 48
Bauman, Zygmunt, 190
Beckingham, Charles, 75
Begin, Menachem, 220
Beinisch, Dorit, 311
Bektaşi Order: and Hacı Bektaş shrine complex, 360; and Hacı Bektaş Veli, 340–41; religious practices of, 86, 94n13, 344; *semah* ceremonies, 344; and state-society relations, 343, 345, 361; suppression of, 342, 346; thresholds as holy to, 355. *See also* Alevi-Bektaşis
Ben Badis, Abdelhamid, 114
Benvenisti, Meron, 214
Berbers, 100, 120
Berger, Agarithe, 102–3, 107, 126n11
Bernadette of Lourdes, 102
Bertram, Anton, 207
Bethlehem, West Bank: Bethlehem 2000 project, 281; Jordanian rule of, 279, 290; Omar Ibn al-Khattab Mosque in, 290; Rachel's Tomb, 209, 237, 245, 248, 264. *See also* Church of the Nativity, Bethlehem
Beyazid II (sultan of the Ottoman Empire), 42
Beyşehir Lake islands, 49
Bhagalpur riots of 1989, 17–18
Bigelow, Anna, 3, 23
Billig, Michael, 176, 189
Bonaparte, Louis-Napoléon, 205
borders: of Jerusalem, 238; as zones of ambiguity and contest, 155. *See also* boundary relations
Bosnia/Bosnia-Herzegovina: and coexistence between Islam and communist ideology, 137; contested sacred sites

INDEX | 405

in Central Bosnian highlands, 135, 138–43, 149–54; foreign Islamic humanitarian organizations in, 131, 147–48, 153, 160n39; intracommunal struggles of Bosnian Muslims, 24, 26, 131, 135–36, 141, 144–48, 149, 150–54, 157n6; Islam in, 24, 131, 135, 136–38, 147, 149, 159n34; and Islamization, 148, 152, 160n40; and Ottoman Empire, 54; shared sacred sites in, 132, 133–34, 135, 136, 157n6; Sufism in, 137–38, 140, 141, 146, 147, 148–49, 151, 159n34; transformations of sacred landscapes in, 131–32. *See also* Ajvatovica pilgrimage; Islamic Community (IC) of Bosnia and Herzegovina; Karići pilgrimage; prayers for rain (*dove za kišu*)
Bosnian war (1992–95), 139, 143, 150
Bouchardon, Edmé, 107
Boudhieh, Ibtissam, 255
boundary relations: across groups, 36, 38–40; fluidity of, 59; and identities, 42–43, 48, 59. *See also* religious boundaries
Bouteflika, Abdelaziz, 119
Bowman, Glenn: on agency, 134–35; on centrality of shared sacred sites, 14; on coexistence, 8, 59–60; on economic benefit of shared sacred sites, 89; on historical continuity in competition for ownership of space, 15; on intrareligious power struggles, 9; on mixing of sites, 30n24; on narratives of shared sacred sites, 12; on state-society relations, 24; on Sveti Nikola, 58
Breslov activists, 248–49, 259–60
Bringa, Tone, 137, 151

Brotherhood of the Holy Sepulchre, 222–23, 224, 228
Brubaker, Rogers, 30n24, 42
Bryer, Anthony, 53
Bulgaria, 337, 362
Burg, Avraham, 267n26
Bush, George W., 285
Byzantine Empire: architecture of, 104; cultural exchanges with Seljuk Empire, 48–51; and Ottoman Empire's conquest of Constantinople, 47; and shared sacred sites, 4, 46, 361

Cardio Maximus, 171, 194n20
Casola, Pietro, 202
Catholic Church: accommodation of, 7; in Algeria, 10, 23–24, 98–101, 114, 119, 120, 123, 124; and Church of the Anastasis, 206; and internationalization of "Greater Jerusalem," 221; and Israel, 220, 221–22, 225, 227, 228; and Jerusalem, 203; and mixing of communities, 22; and Ottoman Empire, 227. *See also* Latin Franciscans
Cave of the Patriarchs, Hebron: and interreligious relations, 250, 251, 252, 264; as Israeli national heritage site, 245–48; and Muslim narrative of Joseph's Tomb, 252–53; role of religion in violence relative to politics, 237
cemeteries: discrimination in treatment of, 317, 324–26; and Islamic Movement, 317; as sacred space, 300, 303, 318–24. *See also* Mamilla Cemetery, Jerusalem
Center for Constitutional Rights, 329
Central Africa, and conversion to Christianity, 108–9

Central Conference of American Rabbis, 324

centrality of shared sacred sites: and coexistence in shared sacred sites, 13; and conflict in shared sacred sites, 12, 13–14; and indivisibility of shared sacred sites, 13, 16; malleability of, 263; marginal sites distinguished from, 13; and perceived threat, 13–14, 29n15; questions concerning, 3, 13–15; and violence, 237, 248, 263

Certeau, Michel de, 124

Chapel of Adam, Jerusalem, 205

Chapel of the Ascension, Jerusalem, 200, 209

Charlemagne, 229n7

Charles X (king of France), 98

Choniates, Niketas, 48–49

choreographies of sacred spaces: and centrality of shared sacred sites, 14; changes in, 8, 135, 145, 147, 156–57; and coexistence in shared sacred sites, 22; and conflict in shared sacred sites, 170; contradictions in, 135; and indivisibility of shared sacred sites, 17; influence of nonstate actors on, 12, 27, 98; and interreligious relations, 125–26; and intrareligious power relations, 131–32, 135–36, 144, 145–49, 156; and Museum of Tolerance, 299, 300; in Ottoman Empire, 59, 60, 199, 228–29n1; and political factors, 97, 131, 236, 246, 249; and prayers for rain, 136, 141, 149–54; and spaces of temporary submission, 76, 80–81, 91; and state-society relations, 1, 21, 27–28, 123, 125, 199, 214–20, 222, 226–28; strategy of, 124; and tolerance, 299–300, 306

Christians and Christianity: and Arab Palestinians, 109, 275, 276, 277; confessional struggles of, 22, 35, 39, 40; conversion to, 71, 74, 80–81, 82, 91, 92, 107–8, 111–13, 114, 120, 121, 123, 124, 125; crypto-Christianity, 53, 71, 74, 75, 91, 92; in Cyprus, 71, 74, 75, 77, 78–81, 82, 89; erosion of Middle East presence of, 3–4; and hierarchy of holy sites, 292n4; and Holy Land, 274; and Islamization in Balkans, 52–53; and Israel, 4, 227; and narratives of shared sacred sites, 12, 200, 201; Nazareth's Christian population, 278, 279, 280–81, 282, 286, 289, 290; and Nazareth's place in Christianity, 14–15, 277–78, 279, 282; Orthodox Christian celebrations, 150, 200; in Ottoman Empire, 4, 34, 35, 36, 46–57; role of Jews in Christian society, 7; and shared sacred sites in Jerusalem, 9, 163, 164, 199–204, 214; use of Muslim amulets, 77

Christofias, Dimitris, 71

Church of St. George, Madaba, Jordan, 194n20

Church of the Anastasis, Jerusalem: and Armenian Orthodox Church, 200, 201, 202, 204, 206, 230n18; and centrality of shared sacred sites, 15; and choreography of shared sacred sites, 202–4, 207; Christian denominations claiming, 9, 199, 206, 207; and coexistence in shared sacred sites, 14, 27; and conflict in shared sacred sites, 200–204, 217–20; and Greek Orthodox Church, 200–201, 202, 204–5, 206, 210, 222–23, 225, 232n38; and Latin Franciscans, 200,

201, 203, 204, 227, 232*n*38; Ottoman Empire's rules for coexistence at, 59; possessory rights to, 200–204, 207; and religious leaders' negotiation with state, 24; and Russian Orthodox Church, 205, 213–14; as shared sacred sites, 202; and state-society relations, 130, 199, 202–6; and status quo agreements, 199, 200–201, 206, 207, 208–12, 215, 225, 231*n*33; violence in, 232*n*38

Church of the Nativity, Bethlehem: Altar of the Manger, 211; Altar of the Nativity, 211; annual cleaning of, 212; and Armenian Orthodox Church, 212–13, 232*n*39; Christian denominations coexisting in, 9; and Greek Orthodox Church, 212–14, 225, 232*n*39; Grotto of, 211, 212–13, 225; and Latin Franciscans, 212–13, 214; and Omar Ibn al-Khattab Mosque, 290; possessory rights to, 200, 204, 205, 206, 209, 210, 211, 212, 213, 225; violence in, 212–14, 232*n*39

Church of the Transfiguration, Jebel et-Tur, 201, 229*n*4

Chyutin (architectural firm), 311

Cinquin, Anna, 102, 103, 107

Clinton, Bill, 242, 244

coexistence: and antagonistic tolerance, 11, 44–45, 59; conflict as complementary to, 38–39; debates on, 36–37; forms of, 6, 7–8, 37–38, 39, 44; meaning of, 7–10, 37; in Ottoman Empire, 34, 36, 46–47, 49. *See also* peaceful coexistence

coexistence in shared sacred sites: and centrality, 13; and characteristics of specific sites, 11; contingent aspects of, 134, 135; definition and practice of, 2–3; fluctuations in, 1–3, 6, 8, 17, 35, 133; latent conflict in, 6, 26, 45, 133, 336; and Mecca, 14; mediation and negotiation of otherness in, 33, 132; and movement to conflict, 2; multiplicity of forms of, 2, 8, 44; pragmatic forms of, 90, 132, 133; and religious rules, 2; and spaces of temporary submission, 73, 76–84; and state-society relations, 3, 10, 21; types and consequences of arrangements of, 6–11

Cohen, Raymond, 213, 214, 218–19, 231*n*33

Communist system, 137, 159*n*32

Conference of Non-aligned States, 137

conflict: coexistence as complementary to, 38–39; as form of coexistence, 6, 38; post conflict processes, 2, 3; resolution of, 300, 305–11, 326–29, 331; and studies of toleration, 46. *See also* Israeli/Palestinian conflict

conflict in shared sacred sites: and antagonistic tolerance, 133; in Central Bosnian highlands, 135, 138–43, 149–54; and centrality, 13; and characteristics of shared sacred sites, 11–12; and context of shared sacred sites, 2, 5, 8, 25, 28*n*5, 156; and Cyprus, 73, 84–88, 92, 93; and Dar es-Sultan, 217–20; and ethnoreligious groups, 132, 276–77, 283, 290, 292*n*4; fluctuations in, 1–3, 16–17, 27, 133; and Jerusalem, 163–64, 166, 170, 182–83, 190, 191–92, 235, 262, 274, 287; latent conflict of interests, 6, 26, 45, 133, 336; and maintenance of sharing, 3, 9; meaning of, 8;

conflict in shared sacred sites (*cont.*) multiplicity of forms of, 2, 9; and narratives of shared sacred sites, 12–13, 200, 201; and political factors, 2, 87, 97, 131, 148, 152, 220, 235–36, 248, 262; and religious extremism, 237, 248, 256, 259–60; and religious heterogeneity, 73, 84–88, 92, 204; and religious leaders, 23, 24–25, 30–31n29, 31n30, 214, 221–24, 236; and religious practice, 84, 86, 150–51, 152, 154; and state-society relations, 2, 10, 21–22, 27, 235–36, 339; and toleration, 84, 86, 87, 88, 290–91; and violence, 26–27, 28n5, 92, 170, 184, 235

conflict resolution: court as venue for, 326–29; and dispute over Museum of Tolerance, 300, 305–11; and legal regime, 300, 326–29; and scale shift, 300, 328–29, 331

Congregation of the Missionary Sisters of Our Lady of Africa (White Sisters), 108, 109, 110

Congress of Berlin (1878), 136, 206

Constantinople, Ottoman Empire's conquest of, 47, 54, 55

Constantinou, Costas M., 81

context of shared sacred sites: and conflict in shared sacred sites, 2, 5, 8, 25, 28n5, 156; everyday context, 136, 166, 168, 169, 187–91, 192, 200; in Macedonia, 8, 58, 134; in Ottoman Empire, 36

Copts: and Altar of the Nativity, 211; and Church of the Anastasis, 213; and Dar-es-Sultan, 217–20, 226; and Edicule, 211; in Egypt, 4, 10; and possessory rights to Chapel of the Ascension, 209; and Tomb of the Virgin, 211

Cordoba, Spain, 338

Cornell, Svante, 341

Cotton Market, Jerusalem, 174–75, *175*, 177, 188, 195n28

Couroucli, Maria, 57, 77

Crimean War, 9, 206, 207, 228n1

Croats, 132

Crusades, 21, 202, 250, 279, 283

cultural patrimony, sites of, 28n5

Cust, Lionel, 201, 208–12, 217–18, 230–31n25, 231n27

Cyprus: and *bayram* gift, 69–71, 72; British rule of, 10, 75, 81–82, 87; and contested spaces, 73, 84–88, 92, 93; and conversion to Christianity, 71, 74, 80–81, 82, 91, 92; and conversion to Islam, 86; and crypto-Christianity, 71, 74, 75, 91, 92; and difference, 72, 92–93; dominant ethnic groups in, 22, 82–83; and economic spaces, 27, 73, 78, 87, 88–90, 92–93; efficacious power of contested shared spaces, 84, 88; efficacious power of economic spaces, 89, 90, 92; efficacious power of spaces of temporary submission, 73, 76, 77–80, 82–83, 91, 92–93; foundation myths of shared sacred sites, 84–85, 95n39; Greek Cypriots of, 22, 69, 70, 71, 72, 74, 80, 82, 83–84, 87, 88, 90; indivisibility in territorial struggles, 16, 83–84; Islam established in, 73–76, 93n7, 94n15; nationalism in, 20, 72, 76, 82–83, 88, 91, 92; and Ottoman Empire, 70–71, 73; peaceful coexistence in, 70, 71–72, 75, 92; and persons adhering to blend of Islamic and Christian beliefs, 81–82, 95n31; and politics of heritage, 72; shared sacred sites in, 20, 26, 71, 72–73, 74; and spaces of temporary submission, 73, 76–84, 86, 88, 91, 92; state policies in, 70, 72; Tanzimat decree of 1856, 89; and tolerance, 71, 72; Turkish Cypriots of, 22, 69, 70, 71–72, 75, 77, 79, 80, 82–84, 88, 89, 90, 91, 94n15, 95n35

Dar es-Sultan, Jerusalem, 200, 204, 209, 217–20, 226
Derderian, Yeghishe, 224
Dermenghem, Emile, 113, 128n36
Desmarescaux, Etienne, 115
Diderot, Denis, 189
difference: boundaries defining, 42, 132–33; and Cyprus, 72, 92–93; inflexible and fixed markers of, 38, 40, 133; negotiation of, 34, 92–93
Digenis Akrites, Byzantine tale of, 49
Diodoros I (patriarch), 233n76
Dome of the Rock, Jerusalem: and conflict in shared sacred sites, 58, 164; as Islamic holy site, 164, 193n7; and Israeli Muslim tourists from north of Israel, 178, *178*; photographs displayed in al-Wad Street shops, 174; view from Western Wall, *166*
Druze, 275, 276, 277
Duijzings, Ger, 57–58, 137, 149, 159n32, 159n34
Dukat, Yusuf, 252
Dumper, Michael, 223
Dung Gate, Jerusalem, 180
Dupuch, Antoine-Adolphe, 100, 101–2, 103, 107

Durkheim, Emile, 123, 168
Duval, Léon-Etienne, 114

East Jerusalem: and Arab Palestinians, 276, 281; and families buried in Mamilla Cemetery, 307–8, 329; Israel's control of, 17, 188, 214, 222, 241; Jordanian rule of, 279, 303, 324
Edict of Nantes (1598), 39, 41
Edict of Tolerance (1782), 41
Edicule (tomb), Jerusalem, 205, 210, 211, 215
Egypt: and control of physical space within Holy Land churches, 9; Copts in, 4, 10; and Dar es-Sultan, 220; Nasserite Egypt, 218, 219
El Bayarek, 196n35
Eliade, Mircea, 169, 190, 194n12
Elijah, Prophet, 50
Elijah, Saint, 150
Elwan Celebi Tekke, Anatolia, 50
Emmett, Chad, 207
Englezakis, Benedict, 82
Eordegian, Marlen, 216
Erdengiz, Ahmet, 94n15
Erdoğan, Recep, 362
Ethiopia, 9, 217–20
Ethiopian Orthodox church, 217–20, 226
ethnic groups: agency of, 133; conflicts of, 5; in Cyprus, 82–84, 91–92; diversity in Ottoman Empire, 33–34, 47, 60; and nationalism, 82–84, 91, 131, 138, 145, 226, 228, 270, 274, 276, 289, 291; and pluralism, 8; political competition among, 10; separation after collapse of multiethnic empires, 30n24; and state-society relations, 2, 21, 22

ethnographies: and choreography of shared sacred sites, 155–56; and historical changes, 10, 36, 43; and historical contingencies, 133, 156; and intrareligious power relations, 135, 136, 151. *See also* anthropological studies

ethnoreligious groups: and agency of social actors, 131, 133, 134, 135, 155; and antagonistic tolerance, 132; and Arab Palestinians, 270, 288–89; and conflict in shared sacred sites, 132, 276–77, 283, 290, 292n4; and identities, 81; in Nazareth, 270, 275, 276–77, 281, 283, 287, 288–89, 290; and power relations, 154, 190

European Union, 121

Evkaf records, 86

Evyatar, Shmuel, 222

Falasha Jews, 219, 220

Fearon, James D., 29n16

Ferdinand I (king of Bohemia and Hungary), 203

First Intifada (1987), 163, 224, 256

First Lebanon War (1982), 220

Fotic, Aleksandar, 54

France: Catholic and Huguenots coexisting in, 39; and colonial Algeria, 23–24, 98–101; and July Monarchy, 98; and Nointel capitulations, 204; and Ottoman-French Capitulations, 201–2, 203, 227, 229n6; and Our Lady of Africa, 101, 102, 103, 104–5, 121

François I (king of France), 203

French Revolution, 205

French Ultramontanes, 205

Friedland, Roger, 28n1

Fromageau, Jean Eugéne, 104

Fundamental Agreement Between the Holy See and Israel (1993), 221–22

Gaudin, Jean-Claude, 122

Gaza, 214, 276

Geertz, Clifford, 43

Gehry, Frank, 305, 311, 315, 326

George, Saint, 50, 57, 150

Georgians, and Church of the Anastasis, 202, 204

Georgiou, Maria, 78

Gilo settlement, 223

Ginsburg, Yitchak, 255–56, 268n36

Gissin, Ra'anan, 243

Goddard, Stacie E., 16, 30n20

Golan Heights, 214

Goldstein, Baruch, 251, 252

Gracanica, 58

Gradeva, Rossitsa, 54, 55, 56

Greece, nationalism in, 71

Greek-Albanian borderland, 155

Greek identity, 10, 22

Greek Orthodox Church: and Arab Orthodox Society, 234n86; and Bethlehem, 290; and Church of the Anastasis, 200–201, 204–5, 206, 210, 222–23, 225, 232n38; and Church of the Nativity, 212–14, 225, 232n39; and Edicule, 20, 211, 215–16; Holy Cross celebrations, 213–14; and Israel, 222–23, 225, 227, 228, 233–34n76; in Jerusalem, 202, 203, 225; and Ottoman Empire, 57, 227; and status quo agreements, 210, 211, 212, 231n27, 232n38; and Tomb of the Virgin, 211

INDEX | 411

Greek War of Independence, 205
Green, Sarah, 155
Gregorios (patriarch), 205
group competition, and antagonistic tolerance, 10–11, 338
groupism, 42, 133

Habsburg Empire, 22–23, 41, 203
Hacı Bektaş Festival, 352, 353, 356, 357–58, 366n34
Hacı Bektaş shrine complex, Turkey: architectural features of, 347, 354–55; cemetery of dervishes in, 355; closing of, 343; and communal worship, 344, 345, 357–58, 366n36; and Hacı Bektaş Veli's tomb, 346, 347, 349–50, 353–56, 359, 365–66n34; and heterodox practices, 339–40, 343; and living quarters of *dedebaba,* 349, 365n31; as museum, 26, 340, 343, 345, 347, 349, 351, 352, 353, 354–57, 360–61; and Perşembeciler, 357; as pilgrimage site, 342, 347, 354, 360; plan of, *348*; ritual practices in museum grounds, 354–57, 359, 360; and state policies, 343, 351, 352, 353–54, 356, 360–61; Tekke Mosque in, 341, 345, 346, 349, 353; ticketed access to, 352, 353–54, 365–66n34
Hacı Bektaş Veli: as Anatolian mystic, 340–41; as proponent of tolerance, 343–44; tomb of, 346, 347, 349–50, 353–56, 359, 365–66n34
Hadžijahić, Muhamad, 150–51
Hagia Sophia, Istanbul: and neutralization of sacred space in public sphere, 15, 358; transformation into mosque, 338, 362

Hagia Sophia Museum, Iznik, 362
Hagia Sophia Museum, Trabzon, 362
Hajdar-dedo Karić, 138–39, 141, 147–48, 159n28
Hakim (khalif of Egypt), 229n7
Hala Sultan, 85
Hallaq, Wael, 319–20, 334n41
Hamam al-Ayn, Jerusalem, 174
Hamas, 248, 251, 253, 259
Hammad, Tahir, 303–4
Hanafi law, 54, 149
Haram al-Sharif/Temple Mount, Jerusalem: access to, 164–65, 182, 244; and al-Wad Street, 166, 171, 174, 176–77, 179, 182; archaeological sites near, *165*; centrality of, 14, 263; and choreographies of sacred space, 187; and First Jewish Temple, 182; indivisibility of, 17; and interreligious relations, 182–83, 187, 263; Jewish narrative of, 12, 193n6, 263–64; Muslim narrative of, 193n6, 263–64; and political factors, 265; Robinson's Arch, 184; sacralization of space outside of, 14, 165; and Second Jewish Temple, 182; Sharon's 2000 visit to, 26, 164, 196n39, 237, 239, 242–45, 263, 266n11; and Temple Mount Faithful movement, 237–38, 266n6; and underground sites, 183; view from Western Wall, *166*; and violence, 263; and Western Wall Tunnel, 184, 240, 241; Wilson's Arch, 184. *See also* al-Aqsa Mosque, Jerusalem
Har HaZeitim Cemetery, 303
Har Homa settlement, 223, 258
Harmanşah, Rabia, 11, 15, 20
Hasluck, F. W., 50, 53, 74–75, 85, 86

Hassner, Ron: on centrality of shared sacred sites, 13, 265n1; on classification of sacred sites, 11–12; on conflict in shared sacred sites, 133; on identitarian framework, 45; on indivisibility of shared sacred sites, 16, 30n18, 190, 191, 265n1; on religious leaders' role in conflict management of sacred sites, 24–25, 30–31n29, 31n30

Hatay, Mete, 10, 22

Hayden, Robert, 10–11, 22, 44–45, 88, 132–33, 265n1, 338

Hazreti Ömer *tekke*, 85

Hebrew University, Jerusalem, 303

Hebron/al-Khalil, West Bank: and interreligious relations, 274, 287; Jewish settlements of Kiryat Arba in, 249, 250, 251–52, 254; and Palestinian Authority, 245–46, 248–49; religious violence in, 236, 237, 245–46, 249, 250–52; view of "massacre in Hebron," 250–52. *See also* Cave of the Patriarchs, Hebron

Hecht, Richard, 28n1, 219, 220

Hellenism, 52, 71

Henig, David, 24, 45

Henry IV (king of France), 203

Herbert, Mary Elizabeth, 126n11

Herod (king of Judea), 182

Herzog, Chaim, 214

Herzog, Yaakov, 221

Hidrellez, Saint, 50

High Court of Israel: and discrimination in treatment of cemeteries, 317, 324–26; and Mamilla Cemetery, 302, 308–11, 312, 318–24, 326, 327, 330–31; and Museum of Tolerance's message of tolerance, 314–15, 317, 318, 325

High Islamic Council, 283

Hindu nationalist activism, 5

Holocaust, and Museum of Tolerance, 315, 316

Holy Land: archaeology of, 183; and changing phases of conflict in shared sacred sites, 9; control of physical space within churches, 9, 205–6; and domains sacralized by Christian narratives, 200; European invasion of, 289; pilgrimages to, 199–200; as shared sacred site, 14, 238; spatial meaning of, 238; transformation of control over, 274–76. *See also specific sites*

Holy Places Commission, 208

Holy Sepulchre, Jerusalem. *See* Church of the Anastasis, Jerusalem

Hopwood, Keith, 48

Huntington, Samuel, 285

Hürrem Paşa, 350, 365n33

Hussein, Mohammed, 241

Hussein (king of Jordan), 224, 290

Ibrahim Pasha, 217

identities: and boundary relations, 42–43, 48, 59; as changeable, 10, 42, 43, 45, 133; and collective identitarian frameworks, 45, 130, 131, 133–34, 143, 154, 155–57; competition among, 11; and conflict in shared sacred sites, 150, 151, 152; construction of, 36; and Crusades, 283; essentialist notions of, 38, 82, 133–34, 135; multivocality of, 45, 46; and Museum of Tolerance, 317, 318; politics of identity, 42–43, 300, 306, 307, 314, 318, 320, 321, 326, 329, 331n1; and religious boundaries, 91–92, 133; religious

INDEX | 413

identities, 39, 300, 307, 313; religious space representing rhetoric of, 242, 246, 247; and shared sacred sites, 72; situational identities, 45; and state policies, 20; and syncretism, 10; and toleration, 40–41; within shared sacred sites, 44–46
Iliofotoi saints, 89–90
imarets, 56
imperial states: accommodation of, 4; diversity accommodated by, 41, 47; and dominance of religious groups, 22–23; and shared sacred sites, 41. *See also* Ottoman Empire; *and other imperial states*
India, 1, 3, 5, 17, 18–19, 22–23, 130, 337–38, 362
indivisibility of shared sacred sites: and centrality of shared sacred sites, 13, 16; and conflict in shared sacred sites, 12, 16; and desecration of sacred space, 190–91; factors circumventing, 29n16; malleability of, 16, 17; and political factors, 16, 17, 18–19, 30n18, 170, 190–91; questions concerning, 3, 15–19; references to larger spaces, 239; and temporal or functional division, 16
Institute for Palestine Studies, 241
intermarriage: as form of coexistence, 39; and interreligious relations, 338; and Islamization in Balkans, 52; and Ottoman Empire, 51
International Hacı Bektaş Veli Symposium, 366n36
interreligious relations: and al-Wad Street, 27, 168, 179–80; and Catholic Church, 119, 125; and economic benefits of interfaith mixing, 27, 73, 78, 87, 88–90; and intermarriage, 338; and *millet* organization, 34, 60n2; and Our Lady of Africa, 125–26; and political factors, 235–36; and religious leaders, 23; shared sacred sites as indices of quality of, 3, 33, 35; state-society relations, 19; and status quo of shared sacred sites in Jerusalem, 217–20, 222, 226; and violence, 5, 135, 239. *See also specific religions and sites*
intrareligious power relations: and Arab Palestinians, 277; in Bosnia, 24, 26, 131, 135–36, 141, 144–48, 149, 150–54, 157n6; and choreographies of sacred spaces, 131–32, 135–36, 144, 145–49, 156; and Christian shared sites in Jerusalem, 9, 163, 164, 199–204, 214; and conflict in shared sacred sites, 9, 131, 135–36, 154; and religious leaders, 23, 25; and violence, 135
Iraq, 4, 10
Ireland, 16, 30n20
Irenaios I (patriarch), 223, 233–34n76
Islam. *See* Muslims and Islam
Islamic Community (IC) of Bosnia and Herzegovina: and Ajvatovica pilgrimage, 141–42, 145–47; and choreography of shared sacred sites, 154; and dervish orders as "other within," 137–38, 140, 146, 149; founding of, 136–37; and Karići pilgrimage, 139, 140, 148, 149; and Nakşbendi order, 146–47; and prayers for rain, 150, 151, 152, 153; and socialist state, 137–38, 139, 141, 146, 150, 159n32
Islamic humanitarian organizations, 131, 147–48, 153, 160n39

Islamic Movement: and Jerusalem tours, 177; and Museum of Tolerance, 305–6, 317, 326, 327; in Nazareth, 280, 283, 284, 286, 287

Israel: Arab Muslim minority in, 300, 306, 308, 312–18; Arab Palestinians in, 270, 274–77, 278, 281, 287, 288–89, 316; and Armenian Orthodox Church, 223–25, 227, 228; and Basilica of the Annunciation in Nazareth, 279; and Catholic Church, 220, 221–22, 225, 227, 228; and conflict in shared sacred sites, 92, 214–16; and control of physical space within Holy Land churches, 9; Eretz Israel, 180; and Greek Orthodox Church, 222–23, 225, 227, 228, 233–34n76; and illegal settlements, 249–50, 254, 260; Jewish majority in, 287; as Jewish state, 227, 274, 275; and Judaizing the land, 246, 247, 276, 279; justice system of, 300; Labor government of, 240; and massacre in Hebron, 251; and Museum of Tolerance, 299; official attitude to Jerusalem, 188; Palestinian refugees in, 274–75, 278; political authority of, 14; power relations in, 25, 243, 267n23; right-wing parties in, 246, 251; and state-society relations, 24, 228; and status quo agreements, 163, 214–20, 221, 222–23, 225, 226, 232n49; violence controlled by, 244; violence instigated by government actions, 236–37, 243. *See also* Jerusalem; Palestine/Israel; *and other specific places and sites*

Israel Antiquities Authority, 185

Israeli Muslim tourists, 177–79, *178*, 196n35

Israeli/Palestinian conflict: and al-Wad Street, 171–72, 195n22; and Arab's use of religious rhetoric, 238; boundaries of, 163–64; and Camp David negotiations of 2000, 25–26, 240, 242–43, 264; and Museum of Tolerance, 315; and Nazareth, 276, 281, 287, 291; prolonged peace process, 238, 239, 240, 241, 243, 245–46, 249, 251, 256–57; religious violence as byproduct of politics, 235, 236, 237; settlers demonstrating against Israel's restraint in, 247

Israel Land Administration, 222, 223

Israel Land Authority (ILA), 282–83, 285, 308

Istanbul, Turkey, 15, 57, 338, 358, 362

Ivanova, Svetlana, 56

Izetbegović, Alija, 142

Jaffa Gate, Jerusalem, 179
Janissaries, 94n15, 342
Japan, 16, 30n20
Jarayse, Ramiz, 284, 290
Jeffrey, George, 89–90
Jennings, Ronald C., 74
Jerusalem: archaeological sites of, *165*, 179, 180, 182, 183; Christian Quarter, 180; and conflict in shared sacred sites, 163–64, 166, 170, 182–83, 190, 191–92, 235, 262, 274, 287; Damascus Gate, 166, 170, 177, 180; division in 1948, 303; and economic spaces, 89, 202–3; indigenous Christian population of, 227; indivisibility of, 17; Israeli control of, 214–17, 226, 227, 238, 241; Jerusalem Day (May 20, 2012), 265n3; Jewish holy places in, 183; Jewish Quarter, 164, 166,

179, 184; Jewish settlements of, *165*, 178, 179–80, 182, 183, 184, 188, 192, 196*n*42, 197*n*43, 197*n*44, 198*n*56, 223, 233–34*n*76; Latin Kingdom of, 202; malleable borders of, 238; military checkpoints at entrances to shared sacred sites, 164, 170, 171, 172, 177, 179, 184; municipal boundaries of, *18*; Muslim Quarter, 164–66, 171, 172, 173, 177, 180, 183, 184, 188, 190, 192, 239, 240; and National Heritage Plan of 2010, 237, 239, 245–48; and nationalism, 187–88; Old City, 164, *165*, 170, 172, 174, 177, 179, 196*n*42, 197*n*43, 197*n*44, 201, 223, 265*n*3; patriarchates of, 205, 209, 215, 222–25, 227, 228, 229*n*7, 231*n*27, 231*n*33, 233–34*n*76, 234*n*86; role of political and religious leaders in, 24–25, 31*n*30, 214; status quo agreements designating shared sacred sites, 163, 193*n*2, 199, 200–201, 206, 207–14, 217–18, 225–26, 228–29*n*1, 230–31*n*25, 231*n*27; transferring authority to Palestinians in three villages surrounding, 242; as undivided eternal city, 17, 238, 244, 313, 316; and urban development, 304, 315, 320, 321, 325; view of junction between Muslim and Jewish Quarters, *172*; violence in, *236*. *See also* East Jerusalem; *and specific sites*

Jewish Museum of Tolerance, and Mamilla Cemetery, 15

Jews and Judaism: attacks on, 10; and conversion to Christianity in Algeria, 114; Falasha Jews, 219, 220; influence of Jewish settler movements, 163; in Mediterranean, 124; in Ottoman Empire, 34, 36; and Our Lady of Africa, 111, 124; and shared sacred sites in Jerusalem, 163, 164; synagogues distinguished from temples, 198*n*67. *See also* Israel; Palestine/Israel

John Paul II (pope), 281

Jordan: and Armenian Orthodox Church, 228; and Catholic Church, 225, 228; and Mamilla Cemetery, 303; rule of Bethlehem, 279, 290; rule of East Jerusalem, 279, 303, 324; rule of Palestine/Israel, 212, 214, 215, 216, 218, 219, 221, 226, 227, 231*n*33, 234*n*86

Jordan River, 225

Joseph's Tomb, Nablus: centrality of, 14, 237, 248, 260, 263, 264; geography of site as factor in complexity of, 257–58; historical veracity of, 252, 253, 257, 267*n*26; Jewish narrative of, 252, 253, 263; and Jewish settlers, 254–60, 268*n*40; Muslim narrative of, 252–53, 263; political nature of violence in, 253, 254–60, 261, 262, 263, 264, 268*n*37

Judaism. *See* Jews and Judaism

July Monarchy, 98

Justinian (emperor of Rome), 104

Kaaba, Mecca, Saudi Arabia, 14

Kabylia, Algeria, 109, 114, 115, 116, 120, 129*n*47

Kach (Jewish Defense League), 252

Kafadar, Cemal, 63*n*43

Kaftwe, Sekhe Ahmad, 288

Kaleburnu, Karpasia Peninsula, Cyprus, 79

Kaplan, Benjamin, 40

Karama Association, 307–8

Kardus, Abdullah Effendi, 209
Karići pilgrimage: Ajvatovica pilgrimage compared to, 136, 142, 144, 145, 147; as all-male pilgrimage, 140, 143, 146; and choreography of shared sacred sites, 138–41, 147–49; and continuity of Sufism, 151; divine power and good luck associated with, 139; and Islamic Community, 139, 140, 148, 149; media coverage for, 144; multiple actors and discourses of, 156; narratives of, 143–44, 148; rebuilding of, 140, 148
Katholikon, 205
Katinka, Baruch, 301–2
Katsav, Moshe, 305
Kazanjian, Karekian, 223–24
Kazantzakis, Nikos, 200–201
Ketchauoa Mosque, Algiers, 101
Khalidi, Rashid, 324
Khamaisi, Rassem, 14–15
Khidr, 50
Kirklar Tekkesi (Tekke of the Forty Saints), 75, 85, 87
Koca, Şefki, 86
Korea, 16, 30n20
Kosovo, 5, 16, 58, 141, 149
Kosovo Albanians, 132
Kreiser, Klaus, 344
Kroyanker, David, 303
Kurban Bayramı, 69, 93n1
Kyriss, Costas P., 87

Ladies of Sacred Heart, Lyon, France, 101
Landau, Uzi, 266n17
Land Day commemorations, 258
Land of Israel, 246

Latin Franciscans: and Church of the Anastasis, 200, 201, 203, 204, 227, 232n38; and Church of the Nativity, 212–13, 214; and Edicule, 211; and Nazareth, 278; as settlers in Istanbul, 57; and status quo agreements, 210, 211, 212, 231n27, 232n38
Lavigerie, Charles Martial, 100, 105, 108–9, 110, 119
League of Nations, 274
Lefebvre, Henri, 317
legibility, 41, 59, 62n20, 208
Levinger, Moshe, 254
Levy, David, 267n29
Leynaud, Augustin-Fernand, 108, 111–12
Likud, 17, 222, 240, 243, 266n17
linguistic diversity, in Ottoman Empire, 33–34
Lippel, Yisrael, 219
Livnat, Noam, 255
local actors: and boundaries, 43; and building of churches in Ottoman Empire, 54; and coexistence across religious boundaries, 39, 40–41, 52; and state-society relations, 23, 27; and tolerance, 37; and violence in Ottoman Empire, 34
Locke, John, 132
Ludolph of Sudheim, 202
Luke, Harry, 77, 78, 209
Luria, Keith, 39

Macedonia, context of shared sacred sites in, 8, 58, 134
Macedonian Torbeshis, 132
Mahmud II (sultan of Ottoman Empire), 86, 341, 345, 346
Makarios III (archbishop), 83

Makdisi, Saree, 313
Makedonski Brod, Macedonia, 12
Makharias Monastery, Cyprus, 77
Mamilla Cemetery, Jerusalem: debate over use of territory of, 301–5; and discrimination, 317, 324–26; as extinct, 304; intra-Muslim dispute of, 15, 25, 302, 303–4, 321, 326, 330; and Museum of Tolerance, 15, 299, 302, 304–11, 315, 317, 318, 329–31; and Palace Hotel project, 301–2, 320, 331n6; and parking lot, 299, 304–5, 330–31; as sacred space, 300, 329; and scale shift, 328–29; urban plans for development of, 304, 325; venue for resolving conflict of, 326–29
Mamluk period, 89, 171, 203
Mandate Law, 216
Manoogian, Torkom, 224
Marioge, Paul, 115, 116–18
Massalha, Omar, 304
Maurier, Henri, 115–16
Mayer, Tamar, 188
Mecca, Saudi Arabia, 9, 14
Mediterranean: and historical continuity, 133, 134; and Our Lady of Africa, 104–5, 121, 122, 123, 125; religious mixture in, 6–7, 57, 124; shared sacred sites in, 132; syncretism in, 6–8, 57, 124
Mehmet al-Fateh (sultan of Ottoman Empire), 147
Mélanie of La Salette, 102–3
Mercerdarians, 103–4
Mevlana Jala ad-Din Rumi shrine complex, Konya, Turkey: architectural features of, 347, 350, 351, 354–55; and communal worship, 344–45, 358, 359; and heterodox practices, 339–40, 343; international visitors to, 352, 353, 361; as museum, 26, 340, 343, 345, 346, 350–51, 352, 354–55, 359–61; as pilgrimage site, 342, 347, 360; ritual practices in museum grounds, 354–55, 358, 359–60; and Rumi's tomb, 347, 349, 351, 358–59; Selimiye Mosque adjacent to, 345–46, 351, 359; and state policies, 343, 351, 352, 359, 360–61; ticketed access to, 352, 353, 354; tombs of dervishes, 351, 358; view from rose garden, 350
Mevlevi Order: and cenotaphs in Mevlana Jala ad-Din Rumi shrine complex, 351, 358; and *sema* rituals, 344, 345, 359–60, 364n20, 366n40; and state-society relations, 342, 343, 344, 345
Mevlevi *tekke*, Cyprus, 88
Michel, R. L. N., 81
Middle East, 3–4, 124. *See also specific countries*
millet organization, 34, 60n2, 82
Milosevic, Slobodan, 5
minorities: accommodation by, 11; Arab Palestinians in Israel as, 276, 278, 281, 288–89; attacks on, 10; majority's acceptance of, 6, 22, 34; Muslims in Israel as, 299, 300, 312–18, 322, 330; and representation in symbolic landscape, 300, 312–18, 320; rights of religious minorities, 362
Misserghin, Algeria, 101
Missionaries of Africa, 109, 115–16
Mitchell, George J., 244
Mofaz, Shaul, 305

Monastery of Saint George, Büyükada, Istanbul, 57
Monastery of Saints Helena and Constantine, 215
Monica, Saint, 106
Monique, Saint, 107
Monophysite Armenians, 217
Moore, Robert, 37
Moorish architecture, 104
Moses, 50
Mount of Olives, 303, 325
Muhammad, Prophet, 93n7, 193n6, 263, 292n4
Muhammad ibn Ibrahim Aal al-Sheikh, 318–19
Mujir al-Din, 301
Murad IV (sultan of Ottoman Empire), 204
Museum of Scientific Atheism, St. Petersburg, 339
Museum of Tolerance (MOT), Jerusalem: arguments for and against placement of, 299, 312–26; building plan of, 305, 309, 310, 326; cemeteries as holy places, 318–24; cornerstone ceremony of, 305, 306; and discrimination, 317, 324–26; and Mamilla Cemetery, 15, 299, 302, 304–11, 315, 317, 318, 329–31; and message of tolerance, 299, 313–16, 318, 325, 330, 331; and minority representation in symbolic landscape, 300, 312–18, 320; model of, 305; Muslim graves abutting Museum of Tolerance Wall, 312; symbolic meaning of, 313–14
museums: and access to shared sacred sites, 336; and centrality of shared sacred sites, 15; and coexistence, 11; role of, 27; and state policies, 336–37, 339, 362; and unauthorized pluralism, 20. *See also specific museums*
Muslims and Islam: in Algeria, 98, 114–19; and Arab Palestinians, 274–80, 278, 281, 287, 288–89; cult of Muslim saints, 118; in Cyprus, 73–76, 82–83, 84, 85–86, 95n35; and folk Islam, 74, 75, 117, 118, 152; and heterodox practice, 56, 59, 74, 75, 86–87, 94n13, 149, 154, 337, 339–40, 341, 343–44; and hierarchy of holy sites, 292n4; Islamization in Ottoman Empire, 52–54; as minorities in Israel, 299–300, 312–18, 322, 330; narratives of shared sacred sites, 12; and Nazareth, 15, 280–81, 282, 286, 287, 290; in Ottoman Empire, 4, 34, 36, 46–57, 73–76; prayer for Muslims in Our Lady of Africa, 108, 109, 119, 122, 125, 127n23; and rigid Islamist rejection politics, 238; Salafi Muslims, 24, 146; and shared sacred sites in Jerusalem, 163, 164. *See also* Shia Islam; Sufism; Sunni Islam *and specific countries and sites*
Mustafa III (sultan of Ottoman Empire), 204–5, 228–29n1

Nabe-Seian site, Nazareth, 278
Nablus, West Bank: and Jewish settlements, 249, 253–55; and Palestinian Authority, 256, 259. *See also* Joseph's Tomb, Nablus
Nakşibendi Order, 86, 87, 94n13, 146–47, 148
Napoleonic Wars, 205
Nasserite Egypt, 218, 219

INDEX | 419

National Heritage Plan of 2010, 237, 239, 245–48
nationalism: in Algeria, 114, 125; and al-Wad Street, 167, 175, 176, 187–88, 189; customs altered by, 20, 76; in Cyprus, 20, 72, 76, 82–83, 88, 91, 92; and ethnic groups, 82–84, 91, 131, 138, 145, 226, 228, 270, 274, 276, 289, 291; and extremism, 237, 243, 251; as form of group violence, 5; and Jewish settlements in West Bank, 250, 256–57, 258; Zionist nationalism, 247, 267n22. *See also* religious nationalism
national significance, sites of, 28n5
nation-states: and homogenization process, 3, 20, 27, 35, 41, 98; religious diversity of, 3; and shared sacred sites, 41; transition from empire to, 4, 20
Natour, Qadi Ahmad, 307, 319, 321–22
Navarro-Valls, Joaquín, 294n40
Nazareth, Israel: al-Salam Mosque, 278; Arab Christian population of, 275, 277, 289; Arab Muslim population of, 277, 278, 279, 280, 281; and Arab Palestinian citizens in Israel, 270, 275, 276, 277, 278, 287, 288–89; Basilica of the Annunciation, 278, 279, 282, 283, 288, 294n40; Bedouin population of, 287; and centrality of shared sacred sites, 14–15; and changes to status quo relations, 270; Christian churches in, 278, 289; Christian/Muslim tension in, 279–81, 283, 284–85, 287, 288–90, 294n40; Christian population of, 278, 279, 280–81, 282, 286, 289, 290; and conflict in shared sacred sites, 270–71, 273; and conflicts between Arab subgroups, 277; demographic structure of, 279–80; development plan for, 271; ethnoreligious groups in, 270, 275, 276–77, 281, 283, 287, 288–89, 290; heterogeneous religious residents of, 273–74; mosques in, 278; Muslim population of, 15, 280–81, 282, 286, 287, 290; Nazareth 2000 project, 281–82, 284; and outsider involvement, 271, 274, 285, 286, 287, 288, 289, 290, 291; place in Christianity, 14–15, 277–78, 279, 282, 289; Plaza of Paul IV, 282–83, 284, 285–86; population of, 278–79; role of sacred sites in representational function of, 270, 272; Shihab al-Deen site and proposed mosque, 271, 278, 283, 284, 285, 286, 287, 288, 289–91; violence in, 284; White Mosque, 278
Nazareth Illit (Jewish Upper Nazareth), Israel, 279, 280, 285
Nebi Samuel (north of Jerusalem): archaeological excavations at, 261; centrality of, 237, 248; coexistence at, 257, 261, 264; geography of, 262; and interreligious relations, 261
Necipoglu, Nevra, 48–49
Nestorians, 202, 204
Netanyahu, Benjamin, 240, 241, 243, 284
Nevzat, Altay, 75
Nirenberg, David, 38, 61n11
Northern Islamic Movement, 177, 196n35, 305–6, 317, 326, 327
Norton, John A., 341
Notre Dame de la Garde, Marseilles, France, 104–5, 121, 122
Notre-Dame du Ravin, Algiers, 103, 128n36

Nuseibeh family, 207
Nusseibeh, Muhammad Zaki, 307

Ohel Yitzhak Synagogue, Jerusalem, 184, 189
Olmert, Ehud, 222, 304, 305
Ömer (Muslim commander), 85
Operation Moses (1984–1985), 220
Orthodox Church of St. Elias, Tabor, 201, 229n4
Oslo Accords, 163, 172, 240, 248, 251, 256
Osman (sultan of the Ottoman Empire), 47
Ostrog Monastery, 58
Ottoman Empire: and cultural fusion, 46, 47, 48; and Cyprus, 70–71, 73; and frontier societies, 4, 47, 48, 49–50, 51, 59; and Islamization, 52–55, 60; and Mamilla Cemetery, 301; *millet* organization in, 34, 60n2, 82, 205, 226–27; and multivocality of projects, 47; and Nazareth, 278; and Nointel capitulations, 204; policy for populating new territories, 74; rules for rights in shared sacred sites, 59, 60, 199, 203–5, 206, 209, 210, 212, 214–15, 216, 217, 222, 225, 226, 227, 228–29n1, 231n27, 231n33, 234n85; shared legacy of, 4; shared sacred sites in, 4, 12, 20, 26, 33–34, 35, 46–47, 52, 57; toleration in, 5, 21, 34–35, 36, 42, 62n31, 71
Ottoman-French Capitulations, 201–2, 203, 229n6
Oulémas, 114
Our Lady of Africa (Marian sanctuary), Algiers: architecture of, 104, 123; and "Black Madonna" devotion, 102, 107, 113, 123, 128n35; and colonial state, 98–101, 106, 123; and conflict in shared sacred sites, 26, 98; continuity of, 7, 98; creation of, 101–7; evolution of mixed attendance at, 98; and France, 101, 102, 103, 104–5, 121; indigenous attendance at sanctuary of, 110; and indulgences, 106, 108; Jewish women visiting, 111, 124; miraculous healings of, 110, 111, 112, 117–18, 124; and mixed attendance, 111–12, 113, 122; multivocality of symbol of Virgin, 103; Muslim attendance at, 97, 110–11, 112, 113, 114, 115, 116–18, 119, 122, 124, 125, 128n29; Muslim women visiting, 111–13, 115, 128n35; naming of, 103, 126n13; and peaceful coexistence, 98; and pilgrimages, 97, 101, 102, 103, 104, 105, 106, 110–13, 122, 123; in postcolonial framework, 114–19; prayer association of, 107–8, 111, 112; and prayer for Muslims, 108, 109, 119, 122, 125, 127n23; and proselytism, 97, 99, 105, 107–9, 111–13, 119, 120, 121, 125; restoration of, 121–22; sanctuary of, 106–7, 109, 113, 123; statue of, 101–2, 103, 106, 107, 113, 123; as symbol of interreligious coexistence, 125–26
Our Lady of Cruz, Oran, Algeria, 101
Our Lady of Fourvière, Lyon, France, 102, 103
Our Lady of Verdelais, France, 101
Our Lady of Victories, Algiers, 104
outdoor religious gatherings (*dove*), 138, 142, 152, 153, 154
outdoor sacred sites (*dovište*), 136
Özçakıl, Fahri (Mevlevi sheik), 360

Palace Hotel, 301–2, 303, 320, 331n6
Palestine/Israel: British Mandate in, 202, 207, 208–12, 214, 215, 216, 226, 227, 234n86, 274, 283, 300, 301, 302, 304, 322; Christian population of, 4, 227; and conflict in shared sacred sites, 22, 26, 58, 235; Israeli rule of, 214–22, 226; Jordanian rule of, 212, 214, 215, 216, 218, 219, 221, 226, 227, 231n33, 234n86; and politics of identity, 329; shared sacred sites in, 1, 134, 274
Palestine Liberation Organization (PLO), 17, 248, 281, 304
Palestinian Authority: and Bethlehem 2000 project, 281; and Hebron, 245–46, 248–49; and Irenaois, 223; and Nablus, 256, 259; and Nazareth, 287, 288
Panagia (Mother Mary) church of Civisil, Cyprus, 78–79
Panagia (Mother Mary) church of Doros, Cyprus, 77
Pancaroglu, Oya, 50
Patriarchal Cathedral Church of St. George, Constantinople, 205
Paul VI (pope), 279
Pavy, Louis-Antoine-Agustin: as bishop of Algiers, 100, 102, 103; and Our Lady of Africa, 102, 103–5, 107, 110, 111, 122, 128n29; prayer association founded by, 107, 112–13
peaceful coexistence: characteristics of, 6, 7, 33; in Cyprus, 70, 71–72, 75, 92
Peres, Shimon, 249, 267n23
persecution: in Reformation, 38, 39; and studies of toleration, 37, 46
Persians, and Jerusalem, 229n7

pilgrimages: and Battal Ghazi monument, 49; and choreography of shared sacred sites, 201; to Church of the Anastasis, 199–200, 202–3, 205; and economic spaces, 89, 202–3; to Holy Land, 199–200; to Joseph's Tomb, 253; in Kosovo, 58; to Nazareth, 277, 279, 289; and Our Lady of Africa, 97, 101, 102, 103, 104, 105, 106, 110–13, 122, 123; and prayers for rain, 149–50; in Southern Europe, 104; and state-society relations, 202–3. *See also* Ajvatovica pilgrimage; Karići pilgrimage
Pius IX (pope), 106, 205
Poitou, France, 39–40
political factors: and centrality of shared sacred sites, 14, 15; and choreographies of sacred spaces, 97, 131, 236, 246, 249; and conflict in shared sacred sites, 2, 87, 97, 131, 148, 152, 220, 235–36, 248, 262; and Dar es-Sultan, 217–20; in foundation myths of shared sacred sites, 85; and Holy Land archaeology, 183; as identity markers, 5; and indivisibility of shared sacred sites, 16, 17, 18–19, 30n18, 170, 190–91; malleability of political myopia, 237; and prevention of religious violence, 264; and religious nationalism, 238, 248, 250, 256–59, 263, 265; religious symbols and sites used for framing violence, 238, 242, 244–45, 253, 265; and riots surrounding religious sites, 235; of shared sacred sites, 1, 5–6, 236; and state-society relations, 20; and Western Wall Tunnel opening, 239–42, 257–58

political leaders: and religious leaders' role in conflict management at sacred sites, 24–25, 30–31n29, 31n30; and violence, 27
Popović, Alexandre, 159n34
Portugal, 337
power relations: and contested sites, 87–88; and ethnographies, 133; and ethnoreligious groups, 154, 190; imbalance in, 11; and indivisibility of shared sacred sites, 17; instability in, 98; in Israel, 25, 243, 267n23; and Joseph's Tomb, 255; and narratives of shared sacred sites, 12–13; and political leaders, 25; and religious leaders, 24, 25; in shared sacred sites, 122–23, 134, 135, 338; and state-society relations, 19–20; and urban holy sites, 273. *See also* intrareligious power relations
prayers for rain (*dove za kišu*): and choreographies of shared sacred sites, 136, 141, 149–54; and clandestine veneration of sacred sites, 150; and continuity of Sufism, 151–52; and intracommunal tensions, 150, 151–53; and Islamic Community, 150, 151, 152, 153; multiple actors and discourses of, 156; relocation of, 153; and women, 151
Prisons of Christ, Jerusalem, 201, 205
Procaccia, Ayalah, 315–16, 320–21
Prodromos, Saint John, 53
Protestants, 39, 120
Pullan, Wendy, 14, 25

Qadis Law (1961), 322
Qur'an: and Karići pilgrimage, 140, 147; and prayers for rain, 151; references to Virgin Mary in, 105, 111, 124

Rabin, Yitzhak, 251, 267n23
Rachel's Tomb, Bethlehem: as Israeli national heritage site, 245, 248, 264; role of religion in violence relative to politics, 237; and status quo agreements, 209
Radwan, Tarek, 70
Raghib, Ahmad, 302
Reformation, 35, 38, 39
Reiter, Yitzhak, 15, 25, 194n19
religious boundaries: in Algeria, 113; in Cyprus, 75–76, 80, 81, 82–88, 91–92; and forms of coexistence, 39–40, 52; and identities, 91–92, 133; and shared sacred sites, 132–33; and shared sacred sites in Jerusalem, 163–64
religious diversity: increase in, 3; and *millet* organization, 34, 60n2, 82; and mixed worship, 36; in Ottoman Empire, 33–35, 36, 47, 59, 60; and tolerance, 11, 22, 33, 35
religious factors: and centrality of shared sacred sites, 13–14; and exclusivity, 7, 132–33, 338; and extremism, 237, 248, 256, 259–60, 314; and heritage, 238; and heterogeneity, 11, 73, 84–88, 92, 204; and Holy Land archaeology, 183; as identity markers, 5; and indivisibility of shared sacred sites, 16, 17, 30n19; and pluralism, 3, 8, 11, 98; secular factors intertwined with, 14, 24, 76, 339, 340, 362; of shared sacred sites, 1
religious groups: agency of, 133; and local actors, 23, 27; political competition among, 10; and state-society relations, 2, 21–22. *See also* ethnoreligious groups
religious leaders: and boundaries, 43; and coexistence, 46–47; and conflict

in shared sacred sites, 23, 24–25, 30–31n29, 31n30, 214, 221–24, 236; and state-society relations, 23–24, 236, 337; and toleration, 40–41; and violence, 27, 236

religious nationalism: in Algeria, 114, 125; as collective identitarian frame, 130, 131, 154–55; and political factors, 238, 248, 250, 256–59, 263, 265

religious practices: in Algeria, 113; changing nature of, 24–25; and conflict in shared sacred sites, 84, 86, 150–51, 152, 154; and heterodox practice, 56, 59, 74, 75, 86–87, 94n13, 149, 154, 337, 339–40, 341, 343–44, 346–47, 349, 354, 357–58; hybrid practice, 81–82, 95n31; and shared sacred sites, 46; and spaces of temporary submission, 76

Revocation of the Edict of Nantes (1685), 39

Richard the Lionheart, 283

Rifa'i order, 141, 149

Rizokarpasos, Karpasia Peninsula, Cyprus, 79

Roma, attacks on, 10

Roussos, Sotiris, 222

Rumi, Mevlana Jalal ad-Din: humanist and modern philosophy of, 344; international fame of, 352; as mystic, 342; as proponent of tolerance, 343–44; tomb of, 347, 349, 351, 358–59. *See also* Mevlana Jala ad-Din Rumi shrine complex, Konya, Turkey

Russian Orthodox church, 9, 205–6, 213–14

Sabbah, Michel, 225

Sabri, Ekrema, 288

Sacred Esplanade, Jerusalem, 12

sacred spaces: areas adjacent to, 191–92; cemeteries as, 300, 303, 318–24; Eliade on, 169, 190, 194n12, 194n14; neutralization in public sphere, 15, 191; permeability of, 168–70, 191, 192; taboos associated with, 190; urban holy sites, 271–74, 291, 292n4. *See also* choreographies of sacred spaces; shared sacred sites

Sadat, Anwar, 220

Saint Anna Chapel, Kaleburnu, Cyprus, 79

St. Helena Chapel, 217

St. Isaac's Cathedral, St. Petersburg, 339

St. James Brotherhood, 224

St. John's Hospice, 222

Saladin, 202, 283

Salafi Muslims, in Bosnia, 24, 146

Salah, Ghassan Mohammed Said, 255

Salah, Raed, 177, 188, 196n39, 317, 326

Sambi, Pietro, 294n40

Sarıönder, Refika, 343–44

Sartawi, Mahmoud, 288

Saudi Arabia, 9, 14, 152, 153, 288

Sayf, Durgham, 318

scale shift, and conflict resolution, 300, 328–29, 331

Schabel, Chris, 79

Schwarzenegger, Arnold, 305

Scott, James, 208

Scribner, Bob, 38

Second Intifada (2000–2006): and Camp David negotiations, 26; and Israeli nationalists, 265; and Joseph's Tomb, 248, 258, 259; and Nazareth, 287; and Sharon's visit to Haram al-Sharif, 164, 239, 244–45, 263; and status quo agreements, 163

sectarianism, 133

secular factors: and al-Wad Street, 166–68, 188, 195*n*29; religious factors intertwined with, 14, 24, 76, 339, 340, 362; and state-society relations, 337, 362

secular space: al-Wad Street as, 166–68, 188, 195*n*29; museums as, 337, 339; and sacred space, 169–70, 189

Selim (sultan), 345

Selim II (sultan of Ottoman Empire), 54–55

Seljuk Empire (1077–1307): and Anatolia, 50–51, 53, 59; cultural exchanges with Byzantine Empire, 48–51; and Ottoman Empire, 47, 48; and shared sacred sites, 4, 46

sema, and Mevlevi Order, 344, 345, 351, 359–60, 364*n*20, 366*n*40

Serbs: Great Serbian Migrations, 21; and Karići pilgrimage, 139; Ottomans defeat in Kosovo, 5; and shared sacred sites, 132

Serry, Robert H., 245–46

Seven Arches Hotel, 332*n*13

Seven Arches of the Virgin, Jerusalem, 205

Sewell, William, Jr., 43

Shalom, Silvan, 305

Shamgar, Meir, 309

Shamir, Shimon, 308

Shamir, Yitzhak, 241, 254

Sharansky Commission, 285

shared sacred sites: and agency of social actors, 131, 133, 134, 135, 155; anthropological studies of, 8; centrality of, 3, 12, 13–15, 29*n*15, 45, 237, 248, 263; characteristics of, 11–19, 33, 45; and choreography of daily life, 2; competitive sharing situations, 10, 22, 132, 135, 199, 337, 337–39; and diachronic and synchronic temporalities, 44, 45, 58; dynamic history of, 1, 46; economic benefit of, 27, 73, 78, 87, 88–90, 92, 202–3; efficacious powers of, 72–73, 76, 77–80; foundation myths of, 84–85, 95*n*39; identities within, 44–46; indivisibility of, 3, 12, 15–19, 29*n*16, 30*n*18, 45, 190–91, 239; malleability of, 264; management of, 9, 236, 245; motivation for changes to, 10; multiple spatial meanings of, 238, 271–72; multivocality of, 132, 153; narratives of, 12–13, 200, 201; in Ottoman Empire, 4, 12, 20, 26, 33–34, 35, 46–47, 52, 57; role in geopolitical transitions, 271–72; vulnerability of, 13–14, 16, 19, 29*n*15, 45. *See also* coexistence in shared sacred sites; conflict in shared sacred sites

sharia: and holy places of Religions of the Book, 207, 210; and land practices, 54, 300; and Mamilla Cemetery, 301, 302, 303–4, 307, 308, 309, 318–24, 330; spread of, 55–56

Sharon, Ariel: home spanning al-Wad Street, 180, *181*; and Irenaios I, 223*n*76; and Jewish settlements, 254; and Landau, 266*n*17; and Nazareth, 285, 287; and Sharansky Commission, 285; visit to al-Aqsa Mosque in 2000, 26, 164, 196*n*39, 237, 239, 242–45, 263, 266*n*11

Shavit, Shabtai, 309

Shepherds' Fields, Beit Sahour, 201

Shia Islam: and Bektaşi Order, 344; in Cyprus, 94*n*13; in Kosovo, 149

INDEX | 425

Shihab al-Deen, 283
Shomrei Mishpat, 324
Silwan/David's City, Jerusalem, 165, 180, 183
Simmel, Georg, 38
Simon Wiesenthal Center, 313–14, 315, 316
Simon Wiesenthal Museum of Tolerance, Los Angeles, 299
Six-Day War, 221
Smith, Jonathan Z., 194n14
Society of Missionaries of Africa, 108
Solomon (king), 182
South Asia, 92
Southern Islamic Movement, 196n35
Soviet Union, 339
space: meanings of, 169, 300, 312–18. *See also* sacred spaces
Spanish Inquisition, 42
state policies: and absent state, 21, 30n26; changes in, 43; on conditions for non-Muslim worship in Algeria, 121, 129n47; in Cyprus, 70, 72; and diversity, 21; and Hacı Bektaş shrine complex, 343, 351, 352, 353–54, 356, 360–61; and macro-historical transformations, 20; and Mevlana Jala ad-Din Rumi shrine complex, 343, 351, 352, 359, 360–61; and museums, 336–37, 339, 362; nature of, 19; and power relations, 25; and prevention of religious violence, 237; and shared sacred sites, 20–21, 36; and toleration, 37, 40–42
state-society relations: and choreographies of sacred spaces, 1, 21, 27–28, 123, 125, 199, 214–20, 222, 226–28; and coexistence in shared sacred sites, 3, 10, 21; and conflict in shared sacred sites, 2, 10, 21–22, 27, 235–36, 339; cultural and ideological understanding of, 41; and Dar es-Sultan, 217–20; and legibility, 41, 59, 62n20, 208; nature of, 19–26; in Ottoman Empire, 34; and religious groups, 2, 21–22; and religious leaders, 23–24, 236, 337; and riots surrounding religious sites, 235; role of, 3, 20–22; and secular state, 337, 362; and tense coexistence, 39

Stewart, Susan, 176, 179
Stoyanov, Yuri, 53
Street of the Chain, Jerusalem, 171, 172
sub-Saharan Africa, 108, 120
Sufism: in Bosnia, 137–38, 140, 141, 146, 147, 148–49, 151, 159n34; and dervish orders, 51–53, 56, 78, 80, 85, 86–87, 88, 137–38, 140, 141, 159n34; in Kosovo, 141, 149; missionary aims of, 86; in Ottoman Empire, 339–40, 342; in Turkey, 342–43. *See also specific orders*
Sunni Islam: and Bektaşi Order, 341, 345; in Bosnia, 147, 149; in Cyprus, 74, 86–87, 94n13; and *namaz*, 345, 359, 365n26; in Ottoman Empire, 51, 54; in Turkey, 337, 340, 342, 351, 352, 353, 360, 361–62
Supreme Muslim Council, 301, 302, 303, 330
Suriano, Francesco, 202
Svanberg, Ingvar, 341
Svensson, Isak, 30n19
Sveti Nikola, Macedonia, 58
syncretism: in Cyprus, 75, 81–82, 90; as form of coexistence, 6, 46; and identities, 10; in Mediterranean, 6–8, 57, 124; and Ottoman Empire, 47, 48, 51,

syncretism (*continued*)
52, 53, 55, 56, 57, 63n43; and shared sacred sites, 1, 4, 134, 199, 338; state emerging within syncretic environments, 21, 338

Syria and Syrians, 4, 211

Taba, Egypt, 220
Taha, Hamdan, 245
Tanyeri-Erdemir, Tuğba, 11, 365–66n34
tarikat, 343, 364n17
Tariq al-Wad, Jerusalem. *See* al-Wad Street, Jerusalem
Te Brake, Wayne, 40
Teissier, Henri, 118, 119, 120
Tekinalp, V. Macit, 62n31
Temple Mount. *See* Haram al-Sharif/Temple Mount, Jerusalem
Temple Mount Faithful movement, 237–38, 247, 266n6
territorial struggles: as cases of indivisibility, 16, 30n20, 83–84; context of, 5
terrorist attacks: in Algeria, 114–15, 117; and indivisibility of shared sacred sites, 18; Palestinian expression of politics through, 247, 251; of September 11, 2001, 285
Theodore, Saint, 50
Theophilus III (patriarch), 223
Tilly, Charles, 42–43, 45
Tito, Josip Broz, 137
Toft, Monica Duffy, 16
tolerance: as abstract value of, 299, 300; and al-Wad Street, 176; antagonistic nature of, 8; AT model of, 44–45; and choreography of sacred spaces, 299–300, 306; competing narratives of, 314; as form of coexistence, 6; negative definition of, 22, 132; periods of relative tolerance, 2; and religious exclusivity, 7; and shared sacred sites, 3, 73, 336, 337; toleration distinguished from, 37. *See also* antagonistic tolerance (AT); Museum of Tolerance (MOT), Jerusalem

toleration: in Bethlehem, 290; and conflict in shared sacred sites, 84, 86, 87, 88, 290–91; debates on, 36–37; and economic spaces, 27, 73, 78, 87, 88–90, 92; legacies of, 19; and majority's acceptance of minorities, 6, 22, 34; meaning of, 37, 41, 46; in Ottoman Empire, 5, 21, 34–35, 36, 42, 62n31, 71; and shared sacred sites, 1; and spaces of temporary submission, 91; and state policies, 37, 40–42

Tomb of Samuel, Nabi Samwil, coexistence at, 194n19
Tomb of the Virgin, Jerusalem, possessory rights to, 200, 204, 205, 206, 209, 210, 211
Toubasi, Marwan, 223
Treaty of Berlin (1878), 206, 207, 216, 220
Treaty of Paris (1856), 206, 216, 220, 225, 228–29n1
Trebizond, 64n50
Trinitarians, 103–4
Trumpeldor, Joseph, 267n22
Tura'an Village, Israel, 277
Turabi *tekke*, Cyprus, 85, 87
Turkey: charm offensive politics, 84; and conflict in shared sacred sites, 26, 337; continuity with Ottoman Empire, 20; and Cyprus, 83–84; inconsistent ideological stances toward religious practices, 340; museums of, 15, 337; Orthodox Christians in, 4; as secular state, 337, 342, 343–44, 361,

362; Sunni Islam in, 337, 340, 342, 351, 352, 353, 360, 361–62. *See also specific sites*
Turk identity, 10, 22
Twal, Fouad, 225
Twelve Imans, doctrine of, 94n13

Ulusoy family, 356
UNESCO, 304, 331, 352
United Nations, and Mamilla Cemetery, 329
United Nations Conciliation Commission for Palestine, 211, 220–21, 233n64
United Nations Human Rights Council, 329
United States: and Nazareth, 285, 288, 291; and Protestant missionaries, 120
United States Supreme Court, 337
urban holy sites: defining, 271–74; dynamisms of, 273; hierarchical rankings of, 272, 292n4; and toleration, 291

vakif institutions, 56
van der Leeuw, Gerard, 273
Vatican: and building of Nazareth mosque, 285, 288, 291, 294n40; and control of physical space within Holy Land churches, 9; and Israel, 221, 225
Vatican II, 119, 125
Vazken I (Armenian Orthodox Church), 224
Veled, Sultan, 342
Vesely, Dalibor, 189
Via Dolorosa, Jerusalem, 166, 184
violence: in Algeria, 114–15, 116, 117, 125; and antagonistic tolerance, 338–39; and boundaries, 38–40; and centrality of shared sacred sites, 237, 248,

263; characteristics of, 33; communal violence, 1; and conflict in shared sacred sites, 26–27, 28n5, 92, 170, 184, 235; defensive violence, 213–14; and denial of access to shared sacred sites, 13, 271; distinction between varieties of, 9; and Edicule, 215; as form of coexistence, 39; history and memory of, 9; and homogenization process, 3; and impact of state policies, 10; and indivisibility of shared sacred sites, 17–18; and interreligious relations, 5, 135, 239; and intrareligious power relations, 135; in Jerusalem, 236, 239–48; in Nazareth, 284; political goals of religious violence, 236, 239, 262; and political riots surrounding religious sites, 235, 236; and power parity, 11; prevention of religious violence, 236, 237, 264; and regulation of community relations, 38; in shared sacred sites of Jerusalem, 163, 164, 184; state's control of religious violence, 235, 237; and status quo regulations in Jerusalem, 208, 212–13, 214, 215–16, 218, 232n38, 232n39; and studies of toleration, 37–38, 46; in West Bank, 236, 237, 243, 245, 248–62
Virgin Mary: in Cyprus, 77, 78–79; multivocality of symbol of, 103. *See also* Our Lady of Africa (Marian sanctuary), Algiers
Vryonis, Speros, Jr., 52
vulnerability of shared sacred sites: and centrality of shared sacred sites, 13–14, 29n15; as characteristic of shared sacred sites, 45; and indivisibility of shared sacred sites, 16, 19

Wahabis, 114, 146, 154
Wailing Wall. *See* Western Wall/Kotel Ha-Maaravi, Jerusalem
Wallez, Peter, 121
waqf (land and building endowments): and Arab Muslim minority in Israel, 300; and Brotherhood of the Holy Sepulchre, 223; and Greek and Armenian churches, 228; and Mamilla Cemetery, 301, 304, 307, 308, 322, 323, 324; in Nazareth, 276, 283–84, 285, 286, 288; and Seven Arches Hotel, 332n13
Warren, Charles, 240
West Bank: and Arab Palestinians, 276; and Armenian Orthodox Church, 224; and centrality of shared sacred sites, 14, 248; Israeli control of, 214, 216, 226, 227, 237, 238; Jewish settlements in, 249, 250, 253, 256–57, 258; links to Jewish settlements in Old City, 196n42, 238; and National Heritage Plan of 2010 sites, 237, 245–48; shared sacred sites in, 237, 262; violence in, 236, 237, 243, 245, 248–62; West Bank Muslims barred from Jerusalem, 177. *See also specific sites*
Western Europe, studies of toleration in, 37–41
Western Wall Heritage Association, 185
Western Wall/Kotel Ha-Maaravi, Jerusalem: access to, 164; and al-Wad Street, 166, 170–71, 179, 180, 182; defense of, 188; and indivisibility of shared sacred sites, 19; as Judaism's holy site of prayer, 164, 193n8; location of, 164, 193n9; and narratives of shared sacred sites, 12–13; and status quo agreements, 209; view of, *166*

Western Wall Plaza, Jerusalem, 184, 185
Western Wall Tunnel, Jerusalem: and choreography of sacred spaces, 189; and conflict in shared sacred sites, 184, 239–42; and Holy of Holies, 185, *185*, 190, 198n68; interpretation of archaeological site, *165*, 168, *172*, 179, 183–84, 185, 187, 189–91, 198n53, 240; Jewish religious content of, 184–85; and Ohel Yitzhak Synagogue, 184; religio-political identities in, 191–92; view of, *186*; violent incidents on opening of, 236–37, 239–42, 247, 257–58
White Fathers missionaries, 108–9, 110, 116, 118, 119, 120
Wiesenthal, Simon, 316
Wolper, Ethel Sara, 50
World Trade Center "Ground Zero," New York City, 273

Yom Kippur War (1973), 220
Yugoslavia: ban of dervish orders in, 137, 147; end of Yugoslav communism, 143; and Islamic Community, 150
Yugoslav National Army, 139–40

Zachariadou, Elizabeth, 51
Zibde, Muhammad, 308, 323
Zionism, 188, 313, 317
Zociste Monastery, 58

GPSR Authorized Representative: Easy Access System Europe, Mustamäe tee 50, 10621 Tallinn, Estonia, gpsr.requests@easproject.com